UTOPIAN VISTAS

Lois Rudnick

LOIS PALKEN RUDNICK

UTOPIAN
V I S

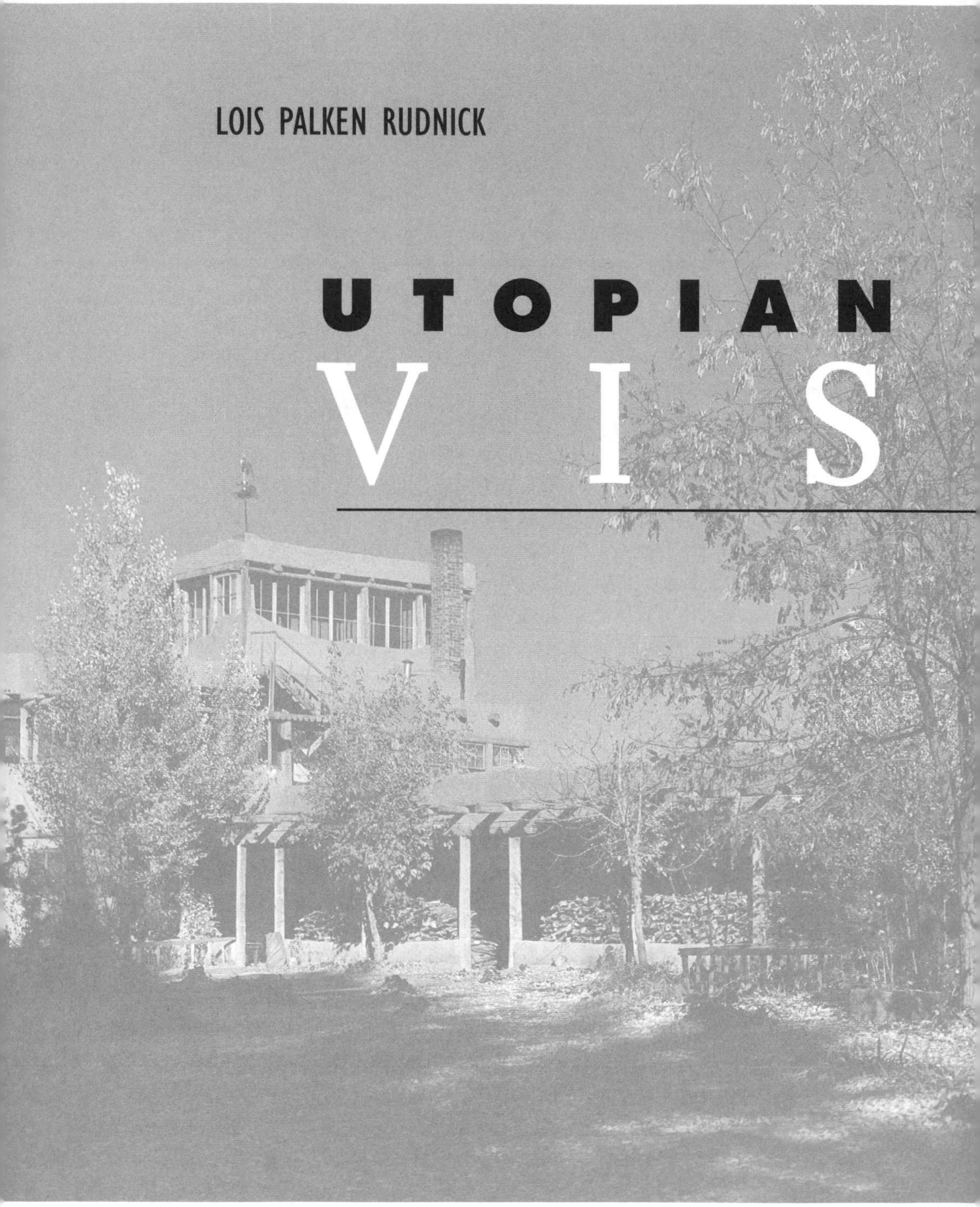

T A S

THE MABEL DODGE LUHAN HOUSE AND THE AMERICAN COUNTERCULTURE

University of New Mexico Press Albuquerque

 Second paperbound printing, 2000.

**Library of Congress
Cataloging-in-Publication Data**

Rudnick, Lois Palken, 1944–

Utopian vistas: the Mabel Dodge Luhan
House and the American Counterculture /
Lois Palken Rudnick.

p. cm.

Includes bibliographical
references and index.

ISBN 0-8263-1926-2

1. Luhan, Mabel Dodge, 1879–1962
—Homes and haunts—New Mexico—Taos.
2. Mabel Dodge Luhan House (Taos, N.M.)
3. Intellectuals—New Mexico—Taos.
4. Taos (N.M.)—Intellectual life.
5. Radicalism—New Mexico—Taos.
I. Title.

CT275.L838R835 1996
978.9'53—dc20
95-32546

CIP

Designed by Sue Niewiarowski

*Title page spread
photograph by Ernest Knee,
Mabel Dodge Luhan House.
(Private collection,
courtesy of Eric Knee.)*

For my father, George Palken (1916–1992),
whose appetite for life fed my hunger for connections

CONTENTS

ACKNOWLEDGMENTS

This book started out as an afterthought to my biography of Mabel Dodge Luhan. It soon took on a life of its own, which has possessed me for the past ten years and never would have been completed without the help of numerous individuals. My book builds on the work of MaLin Wilson, who in 1980 received an NEH pilot grant to pursue a project that she called "Mabel & Co.," which involved documenting the artists Mabel Dodge Luhan brought to New Mexico. MaLin loaned me her notes, her slides, and her chronologies. Her generous spirit has supported me throughout, including reading parts of my manuscript. Other New Mexico colleagues whose critical eyes have improved my text are William deBuys, Marta Weigle, and Sharyn Udall. In Boston, thanks go to the women in my feminist biographers group for their continued support and helpful criticism: Joyce Antler, Megan Marshall, Fran Malino, Sue Quinn, and Judith Tick. And to my wonderful daughter, Deborah, who helped with the editing.

The last few chapters of my book could not have been written without the interviews I conducted with many individuals whose lives were involved in the history about which I write. Many thanks to the following for sharing their memories and interpretations of the past: Larry Bell, Bob Campagna, John Candelario, Pop Challee, Susan Chambers-Cook, Barbara Chavez, Ray Christine, Jamie Cloud, John Collier, Jr., Eliseo and Emily Concha, Gary Cook, Regina Cook, Ron Cooper, Cynthia Darden, Peggy Davis, Jan Drum, Laurie Eastman, Ben Eastman, Ben Elkus, Bonnie Evans, Eya Fechin, Dean Fleming, Tish Frank, Leo Garen, Bill Gersh, Natalie Goldberg, Charlotte Hopper, Duane Hopper, David Hopper, Dennis Hopper, Larry Houghteling, Steve Hughes, Nancy Jenkins, John Kimmey, Lisa Law, Jack Loeffler, Agnesa Lufkin, Al Lujan, Ernesto Lujan, Lorencita Lujan, Marie Lujan, Rick Klein, Terry Klein, Doug Magnus, Josephine Marcus, Jane Mingenback, Bennie Mondragon, Ed Morgan, John Nichols, Kitty Otero, George Otero, Ashley Pond, Kenneth Price, Tony Price, Peter Rabbit, Tally Richards, Pepe Rochon, Orlando Romero, Robert Romero, Arnold Emerson Rönnebeck, Alice Rossin, Loy Sue Siegenthaler, Pat Smith, Robert Sparks, Lupe Suazo, Larry Torres, Soge Track, Frank Waters, Karen Young.

I also want to thank the National Endowment of the Humanities for a fellowship that provided me with a year to work on this book, the John Sloan Foundation for a grant to help pay for the illustrations, and the University of Massachusetts at Boston for various research and travel grants related to the book. Last but not least, I am grateful to the owners and staff of Las Palomas for making me a welcome guest in their home. And to my editor, Beth Hadas, who has the patience of twelve saints.

But it must never be forgotten that everyone is unconsciously tyrannized over by . . . the wants of dead and gone predecessors, who have an inconvenient way of thrusting their different habits and tastes across the current of later existences.

Edith Wharton, *The Decoration of Houses*

Every continent has its own great spirit of place. Every people is polarized in some particular locality, which is home, the homeland. . . . Men [and women] are free when they are in a living homeland, not when they're straying. . . . Men [and women] are free when they belong to a living, organized, believing community. . . . not when they're escaping to some wild West.

D. H. Lawrence, *Studies in Classic American Literature*

PREFACE

The English poet William Blake wrote of seeing "a world in a grain of sand." For nearly twenty years, the Mabel Dodge Luhan house, in Taos, New Mexico, has been my grain of sand. While I won't assert that its history reflects the cosmos, I will claim it as a fascinating microcosm for examining the lives and works of American and European visionaries who sought to heal the spiritual and social wounds created by modernity and postmodernity.

The story of the three generations who have possessed the house and land, and been possessed by them, is of more than local interest because it reflects recurrent patterns in the history of American countercultures. I use the term counterculture here in a much broader sense than is typical, to define an oppositional stance taken by American reformers, radicals, writers, and artists who have contested the mainstream development of American society and culture—its rationalist bent, its class, gender, and ethnic differentiations and subordinations, and its corporate, imperialist, and materialist ethos. I distinguish these cultural radicals from more doctrinaire political radicals because of their interest in exploring psychic along with social change.[1]

There have been three historical "moments" during which countercultural rebellion has become particularly salient in American history in terms of gaining the attention, and to some extent influencing, the dominant culture. To borrow historian William McLoughlin's theorizing, these have occurred at "periods when the cultural system has had to be revitalized in order to overcome jarring disjunctions between norms and experience, old beliefs and new realities, dying patterns and emerging patterns of behavior."[2]

For the purposes of this book, the first and most important of these moments was the mid-nineteenth-century movement known as Transcendentalism (1830–50). The second occurred in the wake of the United States maturing into a major capitalist-industrial empire (1900–1920). It spurred the post–World War I expatriation to New Mexico by Anglo writers, artists, and reformers. The third occurred in the 1960s, as a protest against racism and imperialism, and the exploitation and abuse of the environment. It led to northern New Mexico's becoming a central site of the commune movement. The Mabel Dodge Luhan house has played an important role in the twentieth-century's two countercultural moments and in the legacies of those movements that I discuss in the final section of this book.

Indigenous American radicalism has often had both a utopian and a spiritualist cast, with an ever-receding and mythical West as the locus for prophetic pronouncements and experiments. This imagined, redemptive West has, of course, always existed alongside a very different West, one of violence, racial oppression, and capitalist development that has particularly marked the geographic west of the United States. There is no contest about which of these Wests has won most of the victories in American history.[3] Nevertheless, it is exhilarating to hear the voices and see the visions of those who have struggled to construct more humane alternatives, even when their behavior has sometimes fed and encouraged the opposition.

In the relatively isolated, sparsely populated state of New Mexico, creative men and women, both native and expatriate, have found inspiration for challenging how we perceive and relate to one another and how we build the communities in which we live and work. The counterculturalists have come, for the most part, from the same powerful centers on the East and West coasts that have produced what sociologist G. William Domhoff calls America's "ruling class," with its interlocking networks of families, schools, and economic and political connections. The counterculture has had its own alternative networks in the twentieth century: in the Northeast, it is Greenwich Village versus Wall Street, with satellite colonies in Woodstock and Provincetown. On the West Coast, it is North Beach versus San Francisco's Bohemian Grove, with satellite colonies in Mill Valley and Carmel.[4]

A surprising number of these countercultural types have spent time in northern New Mexico—and at the home of Mabel Dodge Luhan. They provide us with a glimpse of a much less known but valuable history of the search for alternative communities and cultures. This history is intimately connected to the physical and cultural landscapes of northern New Mexico, which have encouraged forms of holistic thinking that continue to inspire men and women to dream of refashioning the world anew.[5]

UTOPIAN VISTAS

Petroglyph rock, Courtyard, Mabel Dodge Luhan House.

Introduction

The story begins like this. Five hundred years ago, the large petroglyph rock that marks one border of the courtyard of the Mabel Dodge Luhan house, in Taos, New Mexico, was placed there by the Tiwa Indians to help anchor the energy of Pueblo Mountain, from whose Blue Lake they trace their origin as a tribe. The petroglyph rock has had an additional function over these years. It has been used as a navigational guide for extraterrestrial visitors because the site also marks the entranceway to other dimensions.

The story continues. At the time the Spanish conquistadores arrived in Taos in 1540, the Indians who were living on this sacred site failed to heed the warnings of their arrival, and thus lost both their home and their land. They were later reincarnated as the codirectors of Las Palomas de Taos, who were brought together in the 1980s and given another chance to serve as stewards of the land, called on once again to protect it from danger.[1]

I can think of no better way to begin a cultural history of the Mabel Dodge Luhan house than this "reading" given by Gilberto Sanchez, an Hispanic psychic and healer, who visited there in May 1989. If any house in the history of Anglo-American civilization deserves to have its own creation myth, it is this one. From its origins in 1918 through the present, the house has attracted so many creative men and women—painters, poets, writers, musicians, social and educational reformers, filmmakers, philosophers, psychologists, and psychics—that I have at times been tempted to attribute its magnetic attraction to the spiritual energies many Taoseños believe are released by the pueblo's sacred mountain.

In December 1991, the Mabel Dodge Luhan house was designated a national historic landmark, one of over two thousand in the country. Among the private homes that have achieved this status, I have not located any with a similar history. Most served as the family homes of prominent individuals in the arts, sciences, or industry and are now private residences, renovated businesses, or museums. None, as far as I know, are able to claim possession by three generations of messianic owners who have imagined their home as an alternative creative space that would transform mainstream American culture. These utopian vistas, and their dystopian undersides, make the Luhan house—and its surrounding Taos environs—a rich site through which to explore the American counterculture in the twentieth century.[2]

In her essay "The Anthropologist as Hero," Susan Sontag provides a philosophical context for my study when she writes of homelessness as *the* existential condition of educated western men and women in the twentieth century.

The felt unreliability of human experience brought about by the inhuman acceleration of historical change has led every sensitive modern mind to the recording of some kind of nausea, of intellectual vertigo. And the only way to cure this spiritual nausea seems to be, at least initially, to exacerbate it. Modern thought is pledged to a kind of applied Hegelianism: seeking its Self in its Other. Europe seeks itself . . . among pre-literate peoples, in a mythic America; a fatigued rationality seeks itself in the impersonal energies of sexual ecstasy or drugs. . . . The "other" is experienced as a harsh purification of "self." But at the same time the "self" is busily colonizing all strange domains of experience.

Although philosophers have contributed to the statement and understanding of this intellectual homelessness . . . it is mainly poets, novelists, and a few painters who have lived *this tortured spiritual impulse, in willed derangement and in self-imposed exile and in compulsive travel.*[3]

Northern New Mexico is one of the germinal sites for understanding the role this "intellectual homelessness" has played in the development of American modernism, comparable in its impact and importance to that of African and Asian cultures on European modernism. On the one hand, American modernists desired to break down the essentialist truths and polar oppositions of western society, especially of nature and culture, that they believed helped to create the political, social, and moral disorder of

Ansel Adams, *Taos Pueblo,* n.d. Yale Collection of American Literature, Beinecke Rare Book and Manuscript Library, Yale University, MDLC.

Anglo civilization. On the other hand, they desired "a there that was always there," an essential, noncontingent, and transhistorical truth that would substitute for the anxiety of temporality and subjectivity. The physical and cultural landscapes of New Mexico seemed to have most of the requisite attributes for serving the American modernist agenda: to create a modern American culture that would cure the malaise of modernity.

Those who lived and worked at the Luhan house have had much to do with constructing the image of Taos as a multicultural Eden, whose indigenous peoples live in peace and harmony with the land. This image has lived side by side with the much less recognized economic reality of northern New Mexico as a place where the majority of people live in poverty, as well as with the often-ignored social reality of Taos as a triethnic community marked by interethnic prejudice and conflict. The dual image of Taos as Shangri-la, and as what the writer John Nichols calls a "third world country," certainly has parallels elsewhere within the United States. But perhaps nowhere have the extremes existed in such striking contrast.[4]

Ernest Knee, *In Back of Mabel's House,* 1933.
Photo courtesy of Santa Fe Lightsource and Eric Knee.

In his essay "Healing, Imagination, and New Mexico," Stephen Fox describes how the state has been subject to various kinds of utopian and dystopian fevers ever since the mid-nineteenth century, when the land and climate began to be promoted for a variety of uses, including the improvement of mental and bodily health. William deBuys's history of New Mexico clarifies the ways in which, over the past two hundred years, "enchantment and exploitation" have accompanied one another. My history of the Luhan house suggests the complex cyclical nature of this pattern: each of the three generations who owned it began with utopian visions that became increasingly commodified, due to factors that were both within and beyond their control.[5]

Los Gallos

Mabel Dodge Luhan (1879–1962) spent much of her life searching for a home in which she could end her sense of being orphaned in the twentieth century. Both the nature and content of her quest place her within one of the most significant traditions of American women's utopian and reformist writing and activism. This tradition began in the nineteenth century with the idea of the home as "a haven from the heartless world" and evolved into a vision of the home as a model for national redemption, of the world *as* home. Luhan completed her search in Taos, New Mexico, where she built the three-story, twenty-two-room Big House, five guest houses, and a twelve-hundred-foot gatehouse, situated on twelve acres contiguous to Taos Pueblo.[6]

Before coming to New Mexico, Luhan had attained an international reputation as a cultural catalyst during her years as an expatriate in Florence, Italy (1905–12), a reputation that expanded dramatically during her tenure in New York City, at 23 Fifth Avenue (1912–17), where she established one of the preeminent salons of the Greenwich Village avant-garde. The disillusionment that she and her radical friends experienced with U.S. entry into World War I in 1917 led to a postwar search for new systems of belief and modes of living that drove many American writers and artists to expatriate themselves in Europe.

Luhan brought many others to the Southwest, where she planned to make her home in Taos the center of a "new world plan" that would regenerate Anglo civilization from its urban-industrialist bias, its individualist and materialist credo, and its Eurocentric vision of culture. Through her marriage to Antonio Luhan, a Pueblo Indian, she hoped to serve as "a bridge between cultures." Together, they would attract the nation's great writers, artists, and activists to discover the social and cultural benefits to be gained from native communities whose religious, aesthetic, and work values were organically integrated with their physical environment.[7]

Those whose lives and works were affected by their visits to the Luhan house and its environs include writers Mary Austin, Myron Brinig, Witter Bynner, Willa Cather, Harvey Fergusson, Aldous Huxley, Spud Johnson, D. H. Lawrence, Oliver La Farge, Jean Toomer, and Frank Waters; painters, sculptors, and photographers Ansel Adams, Dorothy Brett, Andrew Dasburg, Miriam DeWitt, Maynard Dixon, Nicolai Fechin, Laura Gilpin, Marsden Hartley, Ernest Knee, Ward Lockwood, John Marin, Georgia O'Keeffe, Agnes Pelton, Ida Rauh, Arnold Rönnebeck, Maurice Sterne, Paul Strand, Rebecca Strand, Cady Wells, and Edward Weston; musicians Carlos Chavez, Dane Rudhyar, and Leopold Stokowski; theatre designer Robert Edmond Jones and dance choreographer Martha Graham; social theorists, anthropologists, and folklorists John Collier, Carl Jung, Jaime de Angulo, Elsie Clews Parsons, and Ella Young.[8]

Many who came to the Luhan house were at a critical point in their lives, physically, psychologically, or vocationally. For them, the house functioned as a kind of life crisis center: breaking down and healing, making—and sometimes unmaking—love affairs and marriages. Because several visitors often stayed with the Luhans simultaneously, the opportunities for mentoring, cross-fertilization, and feuding were enormously rich, as attested to by the myriad letters and portraits of the Luhans and their guests that appeared over the four decades they inhabited the house. In remarking that Mabel Dodge Luhan had "talons for talent," Ansel Adams drolly summed up the double-edged climate that generated much of the creativity and conflict that occurred there.[9]

Although there were marked differences in temperament, style, and practice among those who visited the Luhan house, many of them can be included within the concept music historian Judith Tick has called "transcendental modernism." An aesthetic based on "an eclectic legacy of ideas which has been linked in American intellectual life since the turn of the century," it included "theosophy, Eastern religious philosophy, nineteenth-century American Transcendentalism, and the imaginative tradition of Walt Whitman." Among Luhan's coterie were an unusual number of pioneers in the arts and social theory who shared her desire to be a "prophet of a new order of man." Believing that cultural vision was central to social revolution, they advocated the preservation of the world's relatively pristine natural environments and the native peoples who inhabited them as necessary to the well-being of modern society.[10]

The Anglo visitors to the Luhan house helped establish what has become a tradition among many twentieth-century New Mexican artists who have shared the belief that they are "relatively free to draw on . . . the symbolic resources" of all three cultures. As Ronald Grimes explained in his study of public ritual and drama in Santa Fe during the 1970s: "The artist is likely to view his own use of symbols as less ideological, hence less exploitative, than the uses of the civil servant, the businessman, or the priest, because he views art as a universal language which is not a means but is its own end."[11]

Most of Luhan's visitors appreciated the wisdom and cultural integrity

Mabel Sterne and Tony Luhan, c. 1918. MDLC.

of ethnic groups barely acknowledged by most other Americans, who did not credit them as participants in, let alone shapers of, American civilization. In their own work, these artists sought not so much to imitate or appropriate native cultures as to adapt certain native aesthetics to their own modes of self-expression in order to make their art and theory more than just a matter of personal vision.

Yet for all their support and understanding, and the often progressive nature of their vision, the relationship of Luhan and her peers to the surrounding Hispanic and Native American communities was an ambiguous and problematic one that evokes the type of serious political, social, and ethical issues raised by other Anglo patronage cultures. They may not have created what folklorist Marta Weigle has called the "Disneyfication" of the Southwest—the commercialization of native arts, and the tourist and real estate industries that have increasingly made Taos a playground for wealthy Anglos who control the economy. But they certainly contributed to these developments. In portraying Taos as a pristine utopia filled with exotic native "others," they helped to attract the very kind of people they most wanted to keep out. By creating art and literature that rarely referenced the

Dennis Hopper on roof of Big House, n. d.
Photo courtesy of Tony Maguire, Turtle Island Archives.

daily social and economic realities of Hispanics and Native Americans, they helped mask the interethnic, racial, and class strife that has been a persistent reality of the region.[12]

During the 1960s and 1970s, the turmoil generated by the clash between utopian dreams and their opposing realities, in the second incarnation of the counterculture that swept over northern New Mexico, made the Luhan house, once again, a center of creativity, conflict, and controversy.

The Mud Palace

In March 1970, Dennis Hopper purchased the Mabel Dodge Luhan house from Mabel's granddaughter, Bonnie Evans. Hopper dubbed it "The Mud Palace" and owned it until 1978. He discovered the Luhan property while he was making the seminal 1960s countercultural film *Easy Rider* (1969), more than half of which was filmed in northern New Mexico. Hopper's life was as self-consciously emblematic of his era as Luhan's was of hers. Just as she had, Hopper arrived on the Taos scene at an epiphanal moment, though his was to prove more destructive and self-destructive than creative. Taos exacerbated what had been for many years a life lived, to borrow Susan Sontag's words, in "tortured spiritual impulse, in willed derangement."

Before moving to New Mexico, Hopper had been an active member of the Los Angeles art scene, as a poet, painter, and photographer, as well as a major early collector of Abstract Expressionism, California Assemblage, and Pop Art. Just as the Mabel Dodge salon was a central meeting place for the Greenwich Village avant-garde in the 1910s, Hopper's home in Bel Air became known as a haven for Pop Art in the 1960s. When he moved to Taos, he hung the walls of the Luhan house with the late modernist and postmodern descendants of her generation: Wallace Berman, Bruce Conner, Ed Kienholz, Roy Lichtenstein, Robert Rauschenberg, Ad Reinhardt, and Andy Warhol.

In the late 1960s, northern New Mexico once again began to attract artists, writers, and social visionaries who felt alienated by urban, industrial culture and by U.S. involvement in another war, this time in Vietnam. Along with them came hordes of disaffected youth, many of them urban hippies eager to "get back to the land." By 1970, there were some twenty-seven communes in Taos county, one of the largest geographical concentrations in the nation. Most local Taoseños had a hard time differentiating Hopper's Mud Palace from the surrounding hippie communes.

As soon as he moved in, in May 1970, Hopper turned the house into a collective, where he worked for fourteen months editing his first solo film project, *The Last Movie.* Filmed in an Indian village in the mountains of Peru, the movie is an apocalyptic study of the decline and fall of the American empire, in which the Indians sacrifice an Anglo, played by Dennis Hopper, in order to reclaim their land. The movie was intended to establish Hopper's home in Taos as the American center of independent filmmaking—a counter-Hollywood. *The Last Movie* has uncanny parallels with Mabel Luhan's imagined subversion of Anglo-American civilization as well as with some of the fiction written by D. H. Lawrence as a result of his travels in New Mexico and Mexico. Hopper, in fact, saw himself as Lawrence's successor. He would do with film, the most important medium of his time, what Lawrence tried to do with language—revolutionize the consciousness of his generation.

Through the portals of the Mud Palace Hopper brought the stars of his era, most of them artists, poets, songwriters, actors, and musicians: Leonard

Cohen, Bo Diddley, Bob Dylan, Peter Fonda, Kris Kristofferson, Jack Nicholson, Joni Mitchell, Michelle Phillips—whom Hopper married in the solarium on Halloween—Nicholas Ray, Susan St. James, and Alan Watts, among the more notable. Indians from the pueblo visited frequently, and Hopper befriended Reies Tijerina, the militant leader of the Hispanic Alianza.

The artists Hopper collected and emulated shared with those of Luhan's generation the credo that "art is an experience, not an object." They believed that the artist is a "truth-sayer," and that art should have a high moral—and even religious—purpose. The post–World War II aesthetic of Hopper's generation was marked by its countercultural revulsion toward bourgeois civilization, scientism, and materialism, and by its search for "rock-bottom truth in an era when the work of man so often seemed a force of ugliness and destruction." Hopper's inner circle was more than alienated, however. They were outlaws who resisted the political and aesthetic conformity of the McCarthy era and the Hollywood code by violating every respectable norm. The art they produced was angry, outraged, and outrageous; it savaged middle-class American society with wit, fury, and blistering nihilism. They took the detritus of bourgeois consumer culture and twisted it into parodies in their sculptures of rusted tin, nylon stockings, and their art "prints" made on Xerox machines. At its best, the art they produced was powerful and disturbing; at its worst, it was a frightening emblem of the atomic age that art historians believe unleashed it.[13]

Hopper brought that rage with him to New Mexico, where, among other things, it affected his relationship with Hispanics who were far less willing to tolerate Anglo patronage than they had been during Mabel Luhan's era. Their criticism of Luhan was rarely made public, although her Anglo friends and artist colleagues were more than happy to publicize her flaws to the world in thinly veiled caricatures and biographical portraits. Hopper faced a very different Taos, one that threatened his life, not just his image. Hispanics were literally up in arms over an invasion that accosted their values and threatened their livelihood. Before Hopper's arrival, the business community and town government had given clear public signals that the hippies should "go back where they came from." Although Hopper looked like a hippie, the way he threw his money around and swaggered about town, and his attempt to make a citizen's arrest of some local youths who were harassing him, infuriated many members of Taos' Hispanic community. He became for them—ironically, to say the least—a symbol of the Anglo establishment.

Luhan and Hopper seemed to be saying "No" to the direction of American civilization by fleeing the city and retreating to a premodern, rural society. But their utopianism reveals the kinds of contradictions that have often subverted the ideal of community in American history. Both were determined to redeem the world in *their* own image, and their narcissism confused their politics and muddied their social vision. Luhan continually fought "progressive" forces in Taos who threatened to modernize "her" community, which she believed included Taos Pueblo. Hopper exploited Indians in film and abused women in his life in ways that violated his own radical intentions.

The most striking photographs of Hopper during his early Taos years show him in three contradictory personae: the classic Hollywood cowboy; Jesus Christ; and Charles Manson, the psychotic instigator of the Tate-LaBianca murders, who was planning a hippie takeover of American society and whose biography Hopper contemplated making on film. These images mark the way in which Hopper's life signified the decline of the traditional macho myth of the American West, as well as the devolution of the 1960s counterculture. Hopper had admired and played the role of the gun-toting loner in numerous TV and film westerns. But he was also a child of postfrontier America and enough of a Beat to want to kick that hero offstage. Hopper was a lot like James Dean in his debut film, *Rebel without a Cause,* a movie in which Hopper also appeared. He was a rebel with and without a cause, whose ambiguous self-presentation suggests the symbiotic relationship between the messianic savior and the mass murderer.

Las Palomas de Taos

Were I mystically inclined, I would attribute my coming to the Mabel Dodge Luhan house in July 1977 as fated. I arrived having recently completed my doctoral dissertation on Luhan, and just as I was about to begin a tenure-track position in the English Department of the University of Massachusetts at Boston. There was no way I could know at the time that the trajectory of my scholarly career would become intimately involved with both the history and future of this house. I arrived at the tail end of Dennis Hopper's reign, when the house looked like a defunct hippie commune, uncared for and filled with the junk of its last renters.

There is no doubt that the Luhan house breathed an audible sigh of relief when it was sold in January 1978 to Kitty and George Otero. If Dennis Hopper's generation reflected a darker version of Luhan's iconoclasm, the Oteros and their colleagues reflected the more benign reformist elements of the utopian heritage she established. When I returned in 1980, the house was undergoing both renovation and revitalization, as the Oteros turned it into a center for the development of global and multicultural education. The log cabin that had served as Hopper's editing room now held workshops for teachers; the garage that had once housed the famous *Easy Rider* motorcycles was converted into two new bedrooms for the clientele who participated in the educational and cultural programs created by Las Palomas de Taos, a nonprofit foundation.

As an antiwar activist and feminist who taught in a large, urban, working-class university that served diverse students, I found the Oteros' interest in democratizing schools and revitalizing teachers highly compatible with my own concerns. The Luhan house was a lot less glamorous than in the heyday of Luhan and Hopper. But its heroes, if there were any, were the ordinary folk who must be counted on for any lasting cultural transformation—teachers, administrators, parents, students, and community leaders from New Mexico and other parts of the nation. It did not take me long to find ways of fitting my own research and teaching interests into the workshops on schooling and on Southwest cultures, and to work out a barter arrangement by which I traded talks on the history of the house and its inhabitants for room and board. It took me much longer to break through my highly romanticized vision of New Mexico, which had been shaped primarily by Mabel Luhan's writings and reinforced by the compelling beauty of the land.

My life as a scholar and teacher has followed a path not dissimilar to the history of the Mabel Dodge Luhan house. I am part of the first generation of scholars who began to look beyond the story of the American past that had enshrined Puritans as the progenitors and New England as the fountainhead and locus of American life and letters. We were in graduate school when the histories and literatures of women and minorities were beginning to change university curricula, and when new critical theories were beginning to transform the way we read, what we read, and what questions we asked of the past.

The revisionist history of the American West that came of age in the 1980s embraced the cultures of women, Chicanos, Indians, and Chinese, and explored the frontier's connection to urban history, industrialism, and tourism. The Southwest was one of the last literary-historical frontiers to be reexamined. Like Mabel when she first discovered New Mexico, I felt that I had come upon territory where my imagination was among the first

George Otero leading teacher workshop, 1979.
Photo courtesy of Las Palomas de Taos.

to "play," as I contributed to reconstructing the all-but-forgotten history of the early twentieth-century Anglo artists and writers who lived and worked in New Mexico, establishing their place in the development of twentieth-century American culture. But the very forces that helped me stake my claim to this territory led to other discoveries as well, some of which revealed myths that my recoveries perpetuated.

Two incidents stand out in my memory, as I moved toward a more complex and tragic vision of a land that had soon begun to feel like my second home. In 1980, I gave my first talk at the Luhan house, on the relationship between Mabel and D. H. Lawrence. Seated on the stairs outside of what had once been Mabel's bedroom, I spoke to a courtyard overflowing with local Taoseños. That was the first weekend I had ever spent in Taos, and it was punctuated by the murder of a young teenage boy who had stopped late at night to urinate and was shot and killed by the man on whose property he was standing. The next day, as I was giving my talk, a fourteen-year-old runaway Anglo girl, who worked part-time at the Luhan house and lived with an Indian at Taos Pueblo, was being pursued by her knife-wielding lover in the kitchen, behind the stairs where I spoke.

Although I was shocked by these events, I did not make much of them. Only after spending a lot more time in and around Taos did I come to understand the acts of violence that punctuated this seeming rural paradise and to learn about the poverty and despair that were a part of daily life in what is billed as one of the most idyllic communities in the United States. I discovered the third world that lives next door to the first world, an often invisible shadow to the tourists who are the mainstay of one of the poorest economies in the nation.

The second incident was more public and personally embarrassing. In 1983, I came to the University of New Mexico as part of a team of women scholars who were working on a book about Native American, Hispanic American, and Anglo-American women's responses to southwestern landscapes. I was speaking at a university-sponsored forum on the subjects of my research, which now included writers Mary Austin and Alice Corbin Henderson, as well as Mabel Luhan. The moment my talk was through, there was an immediate outburst from a woman in the audience. She shouted that Mabel was a "rich bitch" who had come to New Mexico and exploited it for her own ego. An older, less strident, but equally indignant woman then stood up and said it was Mabel's writing that had brought her to New Mexico, now her beloved home. Later, I learned that another member of the audience had complained to one of the organizers of the conference about "the woman from Massachusetts" being brought in to talk about New Mexico.[14]

Although it is easy for me to laugh at this incident now, at the time I was mortified to think that I could be viewed, like Mabel, as a cultural imperialist. But the shock may have been just what I needed to begin to examine the limitations of my research. Over the next few years, I read the works of William deBuys, John Bodine, Charles Briggs, Sylvia Rodriguez, and Marta Weigle. They have retold the story of New Mexico from the kinds of perspectives that I was bringing into my classrooms in Boston, but that had not yet affected my writing on New Mexico. Their critical perusal of race and class relations helped me recognize the less benign impact of the Anglo artists and writers who had helped turn the state into an "exotic" colony. Sylvia Rodriguez's criticisms of the art colonists' aesthetic blindness to the economic and racial oppression experienced by the majority of northern New Mexicans no longer allowed me to just celebrate their contributions to American art history.[15]

In *Taos and Its Artists* (1949), Mabel Luhan wrote that during her forty-year residency, Taos served as a "fabulous honeycomb, irresistible and nourishing," to artists, writers, and social activists. While there is no doubt about the truth of her assertion, her view of Taos has been qualified in ways that

Filming of *Twins*, June 1988, Courtyard, Mabel Dodge Luhan house. Photo courtesy of Bob Campagna. (Danny DeVito and Arnold Schwarzenegger are in the center.)

make for a much more complex and conflicted vision of its place in the lives of its inhabitants, as well as its role in regional and national culture.[16]

In its most recent history, the mission of the Luhan house has been broadened beyond the elitist core of Luhan's cultural "honeycomb" to include members of the region's three major ethnic groups as leaders, staff, and learners. Yet its leadership has been no less utopian in orientation. They have been strongly committed to a belief in the house's "spirit of place" as a transformative environment. In the words of Susan Chambers-Cook, their goal has been to create "a living-learning laboratory" that can serve as a model to lead Americans into the twenty-first century with a clearer consciousness of their relationship and obligation to the planet and its global village.[17]

Like their predecessors, the owners and directors of Las Palomas have also experienced—and created—turmoil and dissent within the smaller and larger communities they inhabit. They have suffered frequent staff turnover and the suspicion and hostility of members of the local community. Las Palomas has existed for most of its life at the edge of financial crisis, a situation primarily due to economic circumstances beyond its control. But its fiscal instability worsened when George Otero began an ambitious building program in 1989 and Susan Chambers-Cook reoriented their offerings in a more New Age direction. In fact, it is Otero and Chambers-Cook whom the psychic Gilberto Sanchez claimed were brought back to save the endangered site. It is at least in part due to the financial results of their expansionist dream to create a wider venue for their social philosophy that the Luhan house was first put up for sale just at the moment when it achieved its status as a national historic landmark.[18]

Whether or not one believes Gilberto Sanchez's reading of the petroglyph rock that resides in the courtyard of the Mabel Dodge Luhan house, there is no doubt that the house has earned a place within the history of utopian ventures in American culture. Its legendary status has even infiltrated contemporary popular—some might say schlock—culture.

In the 1988 Universal Studios movie release *Twins,* Arnold Schwarzenegger and Danny DeVito outwit a diabolical scientist at Los Alamos, who tricked their mother into being part of a genetic experiment to produce the perfect child. Schwarzenegger is the ideal specimen the scientists hoped for, whom they rear in secret; DeVito is his unexpected, unwanted, and very unidentical "twin." When the two orphans find out who their mother is, they set off to find their home. It turns out to be the Mabel Dodge Luhan house. Named Whispering Pines, it is an artist's colony administered by the Benedict Foundation, a creation of the painter Marion Benedict, that provides free shelter, food, and a creative environment for artists and craftspeople. DeVito, who has lived his life as a con artist, is ecstatic to find out that "Mom is rich." But Mom won't accept them at first, because she doesn't believe their story. They have to win her back by displaying the kind of old-fashioned moral values that earn them the right to a family and a home.

It is unlikely that Susan Sontag would give *Twins* high aesthetic marks. But she would recognize its mythic story line as part of the continuing saga of spiritual homelessness and the search for redemption in the twentieth century. (In her list of twentieth-century cures, the plan to produce the perfect human would fall under the attempt to solve "humanistic problems" through "scientific 'value neutrality.'") It is equally doubtful that Mabel Luhan would have approved of the movie. But she might well have recognized the text as a pop version of her own—and her heirs'—century-long quest to create a world in which we can be "at home." It is that quest, and its meaning and consequences for twentieth-century American culture, that I undertake to explore.

PART 1

The Mabel Dodge Luhan Years

Los Gallos (1918–1962)

When the magnetic center, the Purpose, the clear Vision and the Will are there, one by one the individuals are drawn into the magic circle.
Dane Rudhyar to Mabel Dodge Luhan
July 2[, 1925]

I like what Mabel has dug up out of the Earth here. . . . No one who hasn't seen it and who hasn't seen her at it can know much about this Taos myth—it is unbelievable—One perfect day after another.
Georgia O'Keeffe to Henry McBride
[1929]

I feel that Taos is one of the great magnetic centers of the world.
Leopold Stokowski to Mabel Dodge Luhan
January 6, 1938

CHAPTER ONE

Anglo Expatriates and the

New Mexico Landscape

In the first decade of the twentieth century, New Mexicans had to fight to enter the union because their predominantly Hispanic and Indian populations gave them a presumably un-American ethnic cast. By the 1920s, the postwar influx of some three hundred Anglo expatriate artists, writers, and social visionaries was well underway, a number of them claiming that the two indigenous groups legitimized New Mexico as *the* most American of places.[1]

A generation earlier, Walt Whitman, the poet who arguably had the most profound influence on the first generation of modernists that came to New Mexico, anticipated their vision. Although it is doubtful that Mabel Luhan and her peers knew of Walt Whitman's prophetic letter, written in 1883, on the 333d anniversary of the founding of Santa Fe, they shared his point of view:

We Americans have yet to really learn our own antecedents, and sort them, to unify them. They will be found ampler than has been supposed, and in widely different sources. Thus far, impressed by New England writers and schoolmasters, we tacitly abandon ourselves to the notion that our United States have been fashioned from the British Islands only, and essentially form a second England only—which is a very great mistake. Many leading traits for our future national personality, and some of the best ones, will certainly prove to have originated from other than British stock. . . .

To that composite American identity of the future, Spanish character will supply some of the most needed parts. . . . As to your aboriginal or Indian population . . . I know it seems to be agreed that they must gradually dwindle. . . . But I am not at all clear about that. As America . . . develops, adapts, entwines, faithfully identifies its own—are we to see it cheerfully accepting and using all the contributions of foreign lands from the whole outside globe—and then rejecting the only ones instinctively its own—the autochtonic ones?[2]

Why were so many of the men and women who came to New Mexico after World War I searching for the "real" America among cultures that had been ignored, rejected, or despised by the mainstream? There are myriad reasons, most of them intimately tied to patterns of disruption and change within the dominant culture, as well as to the continuing historical search to define a national character and culture that had its roots in the early national period. At the turn of the twentieth century, during the period when the United States emerged as a leader among the urban, industrial empires of the world and experienced its most intensive waves of immigration, economic upheaval, and class divisions, the search for a national character and culture became seriously contested. Many Americans sided with the social scientists, political analysts, and journalists who defended the superiority of the Anglo-Saxon and Teutonic heritages as the ground of American democracy and the guarantor of its continued health and prosperity.[3]

A minority of social reformers and social scientists, many of them first-generation immigrants and African Americans, believed in a more inclusive idea of national identity. They argued that the continued social and political health of the nation was dependent on the cultural "gifts" and economic benefits of immigrants and people of color. In his essay "Transnational America," published in the *Seven Arts* in 1917, the cultural nationalist Randolph Bourne wrote that the 15 million or so immigrants who had come to the United States in the past two decades were helping the United States to become a model of multiculturalism, an emblem to the world of how to end the centuries-long battles among nationalities and religions that had devastated much of the earth. Some of the future leaders of New Mexico's cultural renaissance were fleeing these very immigrants in whom Bourne had such faith. But most shared his belief that non-Anglo, nonwhite cultures had laid the groundwork for a revitalized American civilization.[4]

The Anglo expatriates who came to New Mexico were adrift in the social and cultural turmoil of the modern era; in fact, they were instigators of some of that turmoil, nay-sayers to the hierarchies and polarities of the Victorian age that had placed men and women, black and white, intellect and emotion, in opposition. For the Victorian elite, art was imitative and culture the preserve of the educated and upper classes, who used it to define and consolidate their control over the so-called barbaric lower orders. For the cultural radicals in Luhan's circle, art was intended to be psychically and socially transformative.[5]

In pre–World War I America, New York City was the base of operations, Greenwich Village the home, and Alfred Stieglitz the most important articulator of this countercultural vision. He was also the common denominator connecting many of the innovative artists who made up the first generation to visit the Luhan house. Through his patronage of the European and American avant-garde at his 291 studio in New York, his editing of the avant-garde journal *Camera Work,* and his photography, he developed a coterie who shared his belief that modern art could heal the psyche of the alienated artist, as well as the divisions within society itself. We cannot fully understand the attraction of the early modernists to New Mexico without understanding Stieglitz's credo, although, like Emerson, he was more bourgeois than his most important disciples, and he himself never visited New Mexico.[6]

Stieglitz exemplified the American intellectual's ambivalent stance toward European civilization. He accepted it as both the repository of a rich, traditional past and the heartland of revolutionary theories in social and aesthetic thought and practice. But no one argued more eloquently than he for a "native" American culture that would establish its own viable traditions without imitating or emulating Europe. Stieglitz's dictum was that Americans must create their own authentic art out of a fully realized sense of place. Those who went to New Mexico seem to have adopted this credo more determinedly than other artists who came under his influence.[7]

The entrance of the United States into World War I, especially the war's impact on the home front, had a profoundly adverse impact on a large number of the cultural radicals who formed the vanguard of modernism. Wartime hysteria and repression were directed at anyone who was less than "100 percent [Anglo] American." The censorship of the press even affected art journals like *Camera Work,* which issued its last number in 1917. The war exaggerated the fears over whether there was an American culture or whether it would continue to exist. Conservatives argued that

America's ethnic hodgepodge prevented it from producing a "real civilization," whereas radicals feared the "dreary homogeneity" of the "100 percenters." The disillusionment of the Luhan circle was in good part due to the fact that many of them had believed they were helping to usher in a brave new world of social justice and aesthetic freedom. Even if they did not have precisely the same political or cultural agenda, most of them were supportive of the rights of women and minorities to a fair share of the nation's economic wealth and acknowledged their contributions to American civilization.[8]

Artists' Colonies and Utopian Communities

In rejecting the city, at least as their source of inspiration, and in establishing residence in one of the least- populated and most remote regions of the United States, the expatriates who moved to or sojourned in New Mexico were not rejecting modernism. Nor were they necessarily abandoning the reformist spirit that had inspired their work. What they rejected was the possibility that the urban landscape could provide the conditions and means necessary to their personal, aesthetic, and social visions. The city was the home of machine civilization, a turbulent reminder of the power of the nation-state to steamroll its populace into "mindless conformity" and to reduce human life to rubble in its capacity to make war. It was also the home of the uprooted immigrants and African Americans that some of them associated with the chaos of the urban centers they inhabited.[9]

Santa Fe and Taos were neither the first nor the only "colonies" established by twentieth-century artists who envisioned a sense of place that would nourish their work and their lives. Karal Ann Marling has discussed the burgeoning of these colonies between 1890 and 1910 in Provincetown, Old Lyme, Woodstock, Carmel, and other rural spaces scattered across the United States. Artists and intellectuals took "to the woods and dunes and deserts as a way of life around 1900, many settling permanently in remote outposts and trying to forge a meaningful communal existence." They established studios, galleries, and schools that often involved a variety of different arts and crafts, including painting, weaving, sculpting, bookbinding, and furniture-making. Marling distinguishes between two types of colonies: those that sprang from the Barbizon school, whose painters moved to rural areas to paint "in plein air"; and the "intentional colonies," influenced by the arts and crafts movement, which "arose as a result of advance planning on the part of founders with a mission—founders determined to construct countercultures, away from the blight and turmoil of industrial cities, where circumstances favorable to the creative life could be cultivated, and from which positive humanizing influences for social betterment would emanate." Like Woodstock, the Taos colony that Luhan helped to establish derived from both impulses—the desire for "a formalized Utopian structure and the cult of the picturesque." It is no accident that Andrew Dasburg, who worked and taught at Woodstock in the 1910s and 1920s, became a leader of the modernist movement in New Mexico, nor that Luhan, Dasburg, and Hartley had been part of the Provincetown colony.[10]

What distinguished the colonies that were established in Santa Fe around Alice Corbin Henderson and Mary Austin, and in Taos around Mabel Luhan, was that they did not view themselves as segregated from their surrounding world. Their agendas were more ambitious and outward looking as they sought a national audience for their alternative models of community and culture. In this respect, they shared ideals with some of the anarchist and mystical counterculture communities that Laurence Veysey discusses in his illuminating study, *The Communal Experience.* Most historians of communal movements argue that political and religious utopias represent two different and conflicting traditions. But Veysey demonstrates the connections between them at the turn of the twentieth century, which are particularly pertinent to understanding the visionaries who were attracted to Mabel Luhan's Taos circle.[11]

During the Progressive Era, the ideas and programs of mystics and anarchists shared space in the same journals and were sometimes touted by the same radical individuals and groups. New Thought, for example, was an eclectic mix of Eastern religions—Hindu, Buddhist, Vendantist, Sufi, Zen—and the more occult strains of Christianity, whose adherents increased dramatically in the early twentieth century as they became increasingly alienated from mainstream Protestantism. This broader movement relied on an all-loving God who offered a continuous supply of divine sustenance and the promise of "at-one-ment" with the universe. Although much of New Thought emphasized a passive giving up of mind and will, there were also elements within it that stressed the active evolution of consciousness to higher and higher stages, eventuating in the "cosmic consciousness" that Luhan and many of her friends were bent on achieving.[12]

At the turn of the twentieth century "theosophical pronouncements" often had "a definite utopian ring to them, as the idea of service to mankind was translated into the concept of the spiritual leader who 'may guide the civilization and races of men in their evolution, enabling them to attain far higher ground than would otherwise be the case.'" Interesting parallels exist between the millennium anticipated by Marxist visionaries that would follow the overthrow of capitalism and the New Age that was dreamed of by the leaders of New Thought. For many of the prewar radicals there was no necessary contradiction between using one's energies to affect "outer existence through social action" and using them to affect "inner [existence] through meditation and self-mastery." Thus Mabel's colleagues in Greenwich Village could simultaneously involve themselves in radical action and journalism, psychoanalysis, Christian Science, and other New Thought practices.[13]

A number of contemporary critics have held Luhan's generation of cultural radicals at least partially responsible for "the triumph of the therapeutic" and "the culture of narcissism." But as Veysey points out, it has been typical of American cultural radicals to try to embrace both self-expression and the communitarian impulse. While "it can indeed be radical to work politically for a redistribution of wealth . . . [which] directly challenges the centers of social and economic power . . . this kind of radicalism offers no sense of a profound alternative to existing styles of living or patterns of human relationship." Since the middle of the nineteenth century, American cultural radicals have engaged in a wide range of not always compatible beliefs and activities. Underlying these sometimes contradictory desires is a search for a coherent worldview that will sanctify the human community, provide meaning and order in the universe, and maximize individual consciousness.[14]

Certainly Luhan and some of her cohorts can be justly criticized for the self-indulgence of their quests for evolutionary consciousness and mystic self-gratification. Although they did not see their personal journeys of self-realization as incompatible with a larger social agenda, they also did not recognize the contradiction between their arrogant belief in themselves as spiritual leaders who would light the way for the masses and their presumed commitment to democratic forms of community and culture. Yet it was their belief in themselves as transformers of culture that inspired some of their best work and led to the recognition and valuing of Hispanic and Native American arts. Luhan's seemingly absurd faith in the New York occultist who defined her mission in life as making known to the world that Taos was "the beating heart of the universe" helped to generate the synergistic creativity that took place there.[15]

Woody's Mill on the Road to Taos, c. 1920s.
Photo courtesy of Museum of New Mexico.

The Flight to New Mexico

The transcendental modernists who came to New Mexico were seeking to heal what T. S. Eliot called *the* disease of modernity: "the dissociation of sensibility," whose origins he traced to the French philosopher Descartes and to seventeenth-century Europe's scientific revolution. Antiscientistic, they believed that New Mexico was a place that would help them to reunite body and mind and spirit and matter, because it called forth the experience of art as generation. In the process of reintegrating themselves, they would discover the means by which their art could do the same for the culture at large. D. H. Lawrence spoke of New Mexico as the possible site of his utopian colony "Rananim," where men and women would learn to live simply and in harmony with one another and with the land.[16]

Edward Curtis, *Red Willow* [Tony Lujan], 1905.
Photo courtesy of the Gallery of the North American Indian, Santa Fe.

Disgusted by the mass culture purveyed to an increasingly consumption-oriented mainstream, artists Marsden Hartley and Maynard Dixon hoped to replace the homogenized "melting pot" advocated by assimilationists with a national culture that was rooted in regional and ethnic cultures. In 1919, Hartley wrote of Native American art: "The red man is the one truly indigenous religionist and esthete of America." Twelve years later Dixon wrote about the best-known work from his Taos period, *Earth Knower:* "You can't argue with those desert mountains—and if you live among them enough—like the Indian does—you don't want to. They have something for us much more real than some imported art style."[17]

Equally disdainful of American capitalism and Russian communism, reformers Mary Austin and John Collier searched for alternative models of community in the village socialism that they associated with Pueblo, and with certain aspects of Hispanic, culture. In 1922, Collier wrote of Taos Pueblo as "The Red Atlantis." In a 1925 essay Austin wrote for the reformist journal *Survey Graphic*, she stated that the "apostles of a new social order" should not go to "the cafes of Prague or the cellars of Leningrad," but to New Mexico to discover "the most interesting possibility of social evolution that the world scene at present affords."[18]

Writers Jean Toomer and Frank Waters scoured the world's myths and religions searching for what Carl Jung called "the reconciling symbol" that would bring inner peace and promote social harmony and ecological consciousness. Toomer discovered in New Mexico fertile ground for his dream of "blending . . . all peoples into one American race." In his notes on Taos he wrote, "Here is the possibility of a new people. Men and women in spirit to match the grandeur of this earth." After moving to Taos at the behest of Mabel Luhan in 1937, Waters spent much of his life's work pursuing the correspondences between Southwest Indian and Eastern religions in an attempt to promote a humanistic faith that is "built on the premise that man's psyche and the cosmos are related to each other as inner and outer worlds."[19]

Dance and theatre innovators Robert Edmond Jones and Martha Graham identified traditional Indian and Spanish rituals as "total" art forms that could serve as inspirations for avant-garde forms of expression. Dreaming of a drama that could give life to "the vision of the living soul of the world," Jones imagined an adobe "theatre of the new world" to accompany Mabel Luhan's call to the nation's "Greeks" to make the Southwest their home base. Graham's interest in creating modern American dances that would have the mass appeal of folkloric art was provoked by her witness of Hispanic and Indian dances during her visits to New Mexico in the early 1930s.[20]

For theosophist and modern composer Dane Rudhyar, the Southwest's indigenous arts became models for the promotion of psychic health and international peace and understanding. Rudhyar intended his music to help create an "emotional transformation" in his listeners that would allow them to overcome their egos and the "ghosts of the personal past." At the same time, he wished to bring "social significance" back to music by promoting the "planetarization of consciousness" through his advocacy of world music. Leopold Stokowski argued for recording the music of Indians throughout North and South America, as a means of laying "the foundations of world culture" and world peace in the post–World War II era.[21]

Perhaps John Collier best summed up the millennial promise these Anglo expatriates from mainstream America constructed from the Native American cultures of the Southwest: "If our modern world should be able to recapture this power, the earth's natural resources and web of life would not be irrevocably wasted within the twentieth century. . . . True democracy founded in neighborhoods and reaching over the world would become the realized heaven on earth. And living peace, not just an interlude between wars, would be born and would last through the ages."[22]

The Physical Landscape

What was it, specifically, about the sparsely populated and little-known terrain of northern New Mexico that inspired such visions and visionaries? First and foremost was the identification with the land. To attract D. H. Lawrence to Taos, Mabel Luhan wrote him that it was "like the dawn of world," suggesting both its possibilities for spiritual rebirth and for aesthetic inscription. Robert Rosenblum has pointed out that after the man-made debacle of World War I, the "sacrosanct world of prehistoric nature" moved to a central place in the worldview of American artists. Northern New Mexico offered just about the best that was available of that commodity, as a landscape that had always been "associated with the world after history had come to an end." The insistence of its dramatic geography and climate put humans in their place, at the same time that it challenged them to find the creative resources to match its power.[23]

The New Mexican landscape provided the traditional western myth in a new guise. Instead of the lone cowboy going off into the wilderness to prove himself a man by wielding his gun and pitting himself against an unforgiving land on the fringe of civilization, artists pitted their paintbrushes, pens, and cameras against a landscape so overwhelming in its grandeur that it could have easily eclipsed personal vision and individual creativity. At the same time, the land beckoned them with the promise that their egos would find a connection to something larger than themselves. Sharyn Udall has noted that the idea of the Southwest as a "spiritually-charged land . . . found new currency after the turn of the century among . . . pioneers of modernism" for whom "traditional pictorial means could not adequately express their spiritual, utopian and metaphysical ideas. Their search for other forms produced a new artistic litany, in which symbolic and allegorical content assumed a new purity, with emphasis on color and light as bearers of meaning."[24]

Among the mystically inclined who were drawn to the Luhan house, the obvious topographical parallels between Taos, Tibet, and other Asian terrains suggested that New Mexico was the link that connected West and East, Europe and Asia. In her book *Taos and Its Artists* (1947), Mabel Luhan asked her readers to consider whether the name Taos could have derived "from the small band of devotees who followed Lao-tze westward out of China, imbued with the teaching of the Tao," whose "non-aggressive, moderate politesse of the heart" she found consistent with Pueblo ideals of conduct. Mabel fancifully linked the settlement of Taos and the Pueblo religion with the Tao, while associating her environment with both the Old Testament's Eden and the mythical Himalayan kingdom of Shangri-la.[25]

In Taos, the Sacred Mountain provided artists and writers with a source for their own creation myths and re-visioning of America. As early as 1927, John McGinnis, writing about Taos for the *Southwest Review,* noted that Taos artists were painting the mountain so industriously that "it seems destined to become as familiar in America as the Prudential Company has made the Rock of Gibraltar." Jean Toomer was told by the Taos Indians that the mountain was "the gateway to Heaven." British clairvoyant Geoffrey Hodson, who visited Taos in 1930, announced that "the spirit of a diva lived in the mountain and radiated creative energy" that was measurable—"three feet off the ground in Taos and extending south to Santa Fe where its power diminished to six inches."[26]

Along with the terrain, the climate of northern New Mexico was believed to have healing powers, especially for those with lung diseases. In 1916, Alice Corbin Henderson, an associate editor of *Poetry,* one of the important modernist "little magazines" of the era, came from Chicago to Santa Fe for her health. She wasted no time in making connections between the physical and spiritual healthfulness of the southwestern landscape, which included new ways of thinking about the metaphor of land as woman. The verse that opens her first book of New Mexico poems, *Red Earth* (1920), contrasts the worlds of the city and the desert in terms of male and female identities. The city is youthful, strident, aggressive, gigantic, and noisy—the prototypical attributes of the American man who seeks to shape the landscape to match his materialist visions. The desert, on the other hand, is ancient, peaceful, and religious, its habitats scaled for survival:

After the shout of the giant,
Youthful and brawling and strong
Building the cities of men,
Here is the desert of silence, . . .
An old, old woman who mumbles her beads
And crumbles to stone.[27]

If northern New Mexico was particularly attractive to women writers, artists, and reformers such as Alice Corbin Henderson, Mabel Luhan, Mary Austin, Willa Cather, Georgia O'Keeffe, Elsie Clews Parsons, and other "daughters of the desert," it was because no one had mastered this vast, spacious, and thinly populated expanse of desert, mesa, and mountains. Indeed, that it could not be mastered was attractive to their sense of themselves as women who were seeking to make their own imprint on American culture and as ecologists who believed that their fellow Americans needed to learn how to engage in a nondestructive relationship with the land. The very grudgingness of the land, its indifference to human presumption and its ability to take back its own, challenged them to tackle it on its own terms and to grow through their own inner resources.[28]

The Cultural Landscape

Northern New Mexico became one of the important sites for the gender wars that Sandra Gilbert and Susan Gubar have discussed as marking the emergence of modernism in the early twentieth century. The battle of the sexes sometimes took on a larger-than-life-size scale around the female-dominated magnets of Santa Fe and Taos, in part because strong women were controlling what had been traditionally male-dominated space, in this case the cultural being coterminous with the physical frontier. Male prophets D. H. Lawrence and Jean Toomer met their female matches in Mabel Luhan and Mary Austin, who laid claim to New Mexico's terrain as their own fertile ground on which to rebuild the world. Lawrence savaged Luhan as "The Wilful Woman" who sought to establish her own empire of the spirit, while Toomer complained that the spirit of place in Taos seemed to attract matriarchs in greater numbers than made him comfortable.[29]

For the male and female prophets who came to New Mexico, its greatest attraction was the relationship of native peoples to their land and the cultural practices that were generated from that relationship. Both groups practiced an essentially subsistence economy based on agriculture, pastoralism, and hunting that took little from the land other than what was needed to feed and clothe themselves. Their arts were central to their daily life—work, play, and religious expression—and were created for beauty as well as use.

The modernists who came to New Mexico were attracted to the abstraction and stylization that were essential to traditional Pueblo and Hispanic arts. But more important than any specific designs that influenced their work was their fascination with preindustrial communities for whom the arts were not compartmentalized into separate disciplines and relegated to museums and theatres for passive viewing on evenings and weekends. As distant as the Anglo expatriates were from Hispanics and Indians in their class background, education, and life experiences, as practitioners of the arts, they were marginalized citizens within mainstream American society.

The radical visionaries among them were doubly marginalized by the war. Their dreams of transforming America from its urban centers had proved illusory, as had their belief that artists and intellectuals could affect the nation's economic and political power structure. The New Mexican landscape was as physically unlike Europe and the East Coast as one could imagine; it was culturally distant as well. It offered them a chance to reconstruct their vision of themselves and their roles in the formation of a national culture, on an untested and relatively uncontested terrain. Their hyperbolic insistence that Native Americans and Hispanics had produced the only original art in the United States, and thus that their cultural formations must serve as the foundation for national cultural self-definition, can partly be explained by these factors.[30]

Given the fact that most Americans used the arts for entertainment and leisure, not for personal and social salvation, it is not surprising that the

Anglo expatriates who came to Taos identified with two of the least privileged ethnic groups in the United States. In arguing for the importance of Hispanic and Native American peoples and cultures, they were arguing for the importance of themselves. Those who believed in the transformative power of art found compelling the aboriginal notion that art was *effective* rather than *affective,* that is, intended to induce change in people, the land, or the climate, and to bring the listener-participant into "harmony with the essential essence of things." What Dickran Tashjian says was true for Marsden Hartley, applies to many others. They were interested in artists learning the *principles* of Native American esthetic, not in their "going native." "With his painting thus revitalized, the modern artist might regain a central place in his society and culture."[31]

Pueblo ceremonials inspired many Anglo writers and artists, not only because Indian rituals suggested new ideas for American art and theatre, but also because they seemed to reflect the "generative spirit" of human cultural patterns. These patterns were rooted in the belief that the landscape was sacred. "The land and sky were living things which the Pueblo people supplicated through elaborate ritual to ensure the orderly progression of the seasons and the stability of their communities." The Pueblos' belief that humankind emerged from and was akin to the earth, and was one of many species in which divinity was immanent rather than transcendent, encouraged Anglo artists and writers to rethink their own relationship to the land, their bodies, and to the human community.[32]

Although Hispanic arts and ritual were not as influential in the aesthetic discussions and productions of Anglo artists, writers, and reformers, many were influenced by and aware of parallels between the two cultures. Land was not sacred in the same way for Hispanic farmers as it was for Pueblo Indians, but it was "the mother and protector of their traditional subsistence pastoralism." Although families owned individual plots, there were large areas used in common. Hispanics conceived of land "as a communal thing, belonging not to individuals but to whole villages as a collective possession."[33]

Traditional Hispanic art was religious in purpose, and religion permeated their households as well as their churches. The carved and painted bultos and retablos shared the ahistoricity of Pueblo imagery. Statues and paintings did not retell earthly events; rather they portrayed eternal conditions. Santo art did not exist for art's sake. It was "an instrument within a network or system of such related activities as prayer, penance, pilgrimages, processions . . . through which the adept can exert a powerful persuasive force on the sacred powers . . . " Like Pueblo ceremonial art, the santos represented an art in which the spiritual was incarnated in the material and physical.[34]

Several of the artists who worked at the Luhan house—O'Keeffe, Adams, Wells, Strand, and Graham—were fascinated with Penitente art, music, and ritual. Although the brotherhood served primarily as a community service organization, it was the Penitente celebration of Christ's passion, involving self-flagellation, imitation of the stations of the Cross, and a simulated crucifixion that most attracted these Anglo artists. Prurience and sensationalism may well have played a role in their attraction to these rites, but there was also a genuine reverence for what they understood as a folk celebration of the archetypal experiences of death and renewal. Two of the dances that helped to establish Martha Graham as one of America's premier modernist choreographers were in part inspired by what she gleaned of Penitente ritual in her trips to the Southwest.[35]

Social, Political, and Economic Contexts

The Anglo expatriates' hunger for spiritual and psychic renewal often blinded them to the more unpleasant social, political, and economic realities that surrounded them. Some of the artists contributed to these realities with the patronizing attitudes they displayed toward Hispanics and Indians, who made up the bulk of the servant and day labor population in Taos. In the 1920s and 1930s, artists typically hired Indian models at fifty cents a day, while domestics earned a dollar a day during the depression. Although many individual Anglos had good friends among these groups, there was no real social integration, even at Mabel Luhan's house, where members of the three ethnic groups were sometimes invited to parties, but where most of the Indians and Hispanics on the premises were servants or entertainers.

Many of the Anglos who were part of the Santa Fe and Taos writers' and artists' colonies worked in very responsible ways, privately and publicly, to alleviate hunger and disease through charitable gifts and, more broadly, through helping to create markets for the work of Indian and Hispanic artists and craftsmen. Yet their attitudes, particularly regarding land rights and modernization, were not always in the best interest of either group. Their allegiance to the Indians as innocent victims of the long-ago Spanish conquest—what the anthropologist John Bodine has called "selective ethnophilia"—helped to exacerbate generations-long tensions between those groups. The claims work in which Mabel Luhan, John Collier, Mary Austin, and others were involved throughout the 1920s resulted in depriving many impoverished Hispanics of the little land they still held.[36]

Perhaps the worst that can be said of them is that in constructing their own landscape, the Anglo expatriates never attended to the other "landscapes" that existed in Taos: those that bore the scars of mining and forestry, as well as the scars of racism, poverty, and alcoholism. That they painted what they wanted to see is hardly surprising. That they excluded these social realities because they feared that their work would not sell seems unlikely, given their overwhelming psychic investment in the beneficent aspects of the landscape and the larger sociocultural agenda of their modernist aesthetic. Nevertheless, it cannot be denied that their work supported and encouraged the promotion of the tourist trade, which mostly benefited Anglos.

As early as the first decade of the twentieth century, New Mexico's best real estate was in the possession of Anglo speculators and Hispanic *ricos* who, after decades of corruption and lawlessness, had stripped the majority of Hispanic villagers of their patrimony. During the territorial period, 80 percent of the land grants claimed by Hispanic settlers were lost due to federal adjudication. More than half the public domain was allocated to the National Forest, resulting in the subsequent decrease of grazing land for Hispanic villages and wilderness uses for Indians and Hispanics. During this same period, the Pueblos lost much of their land as a result of the federal government's decision to assimilate them to individual land ownership. A reversal of federal law in 1913 began the restoration of tribal lands. This process was aided by the incoming generation of Anglo expatriates, although their commitment to conservation and preservation of the land also worked to undermine the economic progress of the Indians.

Just at the time Mabel moved to Taos, it "seems to have gone from a valley of golden promise to an economically stagnant backwater, awaiting touristic [and artistic] discovery." By the 1920s, one male in every Hispanic family left home to work. The Great Depression brought a final collapse of the pastoral subsistence economy, while jobs in the mines dried up. In 1935, 60 to 70 percent of northern New Mexicans were on relief.[37]

The Building of Los Gallos

It is one of the many complex ironies associated with Taos's utopian image and its grimmer socioeconomic realities that the material out of which its built environment is created—adobe—guarantees its charm to the outside observer at the same time it disguises the economic hardship that often lies within. For centuries, adobe was the most democratic of building materials—anyone could afford and use it. (Only recently has adobe construction in the Southwest become unaffordable by all but the most affluent.) Adobe is also one of the few architectural forms that "fits" the landscape.

Adobe's organicism and low cost were two of its most appealing aspects to the Anglo expatriates. It was a perfect medium for both community and self-expression: homes made of the earth that took little from the land and were, at least in the beginning, unpretentious and humble in form. To live in an adobe home was not to close oneself off from the world and assert one's dominance over the elements; rather, it was a means of inhabiting space that broke down the division between inner and outer worlds. To borrow a phrase used in another context by the French philosopher Gaston Bachelard, adobe allowed one to be "housed everywhere but nowhere shut in." Although it was used by Hispanics and Indians in fairly standardized ways, it could also easily be adapted to individual needs and tastes. Mabel Luhan's home is, perhaps, the prime example in early twentieth-century Taos of the malleability of adobe in meeting the dual needs of tradition and personal desire.[38]

Los Gallos was the first home to be built in Taos in the Pueblo, or Spanish revival, style of architecture. As several architectural historians have noted, the Southwest was the first region in the United States to generate a revival of its own indigenous styles, a revival that was instigated by the Anglo expatriates who came to New Mexico and wanted to preserve the architectural styles, as well as other indigenous aspects, of native cultures. Akin to the Arts and Crafts movement, the style was part of the international reaction in the early twentieth century "against the processes of cultural standardization." In 1912, the desire to promote tourism and to find an architectural image to represent the newly formed state of New Mexico combined with romantic aesthetics to bring "New Mexico regionalism to a mature form that would have a broad and lasting impact." Just at the same time that ethnologists and poets were beginning to write about the significance of Indian art and ceremonials, publicity got underway for the promotion of the Santa Fe–Pueblo style as "a strictly American style of architecture."[39]

The revival style blended Pueblo and Spanish prototypes and featured "clustered, irregular massing, flat roofs, and the setback of successive sto-

Mabel and Tony Luhan, [1920s?]. MAC.
Photo courtesy of the Huntington Library, San Marino, California.

ries. A heavy, massive effect—with softly rounded corners, and thick battered (sloping) walls and parapets . . . projecting roof beams and portales with round log columns and carved capitals . . . wood grills, pueblo-style ladders, with borrowings from church architecture . . . " Mabel Luhan's house met what Jerome Iowa calls "the overall intention [of the revival architecture] to create a visual effect rather like ancient Taos Pueblo, but with a lot more amenity."[40]

Mabel was especially interested in the melding of the material and the spiritual in Pueblo architecture. Vincent Scully has pointed out that Pueblo villages are "always related to specific sites with their special sacred or, at least, religiously functioning landscape forms," so that their architecture is the "setting" and "physical vehicle" of their ceremonial system. Taos Pueblo "echoes the mountain and abstracts it to the measure of human units." Pueblos refer to making an adobe house as "raising" it, the way one "raises crops or children. . . . It is an act of creation that is an extended family and clan matter."[41]

In May 1918, some six months after they met, Tony Luhan encouraged Mabel to buy twelve acres of beautiful meadow, orchard, and high land bounded on two sides by Taos Pueblo land. On June 22, she signed the deed that transferred the land and a small four- or five-room adobe house from Manuel Trujillo to herself for fifteen hundred dollars. Tony supervised the Mexican and Indian work crew who built the additions. The house was raised to three stories on one end to mimic Taos Pueblo's multistoried adobes. The sun porch, or solarium, which looks out on the four directions, has perfectly framed views of the Sacred Mountain.

While Tony worked on the structure, Mabel designed the interior, which displayed the many worlds she had known within the rooted context of the adobe shelter that defined her new worldview. Louis XVI sofas and Second Empire armchairs shared space with Cedar Rapids oak and pine trestle tables; straw-seated Mexican chairs with bentwood chairs, seated Buddhas with standing Virgins, Navajo rugs with French silk wall hangings. As Agnesa Lufkin explained, "The house [is] . . . a synthesis of the past history and contemporary state of Taos with the past history and contemporary state of Mabel. Taos: Indian, Spanish Anglo, New Mexican. Mabel: Mabel Ganson Evans Dodge Sterne Luhan of Buffalo, Florence, New York, Taos."[42]

Mabel saw in the dwelling's construction the possibility of her own regeneration:

> *Working with earth was a noble occupation. To loosen it and make the adobe bricks, mixing the wheat straw from last year's harvest with it thoughtfully, laying them in rows to dry while the rock foundation is being built, and then fitting them carefully upon each other with the rich dark mud between that will turn as hard as stone, all of it is a sacred matter, for the wonder of creation is in it, the wonder of transformation which always seems of greatest significance to Indians. To take the living earth from under their feet, undifferentiated and unformed, and shape it into a house, with length and breadth and height, each person's house different, yet always basically the same as others . . . is wonderful.*[43]

Throughout the summer, the adobe shapes emerged from and blended into the landscape of chamisa, sage, and low hills. Mabel left the five original 150-year-old rooms as she found them, except for the arched doors and wood floors that she added. The arched doors were not part of the Pueblo

Mabel Dodge Luhan, n.d.
Courtesy of Woodrow Wilson Fine Arts.

revival style, but according to architect Beverley Spears, "they have a certain romantic Spanish flavor" that probably seemed appropriate to Mabel. The first room built was the Big Room, two large rectangular areas that have elements of both the informal and the grand. At the east end of the room, a high-ceilinged, formal fireplace is flanked by two windows, a fashion of the day that was not characteristic of Pueblo revival architecture.

The ceiling was fitted with cedar saplings, layered with sweet clover and sage to spread the wet mud on, the inside and outside worlds continually intermingling. Mabel furnished the room with French, Italian, and Oriental sofas and chairs, whose pale grays and yellows were accented with bright magenta and emerald green pillows. Indian blankets hung on the whitewashed walls and santos decorated the mantelpieces. Always in the room there was the fragrant smell of flowers: sweet peas, roses, and bowls of gladioli.[44]

Los Gallos. Spud Johnson, Laughing Horse Press Papers, Center for Southwest Research, General Library, University of New Mexico.

The Big Room and the bedroom above it, where Mabel slept, formed a wing, and Tony and Mabel decided to build a portal that sheltered the other rooms with which they connected. Mabel stained the cut edges of the lumber they used with a mixture of her own invention. The Pueblo artist Awa Tsireh painted a striking mural on one wall, and Mabel used Mexican tiles with an aptly chosen motif from *Don Quixote* to decorate another. The roof sported brightly colored ceramic chickens, which she bought in Mexico and which gave the estate its name, Los Gallos. (It was originally called Las Cruces until too much of the mail got misdirected to the town by that name in the southern part of the state.)

The dining room was built a few years later, its floor and ceiling much lower than in the Big Room. Reminiscent of the Villa Curonia, the room led down from the Big Room with five round, tiled steps into a larger room, whose floor was laid with burnt sienna and black tiles that were made by the painter William Penhallow Henderson, the husband of Alice Corbin. The room was graced with long French windows and a ceiling painted in earth colors and striped to look like an Indian blanket. In the center of the room was a heavy oak table surrounded by handsomely carved leather-studded chairs.

Beverley Spears feels that the dining room fireplace, built by Tony, is "a dramatic departure from the conventional," adding that all the fireplaces in the house are important "because of their large size and key locations. They are sensuous as is the entire house." Onto the dining area, Mabel added a large kitchen whose windows took advantage of the sunlight, as did every room where she could capture light. Male guests took their breakfast there, seated at a large table covered with bright blue oilcloth that stood beside the huge wood-burning stove. Women guests often breakfasted in bed.[45]

In 1921, Mabel built the sunporch as a third story above her bedroom. There she could lie on a serape on the bare, bright blue floor and view the Sacred Mountain to the north and the Colorado mountains to the east. (In the late 1920s she enclosed the room with glazed windows). The Rainbow Room, in which Mabel did much of her reading and writing, was added in 1925. The Russian émigré artist Leon Gaspard painted the latillas, which added a playful element to the room along with the ogive arch doorway. Here as elsewhere in the house, the windows are low, increasing the sense of compactness and shelter.

The Big House was surrounded by a broad courtyard, which was itself surrounded by massive adobe gates. They incorporated a hand-carved balcony that had been discarded by the priest of the Saint Francis de Assisi Church and salvaged by Mabel's artist friend Robert Edmond Jones. Mabel trained Manuel Reyna, the husband of her maid Albidia, in woodcarving, and he did the elegant carvings on the interior doors in the house (as well as the posts on her bed). Her friend and neighbor, the trader Ralph Meyers, carved the salomonic columns that hold up many of the roof-support beams. The house was, in more ways than one, a communal and community effort.[46]

At the edge of the courtyard ran the acequia, shaded by willows and cottonwoods and straddled by a summer porch for reading on hot summer days. By the 1930s dwarf fruit trees, sickle pear and apple, and masses of iris, delphinium, and tall hollyhocks flourished there. Across the acequia was the alfalfa field and vegetable garden where the Luhans grew their own carrots, beets, onions, cabbages, cucumbers, cantaloupes, and watermelon. They had pear, peach, apricot, and plum preserves from their trees, pork from the pigs they kept, squabs from the large dovecotes in the courtyard, and wheat, oats, rye, and potatoes from the fields and ranches that Tony owned in Prado, Placitas, and Tienditas.

By the late 1920s, the Luhan estate included corrals, stables, barns, and a twelve-hundred-foot gatehouse where Mabel's staff of servants lived. The Big House, which had electricity and plumbing installed, had grown to seventeen rooms, was 450 feet long, and had more than 8,400 square feet of living space. During the 1920s, Mabel built five more guest houses—the St. Theresa House, the Pink House, the Two-Story House, the Tony House, and the Stu-

The Big House [1921?]. MDLC.

dio. In the 1930s, she built a mansion in Ranchos de Taos for her son, John Evans, and his second wife, which she donated to the county for a hospital, and in the 1940s, she purchased the River House at Embudo. She also owned property in Placitas, north of Taos, which she rented out to writers Myron Brinig, Spud Johnson, and Frank Waters. In 1948, Mabel added her last house to the main property, in which she lived until her death in 1962.

Writing about the Big House in 1961 for *New Mexico Architect,* Bainbridge Bunting commented on the "extraordinary" way in which Luhan had been able to fuse "into a harmonious design . . . [the] disparate elements and inspirations" of the house that she built. Beverley Spears feels that it derives its character as much from its setting, ambience, and lifestyle as from the architecture: "In the architecture as well as the setting, a collection of contrasting features are put together in a nonchalant but charming way. Diversity goes along with the eclecticism to create the richness and ambience of the spaces. The result is a composition which feels casual and comfortable but has drama and vitality."[47]

Gatehouse and front gates. MDLC.

Bainbridge Bunting has said of adobe that "as soon as a building is constructed it begins to disintegrate and requires constant repair." The same was true of Mabel Luhan's personality, which made adobe a wonderful medium for self-expression, since she could constantly reconfigure and make additions to her estate to suit her changing needs. John Collier, Jr., who spent much time in his youth visiting Mabel with his family, felt she was a "great designer" whose strongest quality was her aesthetic sense.

Unlike the traditional Indian usage of adobe, which shows no imprint of the individual ego, Mabel designed each of her eight houses spontaneously and intuitively, probably with no total plan. She lowered windows so that people could see out when seated and deepened the traditional shallow

Front gates, which incorporate the balcony of St. Francis of Assisi church, rescued by Robert Edmond Jones. MDLC.

Spanish adobe fireplaces. Her houses, Collier wittily remarked, were "an extension of her interior design." He remembered the Big House as mysterious and magical, full of blazing color, the heavy furniture contrasting with "exquisite, tactile pillows and curtains." Mabel was a "master" at the assembly of colors, including her clothing, which was as carefully selected and created as her interiors.[48]

Los Gallos Imagined: Home as Metaphor for a New World

It was in New Mexico that Mabel found her voice as a writer, in good part due to her relationship with Tony Luhan, which gave her the rationale and the support she needed. What Tony got out of their relationship

The Big House, front and back (facing page) (1930s). MDLC.
Photo by Ernest Knee.

is less clear, just as trying to find the "real" Tony Luhan amid the various and conflicting portraits of him is far more difficult than uncovering the "real" Mabel Luhan. There is no doubt that Tony suffered more than Mabel did in certain respects, especially in the first years of their relationship, when he was forced to give up important tribal duties. But his marriage also brought him economic benefits, as well as political power, which would not have been possible had they never married.

By the mid-1930s, Tony not only had his own house on Mabel's property and his own "doings" with his Indian friends, but two ranches and two mistresses. More importantly, as was recognized by Taos Pueblo about this time, his being a friend and adviser to John Collier had allowed him to serve the Pueblos well in their self-organizing to protect their lands and cultures. Tony's illiteracy and lack of formal education did not prevent his

having a powerful spiritual influence on such visitors as Willa Cather, Georgia O'Keeffe, and Frank Waters, although he was laughed at (in private) by other visitors, such as Ansel Adams and Edward Weston (who nonetheless portrayed him as the dignified "noble savage" in their photography).

Like Mabel, Tony was—and still is—seen by individuals at Taos Pueblo as both a blessing and a curse, for he sometimes behaved more as a padrone than as a community leader (see chap. 8). It is clear that Tony learned to negotiate two entirely different worlds and cultures with aplomb, that he was vain and proud, but also generous, earthy, and good-humored. When white folk came knocking on his door in the hopes of receiving the age-old wisdom of the Indians, they were more than likely to get an earful about the automobiles he loved to drive.[49]

Mabel had the most to do with creating an image of Tony as a Native American seer and sage. She believed that Tony's organic consciousness, merged with her more cerebral one, would allow her to articulate the wisdom of Pueblo culture in terms that would effectively convince modern

Courtyard (1930s). MDLC.
Photo by Jane Hardy.

Anglo men and women of its value. Thus, when she wrote her memoirs, she constructed her autobiographical persona as a symbolic self who represents the decline and fall of Anglo-American civilization, while Tony represents the vehicle for rebirth offered by the Indian Southwest.

The five volumes of Luhan's memoirs (I include *Winter in Taos*) are tied together by one theme: a woman's search for a universe in which she can be "at home." With each volume, the dwellings in which she lives serve as objective correlatives for the state of her interior being, as well as stages for the larger society and world onto which she inscribes her being. Thus she tells her readers in volume one, *Background:*

I have never had a room merely "arranged" in any house I have ever lived in, from the time I first wrestled with death in our house—wrestled and

Front door, Big House (late 1920s–early 1930s).
Photo by Linda Musser, courtesy of Kit Carson Historic Museums. (Note MDL inscribed in carved paneling on door and the Don Quixote tile motif on the right.)

won a room to "fix up," above on the third floor. . . . So the houses I have lived in have shown the natural growth of a personality struggling to become individual, growing through all degrees of crudity to a greater sophistication and on to simplicity. Of all these houses I shall try to tell, for they are like the shells of the soul in its progressive metamorphoses—faithfully revealing the form of the life they sheltered until they were outgrown and discarded.[50]

Mabel's palacio in Florence was intended to be the antithesis of everything she had loathed growing up in Victorian Buffalo, where her mother's garden, with its rigid rows of perfectly organized flowers that came up wilfully, one species after another, "was a symbol for the rest of our house. It was all ordered and organized, nothing was left to fortuitous chance, and no life ever rose in it taking its own form." In her Florentine villa, each

Living Room. Photo by Linda Musser, courtesy of Kit Carson Historic Museums.

room was designed to correspond with the various moods in the *fin-de-siècle* house of her emotions: the dining room, where she entertained expatriate royalty and artists, was voluptuously Renaissance; the bedroom, a deep midnight blue, was complete with a trapdoor in the ceiling meant for a rapid descent of a lover; the pale yellow sitting room was eighteenth-century bluestocking, suitable "to the gay tristesse that always trembled there," along with the latest Henry James novel.[51]

Dining room stairs, looking into living room.
Photo by Linda Musser, courtesy of Kit Carson Historic Museums.

Mabel's home at the edge of Greenwich Village was also a testament to her then current mode of consciousness and that of the avant-garde world she represented. Its interior was a tabula rasa, a "slate" of white walls, muslins, velvets, silks, and damasks that dramatized her desire for a cosmos that was dedicated to wiping out the past, her own as well as the oppressions of the collective human past. Unlike the Villa Curonia, which

William Penhallow Henderson. *Interior, Mabel Dodge Luhan House.*
Oil on canvas, 6 x 8 inches.
Photo courtesy of Owings-Dewey Fine Art, Santa Fe.

was largely a stage setting for the shifting personae that Mabel enacted, or 23 Fifth Avenue, much of whose classical European decor actually denied the modern world, Luhan's Taos home integrated the elements of her past and present into what most (but not all) visitors agreed was an eclectic but harmonious whole.[52]

In the final volume of her memoirs, *Edge of Taos Desert,* "the purity and freshness" of the New Mexican landscape cleanse Mabel of the waste and sickness of civilization, while providing a powerful stimulus to her imagination: "There was no disturbance in the scene, nothing to complicate the forms, no trees or houses, or any detail to confuse one. It was like a simple phrase in music or a single line of poetry, essential and reduced to the barest meaning." As her relationship with Tony slowly unfolds throughout the volume, Mabel establishes his love as a paradigm for a revision of male-female relationships. Unlike her previous lovers (and many of the male artists she gathered round her in New Mexico), Tony does not tap her creative energies for his own use, nor does he enshrine her as an idealized (or demonized) other. He is presented, instead, as devoted to helping her integrate her feeling, thinking, and acting selves. In this role, he is as much parent as lover, as much female as male. His home at the pueblo is "impregnated with a fullness of life" that comes to fruition in the nine months of "gentle organic growth" during which he sees her "into being."[53]

Unlike the Anglo male modes of knowing Mabel had always imitated—prying, penetrating, analyzing—Tony teaches by suggestion and example and relies on an intuitive sense of his surroundings. Mabel describes the joint building of their adobe home as a revision of the myth of domesticity. The shelter grows literally out of the land and figuratively out of their love. Tony designs the structure and Mabel the interior, but so intimately do outside and inside partake of one another that no firm boundary separates their work.

Luhan's memoirs are rooted in the tradition of the conversion narrative, one of the paradigmatic genres of American literature, in which the hero imagines history as a journey from imperfection to perfection, in a search for a paradise to be regained. Her last volume culminates in an Indian captivity narrative, but one that turns the tables on four hundred years of Anglo-American writing: from the seventeenth-century Puritan women that symbolized God's "chosen people" in the hands of the Indian anti-Christ, through the nineteenth-century dime novels where pioneer women shoot to kill the savage "beasts" who threaten their chastity. For Luhan, it is the

Dining room. MDLC.

Anglo world that represents the anti-Christ, or in her more secularized imagination, the exploiter of the earth and the destroyer of human community. The light of true faith lies in the hands of the Indians, and it is brought to the Anglo world by one of its own, who has been captured and redeemed by the Indian worldview.[54]

Luhan's most persuasive testament of this philosophy is her utopian domestic novel, *Winter in Taos* (1935), in which she integrates Pueblo and Anglo traditions. The metaphor of inside-outside binds the book, which is also organized by the cyclical rhythms of Pueblo life. Luhan centers herself in the season the Tiwa call the Time of Staying Still, the interregnum between Mother Earth's death and her rebirth, when no nails or wagon wheels are allowed in the pueblo to interfere with her rest before gestation. Tony is the "medium" who sets the tone of daily living and teaches Mabel how to discipline herself in accordance with the dictates of each season. Hers is the "painterly eye" that composes the seasonal cycles out of her rich "harvest of memories," which is connected to the harvesting of wheat by

Tony's "peyote" fireplace. MDLC.

the Indians. They "bloom from the grain" they consume, partaking of the "season's life," the grain becoming "flesh of their flesh" as it passes through their hands from sowing to reaping to eating. Luhan celebrates the kind of domesticity in which men and women work and live off the land in a cooperative effort that integrates physical, emotional, and spiritual nourishment.[55]

The Pueblos' sense of shared life with one another and with the rest of creation was the key, Luhan believed, to the redemption they offered Anglo-Americans. During planting and harvest times, the young Pueblo men restored the balance of nature by running in relays that give "back to earth and sun what they have received. In due time they will harvest it again, in wheat and corn, and fruit. The everlasting exchange goes on—between man and the earth, one and inseparable, but infinitely divided." When she watches the tall twisters of yellow dust that move across the land, she

Mabel standing in front of living room fireplace. MDLC.
Photo by James Abbe, Jr.

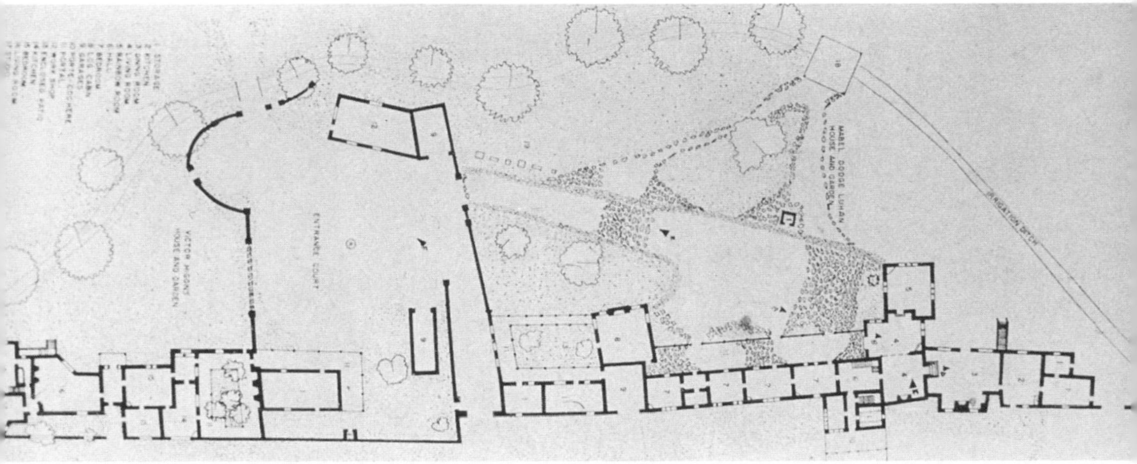

Floor plan, Big House (1961).
John Gaw Meem Archive, Bainbridge Bunting Collection, Center for Southwest Research, General Library, University of New Mexico.

thinks of the column that led the Israelites "toward the Promised Land." At the end of *Edge of Taos Desert,* Tony tells Mabel that he will give her "a new life, a new world—a true one, I think!" In *Winter in Taos,* Luhan gave her Anglo readers the chance to enter imaginatively into a new Eden that has been regained by the interracial partnership of a restored Adam and Eve.[56]

What constitutes the "home" where Luhan finds her imagined peace is not "the traditional conception of female space as 'home space'" that is rooted in a sentimental and limiting domesticity. It is, rather, "a complex figure of adaptation and interdependence between the human and natural" worlds. As Annette Kolodny has pointed out, to mythologize the entire natural world as home and to view the built environment as a rational and intuitive space constructed by both male and female, is to radically reconceptualize both terms—home *and* world.[57]

Los Gallos was created with the utopian intention of altering human consciousness and human relationships through the built environment. It evolved into a rather lavish hacienda with many of the "civilized" comforts and human ailments of the world it claimed to reform. This is less interesting, however, than the fact that it was able to nurture so much creativity over so long a period of time. For most who came, the Luhan estate was

Living room.
John Gaw Meem Archive, Bainbridge Bunting Collection, Center for Southwest Research, General Library, University of New Mexico.

a physical and spiritual oasis. Visitors took what they needed from Tony, Mabel, from her home and the surrounding landscape, and moved on. Whether they established themselves permanently in northern New Mexico, or returned to the East or West coasts, they typically left Taos with their social ideals, their art, and themselves, revitalized.

Living room fireplace. (Note bowl of tulips on right.)
John Gaw Meem Archive, Bainbridge Bunting Collection, Center for Southwest Research, General Library, University of New Mexico.

Mabel Dodge Luhan, *Tulips*. Harwood Foundation Museum, Taos.
(Mabel painted several still lifes, mostly of flowers, according to John Collier, Jr.)

Dining Room
John Gaw Meem Archive, Bainbridge Bunting Collection, Center for Southwest Research, General Library, University of New Mexico.

The St. Theresa House. MDLC.
(Note bust of Taos Indian by Maurice Sterne.)

The Two-Story House. 1920. MDLC.

The Studio. MDLC.

The Pink house. MDLC.

The Tony House. MDLC.

Interior, the Tony House. Photo courtesy of Kit Carson Historic Museums.

La Posta, Ranchos de Taos. MDLC.
(Donated by Mabel Dodge Luhan as hospital to Taos County, 1936.)

Mabel's last home, built in 1948.
Photo by Mildred Tolbert, courtesy of the Harwood Foundation Museum, Taos.

Portrait of Mabel
Walter Mruk, untitled.
Oil on canvas, 24 x 35 inches.
Photo courtesy of Stanley L. Cuba.
(Cuba's explanation:
Mabel, the padrona, is standing on the mesa overlooking the Rio Grande.
The Indian on the lower left appears to be Tony.
Mruk peeps over the mesa at Mabel, while a host of admirers look on.)

"Just a minute. I'm going to ask him a question or two about Mrs. Luhan."

Portrait of Mabel
Drawing by Helen E. Hokinson; © 1938, 1966.
The *New Yorker* Magazine, Inc.

Mabel and Tony Luhan, early 1950s?
Photo courtesy of Las Palomas de Taos.

Dorothy Brett, untitled
Mabel and Tony
being assumed into heaven.
Given to Mabel by Brett on her
sixty-fourth birthday, 1964.
Private collection.

CHAPTER TWO

Visitors, 1918–1929

Maurice Sterne

Were it not for Maurice Sterne there would have been no Mabel Dodge Luhan. It was Mabel's discontent with Sterne, even before their marriage vows were spoken in August 1917, that encouraged her to send him west to find new subject matter for his art. A Russian émigré, Sterne had studied in Paris in the early 1900s, where he was impressed by Cézanne but repulsed by what he felt was the unnatural subjectivism of Picasso and Matisse. He left Paris in 1907, moving to Greece, Russia, Germany, and the Far East in search of a "Garden of Eden" where life would be simple and "where beauty might exist as part of daily living, rather than as an escape from it." Sterne was a conservative modernist who sought to develop an art that would convey the essential forms and rhythms of nature and the human body. Before coming to New York, he found what he wanted in Bali, a culture that had the quality he had hitherto found only in great art, and that Mabel would soon find in the Taos Indians: "completeness."[1]

Sterne's initial response to New Mexico was euphoric. Like most of the European émigrés who came after him, he was searching for the "real" America, and believed that he found it when he "discovered" Indian country. Not long after his arrival, he lured Mabel from New York with the following prophecy:

Dearest Girl—
Do you want an object in life? Save the Indians, their art—culture—reveal it to the world!

When Mabel found Santa Fe too crowded after her December arrival (Alice Corbin Henderson had already staked her claim as the city's resident Anglo muse), she insisted that she and Maurice go to Taos. Her attraction to the spirit of place was immediate, and in January 1918 they rented a house. Sterne immediately set to work fulfilling Mabel's desire that he turn to sculpture.[2]

In August 1918, Sterne had an exhibit at the Museum of New Mexico of three paintings, *Pueblo Indian, Head of Indian Girl,* and *Taos Indian Woman,* and one sculpture, *Pueblo Indian,* that he produced during his nine-month stay in Taos. The bronze portrait bust sat on the gatepost between the Big House and the St. Theresa House in the early 1920s. Form and rhythm were the defining elements of Sterne's draftsmanship, which is marked, as Mabel had noted, by his interest in "sculptural value." His Indians' heads are forceful and enigmatic, conveying the same sense of mys-

Maurice Sterne, *Taos Indian,* 1918?
Oil on canvas, 15¼ x 11 inches.
Roswell Museum, gift of Marshall and Winston, Inc.

tery that attracted him to the Balinese. Although somewhat Europeanized in their features, they are also unromantic and unsentimental, setting them apart from the portraiture of the Taos School of artists.

Sterne's corpus was small, but it foreshadowed that of many other artists who became part of the Luhan circle, particularly his use of postimpres-

Andrew Dasburg, *Bonnie Concha, Taos Indian,* 1927.
Oil on canvas. Photo courtesy of the Denver Art Museum.
(Concha was the father of Lorencita and Reycita Lujan, who worked many years for Las Palomas.)

sionist techniques that became more traditional under the influence of the New Mexico landscape, and his incorporation of music and dance rhythms. Sterne found, however, that he could not handle the physical landscape, which overwhelmed him with a sense of his own human insignificance. He was also forced to struggle with the humiliation of Mabel's intensifying relationship with Antonio Luhan. When she sent Maurice back to New

Andrew Dasburg, *Taos Valley.*
Oil on composition board, 13 x 16¼ inches.
Photo courtesy of Spencer Museum of Art, University of Kansas
(bequest of Mrs. Ward Lockwood, Taos, NM).

York at the end of August 1918, he expressed his rage at her by bludgeoning a wax sculpture, the head of an Indian woman, which had partially melted in the heat of the train. He never returned to New Mexico.[3]

Andrew Dasburg

Although Andrew Dasburg has been called the father of modern art in New Mexico, his work, like Sterne's, became increasingly conservative after he began to paint there. Dasburg had been one of the most radical painters in prewar New York, where his Synchromist portraits of the *Absence* and *Presence of Mabel Dodge* helped establish him as "one of the true leaders of the avant-garde." Mabel's summons of him to Taos changed his career: "Under the influence of the southwestern landscape, his pictorial lan-

Andrew Dasburg, *New Mexican Village,* also known as *Taos Houses,* 1926.
Oil on canvas, 24 x 30 inches. Museum of New Mexico.
Photo courtesy of Museum of New Mexico.

guage ripened and his philosophy of life deepened. . . . Pure form and color were subordinated to the task of measuring the land and people of New Mexico in pictorial terms quite different from, though related to, his abstract work."[4]

In 1920, when he first began spending his winters in Taos, Dasburg wrote Mabel about the way in which Taos fulfilled his spiritual hunger. His sentiment expresses the quest of other postwar expatriates who came to New Mexico: "Taos has the quality of a place in which . . . to find God. In Taos one could create the condition, the form of discipline, that is like the tuning of an instrument of harmony; which we must be to receive and give ourselves the power of the mystic."[5]

Dasburg arrived in Taos at the end of January 1918 and stayed until May. He returned again in 1920 and 1921 with his wife, Grace Mott Johnson,

Ida Rauh, *D. H. Lawrence*, c. 1922. Bronze bust. Harwood Foundation Museum, Taos. Photo courtesy of David Witt.

a painter and sculptor. In the summer of 1921, he moved in with Ida Rauh, who was living in Santa Fe, and who became his second wife. By 1922, he was living with Rauh in Santa Fe, where he set up a summer household until 1932, traveling back and forth between his studio in Woodstock, New York, and his home in Santa Fe, until 1935, when he settled full time in Talpa. He visited Mabel frequently throughout the 1920s and sometimes worked in one of her guest houses.[6]

At about the same time that Hemingway was attempting to create a verbal analog to Cézanne's landscapes in *The Sun Also Rises,* Dasburg was also returning to that paradoxical father of modernism, who took liberties with "reality" in order to uncover permanence. In the best of his 1920s landscapes, Dasburg took natural shapes "toward their nearest geometric equivalent without losing their identity with the actual vista, developing a synthesis between Cubist-derived abstraction and his understanding of the origins of that abstraction." Dasburg's adobes can be viewed as pictorial equivalents to Luhan's prose, which also emphasizes the organic connection between the human and physical environment. This connection is one of the several ways that New Mexico modernists sought to break down the dualities of western culture that had established boundaries between the natural and built environments.[7]

A new temple in a new place.
A sketch by Robert Edmond Jones.

Robert Edmond Jones, Sketch of the "theatre of the new world" that accompanied Luhan article "A Bridge Between Cultures," *Theatre Arts Monthly,* 1925.

Robert Edmond Jones

Robert Edmond Jones arrived in Taos with Andrew Dasburg in 1918. Like Dasburg, Jones was part of the inner circle of the Mabel Dodge salon in her Greenwich Village years. She housed and fed him during these years when he was young and poor, and just beginning to establish himself in the theatre. By the early 1920s, Jones was considered one of America's most innovative stage designers, "the first to win recognition in this century for the scenic designer as an indispensable collaborator in the interpretation of a script." Although it seems that Jones may only have visited Taos twice—in the winters of 1918 and 1920—he maintained close ties with Mabel throughout much of his creative life. Both his work and his aesthetic philosophy were influenced by his brief encounters with Taos.[8]

Jones was a cultural nationalist who proclaimed, "I am distinctly pro-American and I believe that in a few years we will lead the world in stagecraft." But he also had an internationalist vision that was rooted in the "new stagecraft" pioneered in Europe, which involved "the fusion of acting, lighting, setting into a dramatic whole." In a 1924 issue of *Theatre Arts Monthly,* he articulated his Renaissance vision of the artist of the future, which had much in common with that of future Taos visitors Martha Graham and Leopold Stokowski. The artist will make of himself a "transparent mirror—not in a representation of the actual world about him, but in

Robert Edmond Jones, Set design for *Macbeth,* Act V, Scene i, 1922.
Photo courtesy of New York Public Library.

a presentation of light, color, moving form and sound, an abstract evocation and release of desire." Jones called for a new Blake or Cézanne to create dramatic forms that had the qualities of music and dance.[9]

Jones was so taken by adobe forms during his two visits to Taos that he adopted them for his symbolist set design in a 1921 production of *Macbeth,* which "aroused more controversy and critical comments than any others during his entire career." Jones returned to his memories of Taos a decade later, when he created a more conventional but very effective staging for Maxwell Anderson's play *Night Over Taos* (1932), which is set during the American takeover of the Hispanic Southwest in 1847.[10]

Robert Edmond Jones, set design for Maxwell Anderson's *Night Over Taos*. The Billy Rose Theatre Collection, New York Public Library for the Performing Arts, Astor, Lenox and Tilden Foundations.

The play is based on the dramatic confrontation between a noble but tyrannical *rico* who has run Taos as his own personal fiefdom—he expects his women as well as his peasants to do his unquestioned bidding—and the presumably "democratic" American forces that seek to overthrow him and liberate them. What makes the play interesting is the complexity of the hero's character and the politics of his overthrow, as Anderson does not place all the virtue on the side of the Americans. They offer freedom of choice in marriage and self-government, but their spokesman is a man who is mostly interested in how much land he can grab, and he represents the nation he is fighting for. The most intriguing character in the play is Padre Martinez. The Hispanic priest who is vilified in Willa Cather's *Death Comes for the Archbishop* is here the voice of reason and compromise, neither totally good nor evil.

Marsden Hartley, *Last of New England—The Beginning of New Mexico* c. 1918–19.
Oil on cardboard. 24 x 30 inches.
Courtesy of the Art Institute of Chicago, Alfred Stieglitz Collection.

Marsden Hartley

Hartley was another member of the Stieglitz circle whom Mabel had befriended during her Greenwich Village days. A difficult and moody man, he was constantly in need of financial and emotional support and never able to find a resting place that could salve his alienation from modern civilization. Hartley was undoubtedly the most accomplished painter to join Mabel's early entourage. He arrived in Taos in June 1918 and

Marsden Hartley, *New Mexico Recollection*, 1922–23.
Oil on canvas. 23⅞ x 31¾ inches.
Courtesy of Archer M. Huntington Art Gallery,
University of Texas at Austin.
Lent by Mari and James Michener.

stayed with Mabel in her rented house until October, when he moved to Santa Fe, where he lived on and off until November 1919. In this eighteen-month period, his output was prolific, including between fifty and one hundred pastels and several oils. After his return to Germany, he memorialized his obsession with New Mexico in his *Recollections* series.[11]

Writing to Stieglitz about his depression when he came to Taos, Hartley indicated that he was "searching for relief not only from his physical ailments, but also from a period of stagnation in his creative endeavor as well." As was true for other modernists, the New Mexico landscape

Retablos. Mabel Dodge Luhan Collection, donated to Harwood Foundation Museum. Photo courtesy of David Witt.

Marsden Hartley, *Blessing the Melon: The Indians Bring the Harvest to Christian Mary for her Blessing,* 1918.
Oil on board, 32½ x 23⅞ inches. Philadelphia Museum of Art: The Alfred Stieglitz Collection.

Marsden Hartley, *Santos: New Mexico*, c. 1918–19.
Oil on composition board, 31¾ x 23¾ inches.
University Art Museum collection, University of Minnesota, Minneapolis.
Bequest of Hudson Walker from the Ione and Hudson Walker Collection, 78.21.68.

externalized his inner need for psychological structure and certainty: "I want the bigness and the sense of giving of this big country in my system and it is the one way to re[-]create myself."[12]

Almost as soon as he settled in, Hartley began writing prophetic documents about the "Red Man" and the landscape as sources for the renewal of west-

Marsden Hartley, *Cemetery New Mexico,* c. 1924.
Oil on canvas, 31⅝ x 39¼ inches.
Photo courtesy of the Metropolitan Museum of Art.
The Alfred Stieglitz Collection, 1949.

ern civilization and for the creation of American art. In words similar to those D. H. Lawrence would soon publish in his *Studies in Classic American Literature* (1923), Hartley stated that Americans could not create a national culture until they owned up to "our first artistic relative. The redman is the one truly indigenous religionist and esthete of America. He knows every form of animal and vegetable life adhering to our earth, and has made for himself a series of striking pageantries in the form of stirring dances to celebrate them, and his relation to them." Hartley expressed his passion for the Southwest in poetry and prose, as well as in oils and pastels.[13]

Hartley's earliest works were in a realistic vein; as he told Stieglitz, he was eager to get back to nature as a means of grounding his art in the "real." But soon his work began to show the dramatic tension created by his knowledge of abstraction and his renewed interest in landscape. In Taos, he demonstrated "a new understanding of the dynamics of form and space and of color handling that makes the hills, valley[s], and sky throb with inner life." Hartley's sinuous and expressionist landscape forms are highly charged with an erotic power that is concerned not "with the act of sex itself, but with life, the creation of life, richness, and fertility." The New Mexican landscape revealed the process of generation in a way that seemed unavailable elsewhere, just as the Indians' symbolic and mimetic dances made use of that knowledge in a way that promised continued psychic and creative renewal.[14]

Hartley was also interested in the art of the santo, particularly in utilizing "its underlying elements: the naivete, the limited tonal harmonies, the curvilinear rhythms." *The Virgin Blessing the Melon* shows his interest in the power of the santero to embody the spiritual directly in material reality, as well as in the nonorthodox aspects of Hispanic religious practice that suggest the fertility rituals at the root of their pre-Christian spirituality. His most amusing, and enigmatic, still life is his *Santos, New Mexico,* in which a diminutive bulto is juxtaposed with a large female torso. Sharyn Udall questions its seemingly intentional ambiguity: "Does the human form represent a deific benediction of the santos, or could it be a larger-than-life Mabel, hovering over her collection, just as she dominated and mothered her 'collection' of guests? Did Hartley feel like one of her wooden santos, installed as a token of Mabel's aspirations to higher aesthetic concerns?"[15]

When Hartley returned to Germany in the early 1920s, his landscape paintings of New Mexico became increasingly dark, twisted, and tormented, taking on a nightmarish cast that contrasted sharply with the celebratory rhythms of his earlier work. At the same time he repudiated Taos, which he was fond of saying rhymed with "chaos." Gail Scott suggests that these "recollections" reflect the disillusion of "an entire generation of dislocated American expatriates who longed for contact with their native country yet could find there no real nourishment or acceptance."[16]

Agnes Pelton

Agnes Pelton was one the first visitors to stay in Mabel's new home, the first phase of which was completed in December 1918. For Pelton, who arrived in January 1919 and stayed until April (with a return visit in 1922), Taos was a turning point in her life. She had been one of the few women artists represented at the 1913 Armory Show in New York. Mabel had bought at least one of her early works, and Agnes had attended her salon in Greenwich Village.

As was true for Dasburg and Hartley, the Taos landscape encouraged a

Agnes Pelton, *Portrait of Antonio Lujan,* 1921.
Photo courtesy of the National Museum of American Art, Smithsonian Institution, Peter A. Juley & Son Collection.

turn toward realism: "I made studies of the winter in the mountains, and of the Indians in their bright blankets, and discovered that I had that quality of portraiture which conveys the feeling of life—livingness—and for several years I devoted myself to portrait painting entirely." Pelton shared with Hartley a fascination with painting as the embodiment of spiritual impulses, although her brushwork and tonality are far removed from his in their delicacy—a manifestation of the fact that her interest was not in materializing the spiritual but in spiritualizing the material world: "artistic creation is the metamorphosis of the external physical aspects of a thing into a self-sustaining spiritual reality."[17]

Pelton's pastels were given a show at the Museum of New Mexico in the fall of 1919, with Mary Austin providing an introduction at the exhibition's opening. The reviewer for *El Palacio* noted the musical qualities in her landscapes: "The very first alcove the visitor entered was a shimmer of beauty, soft color that fairly sang, the harmonies in the pastels of Miss Agnes Pelton of New York . . . being comparable to symphonies. They were Taos landscapes . . . and portraits of Taos pueblo, all done as it were with joy, with an individualized and poetic realism."[18]

In 1938, Raymond Jonson invited Pelton to become a founding member of the Transcendentalist Painters Group in Santa Fe. Her lyrical and symbolic abstractions are among the finest work the group produced. In that same year, Pelton acknowledged the importance of the Luhans' home—and its female-defined creative space—to her development, when she wrote to Mabel: It "was a positive influence in my life during a long period more or less somber. Its living freshness and the feeling of light as well as beauty seemed—and was—so *new*. Beauty, when I had seen it in houses before—which was seldom—seemed derivative, and usually static: but of course you always infuse life into any place where you are. It is one of your great gifts."[19]

John Young-Hunter

John Young-Hunter was an Englishman who had grown up on romances of the American West, and whose imagination was indelibly impressed by the visit of Buffalo Bill's Wild West Show to London in the early 1900s. In 1918, Tony Luhan helped him buy land that bordered the Luhan estate. Here he built himself a Renaissance banquet hall for a studio to which he brought his wealthy clients. Young-Hunter, a conventional portrait painter who continued to work in the tradition of Sargeant, was one of the few derivative artists to become part of the Luhan circle. The conventionality of his style can be seen in one of the best-known portraits of Mabel Dodge Luhan, in which she looks like a society matron.[20]

Mary Austin

Of all the writers Mabel lured to New Mexico none was more affected by the spirit of place than Mary Austin. Austin's had been a life of hardship and struggle, first with a mother who was indifferent to her, and later with a husband who could not provide for her or their autistic child. She spent much of her early adulthood in the semiarid desert country of south central California, forming friendships with Paiute and Shoshone Indians, and with sheepherders, miners, and cowboys. Here Austin gained the body of experience that fed her most original and powerful work—the naturalist essays and short stories she published in *Land of Little Rain* (1903) and *Land of Lost Borders* (1909).

By the time she arrived in Greenwich Village, Austin was well known for her "translations" of Native American song into poetry, and for her staunch advocacy of the preservation and appreciation of Native American cultures. It is likely that Mabel's first introduction to Native American cultures came through a talk that Austin gave at her salon. Luhan and Austin shared imperious egos and mystical temperaments, as well as the desire to be perceived as "women of genius" and collectors of geniuses. Mary Austin and Mabel shared several important guests, among them Willa Cather, Ansel Adams, and Martha Graham.[21]

Despite their mutual competitiveness as the respective "regents" of Santa Fe and Taos, their friendship was a fruitful one, particularly for Austin. Her life and work were increasingly shaped by her visits to New Mexico between 1919 and 1924, when she finally settled there permanently. Austin arrived in Taos in March 1919, at a point in her life when she was on the verge of nervous collapse because of her continuing difficulty to find either sexual intimacy or financial stability. Mabel encouraged Mary to come to New Mexico by telling her that what she was experiencing was "a metamorphosis . . . a kind of rebirth" and that her turmoil was "only a prelude to the joy of full realization."[22]

When Austin received a commission to do research among the northern Pueblos for the Carnegie Institution, she decided to make Mabel's home her headquarters. She liked Tony, and he became important to her work, both as a chauffeur who drove her around to different pueblos and an informant who added to her folklore repertoire. When Austin returned in 1922, she became deeply embroiled in the Bursum Bill controversy. (The Bursum Bill had been introduced in Congress as a ploy to confirm all non-Indian land claims in New Mexico that were held by Spanish and Anglo settlers who could prove continuous possession.) At Mabel's urging she went to Washington with a delegation of Pueblo Indians to testify against it.

Esther Stineman has concluded that Austin's permanent move to Santa Fe in 1924 was precipitated by Mabel: "Austin considered Tony, Mabel, and their Taos home the emotional and practical nexus of her life in New Mexico." In her autobiography, *Earth Horizon,* Austin wrote that she loved the Southwest because it fed her "pattern-hungry mind . . . the feel of roots, of ordered growth and progression, continuity." She shared her literary ideas with Mabel, while Mabel shared her desire to have her home serve as "a creative centre—not just a place for people to retreat into."[23]

After settling in Santa Fe, Austin helped organize the Spanish Colonial Arts Society, to preserve and support the work of Hispanic artisans. She worked on pilot programs for bilingual and multicultural education and advocated the cultural expression of the "folk" as important to the well-being of modern civilizations. Her 1923 publication *American Rhythm* articulated her theory of the influence of "the landscape line" in the creation of a truly democratic poetry: "All vital poetry, which speaks to how life is actually lived by people and effectively coordinates their psychic life, is shaped by the topography, climate, work, and social patterns of the land where they live." By uniting art, culture, and the environment, indigenous peoples had created aesthetic forms that produced "maximum well-being" in both individuals and society.[24]

In *Land of Journey's Ending* (1924), Austin concluded that the Southwest was the "journey's end" of the American experience, as well as the setting "for the *next* great and fructifying world culture," because it was the only place where long-lived cultures have produced "adequate symbols in art and social forms." Austin's most interesting politicization of this idea was her 1925 *Survey Graphic* article, "The Indivisible Utility," in which she argued for indigenous models of communalism, as opposed to communism, because she was unsympathetic to the foreignness of Marxist theories, as well as to the practice of centralized state bureaucracies. Here she also anticipates contemporary environmentalists in her promotion of bioregional solutions to social and economic problems and the use of appropriate technologies. Austin pointed out that natural factors of land and climate in the Southwest had shaped communities with the kind of environmental awareness and egalitarian values that "would fill the self-constituted prophets of all Utopias with unmixed satisfaction."[25]

Central to the binding of such communities was the *acequia madre* (mother ditch), which symbolized the cooperation made possible when the land necessitates sharing precious water resources. "Rain falls on radical and conservative alike, but the mother ditch makes communists of them all." Austin associated this kind of social and economic communalism with female-centered cultures. "Peace and stability," she wrote in the text for *Taos Pueblo* (1930), "these are the first fruits of Mother-rule."[26]

Austin's vision of Taos Pueblo was, of course, more fantasy than ethnography, the product of her desire to construct a female creatrix as the progenitor of human life. She shared her fellow Anglo expatriates' blindness to the poverty that marred Taos Pueblo, and her belief that indigenous folk arts were timeless was based more on her need for enduring symbols than on historic fact. Nevertheless, there was as much reality as myth in her belief that New Mexico's physical and cultural landscapes could nourish the nation's environmental practices.

In her 1931 novel *Starry Adventure,* Austin satirized Mabel Luhan as a faux primitivist in her character Eudora Ballantine, a wealthy patron of the arts whose home is both strikingly inventive and a mishmash of periods and styles. Eudora talks in a 1920s version of "NewAgespeak": "Don't you think," she says to the novel's young hero, whom she will later seduce, "people who vibrate in the same key can always get at each other?" Eudora ends up married to a land-poor Hispanic aristocrat, merely for the cachet of adding him to her collection of indigenous items. He becomes the final ornament in the restoration of her villa, which is intended to serve as "a playground" for her "fashionable Eastern friends."[27]

John Collier

In December 1920, the Two-Story House was finished, with six rooms and an upper balcony. The Collier family arrived in Taos just in time to be its first occupants. The trip changed their immediate plans to go to Mexico—and the course of their lives. Of all the progressive reformers who came to the Luhan house, John Collier made the most significant political impact on public policy as it affected Native Americans. Throughout the 1920s, he was in the forefront of the fight to protect Pueblo lands and religion, and to promote the benefits of the Native Americans' social system. In the 1930s, as Commissioner of Indian Affairs, he created the Indian New Deal. Although he was highly controversial, and won both praise and condemnation from his Indian constituency, he has justly been called "the greatest of all Indian Commissioners" in the history of U.S. relations with the Indians.[28]

Collier's witness of the Deer Dance at Taos Pueblo inspired the title of his 1921 essay "The Red Atlantis": "Today at Taos," he wrote, "life from infancy to the grave is a rhythm . . . of worship and the quest through art expression for an ecstasy communally realized and associated with practical social aims." This essay launched Collier's crusade against the Bursum

Bill and set forth the reform ideals that he and Mabel would follow throughout the 1920s and 1930s: "recognition of Indian civil rights, conservation of their lands through cooperative enterprise, preservation of their communal societies, and agricultural and industrial assistance programs sponsored by the federal government."[29]

Although Collier knew little about Indians when he arrived, he had spent most of his adult life working to create a culturally pluralist notion of community. In New York City, he headed the People's Institute at Cooper Union, which was devoted to educating immigrants in the utopian theories of the Russian anarchist Peter Kropotkin and the English socialist William Morris, along with promoting ethnic pride through organized festivals and pageants. Collier's activities on behalf of social reconstruction ended in 1917, primarily as a result of America's entrance into World War I. Disillusioned by the antiworker, antiradical, and anti-immigrant hysteria that reached its apex in 1919, he moved to California in the fall to direct the state's adult education program. When he spoke positively of the Bolshevik Revolution during the Red Scare, his budget was decreased and he resigned. It was just at this time that Mabel's letters made their impact.[30]

Among the Pueblos, Collier found alternatives to trends that had vexed him for years: "the uprooting of populations, the disintegration of neighborhoods, the end of home and handicrafts, the supremacy of the machine over man, the immense impoverishment of the age-old relationships between the generations, the increased mobility of the individual, the enormous expansion of commercialized recreation, the quest by mass-circulation newspapers, the movies, and radio for the lowest common denominator." Like other reformers who came to New Mexico in the 1920s, Collier sought to replace mass culture with folk culture. Having seen the degree of paranoia and repression that the "collective mind" was capable of during the war, he lost interest in the social scientific management theories of his progressive intellectual comrades, as well as in the Russian communism that still inspired the more radical members of his generation.[31]

For the next forty years of his life, Collier continued to look at the tribal life of Indians as a source for social democratic alternatives to the class inequities created by urban industrial America. Like Austin, he wished to reshape American democracy by creating an alternative, non-Marxist *native* American radicalism built on *Native* American practices. There were many difficulties with this vision, among them the patriarchal and undemocratic practices of Pueblo tribal politics. Yet Collier's work on behalf of Native American rights was one of the few campaigns of the 1920s that had some success in helping a grossly mistreated and ignored minority during a decade in which the United States grew increasingly racist and ethnically polarized.

One reason for this success was the nature of the coalitions that were formed to defeat the Bursum Bill, to protect Pueblo religious practices against claims that they were obscene, and to help Native American parents win the right to take their children from boarding schools during the time of their puberty rituals. These coalitions were rooted in cultural politics that had broad national appeal, bringing together painters, writers, poets, and reformers such as Mary Austin, Witter Bynner, Andrew Dasburg, Elsie Clews Parsons, and D. H. Lawrence. They drew on Indian and Anglo music, painting, poetry, and exhortation, as well as on traditional lobbying techniques, to effect their cause, which also received support from women's clubs, the Campfire Girls, the Boy Scouts, and a cadre of eminent social scientists.

Tony Luhan played an important role in bringing Collier to the various Pueblo villages to explain the impact of federal legislation, which encouraged the formation of the first All-Pueblo Council since 1680. The council sent delegations (often funded by Mabel) to New York and Washington to lobby. Collier also worked with Taos Pueblo during the 1920s in their attempt to win back the forty-nine thousand acres of land that surrounded their sacred Blue Lake, a campaign that finally achieved success in 1970.[32]

During their first crusade together, Mabel articulated to Collier her vision of her home as "a kind of headquarters for the future . . . [and] a base of operations *really* for a new world plan." Mabel and John planned to save "the whole *culture* and *agriculture* of the pueblos," for their own sake as well as for the sake of the larger society. There was absolutely no doubt in her mind that Americans were on the verge of undergoing a national conversion experience, which would bring them the spiritual peace and emotional plenty that were obtainable only through a return to their lost communal roots.[33]

Although Collier was far more politically savvy and cautious than Mabel in recognizing the amount of time and energy it would take to establish a beachhead in Washington, it is striking how closely he held to Mabel's and his own original vision throughout the rest of his career in politics. The Indian Reorganization Act (1934) and other New Deal legislation that Collier shepherded through Congress in the 1930s marked a major shift in national

Indian policy and reflects the influence of this early vision. It restored millions of acres of land to Indian tribes and helped them gain increasing economic and political control over their lives, while protecting their cultural and religious freedom.[34]

In spite of the reversals Collier's Indian New Deal program suffered at the hands of Congress, including its being all but abandoned by the late 1940s, his sense of the importance of Native American cultures to humanity's survival increased in the post–World War II era. He particularly emphasized how they modeled "emergent social-economic political forms which are predictive of a future world not totalitarian and not ravenous-capitalist." He also believed they could show the way for the integration of Third World countries into the modern age, without the destruction of their natural resources or their cultural integrity. At the end, as at the beginning of his Native American rights work, Collier pointed to Taos to show the way: "Their life and purpose is our world epoch in microcosm."[35]

Elsie Clews Parsons

In the same month that Mabel wrote to Collier about her "new world plan," she wrote to enlist Elsie Clews Parsons in the Bursum Bill campaign. Parsons had visited the Southwest throughout the 1910s, coming to Taos first in the summer of 1921. Over the next twenty-five years, she did fieldwork in the Southwest, publishing the first "modern survey of Pueblo social organization," as well as the first synthesis of material on Pueblo religious traditions. Like Collier, Parsons was drawn to the Pueblos because of what she perceived as their consonance with her own political and social views: "She found in their culture an attractive mix of work and play, little fighting over property, and a cosmic philosophy which preserved social peace and gave people a feeling of security even in difficult times. . . . She was drawn to the way the Indians combined social responsibility with individual tolerance."[36]

Parsons was "one of the founding mothers of American anthropology and folklore," as well as one of the forty-five "daughters of the desert" about whom Barbara Babcock and Nancy Parezo have written: "As scientists, humanists, romanticists, and activists, they were to significantly shape anthropological understandings, public conceptions, and government policies regarding the Native American Southwest." President of the American Folklore Society and the American Ethnological Society, as well as the first woman elected president of the American Anthropological Association (1940), Parsons was "a mentor and role model . . . [who] established a place for women in the field of anthropology."[37]

Parsons tried to serve in this capacity for Mabel, taking seriously her potential contributions to the field of ethnology. She encouraged Mabel to keep a journal of her notes, and to go east for training so that she could contribute articles about Hispanics and Indians in Taos to the *Journal of American Folklore.* Parsons's encouragement was partly motivated by self-interest, as she was a beneficiary of cultural lore that Mabel periodically sent to her; she profited, as well, from her association with Tony Luhan. Like most anthropologists of her generation, she walked a thin line between her professional right to collect information about tribal cultures and her subjects' rights to guard the knowledge of religious ritual whose secrecy they felt was vital to their cultural integrity and survival.

Although her friendship with the Luhans does not seem to have yielded her proscribed information about Taos Pueblo, there is no doubt that Parsons took advantage of her friendship with Indians from other pueblos to gather information that their tribes did not wish made public. In fact, she was quite open about her work with individuals who were willing "to disobey the rules of their culture and divulge secrets" to her, including an Isleta painter who made 140 paintings for her depicting birth, curing, death, and ceremonial cycles. Tony Luhan, who was vigilant about guarding pueblo secrets, was a staunch advocate of Parsons during the first of these controversies.[38]

When the Jemez Indians condemned Parsons publicly for publishing information about their tribe to which she was not supposed to have access, Tony wrote to her: "I know you a long time. You've been a friend to the indians. Their good friend. I know you work, and what you do, but its never bad and not hurt the indians." In her reply to what she called Tony's "loving and loyal letter," Parsons explained to him that for "the sake of the Indians and of all the world, I think that a true record should be made of the *costumbres* before people change them and forget them."[39]

Tony was much less accepting when controversy flared over Parsons's *Taos Pueblo* (1936) monograph, probably because he was under suspicion of being one of her informants. Parsons wrote Tony and Mabel that she had "a great many qualms over publishing" it on their account, and that she realized Tony could not see her reasons for doing so. She somewhat disingenuously claimed—given the outrage at the pueblo and the fact that informants were punished—to have published nothing "*precious* or *valuable.*" On January 7, 1939, she wrote a similar letter to the Governor and Council of Taos in which she disclaimed paying money to Antonio Mirabal for tribal "secrets." The controversy seems to have finally shaken the Parsons-Luhan friendship, for correspondence between them stopped after 1941.[40]

Jaime de Angulo and Carl Jung

Antonio Mirabal was to play a memorable role in the 1925 visit to Taos of one of the twentieth century's most influential psychoanalysts, Carl Jung. The man responsible for bringing him, Jaime de Angulo, was one of the more eccentric members of the Luhan coterie. His life story and Taos connections also provide a link between the Luhan and Hopper generations—between the New Mexico and California countercultures of the 1920s and the 1960s.

Angulo trained himself in seventeen Native American languages, and practiced medicine and anthropology among the Indian tribes on the Pacific Coast. In the 1920s, he was supported with funds from Franz Boas and Carl Jung to work on California Indian languages. In the 1930s, his home became a center for the local bohemia in Berkeley, and in the 1940s, he became a hermit in Big Sur. After being declared clinically insane, in the early 1950s, he moved to Chinatown in San Francisco, where he lived as a drag queen and earned money giving language instruction. The poet Robert Duncan became his live-in secretary in his last years, when he was dying of cancer and writing his best-known book, *Indian Tales,* which Allen Ginsberg helped get published. Angulo was enshrined in the counterculture in the early 1970s, when the Turtle Island Foundation published a seven-volume set of his works.

Angulo met the Luhans through the Colliers in Mill Valley, California, which they frequently visited. He first came to Taos in 1924, while the Lawrences were visiting. Mabel invited him because she shared his enthusiasm for Jung. But Jaime was most attracted to Tony, with whom he hoped to develop the kind of friendship that would allow him to expand his work on Indian linguistics. Jaime wrote one of the fuller portraits of Tony that is extant, made available through his daughter's publication of *Jaime in Taos* (1985). Gui de Angulo notes in the introduction that Tony Luhan "was to be extremely important to Jaime."[41]

It may well have been Tony's suggestion that Taos was the center of spiritual power in the West that convinced Angulo to urge Jung to visit it on his tour of the United States. Angulo recalls Tony's taking him outside to look at the Sacred Mountain after his first night at the Luhan house. Tony said, "Do you feel that something important is going on? They are doing a ceremony for the benefit of the world. Nobody know[s]. It is very secret. . . .

The spirits of this place rule the world. They are on top of it. They are powerful." Tony was more than willing to be rhetorically prophetic, but he was adamant in his refusal to yield any of the "secrets" of Taos religion or language. He informed Jaime, "My box is locked. . . . I will never tell you anything. . . . They'll say I tell everything to the whites, because I married a white woman." Tony used the coyote trickster figure as his analog for prying white folk: "Coyote is very clever, he is very malicious. Coyote wants to know everything. Always to know, to know. . . . Those things belong to the Indians. They are not for the whites. What can the whites do with them? . . . The whites want to know just for curiosity."[42]

Jaime claimed that he would not "sacrifice the pueblo of Taos for the sake of museum anthropology." When Ruth Benedict wrote to him about the possibility of doing fieldwork in Taos, he wrote back that he would never help her get an informant: "You anthropologists with your infernal curiosity and your thirst for scientific data" are killing the inner life of Indian cultures. He concluded that if he ever found Elsie Parsons "ferreting out secrets" about Taos, he would denounce her. It is difficult not to find Angulo's stance hypocritical, given his own attempts to ferret information from Tony, to whom he admitted that he would tell all to "that man in Switzerland" because "he can do things with it."[43]

That man in Switzerland was immensely impressed by what he saw in January 1925 at Taos Pueblo during his brief visit, which seems to have influenced him far out of proportion to its two-week duration. Jung's impressions were at least partly formed by his prior convictions about the necessity for modern men and women to rediscover their "primitive" selves. In words that anticipated Jung's reflections on his visit, Angulo wrote to Mabel on January 16, 1925: "The white American *must* preserve the Indian, not as a matter of justice or even of brotherly charity, but in order to save his own neck. The European can always tie back to his own mother soil and find therein the spiritual pabulum necessary to life. But the American, overburdened with material culture, is threatened with self-destruction unless he can find some way to tie himself to his own mother soil. The Indian holds that key."[44]

In his dramatic account to Mabel, who was away in New York at the time, Angulo wrote of Jung's visit: "I made up my mind that I would kidnap him if necessary and take him to Taos. It was quite a fight because his time was so limited, but I finally carried it. . . . It was a revelation to him, the whole thing. Of course I had prepared Mountain Lake [Antonio Mirabal's Indian name]. He and Jung made contact immediately and had a long talk on religion." Jung's talks with Mirabal at Taos Pueblo were, a biographer later wrote, "the most impressive moment of all Jung's time with the Indians." He recalled them frequently in subsequent years, particularly after World War II, when Mirabal's condemnation of the white man seemed more than ever appropriate.[45]

Jung was impressed by the secrecy with which the Pueblos guarded their sacraments, which he believed helped them to protect the power and cohesion of their community life. In *Man and His Symbols,* he recalled how the Indians preserved what the white man had irrevocably lost:

It is the role of religious symbols to give a meaning to the life of man. The Pueblo Indians believe that they are the sons of Father Sun, and this belief endows their life with a perspective (and a goal) that goes far beyond their limited existence. It gives them ample space for the unfolding of personality and permits them a full life as complete persons. Their plight is infinitely more satisfactory than that of a man in our own civilization who knows that he is (and will remain) nothing more than an underdog with no inner meaning to his life.

Jung suffered from the same romantic impulses that motivated his fellow primitivists. But there was nothing romantic about his appreciation of the Pueblos' claim that they used their religion "for the whole world," nor in his contention that whites who laughed at what they took to be the Indians' superstitious naïveté did so out of their own poverty of spirit.[46]

In his essay "The Spiritual Problem of Modern Man," Jung acknowledged the truth in Mirabal's description of "the racial type" that was the greatest danger in the modern world: "the Aryan bird of prey with his insatiable lust to lord it in every land, even those that concern him not at all." When he wrote of Native Americans and African Americans as white Americans' "shadow selves," Jung anticipated contemporary explorations of the origins of American racism that have focused on the dominance of western rationalism since the Enlightenment. As Jung understood, scientism helped to "substantiate" the categories that subordinated people of color, as well to speed up the rationalization of man's domination of nature, through the identification of whites with reason and will. Somewhat more whimsically, Jung's attempt to "prove" that what was best about modern American culture grew from its indigenous soil led him to claim that Taos Pueblo was the inspiration for the skyscraper: "Have you ever compared the skyline of New York or any great American city with that of a pueblo like Taos? And did you see how the houses pile up to the towers toward the centre? Without conscious imitation the American unconsciously fills out the spectral outline of the Red Man's mind and temperament."[47]

D. H. Lawrence

In the fall of 1921, Mabel sent out her invitation to D. H. Lawrence to come and see "the dawn of the world." She intimated to the peripatetic author that here was the place he might finally be able to call home, and where he could establish his utopian dream of the integrated body and spirit. Of course, Mabel intended Lawrence to serve as midwife to the birth of *her* millennial vision. As a writer who incarnated the "eternal feminine" in his fiction, and as a prophet who shared her apocalyptic insights about the race suicide of Anglo civilization, he had proved his ability to reach the kind of audience she sought to convert. He was, she felt, the one twentieth-century writer who could best "speak" Taos for her and thereby locate it as the center for the redemption of the western world.[48]

The patriarchy-induced horrors of World War I reaffirmed Lawrence's belief in the Great Mother as the source of life-wisdom and psychological well-being. Although he made fun of Mary Austin and claimed to reject Jung, Lawrence's views of the Great Mother were very close to theirs and to Jung's student, Erich Neumann. Neumann described "the Magna Mater" at the center of a mode of perception and symbology through which the world appeared to primitive men and women "as an original and natural unity" and thus "the creative source of the human spirit." Lawrence was trying to achieve through language what Mabel believed the Pueblos had achieved through their ceremonial practices: to arouse modern men and women from their worship of the false icons of money and mechanism and restore them to a nonexploitative relationship with nature and their own bodies.[49]

When Mabel wrote to Lawrence, she whetted an appetite that had already been stimulated by a vision of America as the potential locus of his long-dreamed-of Rananim—a community of like-minded men and women who would practice a simplified economy and live by the organic consciousness that he preached. His coming to America was part of an ongoing life quest, in which he sought the means to personal and artistic regeneration for himself, and to religious, political, and cultural regeneration for western society. Lawrence came with no illusions, however, about postwar American society—its commercialism, mammon worship, and obsession with mechanical contrivances were what he expected to find and what he did find.

Knud Merrild, *Portrait of D. H. Lawrence,* [1922–23?]. Oil on canvas.
Photo courtesy of Saki Karavas.

Nevertheless Lawrence saw America as being at the beginning of a rising cycle of historical importance, which he believed he could influence by redirecting American consciousness toward organic expression. He was impressed by America's lack of a past and traditions, and expressed his belief in the possibilities of a new aesthetic arising from a continent—especially its western half—that had the opportunity to regenerate society and culture by embracing its aboriginal roots: "Americans must take up life where the Red Indian, the Aztec, the Maya, the Incas left it off. . . . They must catch the pulse of life which Cortes and Columbus murdered. There lies the real continuity; not between Europe and the new States, but between the murdered Red America and the seething White America."[50]

It did not take Lawrence long after his arrival in Taos, in September 1922, to decide that Mabel was not going to subordinate her prophetic role in the remaking of America to his. Rather than being an open cultural frontier, he came to see New Mexico as a territory staked out by strong women like Mabel, who claimed its relatively unexplored space for their own imaginative enterprises. In the modernist gender wars described by Susan Gubar and Sandra Gilbert, Luhan and Lawrence were rival generals, and northern New Mexico their seminal—or germinal— battleground.[51]

Whatever the genuine sources of the rancor that Lawrence and other male writers bore toward Mabel Luhan, their portrayals of her tell us more about their own gender and sexual anxieties than they do about her. It is not accidental that she has been imagined dead in a greater variety of ways than any other woman in American literary history. Yet she is almost always presented as attractive, or at least compelling, as well as threatening. Perhaps this double vision has to do with the traditional "quest" theme of the male adventure hero becoming less possible after World War I for these writers, who often adopted female personae in their search for identity.

In retelling Mabel's story over and over, and casting different and sometimes contrary light on it, Lawrence projected his own ambivalence toward giving up his manhood and individuality in order to recover a primal sexual and tribal experience. When his generic heroine risks giving herself up to unconscious forces, as is true in *St. Mawr* and *The Plumed Serpent,* she is rewarded with fulfillment. When she seeks new life out of willful curiosity, the thrill of adventure, or a conscious, prying ego, she is punished with death or rape, as in "The Woman Who Rode Away" and "None of That."[52]

Lawrence's most impressive literary contributions to the construction of New Mexico's "spirit of place" are to be found not in his fiction, but in the essays and poetry that were part of an astonishing output of material, given the brief amount of time—about a year and a half—that he actually spent in the United States. There is no doubt, as he wrote in his oft-quoted essay, that "New Mexico was the greatest experience from the outside world" to affect his consciousness. At his best, Lawrence expressed a genuine appreciation of what the land and native peoples offered to teach modern men and women about how to live in a nonexploitative relationship with their environment: "How is man to get himself into relation with the vast living convulsions of rain and thunder and sun. . . . Our religion says the cosmos is Matter, to be conquered by the Spirit of Man. . . . The real conquest of the cosmos is made by science. The American-Indian sees no division in Spirit and Matter, God and non-God."[53]

Lawrence could also be humorously observant about the absurd behavior engaged in by tourists and seekers in quest of the primitive: "It is all rather like comic opera played with solemn intensity. All the wildness and woolliness and westernity and motor-cars and art and sage and savage are so mixed up, so incongruous, that it is a farce, and everybody knows it." His most entertaining piece in this mode is the fragment of his play *Altitude.* Published posthumously in *Laughing Horse,* it is a light-hearted and good-natured parody of the excesses of Mabel Luhan's and Mary Austin's Indian-loving.[54]

The play revolves around preparing breakfast at the Luhan house, which neither the hostess, nor any of her guests, seem able to handle in the absence of the Indian servants. Austin turns each domestic chore into an archetypal experience. Lighting the fire in the kitchen stove is making "homage to the god of fire." When the young Indian who is sent for water leaves the kitchen, she asks, "Don't you notice, the moment an Indian comes into the landscape, how all you white people seem so *meaningless,* so ephemeral?" Not to be outdone by her rival, Mabel snorts in reply: "It is extraordinary! It's because the Indians have *life.* They have *life,* where we have *nerves.*" When Mary predicts that the next redeemer will be a woman, Mabel retorts: "Meaning yourself, Mary? Why shouldn't I have the revelation?" Mary suggests that "the new revelation will come when . . . some white *woman* gets the perfect rhythm of the American earth," which is certain to occur if Mabel allows Mary to "stay here all summer."[55]

A much more acerbic portrait of the Lawrence-Luhan menage can be found in Paul Horgan's short story "So Little Freedom." It centers on a young writer who worships Edward St. David (Lawrence), while being disgusted with his narcissistic patron, Mrs. Bertha Boree (Mabel). St. David accuses her of "moving in and taking over a whole town, a damned whole contented and centuries-old secure people, and putting them on like a new rag to wear around your shoulders, to show to the rich and famous and talented and frightful people you drag here from all over the world to see your show, your personal mountains, your private desert." Neither the young hero—nor his creator—seem to notice the hypocrisy of St. David's biting the hand that feeds him, nor that he is one of the "frightful people" complicit in her show.[56]

Witter Bynner and Spud Johnson

Witter Bynner would also bite the hand that fed him when he came to New Mexico, though not right away. Writing about his move to Santa Fe in 1924, the poet and playwright expressed the discontent that drove other Anglos to settle in New Mexico: "I was washed clean of the war, I was given communion each night when the sunset would elevate the host of the Sangre de Cristo mountains. I was writing to friends who lived on another planet." Like Austin, Bynner believed the New Mexico landscape would allow him to restore poetry to its early function as a vehicle for teaching men and women how to live. He too hoped to make Santa Fe the capital of southwestern culture, and southwestern culture a contributor to a revitalized national culture. An early supporter of the New Mexico Association for Indian Affairs, he worked to defeat the Bursum Bill, and wrote many essays on Indian art and music.[57]

Before moving to New Mexico, Bynner had been a member of the faculty of the University of California at Berkeley, where he met the man who became his lover and coeditor of *Laughing Horse,* Willard (Spud) Johnson. In California, he learned about the Chinese T'ang poets, whose works he began to translate, at the same time that he adopted the philosophy of Taoism, which he saw as providing a means for living a sane and simple existence in a confusing and overly complex modern world. Bynner found parallels between the worldviews and codes of behavior of the Taoists and the Pueblo Indians, views that he undoubtedly shared with Mabel, who also speculated on these connections.

Taoism is an intuitive philosophy based on a belief that men and women are microcosms whose bodies reproduce the plan of the cosmos. Subject to the ebb and flow of complementary yin-yang energies, they are capable of perpetual transformation, at the same time that they are tied to an underlying primordial essence that connects them to all other life forms. Taosim prefers the female to the male as the source of life energy, encouraging men to "feed on the mother" in them.[58]

Bynner was invited to New Mexico by Alice Corbin Henderson in 1922, and during his first summer he was also a guest of Mabel's. Like many of the men she attracted into her orbit, particularly those of homosexual orientation, Bynner was seeking for a life-giving replacement for the death-dealing patriarchy that led to the holocaust of World War I. When Mabel failed to live up to these qualities, he savaged her in his work. Bynner was initially drawn to Mabel's matriarchal attributes and appreciative of her generosity in providing him with a creative space to work on his poetry. In his 1923 poem "New Mexican Portrait of Mabel Sterne," she is pictured against a background of rainbow waterfalls that join the earth, uniting the physical and spiritual manifestations of the life force.

Within the year, Bynner's admiration changed to full-fledged dislike as the two began a complicated rivalry that lasted for much of their relationship over the next thirty years. The chief source of Witter's anger seems to have been Mabel's appropriation of his lover, Spud Johnson, as her secretary, general factotum, and self-styled public relations agent. Her domineering theatricality, which enraged Witter, charmed Spud, whose one published poetic tribute to Mabel celebrates the creativity with which she intermingled her domestic and psychic "interiors."[59]

In 1929, Bynner pilloried what he viewed as Mabel's perverse feminine wiles in his play *Cake*. Here Mabel's lifelong dream of being queen of her own utopia is given ironic and dystopian fulfillment. Sitting upon a golden throne, wearing a coronet of eagles, an unnamed Lady rules over a "no-man's land" of desires, which she spins from her febrile imagination. These are carried out by her asexual Chamberlain, the Unicorn (whose character is probably based on Spud), whose symbol of emasculation is the eunuch's "horn" he carries in his hand as his "staff" of office. At one point in the play, the Unicorn speaks what may have been Bynner's own voyeuristic visions of phallic revenge as he imagines increasingly horrible ways for the Lady to die.

Aided by her psychoanalyst, who helps to keep her "frontier libido" in good trim, the Lady searches the earth for experience. The cake of the title is a continually transmuted sexual and economic symbol of a female-dominated civilization that is transfixed at the oral stage of self-gratification. Bynner is at his most reactionary when he suggests that the greatest threat to world civilization is the devouring amazon. But his satire is compelling when he uses the Lady to symbolize America's new consumer culture and its relationship to the perversion of America's post–World War I "Christian" mission: as she sweeps the earth in search of riches, she teaches other nations "that the sign of the cross is the dollar sign."[60]

Willa Cather

When Willa Cather remarked that the world "broke in two" some time after 1918, it was the sense of the radical gap between the pre- and postwar worlds that she had in mind. Like Bynner, she saw the postwar United States as cursed by grasping materialism and New Mexico as offering a haven from such concerns. Cather wrote within the tradition of women who use the metaphor of home for a reimagined world. As Meredith Machen has noted, her "sensitivity to houses and other places of withdrawal and protection may have been a function of her persistent notion that the time she lived in was 'out of joint.'"[61]

Cather's interest in using the southwestern materials that she had been storing up since her first trip in 1912 motivated her 1925 trip to New Mexico, during which time she sought to solidify the subject for her next novel. Her lover and traveling companion, Edith Lewis, believed that she got the idea for *Death Comes for the Archbishop* (1927) almost as soon as they arrived in Santa Fe. They were staying with Mary Austin when Mabel wrote Cather a note offering her one of her guest houses. Lewis tells us that Mabel was "very persistent in a quiet, persuasive way." She put them in the Pink House, left them alone except for meals, and provided them with Tony as their guide and driver. Cather had intended to stay for only two days, but she remained for two weeks, returning the following summer for another stay.[62]

According to Lewis, Cather took an instant liking to Tony: "with a noble head and dignified carriage, there was a great simplicity and kindness in his voice and manner." Tony took them on long drives about the country surrounding Taos, during which Cather learned many stories about the land and its peoples. "He talked very little," Lewis recalled, "but what he said was always illuminating and curiously poetic." She was convinced that although the Indian Eusabio in *Death Comes for the Archbishop* was a Navajo, Cather modeled him after Tony Luhan.[63]

In a parallel role to the one Tony played with Cather, Eusabio initiates the French Bishop (who has come to take over the far-flung diocese of New Mexico) into the ways of Indian living and consciousness. Under Eusabio's quiet but exemplary tutelage, Latour learns to integrate French culture, which Cather believed was the finest flower of western civilization, with the intelligence of indigenous peoples whose cultures gained their integrity from their respect for the land in which they lived: "Travelling with Eusabio was like travelling with landscape made human. He accepted chance and weather as the country did, with a sort of grave enjoyment. . . . Father Latour judged that, just as it was the white man's way to assert himself in any landscape, to change it, make it over a little . . . it was the Indian's way to pass through a country without disturbing anything. . . . The land and all that it bore they treated with consideration; not attempting to improve it, they never desecrated it."[64]

Cather can be—and has been—faulted for her elitist bias against the Hispanic Roman Catholic Church, and Padre Martinez in particular. Much more inviting is her vision of New Mexico as "a country . . . still waiting to be made into a landscape," where the aesthetic imagination, rather than economic or political interests, dominates the shaping of the land. Though she was not a member of the Stieglitz circle, Cather shared their quest to create a "sense of place" that provided visual or verbal "equivalents" for the integration of material and spiritual values. Like O'Keeffe's desert flowers, Cather's desert shelters are "reached by two paths: one tactile, physical, erotic; one spiritual, meditative, mystic." Theirs is a sacral ecology that celebrates the primacy of women's embodied literary and artistic voices.[65]

Mabel was able to play a small but important role as catalyst for this process because, as Edith Lewis noted, she was "essentially an artist herself—knew the conditions that contribute to an artist's work, and was able to create them. She had, too, a large ungrudging generosity toward people she admired; one felt she enjoyed helping them toward their aim and seeing them realize their desires." Both Luhan and Cather needed the cosmopolitan society of western-educated men and women. But they agreed upon the necessity of the Southwest as a place of renewal: "Something soft and wild and free, something that whispered to the ear on the pillow, lightened the heart, softly, softly picked the lock, slid the bolts, and released the prisoned spirit of man into the wind, into the blue and gold, into the morning, into the morning!"[66]

Jean Toomer

Like Bishop Latour, Jean Toomer was a spiritual leader who was engaged in a quest for the salvation of humanity. Toomer's faith, however, was rooted in a much broader, catholic perspective. Like Cather, he responded powerfully to the religious qualities of the Taos landscape, but with a great deal more ambivalence toward its seemingly gendered "nature." While he rejoiced in the imaginative possibilities of an unmastered terrain, he was also at times overwhelmed by it, and like Lawrence and Bynner disturbed by the strong women it attracted, who seemed to contain some of the same qualities as the land.

The publication of *Cane* (1923) brought Toomer acclaim as the most gifted African American writer of his generation. That same year, he began his dissociation from the black race. Wishing to be identified as neither black nor white, he claimed to be an American, which he defined as a new race that was evolving from the melding of the many ethnic and racial strains in the United States. Toomer was a Flying Dutchman in search of an identity and a haven. Deserted by his father as a child, and uncomfortable with the personal and social limitations of his black identity, he searched for a father substitute and a role that could both secure and liberate him from the ambiguous paternity that marked his light-skinned complexion. In the fall of 1923, he met Gurdjieff, a Russian mystic whose philosophical system he spent the next three years mastering and teaching.

Mabel first heard the handsome disciple of Gurdjieff lecture in November 1925, in New York, where he offered her a spiritual medicine that promised to cure her of her continuing psychic ailments. Gurdjieff's system appealed to Mabel because it combined a critique of western civilization with a course of self-study that presumably led to total psychic harmony through the mastery of "cosmic consciousness," a project very much connected to her earlier interest in theosophy.[67]

Toomer used Gurdjieffian principles to promote a program that combined individual and social healing. His charismatic messianism, which was noted by many who heard him, was particularly influential on those who hoped to change the world as well as themselves:

Our economic system had run away with itself and was doing damage not only to the proletarians and the petty bourgeois, but to the capitalists as well. All classes and all groups were involved in the mutilation. Our psyches were split and chaotic. Our spirits were shrunken. Our souls were empty. To compensate for this emptiness, to avenge our tortured slow deaths, we had grown fangs and sacks of poison; and we used these fangs—race fangs, sex fangs, class fangs, national and religious fangs, all manner of personal fangs—with typical man-insanity against each other.[68]

Mabel's passion for Toomer almost caused the end of her marriage to Tony, particularly after she convinced Toomer to visit Taos, which he did in December and January of 1925–26. She loaned him fourteen thousand dollars to tempt him to build a Gurdjieff center in Taos, a project that he seemed to entertain over the next six years. Although Toomer did not respond to her passion, nor return her money, he certainly encouraged her interest and exploited her feelings. By 1927, Mabel's ardor had cooled.

Toomer returned to Taos three more times. He visited Mabel with his first wife, Margery Latimer, in 1931, and with his second wife, the photographer Marjorie Content Toomer, whom he married in 1934 in Taos, where they spent the summer. He also rented a house in Taos the summer of 1935, after his break with Gurdjieff. Although Toomer did not spend much time in Taos, New Mexico played an important role in his literary imagination. This is affirmed not only by his more recently published poetry but also by several unpublished manuscripts. In these works, Toomer wrote about New Mexico in ways that add to our understanding of his spiritual and aesthetic development.

A fragment marked "Taos" states: "Here is the possibility of a new people. Men and women in spirit to match the grandeur of this earth." In another fragment: "New Mexico—country for a great myth. . . . A land for instructive center. The unusual women it draws. Matriarchs." The question for him seemed to be, as it was for Lawrence, who was going to inscribe this land with a "new world" creation myth—a male or a female prophet?[69]

Bourne, the poet-quester hero of Toomer's unpublished play *A Drama of the Southwest,* wants to put down roots in New Mexico, but fears its "female fascism—[the] strong resourceful women who like the starkness and the isolation of this country. . . . It's they, these women, who are claiming this land which used to be thought of as man's country." Bourne makes it clear that he wishes to claim this space for the renewal of mankind. He tells his friend Genth, a painter who lives in Taos, that when he reached Raton Pass, he shed the weight of his past twenty years: "As I reached the top and caught that first marvelous sight of New Mexico spreading out, something in me said, 'I must dedicate myself to people, to give them a sense of a new world coming to life.'" Yet Bourne fears settling in Taos because he is likely to make the same mistakes as other Anglos (presumably like Mabel) who hoped to live simply and ended up expanding their material domains.

Toomer was equally concerned with the tendency of the land to overpower his ego: "But what words can I use to affect these mountains? Besides, as I have said, this country takes words away from me."[70] The northern New Mexico landscape did not silence him, however. The 1988 publication of his *Collected Poems* contains poems about New Mexico that use the imagery of the physical and cultural landscapes as tropes for his search for mind-body integration. In "Lost Dance," he says of the dancer:

. . . He can find no source
Of magic adequate to bind
The sand upon his feet, his feet

Upon his dance, his dance upon
The diamond body of his being.[71]

Toomer was a "Unitist," who sought to bring together "the many racial streams warring in him and in America." His most satisfactory achievement of this goal is "Blue Meridian," where he maintains the integrity of his voice while taking his readers through the stages of the mystical journey, from "longing to union." As the "Prophet of a New Order of Man," Toomer claimed he could heal the great divides that fragmented humankind into groups of the dominant and oppressed. He had championed his marriage to Margery Latimer "as symbolic of the new American race," just as Mabel had her marriage to Tony, although the Toomers received much more negative press than the Luhans.[72]

The influence of Toomer's trips to New Mexico on his reformulated American vision is clear in the opening stanzas of "Blue Meridian," and in the refrains that refer to the first peoples inhabiting the continent as those who planted the seeds for a multiethnic national identity. They provide the necessary symbols and myths that can serve as the basis for the new America and thereby help to fulfill Walt Whitman's prophetic vision of the United States as "a nation of nations."

The great red race was here.
In a land of flaming earth and torrent-rains,
Of red sea-plains and majestic mesas,
At sunset from a purple hill
The Gods came down;
They serpentined into pueblo, . . .
To fertilize the seven regions of America.[73]

Native American Artists

Mabel Luhan was an early promoter of Indian arts and crafts. The Luhans' architectural designs integrated Indian artistry into the fabric of their home, from the door carvings by Manuel Reyna of Taos Pueblo, to the beautiful rainbow and drummers mural that Pueblo artist Awa Tsireh painted on the portal of the main house. Awa Tsireh was one of the most influential of this first generation of Pueblo painters, perhaps because of his ability to balance the naturalistic and the symbolic in a way that was at once traditional and modern.

In the early 1920s, Luhan joined with Mary Austin, Alice Henderson,

Paintings reproduced on this page gift of Mr. and Mrs. John G. Evans, in memory of Mabel Dodge Luhan.

a. Trinidad Archuleta, Taos Pueblo, [Buffalo Dance], School of American Research, Santa Fe.

b. Tony Archuleta, Taos Pueblo, [Laguna Annual Mask Dance], School of American Research, Santa Fe.

c. Awa Tsireh, Taos Pueblo, [Dance], School of American Research, Santa Fe.

Andrew Dasburg, and other Anglo patrons to establish the Indian Arts Fund, which was dedicated "to [reviving] the Arts and Crafts of the Indians by giving them free access to the choicest specimens of their tribal handwork . . . [and] to [educating] the people of the United States as to the value of America's only surviving indigenous art." Anglo patrons of Indian artists, and in particular, their sponsorship of the Santa Fe Indian art school founded by Dorothy Dunn, have been criticized for having fostered non-native-inspired art forms and for their attempts to mold Indian artists to fulfill their desires for "primitive" art.[74]

There is no denying the coercive methods used by such enthusiasts as Dunn and the powerful influence of the Anglo-dominated market on what kind of work Native American artists produced and sold. But it is also true

d. Pop Challee, Taos Pueblo, *My Wild Horses,* Millicent Rogers Museum.

that a number of Indian artists of this generation and later produced work of remarkable aesthetic quality and that they, not their white patrons, were responsible for it. As J. J. Brody points out in *Indian Painters and White Patrons:* "Just as the craft revival produced several exceptional artists and many exceptional works . . . so the new art of painting produced several fine artists and a large body of uniquely Indian pictures. These were a curious blend of White preconceptions of what Indian painting should be and the efforts of Indians to shift their aesthetic sights in response to White desires."[75]

Anglo artists brought Indian art to the attention of the eastern establishment—perhaps for the first time when John Sloan included work by Pueblo painters in the Society of Independent Artists Exhibition in 1920 in New York. Sloan explained the dual attractions of Indian art to his generation: "The Indian artist deserves to be classed as a modernist; his art is old, yet alive and dynamic. . . . His work has a primitive directness and virility, yet at the same time it possesses sophistication and subtlety. Indian art is at once classic and modern." By the 1930s, the public relations resulting from numerous exhibits at the national and regional levels, resulted in a substantial market for Indian paintings.[76]

Among the most successful of the Taos painters of the second generation was Pop Challee (Merina Lujan), Tony Luhan's niece. She has been described as "a muralist, lecturer on Indian arts and culture, a vociferous advocate of Indian rights, and a model known for her stunning braided hair and impeccably wild taste in self-designed clothes." Her "fanciful" and "whimsical" work is rooted in the colors and stories she imbibed growing up in the pueblo, when her grandfather told her about the "mythical horse" for which she became famous. (Ten of her paintings and murals became part of the renovation of the Albuquerque Airport in the late 1980s.)[77]

When I interviewed Merina about her relationship with the Luhans, she said that Tony was a beloved figure in their family. He had helped to raise her two sisters, Eva and Mattie Lujan, and provided for their schooling and clothing. She herself spent a lot of time at the Luhan house when she was growing up. Like Tony, Merina's father was somewhat of a tribal outcast, who had married an East Indian wife and lived outside the pueblo for a while. He was also a friend of and interpreter for John Collier. Merina spent a good deal of her childhood going to the studios of Blumenschein, Phillips, Couse, and Bisttram, and watching them paint, although she says she didn't paint before Mabel encouraged her. How Mabel knew she had the makings of a talented artist was unknown to her. "She just knew." Merina was already grown with two children when Mabel paid for her to go to the Institute for American Indian Arts in 1937. Merina insisted that there was no aesthetic "line" at the school at the time she was there—along with Alan Houser, Quincy Tahoma, and Harrison Begay—and that none of them painted alike, or were expected to.[78]

Dorothy Brett

"The Brett"—as she was fondly called by her Taos friends—spent much of the forty years she lived in New Mexico visualizing on canvas her response to Indian ceremonials, which was inspired both by the paintings of Pueblo artists and the actual dances they depicted. The sole convert to Lawrence's prospective Rananim, she arrived with him and Frieda in 1924. She settled in Taos in the 1930s and lived there until her death in 1977, during which time she created an enormous corpus of works. Brett was an endearingly eccentric member of Taos's Anglo art colony, whose feminist spirituality and offbeat countercultural values made her an important presence for all three generations who passed through the Luhan house.

In the 1920s, Brett was the often unwanted "third," played off by Mabel and Frieda in their contest over Lawrence's body and soul. She humbly accepted her role as Lawrence's amanuensis, living in what was little more than an outhouse behind his ranch on Lobo Mountain. After Lawrence's death in Italy, she returned to build her Tower Beyond Tragedy on the mountain. When she ran out of funds, she lived on and off with Mabel, until 1946, when she settled in a house at the corner of Route 86 and the cutoff for Taos Ski Valley.

 Mabel complained that Brett's ear trumpet intruded itself into every con-

Dorothy Brett, *My Three Fates,* 1958.
Photo courtesy of Harwood Foundation Museum, Mrs. Harry A. Batlin Collection.
(From left to right: Mabel, Frieda, Lawrence, Brett)

versation; that in spite of Brett's talk of "sharing and community ideals," she never contributed anything to household expenses; and that she was an incredible slob to boot. Yet Mabel was responsible for providing Brett with both the physical comforts and psychological supports that encouraged her to continue painting over a lifetime during which she received little professional recognition. On Mabel's sixty-fifth birthday, Brett acknowledged the importance of the Luhans in her life and displayed her roguish sense of humor in a sequined collage she presented Mabel and Tony of themselves as angels being assumed into heaven.[79]

Unlike most Anglo artists who used Native Americans as subjects, Brett befriended individual Taos Indians but painted Native Americans collectively. Friends like Trinidad Archuleta were especially helpful in provid-

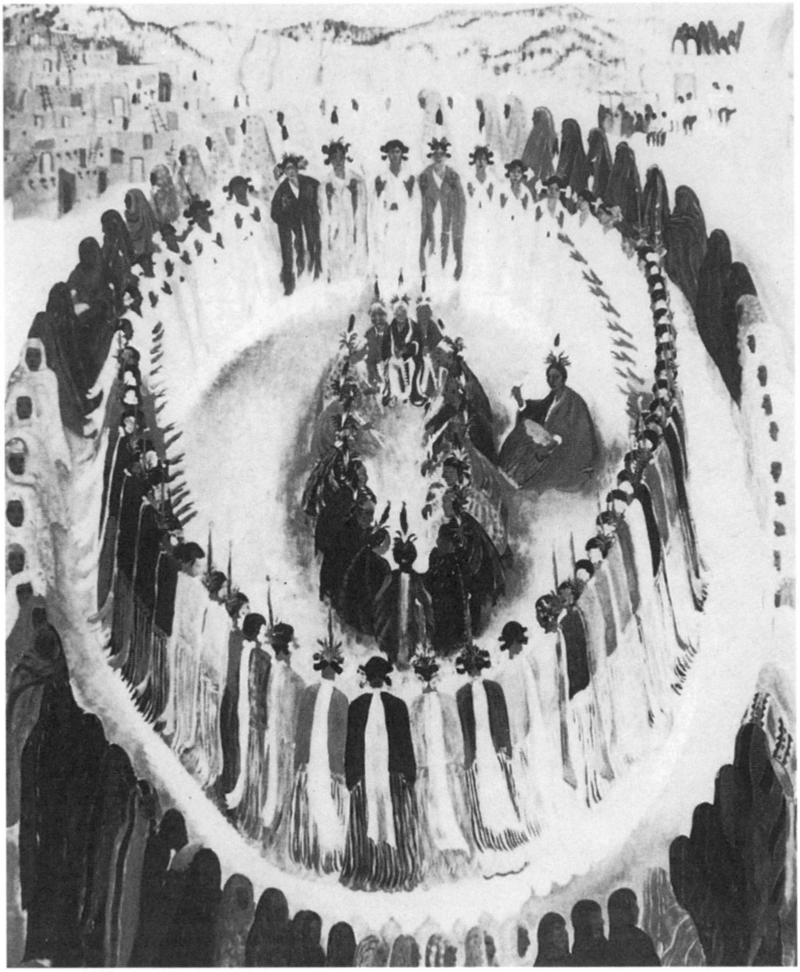

Dorothy Brett, *Women's Round Dance*, n.d.
Photo courtesy of Harwood Foundation Museum.
Photo by Mildred Tolbert.

ing her with the details of dress and dance formations that she needed for accuracy, but her perspective was never that of the prying anthropologist. Brett's style of painting relied on bright, primary colors and "swooping arcs," as well as a belief that painting was an "inward spiritual beauty." It may have been her near-deafness, her living almost totally in a world of silence, that accounts for the paradoxical inwardness of paintings devoted to public forms of worship and celebration: "It is that inner life of the Indian that

Dorothy Brett, *San Geronimo Day,* [1962?].
Oil on canvas, 48 × 54 inches. Photo courtesy of Eric Norby Fine Art.
(Note Mabel, Frieda, Lawrence, and Brett on left).

I have endeavored to paint, his reverence for the earth, the water, the world that feeds him and keeps him alive."[80]

Brett's fluid style and elongated, rhythmic bodies remind one of the postimpressionist paintings of Maurice Sterne. Her attitude toward the dance and the dancers, however, is often closer to Mary Austin's maternalistic feminism, which focused on women's roles in Taos religious and communal

Dorothy Brett, *Stokowski Symphony*, n.d. Oil on canvas, 52 x 24 inches. Photo courtesy of the Mitchell Wolfson, Jr., Collection, Wolfsonian Foundation, Miami.

life. She was especially taken with the "tenderness" of the Pueblo women, which was reflected in their "intense love of children." Some of her most emotionally powerful works depict the women's dances and women and children. Even her series of twelve paintings of Leopold Stokowski, whom she met at the Luhan house in 1932, conveys not the highly charged masculinity that presumably made him a heartthrob to women, but an ethereal and feminized sensuality. The series eventually dematerializes into ab-

Arnold Rönnebeck, *Taos Morada,* 1925.
Lithograph, 9½ x 12¼ inches. Private collection.
Courtesy of artist's estate.

stract renditions of his conducting in which he appears as a virginal flower offering itself shyly to the world.[81]

Sean Hignett has suggested that Lawrence's death, which occurred when Brett was forty-seven, contributed to her personal and aesthetic flowering: "Already New Mexico had fostered in her a forthrightness and self-confidence she had so chronically lacked in England . . . [as the sheltered daughter of Viscount Escher], and her later role as community elder and holy terror, village eccentric and tourist attraction, began to take shape." But it was also northern New Mexico that "released Brett. . . . Gradually I began to emerge, to realize the freedom, the expansion, of living. I began to find myself, my place, and later a purpose." Like so many other women artists who came to Taos, Brett found her voice when she laid claim to the landscape as a domain for her female imagination.[82]

Arnold and Louise Rönnebeck

The year after Brett's arrival in Taos, another European who was seeking the fabled land of the "red man" appeared and was instantly drawn to the magnetic power of the landscape. Arnold Rönnebeck was a German immigrant who moved to America in 1923 and became a peripheral mem-

Arnold Rönnebeck, *Sacred Mountain, Taos, New Mexico*, 1925.
Lithograph, 8½ x 11½ inches.
Courtesy of artist's estate. Private collection.

ber of the Stieglitz circle. An accomplished sculptor who had studied with Rodin, he was also an etcher, painter, and woodcarver. It was as a lithographer, however, that he made his mark in his Southwest landscapes.

Even before his arrival in July 1925, Rönnebeck looked forward to "a wonderful new experience," having met Tony the previous winter in New York. His first visit to Taos had important consequences for the rest of his life, personally as well as professionally. At the Luhans, he met his future wife, Louise Emerson, grandniece of the famous Ralph Waldo. Emerson was the daughter of an engineer for the railroads who, according to his grandson "was quite a character in that he thought that women should do whatever they want to." Louise's father encouraged her to study art at the Art Students' League in New York. When her sister had a nervous breakdown, he sent the two of them to Taos to stay with Mabel. Louise and Arnold married in New York the following winter, with Mabel and Tony in attendance, to Louise's chagrin: "When everyone filed into the church, no one paid any attention to the bride because there was this American Indian sitting there with the ceremonial ribbons in his braids."[83]

Rönnebeck was so smitten on his first visit to the Southwest that he moved there permanently, beginning his career as director of the Denver Art Mu-

Arnold Rönnebeck, *Rain Over Desert Mesas.*
Lithograph. Courtesy of the Denver Art Museum.

seum in 1926, although "his modernist views were neither understood nor appreciated for the most part." Like Hartley and Lawrence before him, Rönnebeck wasted no time in pointing out the importance of Americans returning to the indigenous traditions of Native Americans in order to create an original national culture. He wrote to Stieglitz in October during his first visit, when he prepared several hundred notes and many sketches: "There is a *soul* alive here, & neither mountains nor desert nor human beings are ashamed of it. Of course there are artists besides—but they don't bother you." His observations about Tony and the Pueblos unfortunately represent the worst sort of paternalistic racism that seems to have especially marked European converts to New Mexico. He described them as essentially "children" who were "gentle, pure, innocent . . . only a very small number . . . spoiled by the Dollar, Christian mission or mainstreet Americanization."[84]

Rönnebeck's observations of Mabel as an artist of "creative space" were more on the mark: "She is doing creative work in her own fashion. More under the surface, in an organizing way, holding the threads of peoples lives in her hand, building & enlarging her beautiful house." Rönnebeck's delightful visualization of the Luhan house, which graces the jacket of this book, intermingles the domestic and physical landscapes at their most colorful and dynamic. More than any other artist who took a brush or camera to it, Rönnebeck's rendition captures the Jungian quality of the house as a powerful generator of myth and symbol. So, too, do his pencil sketches of the Tiwa's Sacred Mountain, which seem to envelop a mystical lost kingdom within its center, joining the long tradition of creation myths associated with it. Rönnebeck's expressionism also comes across in his striking lithographs that stylize the climactic extremes of the Taos landscape in what Diane Groff has called "abstract paraphrases." Northern New Mexico provided him, as it did his friend Georgia O'Keeffe a few years later, with the perfect objective correlative for his aesthetic vision, which sought the "timeless inner spirit inherent in all things."[85]

Nicolai Fechin

In July 1926, Nicolai Fechin, a Russian émigré from Kazan, arrived in Taos with his wife and his daughter, Eya, at the invitation of John Young-Hunter. Fechin was a well-known portrait and landscape artist when he visited Taos. Eya remembers meeting Tony Luhan in John Young-Hunter's New York studio in the winter of 1926, where he came to perform for a party of children. Trading his black topcoat and spats for his blanket and moccasins, he sang Taos Indian songs. "He was like a piece of mountain come to life. I was smitten." Once again, Tony was an important lure for foreigners who were seeking the "authentic" America. The Young-Hunters arranged for Mabel to rent a guest house to the Fechins, and, as Eya put it, "Off we went to see the 'real' America."[86]

Taos was a vivid reminder to Fechin of Georgia and the Caucasus Mountains, which he had visited and loved while living in Russia. When Fechin became ill the following winter in New York, he decided to move to Taos. Mabel rented him a studio in the summer of 1927, but he soon decided to build his own home, which may be the finest product of his

Nicolai Fechin, *Medicine Man*, 1926.
Oil on canvas. Photo courtesy of Eya Fechin.

artistic genius. Fechin was a skilled woodworker who carved the interior and most of the furnishings of his new home: the posts, windows, fireplaces, desks, bowls, sculptures, much of it inspired by Russian folk art. The rugged beauty he created with his own hands testified to the fact that he found his "place" in Taos: "he was in love with the land and the natives. His work sang."[87]

Fechin had been trained at the Imperial Academy in Russia, which perhaps accounts for his rather conservative if highly personal style that blends

Impressionism and Expressionism. His paintings are marked by bold color and dramatic, heavy brushstrokes, which create "scintillating, moving surfaces." In 1927, he painted a striking portrait of Mabel Indianized: bold, dark, and regal, she rules from her Florentine chair in a black dress and turquoise jewelry. She dominates her environment with a compelling gaze that invites your curiosity, at your own risk. Fechin's charcoal sketches of artists are often more interesting than his oils, because they lack the sentimentality that sometimes mars his portraits, particularly those of Native Americans. The exception is his *Medicine Man,* a portrait of Dr. Bird of Taos Pueblo, which comes as close as Fechin ever moved to nonobjective form. Fechin may have been influenced by Dr. Bird's reluctance to have his portrait painted because of his belief that if his image was fixed to canvas "a part of his soul would leave and he would be under another man's control."[88]

Paul and Rebecca Strand

Along with the Fechins, Paul Strand arrived in Taos for the first time in the summer of 1926. Strand's presence in Taos over four summers (he returned in 1930, 1931, and 1932) was important not only in terms of his own artistic development, but also because his Taos work helped determine the course of Ansel Adams's career as a photographer. Strand took an immediate dislike to his hostess, whom he hadn't "the slightest interest in photographing." He found her "domineering, destructive, and rather silly in her self-appointed role as the doyenne of Taos." Strand's attitude did not inhibit his taking what Mabel had to offer in the way of food, shelter, studio space, and transportation, although he did pay rent for her guest house.[89]

Strand and his wife, Rebecca, were intimates of the Stieglitz circle, and Stieglitz was an important influence on both of them. In New York, Strand had been working on "the closeup of approachable and relatively small things." His work in New Mexico marked an important shift in his emerging independence, as was later true for Georgia O'Keeffe. Strand came to New Mexico in search of fundamentals and with a determination to capture them in terms that spoke to and of his contemporaries. New Mexico offered the best of two worlds, "where traditional subjects were explored for new freedoms of expression." The "dramatic vastness of the Southwest" presented him with the challenge of trying to simplify and unify its complexity. As he wrote to Stieglitz from Taos in 1931: "I feel that I have gotten more into the spirit of the country and so the photographs are simpler—more direct."[90]

Paul Strand, *Landscape with Cross, New Mexico,* 1932.

In the early 1930s, Strand broke with Stieglitz over the issue of straight photography, taking a somewhat paradoxical stance in which he advocated photography as an objective "instrument of research and reporting on the life of my own time." One only has to look at his Taos photographs to recognize how much his spirit and temperament shape both their content and style. Strand used to watch the sky, wait for a storm, head for Ranchos de

Paul Strand, *Church, Buttress, Ranchos de Taos, New Mexico,* 1932.
© 1971, Aperture Foundation, Inc., Paul Strand Archive.

Taos church and have his camera ready when the storm got there. A friend remembered his cursing what he called New Mexico's "Johnson & Johnson" clouds, the high white cumulus formations. Strand was evidently not averse to tampering with the landscape in order to get the effect he desired. When he found that someone had erected two large basketball backboards at the rear of Ranchos Church, he sought the help of Mexican composer Carlos Chavez, who was staying at Mabel's house. Chavez spoke to the boy who put them up, whom Strand subsequently paid to remove them.[91]

Where Strand parted from Stieglitz was in his desire to connect intimate revelation to a broader and deeper idea of human community. In a 1945 exhibition catalogue, photographer Nancy Newhall remarked on the importance of New Mexico in Strand's search for a vision of landscape in which sociocultural and aesthetic factors were organically related. When he first came to Taos, Strand had been thinking of documenting a community that suggested "a total, cohesive, and shared life," paralleling what Edgar Lee Masters had done in his *Spoon River Anthology*. Like many of the artists who were part of Luhan's creative space, he was "pressing for a totality of vision, a meeting of place and spirit beyond anything he had yet accomplished."[92]

In 1932, when his marriage to Rebecca ended, Paul headed down into Mexico. Carlos Chavez had been so impressed with his New Mexico photographs that he arranged for an exhibition of them and got him a commission to work on art education in rural schools in Mexico. Chavez was also interested in art as a vehicle of social and educational reform, and he encouraged Strand to make films of Mexico's indigenous peoples. This was the beginning of Strand's documentary filmmaking, which became his major occupation in the 1930s.[93]

Becky Strand brought a good deal of color—in both her personality and her art—to Taos, which became her permanent home in the 1930s. The New Mexico landscape had a more profound impact on her than on Paul, for it was here that she first developed her exquisite technique of painting on glass and her colcha embroideries. Unlike most easterners who came to New Mexico and discovered it as a revelation, Becky had been marked deeply by the West as a child. (Her father had been the manager of Buffalo Bill's Wild West Show.) As Suzan Campbell points out, Becky had lived a rather free life on the road with her family, spending a good deal of time in the company of the performers who inspired her notoriously rough manners and language. When her father died in 1902, her mother settled in New York. Here Rebecca met, fell in love with, and in 1922 married Paul Strand.[94]

Although she knew that she wished to make her own "artistic contribution," Rebecca had a difficult time finding her medium, a difficulty compounded by Paul's use of her as a model in his work and her muselike relationship to him. She both painted and wrote while in New York, but it was

Rebecca Strand,
Portrait of Miriam, 1929.
Oil on glass. DeWitt estate.

not until her visit to the Luhans with Georgia O'Keeffe in 1929 that she found an original mode for her artistic expression in the reverse oils that she painted that summer. Strand may well have been inspired by O'Keeffe's work with flowers, but their styles and scale were dramatically different; in fact, the reverse of what one might have expected based on their personalities. Unlike her paintings, O'Keeffe was reserved, whereas the outspoken Rebecca's paintings are notable for their delicate and precise forms, in which energy and color are controlled within tightly compressed spaces.[95]

Mabel drew an insightful contrast between the two artists, when she noted: "The large, unembarrassed flower-forms with which O'Keeffe startled the world, ask for attention, understanding, even assistance; while Mrs. James's flowers are extremely shy and unrevealing, definitely unorganic, reluctantly expressing undefined states of being, never mere explicit and individual sensations." Stieglitz gave Rebecca her first exhibition of her New Mexico works in 1931 and 1932, and she had many more in museums and galleries throughout the United States over the next thirty years.[96]

Miriam DeWitt

One of the twelve paintings on glass that Rebecca Strand produced her first summer in Taos was a flower "portrait" of a twenty-five-year-old woman who was the oldest daughter of Neith and Hutchins Hapgood, two of Mabel's closest friends during her Greenwich Village years. Miriam Hapgood had been in a depression for three years before her parents sent her to Taos, at Mabel's request. Many years later, Miriam remembered the almost instantaneous healing effect that Taos had on her: "The brilliant sun, the clear dry air, the unearthly red rock hills rolling away to mountains, the space—they affect me like a conversion. I know it is where I want to live." Once Mabel convinced the Hapgoods that Taos had cured their daughter, they gave Miriam one thousand dollars for a small adobe that Mabel helped her furnish. Miriam "became a new person" after moving to Taos. Acting in loco parentis, Mabel was her nurse, caretaker, and friend, as well as a demanding and meddlesome elder who encouraged Miriam to marry a man about whom she was ambivalent.[97]

In spite of her less than happy marriage, Miriam recalled the thirteen years she lived in Taos with enormous affection, for it was here that she began to take up painting with some seriousness: "From the roof of the house I do many paintings of the mountain. I am exhilarated by the grandeur of the place. I enjoy the company of Mabel, Tony and their friends; it is the beginning of a long and unbroken friendship. . . . Tony is like a bronze equestrian statue. . . . He moves with measured dignity. When he laughs or jokes, the tranquil, rather stern lines of his face break apart, his eyes become triangular, he looks boyish." The day after her arrival at Mabel's, Miriam met Georgia O'Keeffe, Rebecca Strand, and John Marin. Rebecca's *Portrait of Miriam—1929* is a lovely tribute to what Miriam called "the transformation that is taking place in me that summer." Like Miriam, the sunflower Strand painted is both fragile and vigorous. It reflects tall, thin Miriam's fair skin and fine hair in its coloring, and suggests both her shy nature and the beginning of an eager opening to a new life.[98]

John Marin

John Marin's encouragement was an important factor in Miriam's growing sense of herself as an artist. She recalled his complimenting her on her colors, as they painted in the same vicinity around and about Mabel's house. Marin also painted with Andrew Dasburg that first summer he visited, and his influence can be seen in Dasburg's freer brushwork. Becky Strand and Georgia O'Keeffe suggested to Mabel that she invite this charming and exuberant member of the Stieglitz circle, whose sunny cubist-expressionist visions of the Taos landscape set the mountains on edge and made both sky and ground seem to dance in a dissonant harmony. Marin was a slight, puckish-looking man, whose brown bangs and weather-beaten

John Marin, *The Marin House, John's Horse, Jack, Mabel Luhan Estate,* c. 1929.
Watercolor and pencil on paper, 10½ x 14½ inches.
Photo courtesy of Kennedy Galleries, Inc., New York. Estate of the artist.

gaze greet one with great candor in the portrait that Paul Strand did of him the following summer. He was one of the original members of 291, and Stieglitz had worked hard to help establish his reputation as the greatest American watercolorist of his time.

Ella Young, an Irish poet and folklorist whom Miriam remembered for her assertion that she could project her astral body, remembered Marin as a "slave" of the Sacred Mountain. "Every day he set forth with paper, paint, and pencils, vowing that this time he will escape, he will not be captured by Taos Mountain. He comes back and somewhat shame-facedly exhibits another study of Taos. 'I just looked at it in passing,' he declares, 'and the Mountain held me!'" Like all the other artists who came that summer, Marin was ripe for a change; and like them, too, he extended "the range of his pictorial vocabulary in New Mexico." Just a year before, he had written Stieglitz that he was looking for a new landscape as a means of clari-

John Marin, *Blue Mountain,* 1929.
Watercolor on paper, 14⅞ x 19 inches.
Photo courtesy of Owings-Dewey Fine Art, Santa Fe.

fying and renewing his aesthetic vision: "Seems to me, the true artist must perforce go from time to time to the elemental big forms—Sky, Sea, Mountain, Plain— . . . to sort of re-true himself up, to recharge the battery."[99]

Although Marin had spent several summers on the Maine seacoast, he was immediately impressed by the strikingly different terrain: "He liked the jagged forms of the mountains; was struck most of all by the vastness of space in that lofty region and by the washed clarity of the atmosphere after the showers which occurred almost daily during the rainy season in the summer. He set out to paint space, unbounded space, and produced pictures sharply different from the crowded houses and boats" of his Maine watercolors. Unlike O'Keeffe and Adams, whose works stress stillness, balance, and formalism, Marin's watercolors of Taos capture the ever-changing dynamism of the shifting light and shadow that the clouds create across the

John Marin, *Storm, Taos Mountain, New Mexico* (1930).
Watercolor, 16¾ x 21⅝ inches.
Metropolitan Museum of Art, Alfred Stieglitz Collection.

landscape. His mountains tower above plains that seethe with a motion matched by the drama of the storm clouds that usually hover overhead: "A sunset seems to embrace the Earth/Big sun heat/Big storm/Big everything/A leaving out of that thing called *Man*/With his a moving about/With his talk/With his scribbling."[100]

In spite of his abstract style, Marin's paintings evoke the particularity of each site he visited, as his friend Ward Lockwood noted when he told him he could recognize every place around Taos where Marin painted and could even lead someone "to the exact spot." Another element of his artistic signature was the way in which he merged details of native crafts with the physical landscape, including architectural design motifs of the Luhan house. In *Taos Canyon,* for example, he makes a reference to the twisted

John Marin, *Taos Canyon, New Mexico,* 1930.
Watercolor on paper, 15¼ x 20¾ inches.
Amon Carter Museum, Fort Worth.
(Note the lamppost from the Luhan estate in the lower left hand corner.)

wooden lamp post in Mabel's courtyard in the lower left-hand corner of the painting.[101]

During the two summers he stayed in the Two-Story House, from June to October 1929 and mid-June to mid-September 1930, Marin made nearly one hundred watercolors. When he returned to New Jersey after his second visit, he wrote to Paul Strand that "the East looks screened in. The West is a memory that we are constantly talking about." Marin remarked on the beauty of the Indian dances he viewed, which he called his "greatest human experience," and which may well have influenced his rhythmic integration of the natural and human elements of the landscape.[102]

Georgia O'Keeffe

Marin was stirred to tremendous creativity by his visit to Taos, but it did not permanently change him. For Georgia O'Keeffe and Ansel Adams,

Georgia O'Keeffe, *Taos Pueblo,* 1929.
Oil on canvas, 24 × 40 inches.
Eiteljorg Museum of American Indians and Western Art, Indianapolis, Indiana.
Photo by Robert Wallace.

Mabel's other guests in the summer of 1929, Taos changed the course of their lives. O'Keeffe was a shy and diffident person in public, who very much needed the push that Stieglitz gave her early work, but she was also a very tough, independent, and strong-willed woman. She was completely devoted to her art and self-conscious about her role as a pioneer fighter for women's right to equality in the arts, during a period when women's aptitude for artistic genius was still seriously in doubt among establishment critics.[103]

In the winter of 1928, when Mabel was in New York with Dorothy Brett, hoping to convince Stieglitz to show Brett's Indian paintings at his gallery, she invited him and O'Keeffe to Taos. During the previous year, relations between O'Keeffe and Stieglitz had been strained. Whereas he was happy with his routine, Georgia was growing increasingly restless and eager to find new subjects and new inspiration. In the winter of 1929, O'Keeffe was invited to exhibit at the Museum of Modern Art. She had by now established a national reputation and critics looked expectantly to each of her winter shows. This year her new paintings were her weakest in years and the exhibit was not, by her standards, a success. Mabel invited her to Taos at the

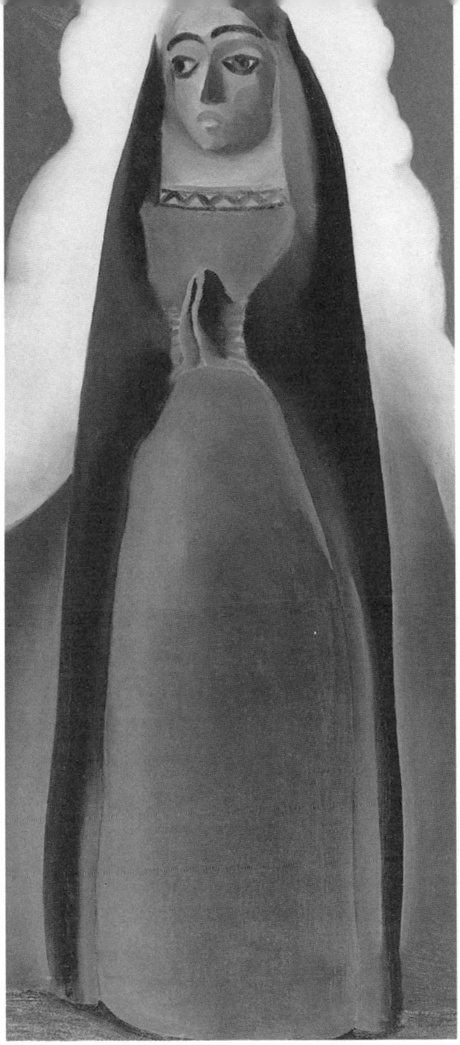

Georgia O'Keeffe, *The Wooden Virgin,* 1929.
Oil on board, 23 × 10 inches.
Courtesy of Milwaukee Art Museum. Private Collection.

lowest ebb in her personal and professional life.

Mabel put Georgia and Rebecca in the Pink House and loaned O'Keeffe the adobe studio. O'Keeffe's response to Taos was immediately positive. She felt completely at home in a landscape whose "bare essentials" called forth her deepest creative instincts. The semiarid terrain, the clarity of light, the vast scale of mountain, mesa, and sky offered her a vision of enduring beauty that she, more than any artist who lived there, has defined for the nation as the symbolic Southwest. Georgia was equally taken with Tony Luhan, for much the same reasons that attracted Willa Cather and Mabel. She befriended him over the summer when she served as his secretary while Mabel was in Buffalo undergoing a hysterectomy.[104]

O'Keeffe's letters about Tony were so effusive in their praise that Mabel suspected she was having an affair with him, not an unreasonable assumption given both Georgia's and Tony's open attitudes toward sexuality. In 1932, O'Keeffe wrote a friend about another Indian who fits the profile of her descriptions of Tony: "[He] is one of the most remarkable people I have ever known—He is wonderful to me like a mountain is wonderful—or the sky is wonderful—but such an uncanny sense of life and human ways—such a child and such a man at the same time—a very grand sort of human being.[105]

It is clear from the similarity of characteristics acknowledged by the three

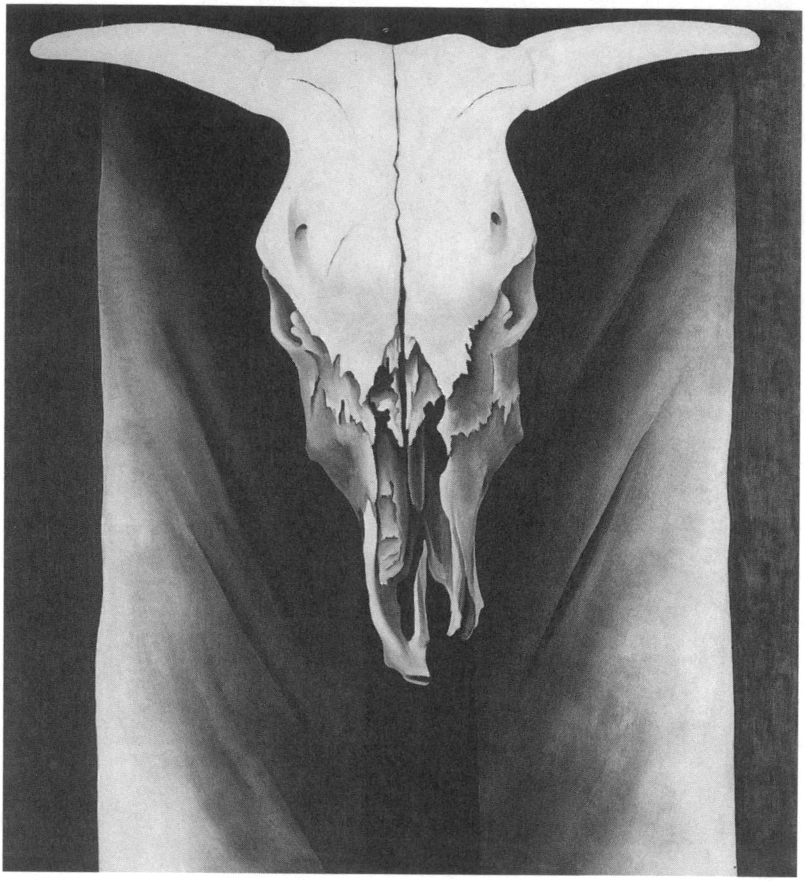

Georgia O'Keeffe, *Cow's Skull: Red, White, and Blue,* 1931.
Oil on canvas, 39⅞ x 35⅞ inches. Metropolitan Museum of Art,
Alfred Stieglitz Collection.

powerful women artists Tony befriended—Mary Austin, Willa Cather, Georgia O'Keeffe—that he helped to shape their creative responses to the New Mexico landscape. All three women paid tribute to his masculinity, but they were particularly attracted by his seeming embodiment of the spiritual force that they believed resided in the land. These ascribed attributes, especially the notion of Tony as "child-man," are endemic to primitivist stereotypes. But they also suggest genuine cultural differences that offered Anglo women who sought success in male-dominated domains an alternative vision of maleness.

Much of the power of O'Keeffe's art derives from her ability to suggest the ways in which art is "life-regenerative." She portrays a spirituality that is embedded in natural forms, and a mysticism that respects the power of polymorphous sexuality. As Elizabeth Duvert has pointed out, she doesn't so much show us "images of flowers but the nature of *flowering*—its openness and receptivity; its response to the energies of water, soil, and sun; its taking of these energies into itself and transforming them." That O'Keeffe's style changed little over the course of her lifetime, especially from the time she arrived in New Mexico, indicates "the ritualistic nature of her attitude toward painting."[106]

Critics have a hard time "placing" O'Keeffe in the canons of modern art. Is she traditional or innovative? progressive or conservative? Most often she is spoken of as one of the few American originals, someone who understood and adapted postimpressionist stylistic elements to suit her own ends. Her originality lies in her return to origins, which are often connected with images of female deities—flowers, fossilized shells, pelvic bones, the moon—associated with birth and rebirth. This helps to explain the paradox of O'Keeffe's creating images of death that are life-giving, as in her series of crosses and cow's skulls.

An important key to understanding the impact of the New Mexico landscape on O'Keeffe's aesthetic vision can be found in the advice she gave a friend: "Try to paint your world as tho you are the first man looking at it." She reacted to New Mexico as though she were the first person to look at it, excited not only by the land but by the opportunity to make her own aesthetic mark upon it. She wished to make that mark nationally, and to be seen as a serious contender among those who were vying for attention in the continuing debate over defining American culture.[107]

O'Keeffe's ambition is most evident in her 1931 painting *Cow's Skull—Red, White, and Blue,* about which she wrote:

As I was working I thought of the city men I had been seeing in the East. They talked so often of writing the Great American Novel—the Great American Play—the Great American Poetry. I am not sure that they aspired to the Great American Painting. Cézanne was so much in the air that I think the Great American Painting didn't even seem a possible dream. . . . I was quite excited over our country and I knew that at that time almost any one of those great minds would have been living in Europe if it had been possible for them. They didn't even want to live in New York—how was the Great American Thing going to happen? So as I painted along on my cow's skull I thought to myself, "I'll make an American painting. They will not think it great with the red stripes down the sides—Red, White, and Blue—but they will notice it.[108]

To wrap a cow's skull in the flag was, of course, a wonderful and complex joke: on the "city men" who found anything that smacked of patriotism vacuous; on the patriots who had held off making New Mexico a state as long as possible because of its empty wastes and dark-skinned ethnics; and on the aesthetes who would be appalled by the mixing of high and popular culture. Finally, it satirized an American mythology that could not acknowledge death as a central icon of the national experience, although it was certainly central to the realities of frontier and pioneer history.

During the two summers that she stayed in Taos, O'Keeffe produced eighteen new works, which Stieglitz showed in the following years to great critical acclaim. Her letters home from her first summer are particularly revealing of the ecstatic nature of her encounters with the land, in which her self-recovery as a woman and her renewal as an artist were entwined. She wrote to the art critic Henry McBride: "I am having a wonderful time—such a wonderful time that I don't care if Europe falls off the map or out of the world. . . . I like what Mabel has dug up out of the Earth here with her Indian Tony crown—No one who hasn't seen it and who hasn't seen her at it can know much about this Taos Myth—It is just unbelievable—One perfect day after another—everyone going like mad after something."[109]

Toward the end of her stay she wrote to Mabel: "I wish I could tell you how important these months have been to me. . . . I am thanking you for much—much more than your house. . . . I had one particular painting—that tree in Lawrence's front yard as you see it when you lie under it on the table—with stars—it looks as tho it is standing on its head—I wanted you to see it." O'Keeffe sometimes hung this painting from a seemingly upside-down perspective. Perhaps her intention was to have us view the tree from its own root system, so that its ethereal spiraling out into the night sky is firmly grounded in the earth—much as Lawrence similarly desired to root his mysticism.[110]

O'Keeffe eliminated any overt human presence in her paintings. But like Marin, all of her canvases bear the mark of a strong and assertive personality. Some of them reflect the imprint of native cultures on the land. Most notable in this regard is her Black Cross series, the genesis of which

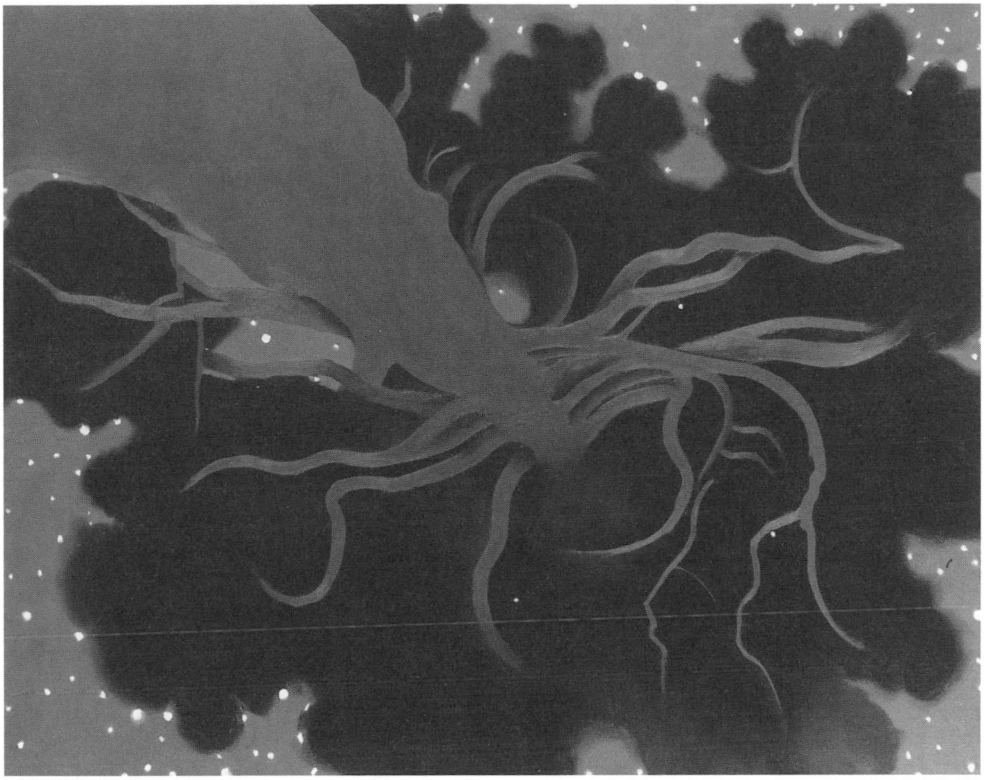

Georgia O'Keeffe, *The Lawrence Tree,* 1929.
Oil on canvas, 31 1/16 x 39 3/16 inches. Wadsworth Athenaeum, Hartford.
The Ella Gallup Sumner and Mary Catlin Sumner Collection.

she described as follows: "One evening when I was living in Taos we walked back of the morada toward a cross in the hills. I was told that it was a Penitente cross. . . . It was in the late light and the cross stood out—dark against the evening sky. If I turned a little to the left, away from the cross, I saw the Taos mountain—a beautiful shape. I painted the cross against the mountain although I never saw it that way." By enlarging the cross and superimposing it on the Sacred Mountain she suggests the multiple ways in which this landscape can be read. Her work speaks of the domination of the Southwest by Spanish Catholicism, but also of how a more ancient and nature-based religion contested and absorbed that power. This multiplicity was also O'Keeffe's, as she escaped the prison house of the East's art establishment, while using the skills they taught her to formulate her own aesthetic vision.[111]

Georgia O'Keeffe, *Black Cross With Red Sky,* 1929.
Oil on canvas, 40 × 32 inches.
Collection of Mr. and Mrs. Gerald Peters.

Ansel Adams

Ansel Adams's Taos experience helped turn him into one of the most popular American photographers of the twentieth century. If O'Keeffe secured the painterly image that many Americans have of the Southwest, Adams did much the same for our photographic vision of the western landscape. It was during his stay at the Luhan compound, during the summers of 1929 and 1930, that his sense of himself as a professional photographer coalesced. Adams, who was twenty-seven years old when he arrived, had spent most of his life preparing for a career as a concert pianist, while practicing photography as an avocation. He had visited the Southwest three times before. During his first visit, in 1927, he spent time in Santa Fe with Mary Austin, who took him to Taos, about which he wrote to his wife, Virginia: "This is the most completely beautiful place I have ever seen. A marvelous snowy range of mountains rises from a spacious emerald plain and this little Old World village nestles close to the hills. Adobe—bells—color beyond imagination—and today, the heavens are filled with clouds." In the summer of 1929 when he returned to Taos to photograph for the Sierra Club, he decided to collaborate with Mary Austin on a verbal-pictorial celebration of Taos Pueblo.[112]

While working with Austin in the summer of 1930, Adams met Paul Strand, whose work conveyed a "luminousness and clarity he had not believed could be captured by a camera." Taos was his "Paris and Rome," and Strand the mentor whose work "hit him like Saul's vision on the road to Damascus." Adams put aside all thoughts of a concert career as well as "the use of soft focus, atmospheric effects, and the simulation of painting that marked many of his early photographs." Like O'Keeffe, he was taken with the solidity and timelessness of adobe and with the paradox created by the combination of weight and light that evoked a spiritual purity embedded in the earth. Taos Pueblo committed Adams to "light and form as the essential building blocks of a picture. Every exposure was made in the most brilliant sunshine which in turn created deep shadows." Shortly after the publication of *Taos Pueblo*, Adams helped found Group f/64 and define "the visual manifesto of straight photography."[113]

In his autobiography, Adams wrote that *Taos Pueblo* might not have been possible were it not for Mabel's hospitality and Tony's assistance in obtaining the permission from the pueblo to make the photographs. Adams paid tribute to Tony in two photographs that represent him in a Pharaonic pose. These are both head portraits, one taken with Tony looking directly out at us, but with the camera somewhat below his face, the other a flattering side view. Both perspectives accentuate his dignity and nobility. Yet Adams does not seem to have been very impressed with Tony. When the Luhans visited the Adamses in California and Tony performed on his drum, "repeating Taos tribal songs ad nauseam," Adams says he found him "pleasant" but "theatrical."[114]

Ansel Adams, *Tony Luhan.* MDLC.

Adams characterized his goal as an artist as "seeking spiritual resonance as moving and profound as great music." In a revealing letter he wrote Mabel after the publication of her *Edge of Taos Desert,* he told her: "Not unlike you, when you first came to Taos, I am confronted with the problem of finding a real way of life, and real and vital simplicity." New Mexico served as his first provocative "equivalent" for creating a modern art built on

Ansel Adams, *Winnowing Grain, Taos Pueblo, New Mexico,* c. 1929.

eternal values. It reconciled the self and the world by its dramatic yoking of earth and sky, body and spirit: "The next morning all was diamond bright and clear, and I fell quickly under the spell of the astonishing New Mexican light. . . . Summer thunderstorms create the dominant symbolic power of the land: huge ranges of flashing and grumbling clouds with gray curtains of rain clearing both the air and the spirit while nourishing the earth."[115]

Perhaps a good part of Adams's and O'Keeffe's popularity, which has increased dramatically during the twentieth century, stems from their suggestion of transcendental spirituality to a secularized public for whom nature carries some of the same symbolic weight once borne by traditional religious iconography. Both artists have been criticized for their "prettification" of the landscape: for their elimination of painful social realities and the depredations of nature by civilization. Yet one can also argue that they helped to restore a much-needed sense of the primacy of the land—of its beauty and power—and of the necessary limits to our human-centeredness, if we are to continue to live on it.

CHAPTER THREE

Visitors, 1930–1950

The sense of mystical unity and timelessness that permeates much of the art, poetry, and prose that came out of the Luhan house in the 1920s can also be found in the work of writers and artists who came in the 1930s. But many of these works also show the effects of depression-age America. These are evident even in the cultural expressions of artists who may seem the most removed from its economic upheavals. The common thread that links the Penitente crosses of Georgia O'Keeffe, the "primitive mysteries" of Martha Graham's choreography, and the Pueblo Indian martyr of Aldous Huxley's *Brave New World* is an aesthetic vision that seeks to purge the materialism and individualism of western civilization.

No "spirit of place" suggested a clearer alternative to these excesses in the 1930s than that of northern New Mexico. In the 1920s, the openness of the landscape and the "discovery" of tribal cultures inspired the imaginative freedom of Anglo artists. In the 1930s, they were more likely to emphasize the spareness of the physical and cultural landscape in their critique of America's economic and spiritual poverty. If one looks at the most innovative paintings, poetry, and performances by Taos visitors during this decade, one realizes that radical revisions of American society and culture were not solely the property of the social realists of the era. There were modernists who were also seeking to meld social vision with new aesthetic forms.

Edmund Wilson

Edmund Wilson, the cynical and sophisticated guru of the eastern literary establishment, could see no redeeming possibilities in New Mexico when he made a trip across the United States during the first year of the Great Depression. He was attracted by evidence of spiritual fakery and by what he felt was the idiocy of white romantics yearning to go native. His description of the Native Americans he encountered are blatantly racist: "They are narrow, unbusinesslike, incurious, illiterate, unhygienic, unscientific." However, he did credit them with a consistency he could not find among his purportedly civilized white fellow citizens: "The Indian's religion and government are the same thing and fit him like a glove—whereas our laws don't fit us anywhere—nor our religion either!"[1]

In Taos, where he met the Luhans, Wilson's attention was captivated by the variety of Anglo carnivores he believed were feeding off the entrails of the human and natural landscape. There was Mona Gibbs, who spent her life "wheedling" Navajos and Hopis into making sand paintings on her patio; Guy Fay and Luell Lamb, who came from Hollywood to film a movie "which will show the struggle between a Navajo and a white man for the love of a covered wagon girl"; and Ellen David, who painted flat landscapes that contrasted sharply with her clothes: "Today she is wearing neat boots, a fancy pink sombrero and a green silk scarf at the neck of her blouse; she has spectacles with yellow rims because with her artist's feeling for color she wants them to go with her blond hair." Wilson had nothing but contempt for these Indian-lovers: "It is as if they felt that the Indians possessed some profound key to life, some integrity, some harmony with Nature, that Americans have lost. And they read into the dances they see unattainable satisfactions—the realizations of poetry and religion which they themselves never know."[2]

Maynard Dixon

Edmund Wilson provided an honest gloss on the least attractive elements spawned by the countercultural invasion of northern New Mexico after World War I. But his was a superficial view in terms of the circumstances of most of the artists who lived and worked in New Mexico. Few had large stock portfolios or bank accounts to sustain them, and a number of them prided themselves on subordinating profitability to the integrity of their work. For Maynard Dixon this kind of pride was reinforced by the impact of the depression on his income.

Dixon arrived with his wife, Dorothea Lange, in Taos in the fall of 1931. As self-employed professionals, they were hard-hit by the depression. Like many other artists, he saw commissions canceled, exhibits dropped, and had a difficult time collecting for work he had sold earlier. Of the one hundred easel paintings he made during the first four years of the depression, he sold twelve. Lange had suggested a change of scene for them and their children. Dixon's daughter by his first marriage, Constance, had been brought by John Collier, Jr., to Taos where she got a job typing Mabel's memoirs and waitressing. It was her glowing reports about Taos that convinced Dorothea and Maynard to leave San Francisco and come to Taos.[3]

Dixon and Lange lived first in Ranchos, then rented a small house in Taos, where they renewed their acquaintance with Tony and Mabel, whom Dorothea called "the queen of the Southwest." Dixon painted some forty works in one of Mabel's studios, including some of his finest: *Earth Knower, Watchers from the Housetop,* and *Round Dance,* whose performance he observed in Mabel's courtyard. He made friends with several Indians at Taos Pueblo, including Antonio Mirabal, whose portrait demonstrates the strength that Dixon, as well as Jung, found in this powerful religious leader.

Maynard Dixon, *Round Dance (At Mabel Dodge Luhan's)*, December 1931.
Oil on canvas. Courtesy of Brigham Young University, Museum of Fine Arts.

When Dixon's and Lange's money ran out in the winter of 1932, Mirabal offered to share food with them.[4]

Although Dixon was influenced by postimpressionism in his use of color and form, his was a fiercely nativist aesthetic. His center of interest in northern New Mexico was the integration of the natural and human landscapes, which defined his westerner's response to the foreign winds that had blown across the Atlantic from France. When modern art first arrived in the United States, he felt he had to make a decision whether to import his ideas or see for himself. "As often before, I went again into the desert to find an answer—and it was not far to seek. Well, there is the empty desert; there are arid mountains, the shimmer in the ashen heat of noon, a reality that appears unreal, challenging the imagination. . . . So my choice was made; I must find in this visible world the forms, the colors[,] the relationships that for me are the most true of it, and find a way to state them clearly so that the painting may pass on something of my vision."[5]

Maynard Dixon, *Antonio Mirabal,* 1931.
Oil on canvas. California Academy of Sciences.
Photo courtesy of Susan Middleton.

Dixon felt that his Taos work was very much influenced by a sense of "something ominous and unavoidable impending . . . of being caught in the slowly closing jaws of a vise, of complete helplessness in the face of fate." Several of his paintings from this period were "a spiritual response to the despair of the Depression and a reminder of man's dependence and identification with the earth." He wrote of his best-known work, *Earth Knower:* "He is a sage, calm Indian who stands against his own background of

Maynard Dixon, *Earth Knower,* 1931.
Oil on canvas, 40 x 50 inches.
Collection of the Oakland Museum, bequest of Dr. Abilio Reis.

mountains, from which he draws his health, wealth, religion and pattern of living. While we get panic-stricken over 'the Market' the Indian puffs his pipe and looks at the sky."[6]

Aldous Huxley

The darkest vision of New Mexico to come out of the 1930s was created by a man who wrote about it before ever seeing it. Aldous Huxley's perceptions were very much colored by his conversations in Italy with D. H. Lawrence, with whom he spent a great deal of time in 1926 and who was an important influence on his thinking and his work. Like Lawrence, he was a prophet manqué who had "repudiated all of the left-over nineteenth-century formulas by which mankind had tried vainly during the decade after the War to support itself—religion, patriotism, moral order, humanitarianism, social reform, science, and (the last of the inebriants), art. Human reason had failed." When Huxley was twenty-one he had met Lawrence briefly and agreed to join him in a dreamed-of utopian colony in Florida. He was moved by Lawrence's criticism of the dualism of modern life that split humanity into warring forces of reason and passion, but he was too much of an intellectual to follow him all the way in his celebration of the irrational. Nevertheless, *Brave New World* is a satire of just "the type of non-human civilization that Lawrence most dreaded," where the price of human happiness is the sacrifice of all genuine human emotion and feeling.[7]

Huxley's scientific dystopia rings damnation on the 1920s and its hedonist display of conspicuous consumption that left England, as well as the United States, bereft of the spiritual and psychological resources necessary to create a meaningful culture and society. His humans are programmed in a genetic hierarchy of intelligence and ability that allows each to serve various functions necessary to the State. They never have to experience pain—either physical or psychic—because of the ready availability of the drug "soma," which puts them into a temporary state of nirvana. "Ford" has taken the place of God, and the ideal of the ultimate good has been reduced to a kind of feel-goodism created through the instant gratification of material and sensory desires: "Ford's in his flivver. All's well with the world."[8]

Bernard Marx, the novel's protagonist, is an Alpha, one of those who represent the highest level of human development. To impress Lenina, a young woman he fancies, he takes her to New Mexico, where they visit a reservation of sixty thousand Indians in their natural "habitat," surrounded by barbed wire fences. They are a kind of exotic human zoo, held in captivity as a reminder of the savagery of life before the coming of the machine Messiah and his assembly line mode of human production. Huxley's futuristic description of Santa Fe as the last comfort stop before the end of civilization is much closer to the mark than he could have known; he describes a plush hotel that offers liquid air, vibro-vacuum massage, synthetic music, and hot condoms in eight kinds of scent.

Huxley's rendition of the Indian reservation is a very different affair. He creates a melange of different tribes, cultures, and customs, blends the architecture of Acoma and Taos, and merges the Hopi Snake Dance with the Penitente rites of self-flagellation. While Huxley's contempt for contemporary Anglo-civilization is clear, his attitude toward the natives of New Mexico is more ambiguous, as one might expect given that his source of knowledge was D. H. Lawrence. He finds the notion of the reservation repulsive, but he seems equally repulsed by the Indians themselves, mired as they seem to him in the darkness of superstition and the filth of poverty. Yet Bernard is moved by a form of worship that is connected to the earth, as well as by the sight of women bearing children naturally. John, the "half-breed" from the reservation whom Bernard takes back to England, is portrayed as a potential redeemer of the modern world.

John is horrified by the ethos of self-gratification that he finds in the Brave New World of England, which he had yearned to see because of his white mother's teaching him Shakespeare. A cross between Caliban and Prospero, he longs for a society in which love has not been reduced to pop-tune sentiments, like the one Lenina sings to him when she tries to seduce him:

Hug me till you drug me honey;
Kiss me till I'm in a coma;
Hug me, honey, snugly bunny;
Love's as good as soma.[9]

When John tries to prophesy a form of primitive Christian morality to this benighted world, he is mocked. Feeling defiled by "civilization," he retreats to a hermitage where he spends hours praying, seeking forgiveness, and practicing self-flagellation, as though he were doing penance for the world. When the media discovers his behavior, people flock to watch him, throw peanuts at him, and egg him on to whip himself more. In disgust, he finally hangs himself. An ironic Christ figure, John has suffered and died for nothing. He serves as a vehicle for Huxley's warning to his fellow humans to redeem themselves before they commit mass cultural suicide.

Five years after the publication of *Brave New World,* Huxley came to New Mexico in search of more fodder for "a practical cookery book of reform" he was engaged in writing. Huxley and his wife stayed from June through September 1937 at the Lawrence ranch, where he finished his treatise, titled *Ends and Means.* The text is an interesting gloss on his novel, for Huxley had the opportunity to observe something of Pueblo life before writing it, and the attitudes he expresses toward the Pueblos here are less exaggerated and grotesque. Although he found the Pueblos too weighted down by "magic rites" and "mental sloth," he believed that they offered an important antidote to the "pride, avarice and malice" of westerners, whose "lust for power" was responsible for so much war and oppression. Huxley ends his chapter on large-scale social reform by asking: "Can we create a new pattern of living in which the defects of the two contrasted patterns, Pueblo-Indian and western-Industrial, shall be absent? Is it possible for us to acquire their admirable habits of non-attachment to wealth and personal success and at the same time to preserve our intellectual alertness, our interest in science, our capacity for making rapid technological progress and social change?"[10]

In the 1960s, Huxley became a guru to the twentieth century's second counterculture, who were attracted by his global consciousness and by his interest in the mind-expanding possibilities of hallucinatory drugs. In his preface to the 1962 edition of *Brave New World,* Huxley speculated upon a third option he could have given his "Savage," one that spoke directly to the hippie youth who were soon to make their pilgrimages to the hillsides of northern New Mexico. He says he could have sent John to the community of exiles and refugees he briefly mentioned in the novel, who had escaped modern civilization and lived within the borders of the reservation. "In this community economics would be decentralist and Henry-Georgian, politics Kropotkinesque cooperative, science and technology would be used as though, like the Sabbath, they had been made for man, not . . . as though men were to be adapted and enslaved to them. Religion would be the conscious and intelligent pursuit of man's Final End, the unitive knowledge of the immanent Tao or Logos, the transcendent Godhead or Brahman."[11]

Robinson Jeffers

In the same year that Huxley wrote his treatise on social reform, a poet who shared his critique of western civilization published the one short poem inspired by his experiences in New Mexico. Unlike Huxley, however, Robinson Jeffers believed that the Pueblos had nothing to offer Anglos because they were too contaminated by their civilization. Jeffers did, however, have empathy for the young Indian men who were embarrassed to dance in front of the tourists and for the tourists who watched them "hungrily": "Pilgrims from civilization, anxiously seeking beauty, religion,/ poetry; pilgrims from the vacuum." But his strongest empathy was with the nonhuman landscape—"the rockhead of Taos mountain"—and the "tribal drum," which limns its music to remind us "that civilization is a transient sickness."[12]

In 1930, Mabel had lured Jeffers to New Mexico from his stone tower in Carmel. He and his wife, Una, returned each summer throughout most of the decade. Mabel hoped that Jeffers would replace Lawrence as the scribe who would convince western society of the restorative powers of the Taos landscape and the Tiwa Indians. She chose as Lawrence's successor a man who had lived most of his adult life in the self-chosen exile of a Tower Beyond Tragedy, the stone house that he built at the tip of the Monterey peninsula, where he lived in fiercely guarded privacy.

When Mabel met Jeffers in Carmel in 1930, he was at the height of his fame, with a wide readership and extraordinary critical acclaim that sanctified him as America's greatest living poet. Despite their vastly different characters and temperaments, the rooted and reclusive Jeffers and the peripatetic and sociable Lawrence shared a kinship. A major theme in both writers' works was the primary theme of Mabel's memoirs: that the solipsistic ego of western man had denied love (what Jeffers called "falling in love outward") and had turned to power for its satisfaction. For Jeffers, as well as for Lawrence, the "original sin" was mental consciousness, what he called man's "distinction" but hardly his "advantage," since it cuts him off from nature and makes him turn inward toward self-love. As a poet of the apocalypse and an heir of the Calvinists, he yearned for the holocaustal destruction that would have to precede the creation of a new world.[13]

Although Lawrence would have recoiled from Jeffers's philosophic doctrine of Inhumanism, they shared a belief in the regenerative power of symbolic language. In spite of his disillusionment with man's essentially corrupt and violent nature, Jeffers's "surge to annihilation" was coupled with "a faith in messianic restitution." Mabel saw him in a role he had already undertaken for himself, that of a sacrificial Christ, whose healing message was ignored by a decadent civilization. By identifying with God's "victimhood," he hoped to teach his fellow humans how to achieve "cosmic selflessness."[14]

Jeffers enjoyed his visits and admired his hostess. But Taos could never become for him what Mabel hoped it would. The center of his belief was an Old Testament God who demanded worship and praise even as he damned man to torture and destruction. It is the Dionysian outbreak of violence at its most ecstatic that consumed Jeffers's poetic energies in his great works, like "Roan Stallion," "The Women at Point Sur," and "Tamar." The destruction of the human family as the incestuous source of self-love—this is the requisite for the illumination and acceptance of the divine tragedy that is life.[15]

Leopold Stokowski and Carlos Chavez

Among the most artistically ambitious visitors to the Luhan house during the early 1930s were the musicians Leopold Stokowski and Carlos Chavez. Mabel had met Stokowski in Phoenix, in February of 1930, and he came for the first of several visits to Taos during the summer of 1931. At the time he visited Mabel, Stokowski was probably the best-known classical conductor of his time in the United States. A fierce cultural nationalist, he challenged the European dominance over American music that was more prevalent in his field than in the other arts. Stokowski made the Philadelphia Orchestra a first-rank world symphony during his twenty-six-year tenure, during which time he was praised and condemned for both his progressivism and his popularization of classical music. His openness to new musical forms transcended his nationalism, however, for he traveled to Asia to study music, and he promoted indigenous music throughout the Americas.[16]

Stokowski's interest in experimenting with the latest technology in sound reproduction aroused Mabel's hopes that he could record Indian ceremonial chants and bring them to the attention of the nation. He responded immediately to the culture and communalism of the Pueblos, writing to Mabel of his eagerness to see her and Tony again in order "to learn all I can about Indian culture and perhaps be able to pass some of it on to others." Stokowski agreed with Mabel that "Taos feels like the *center* of this America," and he was "enthusiastic about the idea of a great center in Taos." He had brought along with a him a specially designed recording machine, but the recordings he made were of poor quality. In August, he wrote Mabel of his difficulty in finding an adequate notation system for transcribing Indian music.[17]

Tony, who was very fond of Stokowski, tried to help, but he had difficulty explaining how he made the music for which he was famous in Taos and Carmel: "I don't read & I never speak to any man about music," he wrote his friend, "but, I listen to the world & the mountain & I learn from them & that comes. You know music is not just sound, it is what you make from own life & heart. Afterwards you make the brain work. I have to think a lot about it." In spite of his difficulties, Stokowski continued to believe that "Taos is one of the great magnetic centers of the world." He said of Tony that he was one of those individuals who holds the "sacred fire" of civilization.[18]

In 1934, Stokowski resigned from the Philadelphia Orchestra and set his sights on Hollywood, in order to find new directions and greater audiences for his music. (He was soon to collaborate with Walt Disney on *Fantasia*). En route, he stopped at Mabel's. When he was asked in 1935 to make a movie about music from all over the world, he told Mabel he wished to include the Indian dances and music of Arizona and New Mexico. Stokowski dreamed of building in Philadelphia a Temple of Music created on Native American architectural principles: "The great building, and we [have] built it here, seems to have sprung from our soil. Perhaps it has roots in Taos. Maybe it is more Aztec than anything else; but, whatever it is, it's our own." Stokowski saw this as a place to synthesize all the musical arts, with a stage for opera and ballet as well as for orchestra, and spaces for outdoor as well as indoor programs. He was, as Daniel Oliver notes, some thirty years ahead of his time in imagining a "performing arts" complex.[19]

The knowledge that Stokowski gained about Indian music and architecture through his visits to New Mexico and Mexico served as an important basis for his most prophetic pronouncements about the role that music could play in establishing the basis for a new world order. Stokowski's most far-sighted articulation of his internationalist vision can be found in *Music for All of Us* (1943), published in the midst of World War II: "In the American continent the music of the Indians is of high cultural value to all those who are interested in rhythm and melody. . . . The most typical of all this music should be recorded, as should the folk music all over the world. Such records will be a permanent monument of the individual culture of many lands, and an important part of the foundations of world culture."[20]

As conductor of the Mexico National Symphony, Carlos Chavez's ambitions for Mexico were similar to Stokowski's for the United States. He was desirous of creating a Mexican classical music that would achieve respectability outside his country, one that was a product of high culture, but that also built on native folk forms. Chavez was equally committed to promoting works of art that spoke to the indigenous populations of Mexico, as evidenced by his sponsorship of and influence on Paul Strand's work when Chavez was minister of education during the early years of the depression.

Like Stokowski, Chavez believed that the task of his generation was to develop what he called "musical theater," a concept that had a progressive sociopolitical dimension. Chavez met Stokowski in Mexico and at the Luhan house in 1931. They worked on the orchestration and performance of Chavez's *Caballos de Vapor,* an avant-garde piece with set designs by

Diego Rivera, which was one of the most exciting modernist collaborations of the period. Stokowski premiered the piece in March 1932 with the Philadelphia Orchestra, where it was received with some measure of incomprehension. Retitled *H.P.* (Horsepower), it was literally and figuratively foreign, in concept, theme, and execution, from what Americans expected in terms of dance and orchestration. And it was politically and aesthetically revolutionary in its subversion of the purported superiority and dominance of the United States over Latin America.[21]

H.P. dramatized the economic relations between the United States and Latin America by contrasting the easy-going rhythms of the South with those of the hectic North. The South was represented by animated pineapples, bananas, coconuts, sugar cane, and mermaids playing guitars. The North was represented by sailors, drab workmen "gyrating before a stock ticker, a set of gasoline pumps, bathtubs, and a ventilator all melded into a materialistic orgy." In the last act, the workers take over their machines in a triumph of the sensuous and lyrical over the mechanical. Chavez's program notes suggest that the purpose of the ballet was to "harmonize" the interdependence of the North and South. But the music indicates more a reversal of fortune, with the native rhythms of the *zanduga,* the *huapango, sones,* and the Argentine tango triumphing over the dissonant city noises and popular tunes like "The Sidewalks of New York."[22]

In working on a series of new pieces in the early 1930s, one of which was called *La Revolución,* Chavez tried to enlist Mabel to send Taos Indian dancers to Mexico City. He wanted them to dance in his new works, but also to express themselves, "from which I am sure will come out one of the greatest choreographic expressions that has ever been known." In 1935 Chavez finished what he called his "Indian Symphony," which he recorded for Columbia Broadcasting. Graciously, he wrote Mabel that he wanted her and Tony's opinion of it. In his last letter to her, he recalled that his stay in Taos "was one of the greatest experiences of my life."[23]

Dane Rudhyar

Perhaps the most transcendental of modernists to appear in Taos, Dane Rudhyar was a true polymath, a man who crossed the fields of modern classical music (he was both a composer and performer), theosophy, Jungian psychology, painting, poetry, and astrology, with several volumes of publications to his name. Born in Paris in 1895, he came to the United States in 1916, where in 1917 he was one of the first to give a public performance of polytonal music. Rudhyar was a pioneer of music therapy, although he meant by that something much broader than its current usage. His ambition was to find rhythmic patterns that corresponded to internal psychological states in order to effect the healing and integration of the modern psyche.

Like Stokowski, Rudhyar was a promoter of "world music," a term he may even have coined in the 1920s. He attempted to base the principles of his music, as his friend Martha Graham based her dance choreography, not on traditional patterns of musical notation but on "the flow of life itself." For Rudhyar, this was not merely a matter of aesthetic or personal choice, but a matter of bringing "social significance" back into music. Rudhyar's ultimate goal was to have music serve as the building blocks of a new civilization, one that was created "on a non-exclusivistic, non-European basis." Although he was trained in the elite heritage of western classical music, he wanted to create a music that spoke to a much broader audience and that incorporated many other traditions. In his desire to democratize classical music, he refused to accept a "system of tonality reflecting the ways of life of the aristocratic classes of the seventeenth and eighteenth centuries, . . . [or] the rigidly intellectual, neoscholastic procedures of the Schoenberg school."[24]

Rudhyar may have first connected with Mabel Luhan through her 1925 article in *Theatre Arts,* "A Bridge Between Cultures." In his first letter to her, he said that he was living near the pupils of Ruth St. Denis. He noted that Miss Martha Graham "is especially attracted by your article" and that she might pass through Taos. He ended his letter with just the kind of messianic prophecy that would most whet Mabel's appetite: "When the magnetic center, the Purpose, the clear Vision and the Will are there, one by one the individuals are drawn into the magic circle." In the early 1930s, he spent a few weeks at Mabel's. Rudhyar tried to interest Mabel in his "Project of Studies in the Evolution of the Social and Individual Psychology of Music," a proposal to study the "correlation of music with psychology" through collaboration with psychologists and anthropologists, and contact with the Indians of Taos and Zuni "because of their strong musical development." He gave some thirty lectures in Taos and Santa Fe during his 1933–34 stay, returning over the following four years, and helping to establish the Transcendentalist painting group that formed in Santa Fe in 1938. In 1945 he married Eya Fechin.[25]

In 1969, Rudhyar coined the phrase: "planetarization of consciousness" to describe the ethos of the "earth-as-a-whole," a Jungian-based concept that he explained as the "unity aspect of consciousness and being, which undertones the consciousness of all individualized units of existence." Like Jaime de Angulo and Aldous Huxley, he was adopted enthusiastically by the 1960s counterculture. Rudhyar festivals were held in California in the 1970s and recordings made of his music.[26]

Martha Graham

In 1934, Dane Rudhyar published an essay titled "The Indian Dances for Power" in the journal *Dance Observer.* In his description of the dance can be found one of the generating principles of modern dance in America as developed by one of its most original—and long-lived proponents—Martha Graham: "A ritual of power. They danced neither for pleasure, nor for show . . . but to release power out of tense drums, tense earth and tense muscles. . . . What is dancing for? I believe it is to generate . . . more vital power in soul, mind and body. Dancing is for the purpose of drawing together by the magic of rhythm . . . the sky and the earth within the human psyche."[27]

Isadora Duncan, the first great pioneer of modern dance, sought to do with dance what George Cram Cook tried to accomplish with modern theatre—return to its Greek roots, when dance and drama were central components of an integrated religion and culture. Ruth St. Denis and Ted Shawn followed her, both of them influenced by Christian Science, New Thought, and the "wisdom of the East." In 1914, they formed the Denishawn Company in Los Angeles and were joined by Doris Humphrey, Charles Weidman, Martha Graham, and Louis Horst. Shawn was interested in many types of dances from all over the United States, including Indian and Spanish dances. They linked dance "with idealistic goals for humanity. The next generation found it but a short step from the metaphysical goals of Denishawn to the social utopian goals of the 1930s."[28]

Graham took modern dance two giant steps further. She gave up productions that depended on theatricality, sumptuous costumes and settings, and created dances based on controversial social themes. The *Immigrant* dealt with immigrants fighting for their rights in a strike; *Chronicle* unmasked American imperialism; and *American Document* made use of the speeches of Red Jacket, as well as excerpts from the Declaration of Independence to chronicle the course of the American Dream.

Graham achieved her first important recognition as a dancer in 1929, when she performed as The Chosen One in the American premier of

Stravinsky's *Le Sacre du Printemps,* conducted by Leopold Stokowski. She began her own company the following year, during which time she also made her first trip to the Southwest. Like other artists who came to New Mexico in the 1930s, what she drew from the physical and cultural landscapes was connected to her response to the depression. She was searching for a new simplicity and honesty, "for intellectual and emotional cleanliness, which in dance meant a commitment to strong unornamented movement. The sinuous flow that had been characteristic of the Denishawn dancer was not the movement with which to meet a moral crisis." Graham became the "high priestess" of modern dance, guided by an austere and puritanical aesthetic.[29]

Graham was accompanied to New Mexico by Louis Horst, her lover and the composer of much of the music that she used in her work. They were tremendously impressed by the landscape and by "the Indian's intense integration and sense of ritualistic tribal drama." They visited Isleta, Santo Domingo, the Santa Fe Fiesta, and they made a trip to Taos. Graham's work was "energized by the strength she found in the rituals of the Southwest Indians," which gave her and Horst "an indigenous American root" for their new choreography and music. Martha focused "on earth and air-borne images, breath and chanting, strict repetitive structuring, and formal, symbolic devices to assimilate into a dance style of her own."[30]

In Santa Fe, Graham stayed with Mary Austin, whose theories about the American Rhythm she greatly admired and with whom she discussed theories about dance drama. Her trip to New Mexico gave her a new impetus to rebel against "the easy beauty" of classical ballet in order to liberate and "restore the 'natural' body so that it could once again dance with freedom and power." It may also have affirmed her belief that music and dance could invoke "Powers of the Spirit" which could bring about a healthier nation and world.[31]

The source of Graham's fascination with Native American rituals was that they were repetitive and traditional, at the same time that they referenced an archetypal, original experience with divinity. The specific movements, which she did not try to imitate, were of secondary interest to the process of generativity and community suggested in the patterns. Graham adapted elements from both Indian and Hispanic dances for the choreography that earned her her first major recognition, *Primitive Mysteries,* which premiered in February 1931 during her second repertory series. Here Graham introduced her prototypical movement, based on the Native

American orientation toward the earth, rather than the balletic flight from it. "'Come down to the earth with your heels!' Martha told her dancers. . . . 'Walk as if for the first time.'" Together, she and Horst had "created their own *Sacre du Printemps.*"[32]

In 1931, when Graham returned to Santa Fe as a guest of Mary Austin and visited several more pueblos, she wrote to a friend that she was at a crossroads in her life. In February 1932, she performed her second work inspired by the Southwest, *Ceremonials,* and the following fall, she received a Guggenheim, the first dancer ever to receive one. In the fall of 1932 she visited New Mexico again, where she also spent five weeks in July 1933, part of the time as Mabel's guest. This time she visited Taos Pueblo. Throughout the 1930s, Graham developed other dance pieces that were directly inspired by her trips to New Mexico, including *Primitive Canticles* (1931) and *El Penitente* (1937).[33]

Graham attracted another passionate devotee of the Southwest to photograph her work. Barbara Morgan's photographs of Graham's dances were really more of an artistic collaboration then a series of photographic sessions. Morgan had come to New York with a friend who was filming a documentary on Graham. When Barbara asked Martha if she were influenced by Southwest Indian dances, Graham replied: "Absolutely, that's one of the greatest inspirations of my entire life." Morgan's interest in Graham's work stemmed from "my many summers of seeing the rituals of the Southwest Indians. . . . And the relationship of the community and the dancing group inviting union of the sun god and earth mother—inviting living forces together—made dance for me not only a theatrical performance but a spiritual embrace of people and the world."[34]

Graham's commitment to an essentially religious aesthetic that is both timeless and bound to the time in which she lived can be seen in *Primitive Mysteries* and *El Penitente.* The first is a story of the Crucifixion. Martha, who plays the Virgin, is the focus of the dance, the one who bears the symbolic crown of thorns, which is created by the bare hands of her female acolytes. Graham's intention was to present "the essence of religion" by abstracting the elements of initiation, suffering, and redemption. "Read purely as a personal statement, the central figure, the initiate might even have been the choreographer herself, as an innovative force bringing creative life to a group or society."[35]

El Penitente is presented more in the manner of a medieval mystery play. The performers enter, and the penitent is flagellated. He has a vision

Martha Graham's *Primitive Mysteries,* n.d.
Photo by Barbara Morgan. Courtesy of Willard and Barbara Morgan Archives.

of the Virgin pleading and of Christ giving his blessing. Seduced by Magdalen, he is tied to the death cart (used in Penitente practices) as a symbol of sin and the fall of man. The penitent then bears the cross on his back, is crucified, and atones. The piece ends in a festival dance. "This process of redemption fascinated Graham," who played the Virgin, Magdalen, and the Madonna. Graham saw herself as a redeemer, both in terms of the role she played for dance theatre in America, as well as in terms of the message she brought to her fellow Americans about the need to rid themselves of the materialism that had created havoc not just with the nation's economy, but with its soul.[36]

Like Stokowski, Chavez, and Rudhyar, Graham wanted to create an art that served both a nationalist and a global agenda. After her trips to New Mexico, she began to draw on myths and rituals from all over the world—Celtic, Christian, Greek, and Egyptian, as well as Spanish and Native American. These she universalized by integrating elements from more than one myth or tradition into the same dance. She also created heroic roles

Martha Graham's *El Penitente*, n.d.
Photo by Barbara Morgan. Courtesy of Willard and Barbara Morgan Archives.

based on the common elements she believed were shared by "the ancestresses" of the world. Just before her death in 1991, she was "brooding" on a new dance that would celebrate the earth goddess in all her incarnations. This may have been intended as her definitive statement on the power of the female in the much-needed regeneration of the planet: "the transmigration of the goddess figure, from India to Babylon, Sumer, Egypt, Greece, Rome, Spain, . . . and the American Southwest."[37]

Ward Lockwood

In his 1940 autobiographical essay, "An Artist's Roots," Ward Lockwood spoke eloquently of the way in which the "art spirit" might help to heal a nation in the throes of more than one kind of depression: "It is the effort to build as fine a thing as possible regardless of material remuneration. . . . It is only the ignorant who smile with disdain upon the struggles of any

Ward Lockwood's painting on book jacket of Mabel Luhan's *Winter in Taos*.
Ward Lockwood Papers, AAA, Smithsonian Institution.

artist, because in the art spirit will be found someday—somewhere—the seed of the cure for most of our social and economic ills." This vision of the arts as having social purpose was made possible by the Roosevelt administration's nationwide support of them during the New Deal, and it could be found in northern New Mexico as well as elsewhere.[38]

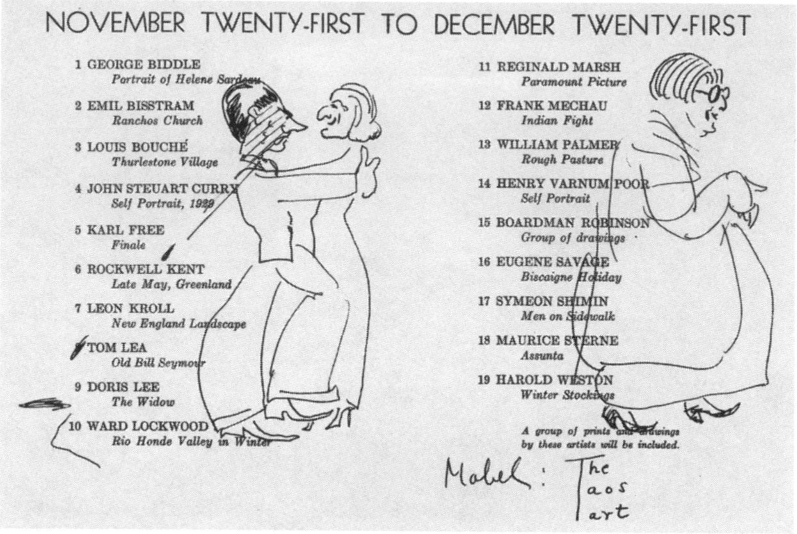

Ward Lockwood, Caricature of Mabel Dodge Luhan on an exhibition brochure, 1930s. Ward Lockwood Papers, AAA, Smithsonian Institution.

Charles Eldridge notes that Taos painters in this period retreated from some of their early experiments to rely more on "native backgrounds as sources for their imagery. . . . This development of a strong concept of 'spirit of place' and a stress upon the mystique of Taos grew during the 1930s." Although their avoidance of social issues in Taos art remains a legitimate cause for complaint during the depression years, when Indians and Hispanics suffered greater poverty than most Anglos, the work of Lockwood and his peers demonstrates that theirs was not an aestheticist response. Their art may have avoided social injustice pictorially, but it suggested a Thoreauvian simplification of living as a means to greater economic and social equality.[39]

Lockwood was one of the more notable among the second generation of Taos modernists influenced by Andrew Dasburg. He came in 1926 to study with Dasburg and returned the next year to build a house, where he stayed until 1938. Like his mentor, his art derived from Cézanne, with a "regard for the essentials that underline all form." This aesthetic that attracted him to Taos was reinforced by the landscape, including the architectural landscape, which may have influenced him as much as his European training. Eldridge notes that in the 1930s Lockwood dropped his impressionist tonalities "in favor of emphatic contrasts of light and dark,"

Tony Lujan, 1930.
Gelatin silver print, 9.8 x 7.3 cm.
Photo by Edward Weston.

an aesthetic choice shared by other New Mexican artists, perhaps inspired by the search for spiritual clarity.[40]

There are suggestive parallels between Lockwood's art and Mabel's writing in the 1930s, which is perhaps the reason she chose one of his paintings for the cover of her book *Winter in Taos.* Eldridge pairs Lockwood's *Midwinter* with a quote from Mabel's book that can serve as a verbal equivalent: "Now, in the frozen immunity of winter, the earth on either side of the road looks like blue glaciers interminably stretching to the mountain slopes, monotonously still except for a sudden splash of black, when a couple of crows land on the dark huddle of a carcass."[41]

Edward Weston

Edward Weston produced many of his finest photographs during the eight years he traveled through New Mexico. Before his first trip, during which he spent two weeks at the Luhan house, Weston had "concentrated on the sharp-focus, reductive style that . . . [became] his trademark" in his portraits of shells, vegetables, and his nudes. Sally Eauclaire argues that his New Mexico photos "catalyzed the modern landscape style that preoccupied him during the final phase of his career."[42]

"E" Town, New Mexico, 1933.
Gelatin silver print, 19.1 x 24.3 cm.
Photo by Edward Weston. © 1981, Center for Creative Photography, Arizona Board of Regents.

Mabel had met Weston in 1930 in Carmel, where she bought three prints from him, including the D. H. Lawrence and Robinson Jeffers photos that she used in her biography *Lorenzo in Taos.* Weston also made several portraits of Tony, one of which also appears in that book. His memory of the responses to his Tony portraits is revealing of the willingness of artists to cater to their patrons, even when it meant compromising the "purity" of their art: "The print [of Tony's head] was extraordinary—about the limit of brilliance of chemical quality, and powerful in presentation of the person. I was more than happy. Now Tony is a rather flabby Indian, settled down into a life of ease, well-fed, middle-aged inactivity. In my print, I gave him a heroic strength he does not possess. So when he lumbered in, I got out the enlargement, anticipating at least a grunt of approval." Mabel

Ovens, Taos Pueblo, 1933.
Gelatin silver print.
Photo by Edward Weston. © 1981, Center for Creative Photography, Arizona Board of Regents.

liked it very much but Tony did not: "I look too old—a hundred years maybe."[43]

In June 1933, Weston drove to the Luhans with two other photographers, Sonya Noskowiak and Willard Van Dyke. When Weston returned to Carmel he wrote in his *Daybook* that he had "some fine new work; landscapes with gorgeous heavens . . . details of various pueblos—the old church at Laguna, the perfectly formed and functional ovens against equally perfect walls of adobe." In January 1934, he noted that his New Mexico landscapes "marked a definite . . . advance, and indicate the next phase of my work." Weston was as excited as his fellow Californian Ansel Adams to be in a place where the sky mattered. Like Adams and Strand, he discovered in landscape photography a way to free his art "beyond the doctrinaire modernism that found its apotheosis in his earlier still-lifes and portraits."[44]

Mabel used six of Weston's photos from this first trip as illustrations for her book *Winter in Taos.* It is interesting that she chose Weston (and Adams) and not Strand to illustrate her work. Harold Jones's comparison of the two helps illuminate why: "Where Strand waited for the elements to reach a climax of baroque dynamics, Weston saw quiet reserve in nature's action. Strand set himself the problem of relating the earth to the sky, which he did through orchestrated dramas. Weston marveled how finely 'the heavens and earth became one.'" Adams's and Weston's photographs reflect the serenity and poise that marked both the theme and form of Mabel's most utopian work.[45]

Ernest Knee

Ernest Knee came to Santa Fe for his health in 1933. He was friends with Edward Weston and Ansel Adams, and he had shared an exhibition with Georgia O'Keeffe at the Chicago Art Institute. Knee was one of the few Anglo photographers who focused on the rural life of Hispanic and Indian cultures. He illustrated several books on the Southwest and authored pictorial books on Santa Fe and Mexico. Knee also made one of the finest photographic studies of the Luhan house. Because the house was too long and rambling to be captured in a single frame, most photographers chose a close up of its most dramatic aspect—the three-story wing with its glass-topped solarium—or a long shot that included the courtyard in front of this wing. (Knee did one of the latter that appears in *Winter in Taos.*) In his oversize photo, Knee made the olive tree outside the log cabin a seemingly magically lit central focus. He cropped the house on both its right and left sides, so that it appears open-ended. The dramatic contrast of dark and light shadings that balance the two sides of the house, and the house and the courtyard, are blended in the tonal balance of a flawlessly unclouded sky. The equipoise of nature and culture, which Mabel played off against the process of growth in *Winter in Taos,* is here given an elegant visual statement.[46]

Cady Wells

Although Cady Wells is one of the least well-known of the Anglo painters to come to Taos in the 1930s, Georgia O'Keeffe wrote about him in a 1944 exhibition catalogue: "I think we are the two best painters working in our part of the country. I think we both love that country more than most people love any place." Mabel wrote of Wells in *Taos and Its Artists* that he

Cady Wells, *New Mexico Landscape,* 1934–35.
Watercolor, 33 x 45.7 cm. The University of New Mexico Art Museum, gift of the Estate of Cady Wells.

was "producing some small but extraordinary studies with a completely original technique and expression. With utmost patience and exquisite meticulousness, he evolves abstract forms that stir our archaic and almost forgotten racial memories."[47]

Wells came from a wealthy family in Massachusetts and, like Ansel Adams, had embarked on a career as a professional pianist. He started painting in the 1920s and traveled a great deal before settling, in 1932, in New Mexico, where he studied with Andrew Dasburg and decided to paint full time. Before buying his permanent home in Santa Fe, he made two trips to Japan that influenced his work. During these early years in New Mexico, he was often a welcome guest at the Luhan house. Like Thornton Wilder, who also visited often during the 1930s, Wells was one of Mabel's few homosexual friends who did not view her as castrating and with whom she maintained good relations throughout her life. Like Mabel, Wells was a generous and often anonymous benefactor of others. He assisted the needy

Cady Wells, *Cross and Morada,* 1936.
Watercolor, 21.125 x 30 inches.
Phoenix Art Museum, gift of Mr. Mason B. Wells.

"up and down Española Valley," established a music scholarship in Aspen, and a trust fund for his good friend Martha Graham to travel in Europe. According to Kate Duncan, many composers, writers, and artists received gifts from him when he heard of their financial troubles.[48]

Wells's artistry demonstrated greater stylistic variety and interest in experimentation than most of his New Mexican peers. Some of his work bears interesting comparisons with O'Keeffe's and Dasburg's, but it is typically less static in form and less reassuring in color. Wells's landscapes are marked by a sophisticated combination of a dynamic calligraphic line and a restrained formalism, while his colors are characterized by the dark moodiness of gray-blues, browns, and blacks, hues that he drew upon from his collection of santos. There is often a wonderful tension between solid structure and driving rhythm, as can be seen in his *New Mexico Landscape,* and in his obliquely askew *Penitente Cross* that seems lashed across the landscape in imitation of the rituals practiced by that sect. Mabel's encouragement of Wells's work may well have been due to the fact that he was not only able to see the landscape freshly but also to refresh her own vision of it.

Myron Brinig

Mabel achieved her final fictional avatar when Myron Brinig sent her to a spectacular death in his roman à clef *All of Their Lives* (1941). The novel pays homage to Mabel's imaginative use of the New Mexican landscape and to the charismatic power of her personality to attract visionaries who were stimulated by the ambience she created. A Jewish novelist who grew up in Butte, Montana, in the 1900s, Brinig wrote realistic fiction about miners, labor organizers, farmers, and businessmen who populated communities not far from the pioneer stage. When he first visited Taos in the early 1930s, he was living in New York City and was spoken of by critics as one of America's leading young writers.

Like Witter Bynner, Myron was a homosexual whose relationship with Mabel began in friendship and affection and turned to loathing, as he came to resent her desire to control creative men. Brinig's sense of threat was not unwarranted, as can be assessed from just one letter of Mabel's on the subject of homosexuality that she wrote to Una Jeffers in 1934. Mabel spoke of Brinig's being one of the "unformed" human beings who symbolized the degeneration of the racial impulse to survive.[49]

Of all the writers who had turned to Mabel's character and life in order to capture modernity's New Woman, no one brought wider scope to this task than Brinig, and his portrait was by no means merely condemnatory. He was fascinated, as well as repelled by the New Woman's liberated powers and found her a useful, if sometimes frightening, surrogate through whom to explore his own creativity and sexuality. A protagonist who transgressed the boundaries of her gender in order to create herself was an ideal cover and persona.

Florence Gresham, the novel's heroine, is in some ways a stereotypical female character—she is the "dark" half of a twinned pair of women neither of whom "was whole by herself." But as is true of many of the dark ladies in American fiction, she takes over the novel and so dominates her "fair" twin that she all but erases her from the text. She comes to maturity at a time when the small-town community is suffering from the deterioration of character presumably caused by the passing of the frontier. She is a transitional figure, a liberated woman who has inherited the male pioneering spirit. As the product of Victorian America, she cannot conquer the world in her own right, but she can conquer men and, because of her financial independence and mobility, rule the world through them. Brinig gives Florence the traditional male hero's hunger for achievement and experience.[50]

Like his predecessors, Brinig identifies the New Woman with the unleashing of uncontrollable forces, irrationally blaming her for the upheavals created by a male-dominated economy and technology. Florence is very much a sister of Lawrence's first new world heroine, Sybil Monde, in her role as the link between the "old" energy (used by men to carve a civilization from the wilderness) and the "new" (usurped by machines and implements of warfare). She is "one of those rare beings of the earth, willful, selfish, stubborn, brave, malicious, witty, and so filled with self-importance that only an earthquake, a flood, or a stroke of lightning would defeat her—some great natural upheaval beyond man's control."[51]

Unfortunately for Florence (and the reader), Brinig chooses to make the capstone of his heroine's life experience her falling in love with a neurasthenic artist who has come to Taos for his health, and who bears more than a passing resemblance to D. H. Lawrence. Laurence Cooper is much less interesting than his original, although he submits to his hostess for much the same reasons: she was "an extremely intelligent woman" who recognized his "true value" as one of the world's few, great living writers. Brinig does recognize the shared pursuit that bonded Mabel and Lawrence and made them such exemplary modernists—their quest for a structure of belief that would anchor their wandering spirits.[52]

When Florence can't have what she wants, Brinig brings her to a flamboyant and melodramatic apotheosis. As she rides across a thirteen-thousand-foot mountain ridge in a storm, where her would-be lover has refused to follow her, she is consumed by a bolt of lightning. Brinig tries to give Florence's death a certain tragic nobility, but without much success. He is much more successful describing the uses she (and her prototype) made of their creative powers in life, as when he notes of her early impact on Taos: "In a few years, when automobile roads would be more numerous and improved . . . New Mexico and the entire Southwest would know the pollutions of hundreds of thousands of tourists; but in 1917, they had not yet begun to arrive in great numbers. In a sense Florence was a pioneer . . . [and] once she arrived in a place, no matter where it might be, it took on her imprint and personality, distinguishable from the rest of mankind."[53]

Laura Gilpin, *Taos Landscape, from Ranchos,* 1938.

Laura Gilpin and John Candelario

Unlike Florence Gresham, Mabel Luhan continued to make an imprint on the Taos landscape at least through the late 1940s. In her seventh and last book, *Taos and Its Artists* (1947), she put together the first published retrospective on the three generations of Anglo artists who had worked in Taos since the early twentieth century, many of them at her invitation. Luhan's short descriptive pieces on the artists focused on what she believed were a defining characteristics of their work, and each artist was represented by a reproduction. The book is more celebratory than critical in its presentation,

John Candelario, *Andrew Dasburg*.
Andrew Dasburg Papers, AAA, Smithsonian Institution
(photographed for Mabel Dodge Luhan's *Taos and Its Artists*).

Laura Gilpin, *Looking Westward From the Lawrence Ranch,* n.d.
Gelatin silver print. © 1981, Laura Gilpin Collection, Amon Carter Museum, Fort Worth, Texas.

but it does mark a serious attempt to look across half a century at a wide variety of artists, some of whom did produce work worthy of high praise.[54]

Mabel hired two notable photographers to work with her on the book, mostly to make portraits of the artists represented: Laura Gilpin and John Candelario. Candelario, who had photographed for *Life, Look,* and *Saturday Evening Post,* was given the Tony House to live in rent-free while he worked on the book. He stayed there for about eight or nine months and continued to photograph after he was finished with her work. Gilpin, too, was an established photographer, the author of several works on the

Laura Gilpin, *Residence, Mabel Luhan, Taos,* c. 1935.
© 1981, Laura Gilpin Collection, Amon Carter Museum, Fort Worth, Texas.

Southwest, including two extraordinary photo essays of New Mexico, *The Pueblos* (1941) and *The Rio Grande: River of Destiny* (1939).[55]

Gilpin did several fine photographs around Mabel's house and in the environs of Taos, including a luminous winter portrait of the Big House, and the best photograph of Mabel taken in her old age. A gentle Mabel looks out at us, but one who is a dominant and domineering figure, and very self-assured. She is at once connected to the landscape, symbolized by her holding of the tree branch, and very much in control of it. Mabel did not, however, endear herself to Gilpin. One evening after Laura finished a long day of work at the house, Mabel invited her to supper. Laura was dressed in trousers and a work shirt, which Mabel had said was fine, but then she "upstaged her guest by making a grand entrance into the dining room—dressed in a green evening gown."[56]

Laura Gilpin, *Mabel Dodge Luhan,* 1948.
© 1981, Laura Gilpin Collection, Amon Carter Museum, Fort Worth, Texas.

In spite of Gilpin's dislike of Mabel, the two women shared similar views of the New Mexico landscape. Gilpin's work was, in fact, closer to Mabel's than the male photographers' who visited in the 1920s and 1930s. She was "interested in the land as an environment that shaped human activity, an approach that distinguished her" from artists like Ansel Adams. For Gilpin, the Southwest "was a peopled landscape with a rich history and tradition of its own, an environment that shaped and molded the lives of its inhabitants." Like Mabel Luhan's and Mary Austin's prose landscapes, Gilpin's visualizations "represent a new humanistic strain in landscape photography that regards people and the physical landscape as an integral whole."[57]

Frank Waters

Frank Waters was an elder statesman among New Mexico's writers and an important link to the second-generation counterculture that began to flock to New Mexico in the mid-1960s. He remained, until his death in June 1995, a staunch and articulate environmentalist. Waters is the author of several novels and nonfiction works, among them two books on native American ceremonialism, *Masked Gods* (1950) and *The Book of the Hopi* (1963). His best-known novel is his fictionalized story of a true incident that took place at Taos Pueblo, *The Man Who Killed the Deer* (1942).

A westerner by birth, Waters grew up at the foot of Pike's Peak in Colorado Springs, lived for a while with an Indian trader on the Navajo reservation, and studied engineering at Colorado College. He first came to Taos in the summer of 1937, rented Spud Johnson's house, and met Tony Luhan at an Indian dance. When Tony invited him to a party at the Luhans', he was skeptical about going because of Mabel's reputation, but he found that "she was friendly and warm and it destroyed my bad impressions of her immediately. I liked her very much."[58]

Frank went back to Mora in the fall, where Tony and Mabel visited him and offered him a house. He moved into her house in Placitas, the one that Myron Brinig later bought, and lived there over the winter. After a year in Los Angeles, he returned, invited by the Luhans to take the room above the garage in Tony's house, where he wrote most of *The Man Who Killed the Deer.* It was during the Luhans' visit in Mora that Waters first discovered the mystical bond that would tie them together. Mabel introduced him to Eastern philosophy, which started Waters on a lifelong search to bring together the philosophies and symbologies of East and West that he believed could heal the first world of its selfish materialism and environmental degradation. Waters's initiation came through the *I Ching,* a copy of which Mabel brought with her to Mora. This ancient Chinese text, translated in English as *The Book of Changes,* is a sacred scripture, on the order of the Koran and the Bible. It centers on a collection of sixty-four hexagrams that are based on the yin-yang symbolism of Taoism.

The hexagrams of the *I Ching* were "considered as cosmic archetypes representing the patterns of the Tao in nature and human situations. . . . An elaborate ritual involving fifty yarrow stalks was used to determine the hexagram corresponding to the personal situation of the questioner." The idea was to make the cosmic pattern of that moment visible in the hexagram and to learn from the oracle which course of action was appropriate to it. When Mabel took out her set of sticks, she and Frank obtained the same hexagram. According to Waters, the odds against the same pattern appearing were 4,096 to one. True to the judgment, the reading changed the path of Waters' life: "Certainly it was oracular, for it led to my move to Taos, and to a close friendship with her and Tony that existed until their deaths."[59]

Waters became one of Mabel's most ardent defenders. The only time he became acerbic in my interviews with him in 1977 and 1986 was on the topic of her reputation. He noted that Mabel was not well liked in the Taos community because she was "too damned independent. She was a generous, kind-hearted woman and she just did so much good but never let it be known." Referring to the portrayal of her in my biography, he informed me that Mabel was "a lot different from the guise that you show of her. She was a lot of fun to be around."

It was Tony, however, who became Frank's primary mentor. Waters has spoken of him in his books and in interviews as being like an "older brother" to him, as well an important influence on his writing. Tony was a kind of "ceremonial uncle," the role in the pueblo taken by the maternal uncle who sponsors his nephew "in its beliefs and rituals." (Frank was clear on the point that Tony did not reveal to him any of the secret rituals connected to Pueblo religion). Waters was as ardent a defender of Tony as he was of Mabel. He acknowledged that Tony was not well liked in town because he seemed "this great big lunk of an Indian, married to a rich wife, driving around in a car, never doing any work." But as he pointed out to me, Tony owned land, oversaw the plowing and harvest of his crops, helped his tribe, and influenced John Collier "very, very much."

Waters accompanied Tony and Mabel to Mexico in April 1940 to attend the First Inter-American Conference on Indian Life, sponsored by the

United States and twenty Latin American republics. Tony was appointed by Collier as a delegate to this landmark meeting, which had been inspired by Mexicans who called for an end to the dominance of white values, "the tyranny of American 'dollar diplomacy,'" and for the redistribution of the 80 percent of the land owned by the wealthy in their country. The conference produced eleven hundred pages of papers on economic, education, and legislative issues and resulted in a permanent Inter-American Indian Institute.[60]

In Waters's memory and writings, Tony is a man of stature, whose "accepting and nonjudgmental" attitudes allowed him to negotiate the white and Indian world. But he is also sometimes out of place and misunderstood in the urban worlds of Washington and New York, where he was perceived as an exotic freak who was stereotyped and discriminated against. Frank remembered going to restaurants with Tony where he held the menu upside down because he could not read. He recalled their visits to nightclubs, like the Cotton Club, where the management would not serve them liquor.

Tony's treatment by a reporter in Washington, where he had come to see John Collier about Blue Lake, indicates something of the rude indignities he must have suffered more than once. The reporter greeted Tony in his hotel room in this manner: "Well, well Chief! Come to see the Great White Father at Washington, eh? Set right here now in this big chair. Got any feathers to put on? No? Well this here red blanket will do right smart. . . . Yessiree. A drink all around now and we'll give you a front page spread that'll knock your eyes out."[61]

Waters had another, moving memory from this trip: his introduction to his country's capital by an Indian who made American history come alive for him. Tony decided to take Frank on a tour of Washington, including La Casa Blanca (the White House), and ended up with him at the Corcoran Art Gallery. As they entered the museum, Waters noted that Tony's face took on "a look of fear, horror, and contempt at a huge figure towering on a pedestal before him." It was a statue of the Puritan, standing on his pedestal, Bible under his arm, "strong and indomitable in his implacable self-righteousness." Tony spoke: "'This—this I think is the White Man,' said Tony decisively. Like his voice, his body had changed. He too stood feet apart, well braced, as if rooted to the earth which begot him, clutching one pigtail in his hand. He had forgotten his pride in the noble marble halls outside, thrown off his mask as a loyal 'American.' He was again all Indian—and he had his back up. 'Now this John Collier. She never see no Indians till I show her. Now I think we call her at home and say she see us now. We wait long enough!'"[62]

It was through Tony Luhan that Frank Waters gained entry to Taos Pueblo, which marked the beginning of his study of Pueblo cultures. (He had written about Colorado Indians in his earliest novel and was part Indian himself.) *The Man Who Killed the Deer* is a sensitive and insightful, if somewhat romanticized, portrayal of the Tiwa community. Based upon the story of a Taos man who killed a deer out of season, it tells the tale of the marginalized Indian, Martiano. He represents the no-man's-land that was often created by the government's policy of taking young Indians away from the tribe and sending them to Anglo-dominated boarding schools that tried to erase their heritage and language.

Deprived of a traditional Pueblo education, Martiano won't conform to the tribal clothing prescriptions, marries outside the pueblo, kills a deer out of season, and then assaults the ranger who discovers him. He is censured by the tribal council for his improper killing and for his refusing to ask the deer's consent. An outcast from both Indian and white society, Martiano slowly begins to work his way back to his wife, whom he has abandoned after the incident, and to his tribe. Eventually he repays his debt, relearns his culture, and sees his son adopted into the kiva.

The novel's most arresting moment occurs when Martiano's young son is taken at puberty by his godfather, Palemon, into the kiva to learn the history of his tribe and his place in the universe. Palemon's lesson represents the philosophical core of Waters's belief system, which permeates everything he has written. Waters's portrayal of this rite of passage has little to do with specific aspects of Taos culture; it is, rather, his interpretation of a generic Pueblo worldview translated into an idiom that he clearly hoped would make sense to his Anglo readers: "You must be taught the laws of world creation and world maintenance, the laws of all life whatever form it takes: the living stones, the breathing mountains, the tall walking rain, as well as those of bird and fish, beast and man."[63]

Thirty years after writing the novel, Waters recalled the way in which it took hold of him: "I remember that fall morning in Taos, sitting in front of the fireplace in the big room above the garage in back of Tony Lujan's house just inside the reservation. The story did not have to be contrived; it unfolded like a flower, its own inherent pattern." The novel served tribal interests in more than just its respectful and intelligent presentation of Indian characters and Tiwa culture, for it included episodes dealing with the tribe's efforts to regain their sacred Blue Lake and its surrounding lands. During the hearings on the Blue Lake Bill in the late 1960s, *The Man Who*

Killed the Deer was sent to members of Congress and various supporting committees and organizations as background material.[64]

In 1973, writing in *Psychology Today* to an audience much more attuned to his message, Waters named his belief system "psychical ecology": "For all these living entities, like man, possess not only an outer physical form but an inner spiritual component. . . . In ruthlessly destroying nature, man, who is also part of nature, ruptures his own inner self. We set ourselves apart not only from the earth, but from the dark maternal unconscious, its psychic counterpart. For man's unconscious is equated to and rooted in nature."[65]

In many ways, Waters's work represents a theoretical summation of the quest that attracted many of the transcendental modernists to New Mexico. It can be read as the philosophical equivalent of what Chavez and Stokowski were trying to accomplish in music, Martha Graham in dance, Jean Toomer in poetry, and Georgia O'Keeffe in painting. Waters was well aware that the landscape he inhabited was a geographical and spiritual space that had the potential to bring the ancient and the modern together in a new synthesis: "Perhaps in no other comparable area on earth are condensed so many contradictions, or manifested so clearly the opposite polarities of life. The oldest forms of life discovered in this hemisphere, and the newest agents of mass death. The oldest cities in America and the newest. The Sun Temple of Mesa Verde and the nuclear fission laboratories of the Pajarito Plateau. The Indian drum and the atom smasher." At the end of *Masked Gods,* as Waters gazes out from his home on the slope of the Sangre de Cristos, he thinks about Taos as a "symbol for the Four Corners" and concludes that here is the likely creative space for the "fusion" out of which will arise a "new faith."[66]

Some twenty years after this prediction, Frank Waters watched a long-haired young man and his wife, dressed in a Mexican rebozo with a baby in a sling across her chest, move up the mountain above him where they built themselves a lean-to. They were the vanguard of the next generation seeking a "new faith": the "footloose young people who had forsaken their homes and schools and jobs, unable to bide our excessively rational and materialistic culture, and seeking a simpler way of life." It was the "exodus of Flower Children from Haight Ashbury to Taos," a western counterpart of the earlier exodus from the East.[67]

Like their predecessors, the second counterculture to arrive in New Mexico was a mixed lot of true seekers and lost souls, who would bring a new batch of tourists and land predators in their wake. They were tribal-minded communalists who hoped to live off the land, but they brought few skills or resources with which to make a living from it. Waters greeted them with tolerance, perhaps because he was a kindly guru figure to them. During this time, he watched the rise of Indian militancy, the closing off of the reservation to Anglos, who now paid fees to enter the pueblo, and the continued battles over land rights between Native Americans and Anglo developers.

As might be expected, the Mabel Dodge Luhan house became a matrix for this second wave, first by passing into the hands of a friend of the hippie subculture, Mabel's favorite granddaughter, Bonnie Evans; and next, through its purchase by one of America's notorious cultural outlaws, Dennis Hopper. Hopper turned Los Gallos into the Mud Palace. Here he plotted his counterrevolution against Hollywood and dreamed of making movies that would "blow the mind" of his generation.

PART 2

Dennis Hopper and Friends:
The Mud Palace (1970–1978)

You there who have seen me but did not realize the Exile,
who have seen this body of a man and a human mask walking
plazas in Taos . . . how could you know my feeling that the earth
and all her Nature, that heaven and all its gods were gunning
for cosmic outlaws, you and I being of the driven band?
D. H. Lawrence, "Imprint for the Rio Grand"

I think of Taos as my home. Taos Mountain is one of the sacred seven.
And there's the sacred Blue Lake. If you drilled straight through you'd
come to Tibet. . . . People come into Taos, have a flat tire, and stay
the rest of their lives—or they can't wait to get out.
It drives some people crazy.
Dennis Hopper, *New Yorker*

CHAPTER FOUR

Dennis Hopper and Post–

World War II American Culture

Interregnum

On August 28, 1946, Mabel Luhan wrote to her friend Alice Sprague with an outline of her future vision for her home. It would be a retreat for "'the movers and shakers' of the earth . . . to relax and recover their energy. . . . They are the scientists, artists, statesmen, creators, promoters of values and changers of the world. . . . These are the people I have always sought out. . . . In my way I also achieved, through a gift of great energy, though small means, certain things on earth." Mabel asked Alice if she could accept this as her "life's work" on the understanding that her home must be "very consciously devoted to an ideal" and that she be willing to "eliminate the unfit in favor of the superior element in the race."[1]

It is almost beyond imagining that Mabel would have accepted the next owner of the Luhan house as a member of her Jeffersonian-Darwinian elect of natural aristocrats. Yet she and Dennis Hopper shared a surprising number of attributes, including "a gift of great energy" employed in service to their gargantuan egos and messianic dreams. It would be eight years after Mabel's death, however, before the next generation of Luhan house utopians staked their claim.

After Mabel's death in 1962, her son, John Evans, and his wife, Claire Spencer, moved into the Big House. John was involved in peace work with John Collier and in public relations for Taos Pueblo, which once again was renewing its attempts to repossess Blue Lake. Evans put his mother's house up for sale in 1967, but he could find no interested buyers. He then convinced his daughter Bonnie, who had been Mabel's favorite granddaughter, to leave her home in the San Luis Valley of Colorado and move to Taos with her four children. The Big House needed a new roof, and when Bonnie agreed to put up the ten thousand dollars necessary for it, John gave her the house. In the summer of 1968, before Bonnie moved in, Dennis Hopper first came by to see the house, in the midst of filming *Easy Rider,* much of which was shot on location in and around Taos.[2]

Bonnie took over the Luhan house in the fall of 1968. She got a job working for Taos's hippie paper, the *Fountain of Light,* in advertising and circulation, but she could not take care of the house on the fifty dollars a week she earned and soon put it up for sale. The one time she remembers making good money was during the spring of 1970 when she rented the grounds for what turned out to be one of the oddest clashes between the Old and New West. The producers of *Gunsmoke* decided to film an episode in the courtyard between the Big House and the St. Theresa House. They asked Bonnie to round up extras (at sixty dollars per day per person, plus rental fees for a dog and some chickens) in order to create a scene that was intended to take place in a Mexican village. Bonnie hired her hippie friends, who arrived in rags. When James Arness, a.k.a Matt Dillon, rode into the courtyard and the hippies scattered on cue, the appalled producer groaned that it looked "like a riot in Haight-Ashbury."[3]

It was during the time Arness was filming that Dennis Hopper came by and purchased the Luhan house. He was accompanied by Michelle Phillips, backup singer for the Mamas and the Papas, and her daughter. According to Bonnie, he appeared very tense and "wigged out." Bonnie regretted having to sell the house, especially to Hopper, and the sale infuriated her family. She justified it by saying that when Mabel was near death she told Bonnie that Taos had been spoiled and she wished to leave it.

The sale also angered Dorothy Brett, who had spent more time living on the premises than any other of the artists or writers of Mabel's generation and felt a proprietary interest in it. The longest-lived holdover from the Luhan years, Brett was perceived in the 1960s as "the first hippie—possibly. The last of the Great Bohemians—probably." According to local reporter Tricia Hurst, hippies "adored her" because she was "their kind of people." Brett was a model of countercultural fashion in her "uniform of Indian trousers and moccasins, bright hued smock held together by safety pins, . . . head band and bright red lipstick."[4]

By the time Dennis Hopper moved to Taos, "the Great Hippie" inva-

Actor Owen Orr and unidentified friend entering front gates of the Luhan house, n. d. Photo courtesy of Walter Chappell.

sion was well underway, and it had taken on a tone far different from the light-hearted one of Hurst's piece on Dorothy Brett. Hopper was ambitious to make films subversive of the imperialist empire of the United States. But he ended up cast in the lead role of a dangerous scenario during which he clashed with local Taoseños who were enraged at the hippies, with supporting roles played by Chicano militants, Hollywood stunt men, and undercover government agents. Before encountering this dramatic moment in northern New Mexico's second confrontation with the counterculture, we must turn to the sociohistorical context that shaped Dennis Hopper, who more than anyone in the film industry of his time came to epitomize the youth rebellion of the 1960s.

Rebels with a Cause

A second generation of escapees from mainstream American culture began to arrive in New Mexico in the 1950s, their numbers increasing exponentially in the late 1960s. They came for many of the same reasons that motivated Mabel Luhan's generation who were, unbeknownst to most of them, their spiritual ancestors. The Greenwich Village rebels were mainly the privileged sons and daughters of the Victorian middle classes, who took up arms against the materialist ethos and aesthetic blandness of their parents' generation in the hopes of revitalizing themselves and the nation's political and cultural life. The countercultural exiles who came to New Mexico in the 1950s and 1960s were also mainly children of the middle classes. Their parents had grown up during the depression, lived through World War II—the "good war"—and then retreated to all-white suburbs in the postwar boom, where they wrapped themselves in a security blanket of economic prosperity.

The 1950s bears comparison with the Victorian Age as a time of political and social conformity, clearly delineated gender boundaries, and an ethos that made "keeping up with the Joneses" the ideal of suburban life. The emphasis on the nuclear family as the stabilizer of the nation grew out of an anxiety far more profound, however, than the economic and political upheavals that shook post–Civil War and post–World War I America. The Atomic Age created the first generation of children to grow up in the United States for whom global annihilation became a routine possibility. This was seen in such ludicrous practices as schoolchildren hiding under their desks to protect themselves from atomic blasts, and in the building of well-stocked bomb shelters in suburban backyards to protect the middle-class nuclear family from radiation fallout.

The Beats were the first post–World War II cultural radicals to react to this "brave new world" by rejecting everything that the middle classes held dear. With their sexual, drug, and aesthetic transgressions, they flung a gauntlet at the bloated Moloch of America's Cold War consumer culture. Allen Ginsberg's 1955 reading of "Howl" in San Francisco was, in many respects, the opening call to this generation of alienated youth who, much more fiercely than their forebears, embraced marginalized groups and antibourgeois practices:

I saw the best minds of my generation destroyed by madness,
starving hysterical naked,
dragging themselves through the negro streets at dawn looking for
an angry fix,
angelheaded hipsters burning for the ancient heavenly connection
to the starry dynamo in the machinery of night, . . . [5]

Dennis Hopper entered adulthood on the edge of the Beat scene, as a poet, painter, photographer, and art collector. His first movie role was as the gang member Goon in *Rebel Without a Cause* (1959), a film that was an important harbinger of the much-broader youth revolt that would explode in the 1960s. Hopper forged a link between the two rebel generations that marked the shift of cultural power from literature to film (and TV), and the shift of the seat of counterculture from New York to California. It was fitting for the role Dennis would one day play that he was a child of the American heartland, with a pedigree that could have been invented by the public relations department of a movie studio. According to his brother, David, the Hopper family tree goes back to Daniel Boone and the Cherokee Indians. Their great-grandfather homesteaded in Dodge City, Kansas, where Dennis and David spent their childhood, playing alongside the descendants of Wyatt Earp.[6]

By the time Dennis was born, in 1936, the family fortunes had declined. His grandparents had twelve acres of land, but his grandfather spent much of his time farming wheat sixty miles away. Dennis remembers his grandparents as his "best friends" when he was growing up, although he spent much of his time by himself. His father, Jay, a traveling postal worker on the railway, was often absent. Jay Hopper spent World War II in China, purportedly doing undercover intelligence work, while his wife, Marjorie, managed a swimming pool in Dodge City. In 1949, when Dennis was thirteen, the family moved to San Diego. As Dennis's brother, David, explains it: "We ended up in California and that was it; there was no more land and no more frontier or whatever. . . . [Dennis] was a fighter, always a little maladjusted and crazy, you know, a fifties cat. You didn't walk down the street if you didn't know how to fight, and usually it took groups of you."

Hopper's antisocial and antiauthoritarian attitudes and behavior can in part be traced to the lie he was told at age five about his father, whose government cover was so secret that his wife was asked to tell her family that he had died. Dennis believed his father was dead—until he returned home from the war. This lie seems, not surprisingly, to have traumatized Hopper. It generated in him a lifelong fascination with the "art" of deception, and it fed a sense of alienation and betrayal that were compounded by the emotional and physical absence of both his parents, and by his mother's religious fundamentalism. Hopper's sometimes violent and abusive behavior toward women, which alternated with a form of mother-worship, can be traced to these factors as well. As a woman friend astutely noted about his treatment of women, the "strong crosscurrents in his character" can be related to his "desperate primary need to be loved. . . . He doesn't really know how to ask for love, because that would involve accepting a woman as an equal. Too dangerous. I think that to Dennis a woman is either a whore or a madonna. Or both. Anyway, he wants you to be a fantasy creature and he leaves you if you try to become real."[7]

Hopper's strained relations with his parents increased during adolescence because of their expectations that he choose a respectable career. He explained his leaving home at age fourteen, soon after his family's move to California, by saying that they told him, "You can become an engineer, a lawyer, or a doctor. If you become an artist or an actor, you'll end up a bum. . . . Which is what happened." Hopper says that his salvation as a child was the movies, which provided him with his first sense of reality. His happiest childhood memories are of accompanying his grandmother to town every week, where she sold farm eggs and used some of the money to take Dennis to the movies: "Ever since the first movie, I thought movies were where it was at. They were total involvement. That's why I find movies dangerous. You're only as good as the movies you see. Or[what] you read. But movies have more impact. Film is writing, painting, a play, music, audience—everything. And also working with light—a mystical area."[8]

Hopper's belief that movies incorporated all of the other arts in a spectacle that was at once emotional, aesthetic, and religious would lead him to argue for film as the most revolutionary medium of his generation. In preparation for what he saw as his fate as the film prophet of his time, he apprenticed himself to each one of the arts that make up film—acting on stage and in television and movies, writing poetry, becoming a painter, photographer, and assemblagist, and when given his first directorial debut, incorporating music into film as a major element of thematic and character development.

Hopper began his acting apprenticeship in 1953 at the La Jolla Playhouse and the Old Globe Theater in San Diego, where he performed Shakespeare. In 1954, he went to Hollywood looking for work in the movies. It was here he met James Dean, who was five years older than he. Dean became his first and most important mentor, affirming for Dennis the Strasberg style of method acting he would use throughout his career—off- as well as on-screen. Dean was a hero to Dennis, the man who had mastered the paradox of art in his ability to make illusion real, to act as though he were not acting, and to create an intensity of character that transcended whatever role he was playing. Dean and Hopper shared a similar family history, as midwestern farm boys desperate to escape the boredom and poverty of rural life and achieve fame. Like F. Scott Fitzgerald's Gatsby, they also shared a passion to reinvent themselves and a naive belief that they could maintain their integrity while engaging in a business whose bottom line was profits.[9]

Hopper's emulation of Dean was not without reason. Dean was a talented actor who spoke to his generation in a way that few others did (and whose cult following his death has all but equaled that of Elvis Presley). He captured the discontent of white middle-class youth who saw the adult world as smothering in its need for material security and social conformity. An ideal combination of toughness and vulnerability, he conveyed the image of a young man sure enough of himself not to buy into the bourgeois dream of economic success, yet sensitive enough to reveal his emotional insecurity about where to locate himself in the world. Hopper and Dean weren't rebels without a cause. What they wanted to bring to their work in Hollywood films "was fiercely hated and vigorously resisted by most of Hollywood's old-line directors, because it threatened to displace the locus of control of the film from the director to some mysterious process within the actor that the director couldn't command."[10]

Dean had studied the Method at the Actor's Studio in New York, a demanding technique that emphasized an actor's creating his character through self-exploration. He taught Hopper not to act but to be natural and "leave yourself open to the moment-to-moment reality." When Dean died in an automobile crash just before the 1959 release of *Rebel,* Dennis was devastated. It was "the most personal tragedy in my life. . . . I had dreams tied up in him and suddenly . . . [they were] shattered." Hopper literally and figuratively tried to take on Dean's mantle, wearing his ring, carrying the weight of his soulful, angry, rebellious consciousness, in fact, doing his best to self-destruct. Hopper went on the set of his next film, a traditional Hollywood western *(From Hell to Texas)* directed by Henry Hathaway, and forced the director into eighty-five takes for one scene because he refused to follow Hathaway's directing. Hathaway epitomized the old Hollywood establishment and Hopper "the new challenge to directorial authority." Hathaway swore that Hopper would never work again in Hollywood, and his film career was virtually over for the next decade.[11]

From the moment he learned of Dean's death, Hopper began to believe that he would not live to maturity, that he too would die a violent death because the kind of art he espoused was one that demanded his own martyred self-sacrifice. The seeds of Dennis's messianism may have been planted by his mother's fundamentalism, but they were nurtured into bloom when he inherited Dean's mantle as "the nation's leading delinquent." Hopper explained to a *Life* interviewer that Dean had once "pulled a switchblade and threatened to murder his director. I imitated his style in art and in life."[12]

If these behaviors don't sound very Christlike, it is because Hopper's messiah was the Jesus of *The Gospel According to Thomas,* a heretical Gnostic text whose philosophy Hopper often summed up in the aphorism "don't lie and don't do what you hate." His Jesus had satanic and hedonistic elements, which helps to explain Hopper's belief that the act of creation is intimately tied to the act of destruction, as well as his fascination with such demonic savior types as Charles Manson. In the mid-1960s, Dennis began to carry around a portrait of Jesus that looked like himself, convinced that he, too, "was going to die in his 33rd year." After his debacle with Hathaway, Hopper turned to other venues for achievement. He went to New York and studied with Lee Strasberg and did some serious off-Broadway theatre and television work. He also spent much time in the Museum of Modern Art until he "knew every painting." At this time, he befriended Andy Warhol, Jasper Johns, Roy Lichtenstein, and other members of the New York avant-garde, whose works he soon began to collect.[13]

In 1961, Hopper returned to Hollywood where he married Brooke Hayward. She was "a princess of the Hollywood establishment," the daughter of Leland Hayward and Margaret Sullivan. But theirs was to be no fairy-tale romance. Dennis was physically abusive to her, as he would be to many other women. And he was verbally abusive to the Hollywood establishment, lashing out at parties about how he would run things when he was in charge. He justified his increasing use of drugs and alcohol by saying that "the great artists had done it, that it must lead to something. It does help you with your senses, and makes your senses like raw nerves. I was working with my nerves." Because of his heavy drinking, his increasing use of LSD, and his violent rages, during one of which he broke his wife's nose, Brooke left him in 1967.[14]

Hopper laid the blame for his turn to violence on his experiences marching with Martin Luther King from Selma to Montgomery in 1963, when he was spit on by "redneck southerners" who called him "a long-haired, nigger-loving communist" (an incident he drew on five years later for one of the most potent scenes in *Easy Rider*). But Hopper was creative, as well as destructive, during these years, turning his hand to poetry and painting, and photographing the leading artists of his times. With the help of Brooke's money, he established one of the finest collections on the West Coast of post–World War II avant-garde art. Their Topanga Canyon home became known as "the Prado of Pop," with paintings that included Andy Warhol's Campbell's Soup Can, and works by Jasper Johns, Roy Lichtenstein, Ed Kienholz, Ad Reinhardt, Frank Stella, Ed Ruscha, Claes Oldenberg, George Herms, and Robert Rauschenberg, along with an eclectic array of the objects that often formed the basis of their art—marquees, billboards, barbershop chairs, and streetlamps.[15]

Just as Mabel Luhan had set out to make herself mistress of her era by supporting and surrounding herself with some of the most interesting artistic innovators of the early modernist era, Hopper was drawn into the radical fringe of the late modernist and emerging postmodernist ferment of the 1950s and 1960s. In a recent assessment of his place in the avant-garde, Walter Hopps said that Hopper's "eye for art was among the best of his time," and that the assemblages and large photo blowups he made in the 1960s were "extraordinary and ahead of their time." Dennis's wide-ranging art collection and his artistic practices fed his growing ambition to make a statement in film that would unveil the illusions of the American Dream. In order to appreciate how Hopper earned his position as a cultural touchstone of his times, one must understand the place of the avant-garde artist in post–World War II America.[16]

The 1950s and 1960s Art Scene

The primary influences on Hopper's aesthetic consciousness were the Abstract Expressionists, although Hopper claims that he was one even "before I knew there was such a thing." Between 1955 and 1961 he did numerous Abstract Expressionist and action paintings, putting the same intensity into his visual work that he had into his acting. Abstract Expressionist philosophy and technique appealed to the qualities and concerns that Dennis found attractive in method acting. The artist forged "his or her own identity in the act of creation," which usually entailed "anguish and struggle." Although that anguish and struggle grew partly out of the subjective necessities of individual artists, they were also related to these artists' response to the post–World War II atomic age.[17]

Luhan's coterie of artists turned to Native American culture at least partly in reaction to the destructiveness unleashed by Anglo civilization in World War I. The Abstract Expressionists turned to Native American myth and to Surrealist practices out of "a profound desire to transcend the particulars of history and search out universal values . . . [that] could make a positive contribution to the America of the future." That contribution was premised on the artist's belief that by reaching into his own collective unconscious he could retrieve ancient symbols that would make his art "a shamanic process for healing."[18]

One can find in Hopper's direction of both *Easy Rider* and *The Last Movie* an Abstract Expressionist aesthetic that suggests belief in the filmmaker's shamanic role, which permitted "no barrier between inspiration and execution, no intellectual editing, no cleaning up to conform to some pre-conceived idea." Hopper was also influenced by the Abstract Expressionists' cultural nationalism, which reads like the second wave of Stieglitz's credo: "the recognition of a body of art as the product of American artists, living in America, and producing an art of equivalent or superior value to European art." During his heyday as a director, Hopper frequently spoke about his desire to make an American art film that was as good as, if not better than, what his counterparts—Bergman, Fellini, and Antonioni—were accomplishing in Europe.[19]

The Abstract Expressionists touted an American art, but like their early modernist predecessors, they were essentially indifferent to and contemptuous of mass culture. Not so the next two generations, beginning with Robert Rauschenberg and Andy Warhol, who were influenced by what Irving Sandler calls "the Duchamp-Cage aesthetic." They engaged vitally with mass culture, whether using it to celebrate or attack American values. In choosing as their subjects ordinary objects like the American flag, conceptual artists like Jasper Johns provoked such questions as "whether they are real or art," and "does re-creation result in transformation?" These were questions that Hopper asked in his own assemblages and that were central to his career as a filmmaker.[20]

Hopper credited Duchamp with being the artist who most influenced his generation: "He said the artist of the future will not be a painter but a man who points his finger and says, 'That's art,' and it'll be art." Dada's satiric rejection of Anglo-European elite culture seems to have had particular resonance in California. Hopper had been part of the Beat scene in Venice since the early 1950s, making friends with the poets Lawrence Ferlinghetti and Kenneth Rexroth, and with other artists. Terry Southern remembers Dennis from this time at an early "happening" in Allen Ginsberg's and Peter Orlovsky's apartment. Orlovsky was playing timpani and chanting, as Ginsberg dipped a copy of the *New York Times Book Review* into honey and put word-images across the wall. While a movie projector was showing Luis Buñuel's *L'Age d'Or* in reverse, a naked woman dropped rose petals and dog hairs into a whirling fan, and Hopper glided around "in a Marcel Marceau manner, grimacing oddly, and at the same time, attempting to take photographs."[21]

Hopper's sensibilities were shaped most strongly by the West Coast avant-garde, whose responses to mainstream American culture were blatantly confrontational, iconoclastic, and nihilistic. His closest circle included artists who "focused on the ultimate destruction of the world." Most of them were associated with Dada and Surrealism, which were introduced to California by Man Ray and Knud Merrild. Knud Merrild, who came to Los Angeles in 1923, provides a link with the Luhan generation, having lived with D. H. Lawrence at his ranch the first winter Lawrence spent in Taos. Merrild wrote that he believed in art as a religious experience, "a state of being at one with the dark gods within us." Hopper would speak in similar, if more hip, terms when he too claimed Lawrence as his progenitor.[22]

Merrild's view of art "was characteristic of a peculiarly West Coast strain of esthetic mysticism" that was "reinterpreted" in the 1950s and 1960s "by the beatnik/Zen/hip spirit." Its advocates fared worse in the Cold War atmosphere of California than was true, in general, for artists back East. Permeated by a "suspicion that modern art was created by degenerate, un-American subversives," an L.A. ordinance spoke of "modern artists as tools of the Kremlin," while in San Francisco much avant-garde activity went underground.[23]

Peter Boswell has concluded that "for most of the fifties, artists were shut out of the American Dream . . . there was little or no market for much of the work that was being produced, particularly on the West Coast. Given this lack of commercial prospects, many artists used junk objects as metaphoric surrogates for their own status" as well as for "a rejection of the prevailing value system of fifties America." It is no accident that Hopper chose to photograph Ed Kienholz as he left a scrapyard looking for "art" material. Kienholz was "above all, the moralist who sees disorder and decadence in contemporary society." Among many other social issues confronted in his life-size satirical sculptures, Kienholz commented on the horrors of illegal abortion *(The Illegal Operation)* and on the racist treatment of blacks (*Five Car Stud,* "a brutal multi-figure tableau of four white men castrating a black victim").[24]

Bruce Connor, the most nihilistic of these artists, was also a favorite of Hopper's. Connor fled the United States in 1962 fearing that the bomb was going to drop and he would be annihilated. In his collages, movies, and assemblages of the 1950s and 1960s he "entangles themes of sex, death, and violence" to suggest "their conjunction in American culture," themes that were to become the holy and unholy trinity forming the basis of much of Hopper's film work from the 1960s through the 1990s. In both Connor's and Hopper's work, it is not always easy to tell how much the artist is criticizing and how much he is revelling in the political, sexual, and moral corruption and decadence his work adumbrates. Both Connor and Hopper present "a vision of suffering that transcends social analysis and strikes at the depths of psychic discomfort."[25]

Other artists in the Hopper circle of influence turned completely away from America's techno-horrors to find alternative belief systems in Buddhism and occult mysticism. Wallace Berman infused his "art with a sense of spirituality" through the incorporation of "religious and occult symbolism." His most famous piece was taken up as a countercultural mantra: "Art is Love is God." Along with Berman and George Herms, Hopper was part of "an expanding circle of poet-painter-collagists. . . . Mystic travellers and drug trippers, they responded to the creative act in a manner consciously opposed to the professional world of studio productions, specialized art issues, and regular gallery exhibitions." They were involved in the development of an alternative art culture that was just beginning to achieve recognition in the early 1960s.[26]

Art historian Barbara Rose has argued that the 1960s were "a period of investigation and redefinition of basic concepts as explosive and experimental as the years when Cubism was formulated." The cultural visionaries of both generations thought in terms of art forms that incorporated theatre, dance, music, painting, and poetry in ritualistic forms. These would serve some of the same purposes as tribal religions in terms of establishing the significance of the individual and of integrating the individual into a broader human community. In the 1960s, these gestures, which more openly flouted mainstream social and sexual mores, included events such as the "levitation" of the Pentagon by antiwar activists, Owen Orr's passing out ten thousand bags of fresh air in downtown L.A. during the opening of his first one-man show in 1968, and Living Theatre's onstage nudity and sexual antics.[27]

By the early 1960s, Los Angeles had become the "second art city" in the United States, as local artists increasingly gained international recognition and critics talked about the "L.A. Look." The development of L.A.'s reputation, as well as of Hopper's art and art collection, was closely related to

Untitled [Ed Kienholz], 1962.
Photo courtesy of Dennis Hopper.

Untitled [Hopper house], 1963.
(Sculpture on right by Ed Kienholz; Mona Lisa, by Andy Warhol; assemblage, by Jasper Johns.)
Photo courtesy of Dennis Hopper.

Andy Warhol cover of *Art Forum,* December 1964.
Photo courtesy of Dennis Hopper.

the creation of the Ferus Gallery by Walter Hopps in 1962, the "seminal vanguard gallery" in Los Angeles. Hopper was "a central figure in the Los Angeles art scene," where his sculpture and mixed media assemblages were widely exhibited. One of his most interesting pieces, done in 1966 and shown at the Pasadena Art museum, would have a place of honor in Mabel Luhan's dining room. Titled the *Bomb Drop,* it was a replica of a World War II control box. "'Bomb Drop' is written across a large sheet-metal phallus with stainless steel balls that switch from positions of 'safe' to 'arm' as colored lights flash from inside the base."[28]

Hopper began photographing in the early 1960s, under the influence of Cartier-Bresson. Like method acting and Abstract Expressionist technique,

Torn Poster Collage cover of *Art Forum,* September 1965.
Photo courtesy of Dennis Hopper.

Cartier-Bresson's theory of "the Decisive Moment" favored untutored spontaneity in service to authenticity. Hopper took his photos in full-frame natural light with Tri-X film and refused to crop them because he wanted to "develop a sense of full-field composition." The unfinished look and raw-edged power of the best of his photographs is most evident in those he took during the Civil Rights march from Selma, Alabama, and in some of his photographs of the Hell's Angels and L.A. love-ins. But Hopper was best known for his *Vogue* and *Harper's Bazaar* "personalities" photos of artists and actors. His status as an avant-garde photographer and a photographer of the avant-garde is attested to by his covers for *Art Forum,* at the time the leading avant-garde art journal on the West Coast.[29]

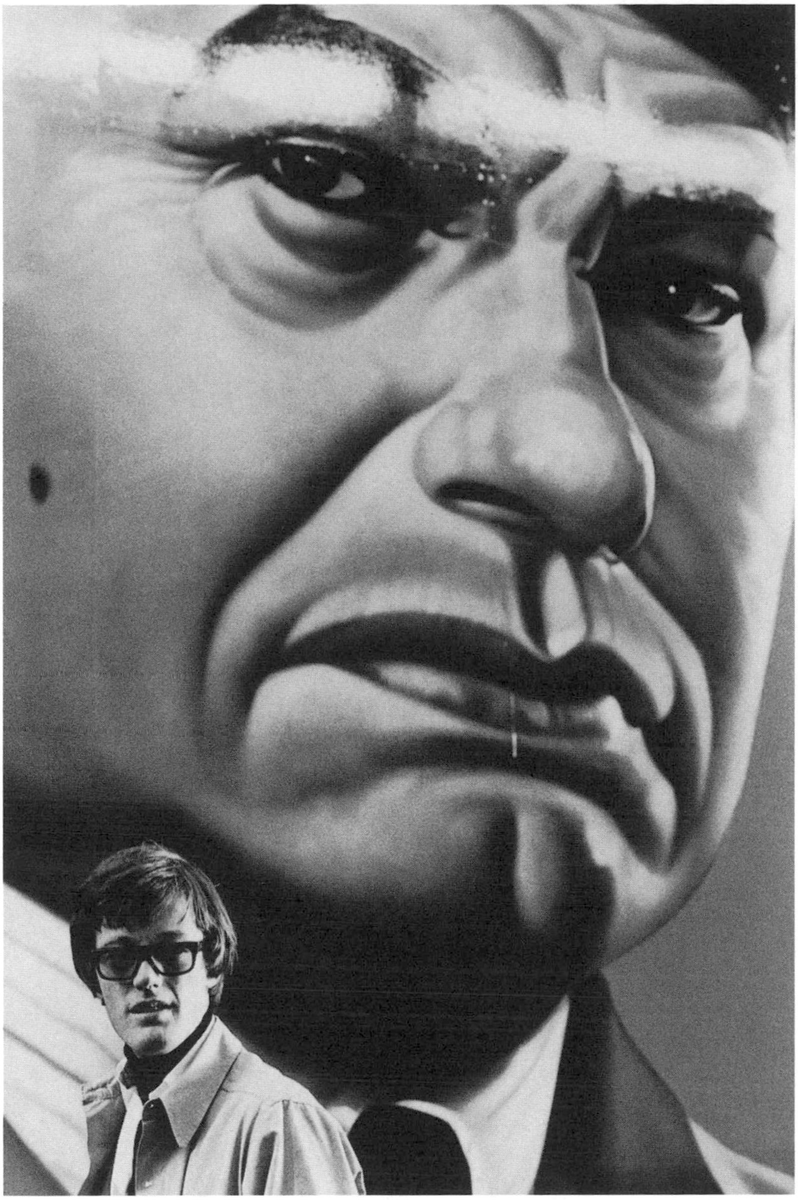

Untitled [Peter Fonda in front of poster of Edward G. Robinson], 1965.
Photo courtesy of Dennis Hopper.

Andy Warhol, *Dennis Hopper,* 1971.
Silkscreen ink on synthetic polymer paint on canvas, 40½ x 40½ inches.
Photo courtesy of Nigel Greenwood Gallery, London.

In the mid-1960s, Hopper became involved with the third generation of the postwar avant-garde, the Pop artists who provided what seemed to art critics and the public alike the most outrageous challenge to traditional aesthetic norms and to the increasingly tenuous line that separated art from life. Pop artists were responding to the power of commercialization and, in particular, to the advertising industry's ability to shape the values and behavior of the American public. Pop artists sought to cater to a taste that was more than coincidentally related to a period "when the present was exalted over the past by a youth-oriented, tradition-defying, anti-authoritarian culture."[30]

Pop artists were the first avant-garde to move outside elite circles. Artists like Andy Warhol became big news, having a routine beat in the popular press and achieving a celebrity status more like that of movie stars. It was Warhol, the king of Pop, who coined the phrase "everyone will be world-famous for fifteen minutes." He did more than any other artist of the 1960s to erase the lines between popular and high culture, and more disconcertingly, between the idea of the avant-garde as the cutting edge of dissent and the co-optation of the avant-garde by commercialism. Warhol chose "the grittiest, tackiest, and most commonplace facts of visual pollution in America that would make the aesthetes and mythmakers of the fifties cringe in their ivory towers"—Popeye, Nancy, Dick Tracy, Campbell's soup cans. At the same time, he achieved just the kind of glamour revered by the haute bourgeois culture his lifestyle and art presumably mocked.[31]

After Hopper achieved fame with *Easy Rider,* Warhol created a silkscreen that enshrined him in his pantheon of media-inspired "post-Christian saints," which included the Beatles, Marilyn Monroe, and Mao T'se Tung. One can read Hopper's love-hate relationship with the movies and with Hollywood in a similarly paradoxical fashion to Andy Warhol's ambiguous embrace and critique of American capitalism. But where Warhol was "cool" in his response to the power of the "entrepreneurial world-view," Hopper was frantic. He wanted his movies to subvert America's consumer culture, at the same time that he wanted the kind of praise and acclaim that could only come to one who did its bidding. These conflicting—and unresolved—desires caused his film statements to be both morally and aesthetically confusing, and damaging to his own revolutionary intentions.[32]

Hopper's landmark film, *Easy Rider,* demonstrates this essential confusion. Here he responded to the darker side of the counterculture, which had always attracted him and which came more to the fore in the later part of the 1960s, along with the increasing escalation of American violence at home and abroad. These factors were felt powerfully by the youth who turned *Easy Rider* into a cult film. They also fed the upheavals that overtook Hopper when he moved to Taos on the coattails of his first real movie success.

Easy Rider

"'Easy Rider' is a southern term for a whore's old man; not a pimp, but the dude who lives with a chick. Because he's got the easy ride. Well, that's what's happened to America, man. Liberty's become a whore, and we're all taking an easy ride."[33]

Easy Rider (1969) was a seminal event in American popular culture: a

Outtake from *Easy Rider,* 1969.
Photo courtesy of the Museum of Modern Art,
Film Stills Archive, New York.
(Wyatt and Billy riding through northern New Mexico.)

film that spoke to and for a generation of rebellious youth and that played an important role in changing the "Hollywood system" it set out to challenge. When Dennis Hopper said he believed "that the revolution will really be fought with the camera, with films, and at a certain point minds [will] be won in the theatre," there was something more than drug-enhanced megalomania in his claim. Drugs were, however, intimately connected with Hopper's faith in the transformative possibilities of a medium that had proved itself a singularly powerful manipulator of Americans. In fact, his comeback in film began when he and Peter Fonda made the 1967 movie *The Trip,* in which they went out into the desert to shoot acid-trip sequences by themselves. About a year later, Fonda got the idea for *Easy Rider* one evening when he was stoned on marijuana.[34]

It is as difficult today to appreciate the liberationist view of psychedelic drugs held by 1960s countercultural advocates as it is to view *Easy Rider*

Outtake from *Easy Rider,* 1969.
Photo courtesy of the Museum of Modern Art,
Film Stills Archive, New York.
(Wyatt and Billy riding through Taos Pueblo.)

and not find embarrassing its stilted, clichéd language and macho on-the-road posturing. In *Storming Heaven: LSD and the American Dream,* Jay Stevens helps us comprehend the revolutionary and spiritual potential that many advocates for the drug subculture saw in dropping acid and smoking pot. What New Thought and Burkean "cosmic consciousness" were to Mabel Luhan's generation, LSD was to the hippies: "a mind detergent capable of washing away years of social programming, a re-imprinting device, a consciousness-expander, a tool that would push us up the evolutionary ladder. Some even claimed LSD was a gift from God, given to mankind in order to save the planet from a nuclear finale."[35]

Stevens reminds us that a clear line did not initially exist between the hippies and their drug culture, and the New Left radicals who were actively involved in antiwar and Civil Rights protests. Many hippies believed that drugs were a means of transforming the self in order to change the world.

Outtake from *Easy Rider,* 1969.
Photo courtesy of the Museum of Modern Art,
Photo Stills Archive, New York.
(Wyatt and Billy at the hippie commune.)

Stevens does not minimize the dangers of LSD and other more powerful psychedelic drugs. But he also makes a convincing case that mainstream America's hysteria toward the drug culture had less to do with the actual damage caused by drugs than it did with the fear that they were politically subversive and were creating nonconformists who would erode America's most basic institutions.[36]

For Peter Fonda and Dennis Hopper the psychedelic experience was both a route to power and a vehicle through which they would storm Hollywood, if not heaven, taking over the "means of production" in order to create their revolution of consciousness. In doing so, they hoped to merge personal, aesthetic, and political ideas in order to work out their own private issues of familial rejection while simultaneously revitalizing American cinema—and potentially American society. Because Hopper saw a close connection between drug use, psychotherapy, and method acting, he encouraged Fonda to explore in *Easy Rider* his feelings about his mother's suicide, which he did in the notorious LSD sequence that takes place in a New Orleans cemetery.[37]

Hopper invested all of himself in the making of the film and yet risked his chances to complete it because of his insistence that he have total control. He continuously cursed and fought with the camera crew, most of whom quit. At one point, after an argument with him, Fonda felt it necessary to hire a bodyguard and to carry a gun. Although Hopper's behavior was irresponsible and immature, one can attribute some of the fierce possessiveness that generated it to his faith in the tremendous potential of his medium: "Film is . . . the Sistine Chapel of the twentieth century, it's the best way to reach people. The artist, not the industry, must take responsibility for the entire work." It was now his generation's turn to "have its say" and "change the balance of power in the good Old American Way." Hopper recognized that mass culture had turned America into a "set" ripe for exploration—and exploitation: "The whole damn country's one big real place to utilize and film, and God's a great gaffer."[38]

In making *Easy Rider,* Fonda and Hopper broke with a number of conventions and helped establish a new wave of cinema productions that were antiestablishment in terms of theme, methods, and cost of production. Made for less than $500,000, *Easy Rider* grossed somewhere between $50 million and $60 million dollars, opening the way for low-budget productions aimed at the youth market. Although Terry Southern wrote the script, with Fonda and Hopper collaborating, much of the movie's action and dialogue were improvised. Fonda and Hopper were not the first to eschew the Hollywood soundstage for the real world, in order to break down the barriers between art and life by shooting on location. But they were among the first to make the crossover between the underground and mainstream film in Hollywood by borrowing techniques—such as flashback and flashforward, quick-cutting, and ironic juxtapositions of visuals and sound—from the European avant-garde for a popular vehicle. They used legitimate actors, but they also hired nonactors on locale who sometimes created their own dialogue. They smoked pot on screen, and they elevated rock music as a major element in the development of character and theme.[39]

Easy Rider expresses the particular moment in American history when it was made: when the flower children who had dropped out and the political activists of various self-styled revolutionary vanguards had little left to say to one another. The summer of love celebrated in Haight-Ashbury in 1967 had yielded to scenes of violence. There were deaths at the Rolling Stones' Altamont concert and the more frightening murders committed by the Manson Family commune, whose leader dreamed of an apocalyptic takeover of America by fomenting a racial civil war.

On the heels of the 1968 assassinations of Martin Luther King and Robert Kennedy, the integrationist Civil Rights groups of the early and mid-1960s, like SCLC (the Southern Christian Leadership Conference) and SNCC (the Student Non-Violent Coordinating Committee) gave way to the segregationist nationalism of the Black Muslims and the Black Panthers. Their militancy encouraged the formation of analogous groups within the Hispanic population, like New Mexico's Alianza Federal de los Pueblo Libres (with whom Hopper would ally himself when he moved to Taos). The idealist social democrats who had founded SDS (Students for a Democratic Society) and drafted the Port Huron Statement, which was intended to revitalize participatory democracy, had splintered into warring factions that included the paramilitary Weathermen.

After years of Americans' protesting an escalating, so-called undeclared war in Vietnam, Vietnamese men, women, and children were still losing their lives and livelihood in massive numbers (an estimated one million by the end of the war). The 1968 Democratic convention revealed that the leaders of America's liberal party were willing to allow police brutality to be used against middle-class youth in order to maintain the status quo. While young American men and women in combat in Vietnam gave their lives to a war that was purportedly keeping the world "safe for democracy," their antiwar counterparts in the United States were harassed and sometimes beaten for using their First Amendment rights of free speech and assembly. It was against this backdrop of political chaos and social fragmentation that *Easy Rider* was made, giving the film a political force that contemporary viewers are rarely able to appreciate.[40]

At the time of its release, many critics praised the film's "integrity and portrayal of American hypocrisy and discrimination," while noting its suggestive parallels to current political events: "Implicit in the politics of 'Easy Rider' are the Chicago Convention, the civil rights struggles, the Berkeley People's Park conflict, the California grape boycott, Viet-Nam. . . . The heroes are the movie's outlaws and its villains 'law-and-order' Americans." It is understandable that the youth of America identified with Hopper and

Fonda. As Jeff Greenfield points out, "By the summer of 1969 the premise that America had declared war on the young seemed in some circles to be almost self-evident."[41]

Easy Rider has not been treated kindly by later film scholars. The film's politics are one problematic element. In spite of its blistering attack against mainstream America's intolerance of those who are "different," and the martyrlike death of its two roadie heroes who just "want to be free," the film's intentions often seem confused and contradictory. It is a western of sorts, part of a long-lived tradition of Hollywood films in which the lone hero stakes out his claim to individuality and manhood against a conformist society. But it also mocks that tradition by having its heroes go east, rather than west, in order to get to Florida, where they hope to retire in luxury.

Captain America, a.k.a Wyatt (Earp), played by Fonda, and Billy (the Kid) played by Hopper, are named after American heroes who are part of the popular pantheon of Anglo-American culture. But they assumed their identities (and costumes) as part of a carnival act, and they are drug dealers who feel they owe absolutely nothing to anyone. If they are subversive of established norms of dress and behavior—wearing long hair, refusing to work, taking dope, having sex when and where they feel like it—their actions and dialogue hardly suggest a revolution of any meaningful sort in terms of the social and political movements of the 1960s mentioned in reviews of the film.[42]

In the southern town where the heroes' deaths are foreshadowed, they stop to eat in a restaurant where they are tormented by the local "rednecks," who cast doubt on both their manhood and humanity. There is little doubt that these plain folk are the incarnation of mindless bigotry and brute violence. But the other options offered by the film are not much more desirable. The farmer who feeds Wyatt and Billy at his long picnic table inspires Captain America to a momentary eulogy to rural life—"You've got a nice place. It's not every man that can live off the land, you know. You do your own thing in your own time. You should be proud." But the viewer can't help but notice the farmer's false teeth, his worn-looking wife, who has borne too many children, and the general lack of prosperity his ramshackle property suggests. The New Mexico commune where Wyatt and Billy stop is filled with gentle people who ask little from the land: "We ask that our efforts be worthy to produce simple food for our simple tastes . . . that we may share it with our fellow man and be even more generous when it is from our own. Thank you for a place to make a stand." Yet when we watch them plant their seeds in the dust-dry soil, we have little faith in Captain America's prophecy that "they're gonna make it."[43]

The one redeeming character is George, an alcohol-befuddled ACLU lawyer played by Jack Nicholson, who offers the only political philosophy in the film. George's first marijuana experience induces a vision of a superior race of "Venutians" who will help turn America into an anarchist utopia: "They are people, just like us—from within our own solar system. Except that their society is more highly evolved. I mean, they don't have no wars, they got no monetary system, they don't have any leaders, because, I mean, each man is a leader. . . . For once man will have a god-like control over his own destiny. He will have a chance to transcend and to evolve with some equality for all."[44]

Just before George is killed by some Ku Klux Klan types, the night following the incident in the restaurant, he says sadly, "This used to be a helluva good country. I can't understand what's gone wrong with it." George's plaintive statement, made to no one in particular, is the key to both the power and the ultimate failure of the movie, a key that also helps to unravel the mystery of why Hopper chose to leave Hollywood to make his "last stand" in Taos, New Mexico. As at least one critic has noted, there is a strong streak of puritanism in this film, which ostensibly loathes everything held dear by white Protestant America. Hopper emphasized the intentional moralism in his addition of a crucial line of dialogue that comes just before the end. When Captain America and Wyatt head out for their last day on the road, Fonda turns to Hopper and tells him, "We blew it."[45]

This line can be read as a commentary on the demise of the counterculture, as well as on "the American experience as a whole." It is reinforced by the symbol of Wyatt's having placed their drug money in a tube located inside the gas tank of his motorcycle. Billy calls attention to this when he says that "everything that we ever dreamed of is in that teardrop gas tank." The money, of course, goes up in flames, along with Wyatt and Billy, in the final scene. Fonda admitted that both Captain America and Wyatt were "bad guys," who peddle dope "because that seems no worse to them than the Wall Street tycoon spending 80 percent of his time cheating the government. . . . My movie is about the lack of freedom, not about freedom. My heroes are not right, they're wrong. The only thing I can end up doing is killing my character. I end up committing suicide: that's what I'm saying America is doing."[46]

Both America, and its eponymous hero, have seemingly hit "the end of the road." The Captain and his sidekick are heirs of a long line of male buddy heroes in American literature and popular culture: Ishmael and Queequeg, Huck and Jim, Sal Paradise and Dean Moriarty, the Lone Ranger and Tonto. Like their forebears, they represent the dualities of mainstream western culture—civilized and savage, mind and body. (Billy is highly strung emotionally and acts like an animal; Wyatt is the "cool" brains of the outfit.) Like those other male pairs, they also represent a homoerotic displacement of the female. Neither Wyatt nor Billy is really interested in women, who are given the most stereotypical roles in the film. Women function primarily as crude representations of sex and death: from the nymphets who go swimming with Billy and Wyatt in the Hot Springs to the prostitutes in the LSD sequence in New Orleans.[47]

The movie's message seems to be that neither mainstream America nor its alternatives offer any hope for redemption, for a place and way to be both free and moral, independent and connected. Although Hopper believed he was urging young people to "go and try to change America," he also warned them: "If you're gonna wear a badge, whether it's long hair or black skin, learn to protect yourselves." Some scholars find the movie nihilistic. But eschatalogical might be a better term for Hopper's vision in *Easy Rider.* When Wyatt's and Billy's bikes burst into flames, and the pillar of smoke is panned from above in the closing scene, the film's religious undertones are reinforced by the contrasting view of an Edenic landscape with a river flowing through it.[48]

Hopper spoke in several interviews about the influence of *The Gospel According to Thomas* on his artistic vision. Thomas's Jesus speaks frequently of having come "to throw divisions upon the earth, fire, sword, war." The movie's ending also has political resonance, as Hopper suggests connections between the incineration of Captain America—whose motorcycle leaps into the air and blows up like a bomb—and the scenes of American planes napalming Vietnam that were shown nightly on television. It is probably not accidental that the murderers refer to Wyatt and Billy as "ginks," intended perhaps as a play on the racist epithet "gooks" that was often used by American soldiers in combat to describe the Vietnamese.[49]

According to Hopper, there was only one place where a man could go to attain what was left of the American Dream. "I've got to get back to the country, to an earth feeling, like when I was a kid. . . . Taos, man, . . . Taos, New Mexico. There's freedom there. They don't mind long hair. The herds mingle." It is noteworthy that the only scenes of genuine and unselfconscious pleasure in *Easy Rider* take place when Billy and Wyatt ride their motorcycles through the southwestern landscape, including their brief stop on the sacred ground of the Navajo in Monument Valley, and their early morning drive through Taos Pueblo. It is ironic, to say the least, that Hopper would invest the bountiful proceeds from this movie in his dream to establish a counter-Hollywood in Taos, only to find himself embroiled in an ethnic civil war among "the herds."[50]

CHAPTER FIVE

The Great Hippie Invasion

They ask why? . . .

Why must man be born in a gray room in a gray house in a gray impersonal concrete city, covered by gray smog, work at a gray job, until succumbing to gray hair and gray dust?

Why must man be infused, permeated, contaminated, diseased, imbued, and in other ways fed with hate against his neighbor, yes, even his loved ones? . . .

We earnestly pray that the good people of Taos will open their hearts and minds and find the wisdom to give the right answers. All America waits.[1]

This heartfelt *cri-de-coeur* from the *Fountain of Light* newspaper reflects the ardent hopes of many hippies who invested the northern New Mexico landscape with a utopian promise that harkens back to Mabel Luhan's first years in Taos. In their May 1969 issue, the editors explained why hippies believed that Taos was a potential center for cultural renewal: it was *the* place in America that could best fulfill their quest for authenticity. "Real food, grown by ourselves for the most part, real and useful products produced by our heads, and hands and hearts. Expressions in art forms that manifest individual energies of human beings rather than the faceless and soulless work of a mechanized existence." By August, they were even more effusive: "The future of America is coming to Taos, which we feel should be viewed as the highest compliment to Taoseños, Indians, Spanish, and Anglos alike . . . for this magnificent valley may well be the amphitheater in which will be enacted the final stage of the future of America."[2]

In 1969, the hippie population of Taos was estimated to be 2,000, at a time when the native population of the town was 3,500. By April 1970, the U.S. Census identified 3,314 hippies in New Mexico, half of them in Taos County (whose population was 17,500). A thousand of them lived on communes, and 4 percent of them on welfare (as compared to 5.25 percent of the general population.) In the summer of 1970, it was widely rumored that there was a plan to buy one hundred thousand acres of land in northern New Mexico "and invite all the freaks in America to come there to live in freedom. It is being financed by asking everyone who was at Woodstock in body or spirit to send a dollar." Taos had come to be, in the words of *Parade Magazine,* "a leading candidate for hippie capital of America."[3]

The Retribalization of America

In his contemporary account of the hippie-commune movement, *Getting Back Together* (1971), Robert Houriet explained its genesis as the

Ken Kesey on his bus Further, at the Great Bus Race, Aspen Meadows, 1969. Photo courtesy of Lisa Law.

desire to return "to the primal source of consciousness, the true basis of culture: the land. There they would again move forward, very slowly, careful not to take the wrong turn and keeping to the main road and to the central spirit and consciousness that modern man had lost along the way." In their search for a lifestyle of "voluntary primitivism," many of those who had started communes in California, Vermont, and New York, began to shift their sights to northern New Mexico by the late 1960s. They wanted to live as far from "civilization" as possible, but in a place that offered them models for rebuilding community. As one anonymous hippie stated: "It was my dream to belong to a tribe, where the energies flow among everyone, where people care for one another, where no one has to work, but everyone wants to do something because we're all mutually dependent for our survival and happiness."[4]

For many years before the arrival of the several thousand young people who inhabited the estimated twenty-seven to thirty-two communes in northern New Mexico, the Taos area had been receiving a small but steady stream of countercultural artists, writers, and activists. In the 1950s, Edward Abbey lived in Taos, where he was editor of the newspaper the *Territorial* before moving on to make southern Utah the staging ground for his militant environmental activism. Gary Snyder also spent some time in New Mexico in the 1950s during the early stages of finding his voice as one of the late twentieth century's finest nature poets and ethicists. Other members of the Beat generation who fled the West Coast and came to Taos were Ed Dorn, Robert Creeley, Gregory Corso, and Max Finstein, who was one of the founders of the most famous commune in Taos, New Buffalo. It may have been at this time that Creeley aptly named New Mexico "the *goyim's* Israel."[5]

Peter Rabbit, a poet who founded the first commune in the Southwest, came to Taos in 1954. He remembers "an amazing literary scene," most of it populated by San Francisco Renaissance and Black Mountain people. Black Mountain College in North Carolina was the most innovative avant-garde arts community in the United States at that time, spawning a cross-fertilization of talented sculptors, weavers, painters, dancers, and musicians, like John Cage, Merce Cunningham, and Josef and Annie Albers. Joan Loveless, a student of the Alberses, settled in Taos during the mid-1950s; she set up the Craft House with Rachel Brown "to promote interest in local crafts" such as weaving, silk screen printing, leathercraft, and woodwork. In the mid-1970s, Joan's daughter would continue that tradition at the Luhan house, where she lived and worked with the Sterling Smiths, a jeweler's commune.[6]

Jack Loeffler, an ethnomusicologist and environmental activist who came to Taos in the 1950s, saw a link between his generation and the hippies who came a decade later. A self-described drop-out jazz musician who had joined the U.S. Army, Jack fled to San Francisco after performing in an army band that played during the testing of an atomic bomb on the Nevada proving grounds. In San Francisco he worked on an oral history project titled "America Needs Indians" with Stewart Brand, who later originated the *Whole Earth Catalogue*. In the early 1970s, Loeffler joined with Edward Abbey to form the Black Mesa Defense Fund, whose environmental activism Dennis Hopper would support while he was living in Taos.[7]

Loeffler views the hippie-commune phenomenon as "one of the great resurgences of anarchist thought in America." He notes its connections to the theories of the Russian philosopher Alexander Kropotkin, whose definition of anarchism could serve as a gloss on much of the commune movement: "The Anarchists conceive a society in which all the mutual relations of its members are regulated, not by laws, not by authorities, whether self-imposed or elected, but by mutual agreements between the members of that society, and by a sum of social customs and habits . . . [consonant] with the ever-growing requirements of a free life. . . . No government of man by man; no crystallization and immobility, but a continual evolution—such as we see in nature." Loeffler attributes the Southwest's attraction for hippies to the Native American Church's use of peyote, through which he and others experienced "the sense of community with a common point of view" that was grounded in the sacredness of one's "place" on earth.[8]

In spite of their identification with Indian tribalism and their generally anarchist spirit, northern New Mexico's communes reflected the wide range of philosophies and lifestyles that one could find throughout America's two thousand communes in 1970. Like most hippies, the inhabitants were ambivalent in their intentions. Did they come to New Mexico, as the board member of one commune was quoted as saying, in order to provide an escape from "the huge cities, the destruction of the environment, and the fear that should revolution erupt they would be trapped in the cities"? Or did they intend to serve as models of sociopolitical and cultural revolution in the United States? Like their forebears in Mabel Luhan's generation, they had an ambiguous relationship to the larger Anglo-American society they alternately hoped to escape and transform.[9]

Drop City

Drop City was the "grandfather" of communes in the Southwest, a harbinger of their promise, their failures, and the kinds of compromises that a few of them were able to make in order to survive. One of the earliest rural communes, Drop City was founded in 1964, in Trinidad, Colorado, by Peter Rabbit, as a "sort of refuge for hip artists who wish to maximize their privacy but still retain neighbors who are like-minded and cooperative." Each family helped the others build their own geodesic dome, thus providing space for family privacy. They adopted Native American rituals, such as the requirement that everyone be present for the birth of each new child, who was welcomed by group chanting, and the Pueblo practice of deer hunting, in which permission is asked of the deer before killing it.[10]

In 1967, teenage runaways and deserters from Vietnam began to inundate Drop City. The arrival of these youthful hordes was partly due to the cross-country missionary tour that Peter Rabbit and his friends, artists Dean and Linda Fleming, took to colleges and universities from New Mexico to

New York. They presented slides and movies of what they were doing and proselytized that the commune movement "was the hope of the world." Like many communalists, the Drop City founders were drawn equally by a compelling desire to help others and to be free of others. When they decided to take all newcomers, in whatever condition they arrived, they subjected themselves to much more than they could handle socially, psychologically, or economically. According to Fleming, "Peter at thirty years old was like the old man. Sometimes they resented him because he tried too hard to keep everything together. . . . He was taking care of a lot of kids and the FBI would come just about every week and they'd hold up these photographs on the other side of the fence and they'd say, 'Have you seen them?' And we'd have all these teenagers with dyed hair and growing beards trying to camouflage themselves."[11]

Lama

Lama began life as the brainchild of two of the founding members of Timothy Leary's Millbrook Community in upstate New York, Steve Durkee and Richard Alpert. Leary's partner in LSD experimentation and philosophy at Harvard, Alpert renamed himself Baba Ram Dass. Alpert claims that his experiences with LSD led him to enter "the kingdom of heaven" where he felt "new states of awareness" that gave a "heightened sensitivity" and "speeding up of the thought process, followed by figure ground shift so that when you looked at people you focused on their relation to you and differences seemed more like clothing." When he discovered the similarity between this awareness and the stages of consciousness described in the *Tibetan Book of the Dead,* he went to India. Here he met Bhagwan Dass, an American who had become a guru and who taught him the philosophy of *Be Here Now.*[12]

Lama's 115 acres were purchased in the winter of 1967. During its first two years some 150 people passed through, most of them participating in such activities as construction—building a solar heater, greenhouse, barn, domed common house, meditation house, cabins—farming, landscaping, kitchen duties, and childcare. A "spiritual smorgasbord" that held the reputation of being an "Ivy League graduate school," Lama attracted people who were both older and more mature than the average commune inhabitant. Lama was—and still is—a rare example of the coexistence of East and West, containing elements of Sufi, Buddhist, Hindu, Jewish, Islamic, Christian, and Native American traditions.[13]

In 1974, Natalie Goldberg, who would become a widely acclaimed author and teach writing workshops at the Luhan house in the 1980s, moved to Lama to learn meditation practices. Natalie began her study of the Zen philosophy, which informs her writing and teaching practice, with Roshi. A year later, she was hired by Lama to teach writing in the hippie alternative school the foundation started in Taos, named Da Nahazali, or Return to Spring, in Navaho. Natalie offered her first adult writing workshops at the same time, charging twelve dollars a week for four weeks, or the equivalent in baked bread or food stamps. "We made writing communal, about relationship. We learned about each other. The aim was to glow, not to publish."[14]

New Buffalo

New Buffalo was the archetypal hippie commune, its symbolic power reinforced nationwide through Dennis Hopper's simulacrum in *Easy Rider.* Max Finstein borrowed from Native American tribal practices and Zionist kibbutzim, and named it after the animal that had provided food, clothes, and shelter to the Plains Indians. Rick Klein provided the fifty thousand dollars necessary to purchase the land (and equipment) in Arroyo Hondo. Rick had been destined for academia as an English professor, but like Richard Alpert, he was "converted" by LSD, and he became a musician instead.[15]

New Buffalo's first year was full of utopian promise and practical accomplishment. Members built a beautiful hexagonal house that had a communal kitchen and a common room with a kiva-like circle sunk four feet in the center. Working from dawn to dusk to create their self-styled pueblo, they planted corn and beans and invited the Taos Indians to come and teach them the ritual celebrations that were appropriate for different times of the year. The New Buffalonians saw themselves as "a lost tribe who had forgotten how to live—to plant, dance, sing, raise children—and how to die." They conducted peyote ceremonies and practiced simple prayers before and after meals to express gratitude for their slim bounty from the land (as depicted in *Easy Rider*). In setting out to revive what they believed was an almost extinct wisdom and lore, they were influenced by one of the bibles that had inspired this generation to move to Taos—Frank Waters's *Book of the Hopi.*[16]

Determined to be self-sufficient, they rebuilt cars and trucks, refrigerators and furniture, and earned money reselling auto parts and salvaging

Toni Law and Richie Moonchild, New Buffalo Commune, 1970.
Photo courtesy of Lisa Law.

metals. They also experimented with finding safe substitutes for chemical fertilizers by testing natural pesticides, a practice that would have important consequences during the 1980s in the pursuit of sustainable agriculture. In that first year, everything seemed possible, including the belief that "we could love one another freely without guilt" and maintain an open commune that would shelter and feed whoever needed them.[17]

But keeping the commune open to all undermined its initial vision. By its third year of operation, New Buffalo had already been through "three generations" and maintained an ex-Hell's Angel as the unofficial bouncer of the hordes of "drifters, parasites, and criminals" who were increasingly attracted to it. Rather than a sacred tribe, the commune devolved into something more like "Gorki's *The Lower Depths,*" with its thirty to fifty people living mostly off of food stamps, sometimes stealing each other's food (including the milk meant for breast-feeding mothers and children), and its leadership made up of "lawless frontiersmen." When a vote was taken in 1970 to close the commune, New Buffalo started on a new, less utopian

New Buffalo Commune, 1967.
Photo courtesy of Lisa Law.

phase of its existence. In 1977, it celebrated its tenth anniversary, twenty adults and twelve children having achieved a modicum of economic stability with the raw milk dairy they established.[18]

Morningstar East, Reality Company, and the Magic Tortoise

In 1967, Michael Duncan bought 720 acres on a mesa north of Taos for $250,000 and issued an open invitation for anyone to come. He declared that the hippies dressed and looked like Indians and "think like they do. What I mean is that . . . we're more mystically oriented. The earth and sky and rain are holy to us, and when we work, we do it so we can live, so we can enjoy these things—not like the crazy, logical middle-class Americans who live only to work, and have fallen out of Nature's grace." What resulted from his open call were two contiguous communes that represented the extremes which the hippie movement had generated: "the political revolutionaries . . . and the children of faith and fantasy."[19]

Morningstar East was a direct offshoot of the California migration from

Morningstar West, which was founded by Lou Gottlieb in Sonoma County as a home for Haight-Ashbury refugees. Gottlieb was a forty-seven-year-old drop-out jazz musician and self-described "prophet of the Open Land Movement" who moved his group to Taos in 1968. At the "opposite geographical and philosophical ends of the mesa to the east" was Reality Construction Company, which had been liberated by a band of young revolutionaries who didn't like New Buffalo's "apolitical, spiritual atmosphere." Where Morningstar East was populated by "mystics, winos, runaways, and hermits," Reality was made up of "Weathermen and outlaws."[20]

Max Finstein founded Reality because he was convinced that a fascist police-state was about to take over America, which would "exterminate all its young radicals. Here they could safely resist and launch liberating forays into the surrounding country." The first summer they moved eighty-five tons of earth, made and sold adobe bricks, built workshops and pens, and raised animals. Bill Gersh, an artist who lived and worked north of Taos until his death in 1994, was a charter member. He remembered coming out to Taos from Berkeley in 1968 as part of the "big exodus" from the East and West coasts for which Taos "seemed to be the focal point." The Native Americans were a big draw for the hippie exurbanites who had taken too many psychedelics "and needed to have more of a . . . concrete identity. Maybe the natives served that function for them. Maybe coming to a place like Taos would give people more of a spiritual backbone; something that had been going for a much longer time than just taking acid in Cambridge, taking acid in Berkeley. . . . This was like a suction cup of energy."[21]

Gersh decided to leave Berkeley when the Black Power movement he'd been supporting made it clear they didn't want whites working with them. He described Reality as a "radical, interracial, legal nut house, with Puerto Ricans, Dominican Republicans, and Blacks from the South, and like, you know, Great Neck Jewish boys and little Jewish girls from Brooklyn who had taken too much acid and a bunch of guys running around thinking that they are going to save the world with this anarchist philosophy. . . . This is way beyond the Wobblies." Their major activity, according to Gersh, was to keep peaceful hippies away so they could maintain their political activities: "We were going to supply the world with food but meanwhile, we never really grew any. We are going out and change the attitude of such and such people, and if they don't pay attention to us, we are going to, you know, blow them away, and we are prepared for this revolution, we know it's going to come." When the revolution didn't come, and when they were

Reality Commune, n.d.
Photo courtesy of Walter Chappell.

rebuffed by local Chicano militants, Finstein left and went to Israel, claiming that "American kids were too soft."[22]

With sardonic humor, Gersh pointed out the absurdity of suburban youth trying to "pick up" the ways of Indians who had one thousand years to build their cultures. Faced with their first cold winter, a lot of them "booked" and went back to Great Neck or "called up their mom for money so that they could go to . . . wherever, someplace where it was warm, and they can act it out without too many clothes." Some of these seekers joined the Native American Church, stopped taking acid and smoking pot, and moved in their next transition to "some form of researching out what Christ's spirit meant to them from when they were little kids. . . . They had dreadlocks in 1969, where their head was crewcut in 1957."

By 1977, according to the *New York Times,* Reality commune was a "cultural ruin, littered with rusting hulks of battered cars and wood-burning stoves"; all that remained of Morningstar was a herd of goats belonging to someone who had left New Buffalo and lived alone with his family. But Reality Construction Company wasn't exactly left to rot. In good hippie-ecological fashion, it was recycled. In 1971, Gersh joined the Magic Tortoise, which consisted of forty acres and four families who have lived on Lama Mountain for twenty-five years as a "community" rather than a commune. Each family built and owns its own home, while sharing the land in common.[23]

Last Resort, Lorien Enterprises, and the Cowboys

For all its revolutionary pretense, Reality offered no real threat to surrounding communities, let alone to the nation at large. But there was a dangerous side to the commune movement in Taos, which would also be reflected in Hopper's lifestyle in the Luhan house. Last Resort was founded by drop-outs from Drop City, a group of liberal arts college graduates who built beautiful homes, devised their own water system, milked goats, and delivered their own babies. But they also practiced a form of peyote philosophy that suggested humans should express their "natural, violent, and unpredictable nature."[24]

Lorien was founded in Arroyo Seco by Rick Klein and Chick Lonsdale, who also owned and managed a free clinic in Taos and the Taos General Store, which provided a free information service that directed itinerant hippies to food and shelter. According to Doug Magnus, a photographer and observer of the hippie scene in Taos, Lorien was a "bandido hang-out" made up of escaped convicts and runaways. He claims that Linda Kasabian fled there to join her husband, Bob, a few days after the Charles Manson-inspired Tate-LaBianca murders in August 1969. Writing for *Rolling Stone* in July 1970, James Dean claimed that Charles Manson and Linda Kasabian had lived in Ojo Sarco a year or two before the murders. Ojo Sarco was the home of the acid-tripping Cowboys. Former Hollywood extras, they walked around with guns, shot them off wherever and whenever the spirit moved them, and ended up in a shoot-out with some local Chicanos.[25]

Manson was one of the most terrifying manifestations of the apocalyptic mood of the late 1960s, and of great fascination to Dennis Hopper, who took on an uncanny resemblance to him during his own dark days in Taos. Like Hopper, Manson imagined himself a Christ figure, telling his friends that he had once died on the cross. He believed that he was paving the way for the Day of Judgment, when his Family—as he called his coterie of hippie worshippers—would reach the biblical 144,000 predicted in the New Testament's Revelation.

Manson combined drugs, sex orgies, and Christian prophecy with Hopi legends about a "bottomless pit" where "tuned-in tribes" went to escape the mass destruction of the earth and lived in a golden city flowing with milk and honey. To this concoction, he added the Nazi's theory of the Master Race and combined it with the Ku Klux Klan's racist fantasies. Manson's murder-by-proxy of six Hollywood actors and producers on August 30, 1969, was intended to be the brushfire that ignited the Apocalypse. The members of his Family who carried out his instructions wrote Black Power slogans with the blood of the murdered men and women, in order to make white America think that blacks had committed the murders. This ploy was intended to start a race war, which the blacks would win. Afterward, they would yield themselves to Manson and his elect, who would become their masters, bring on the Day of Judgment, and live happily ever after.[26]

In his history of the Manson crimes, Victor Bugliosi tracked Linda Kasabian to Taos after the murders. She had left her baby daughter at the Spahn ranch, the Manson Family hideout, because she was afraid that if she and her husband went back, Manson would kill them all. Linda sought the counsel of Joe Sage, a fifty-one-year-old Zen monk who ran the Macrobiotic Church in Taos and who "was campaigning for president of the United States on an anti-pollution ticket." With his help, she managed to find her daughter and return to Taos, but by the time she returned, her husband was living with another woman. Linda left for her mother's home in New Hampshire where, on December 2, 1969, "the news broke that she was being sought in connection with the Tate murders."[27]

Although the Tate-LaBianca murders were only peripherally connected to Taos, the rumors about the Manson Family's presence in northern New Mexico and the actions of outlaws like the Cowboys fed the already burgeoning local suspicion and hatred of longhairs. Closer to home, there were forms of violence and social disruption that had a far greater impact on the populace of Taos, both native and hippie. When Dennis Hopper moved to Taos in June 1970, he became a provoked and provoking symbol of a political and social crisis that was reaching its crescendo.

The Hippie-Chicano Wars

On its surface, the Taos landscape encountered by the second wave of the counterculture that came to New Mexico did not look dramatically different from the one that Mabel Luhan had inhabited. Stephen Fox has noted the "remarkable parallels . . . between Bohemians of the twenties and the advocates of the counterculture of the sixties" whose disenchantment with "the dominant culture and the search for alternative visions and experiences" drew them as "ethnicity-seekers" to native cultures and traditions. The differences between these generations are, however, as significant as their similarities. The majority of hippies who passed through Taos were adolescents or postadolescents who had few skills, little self-discipline, and less understanding of the indigenous cultures they believed they wanted to imitate. Moreover, during the decades that divided them from the heyday of Luhan's generation, there had been substantial changes that made for a very different economic, political, and social climate.[28]

In the 1960s, New Mexico was the third poorest state in the union, and Taos County, and its contiguous counties, Rio Arriba and Mora, were among the poorest of the poor, with approximately one-third to one-half of the indigenous population on welfare and the same proportion living below the official federal poverty line of three thousand dollars. The per capita income was around twelve hundred dollars. (It was thirty-eight hundred dollars nationwide.) Unemployment ranged between 15 and 40 percent, and employment consisted mostly of low-paying service jobs. Schooling was monolingual and averaged 7.1 years for Hispanics, compared with 12.1 for Anglos.[29]

The native Spanish-speaking population had suffered a loss of wealth since the 1920s, when a cash-based economy weakened the security of villagers, who became dependent on livestock ranching and outside jobs for income. The Great Depression brought "the final collapse of their pastoral subsistence economy." At the same time the federal government started curtailing traditional Indian and Hispanic uses of the National Forest, which makes up 44 percent of Taos County, for grazing and timber-cutting. Recreation and retirement interests led to the establishment of Taos Ski Valley in 1956, and to the real estate boom that began in the 1960s.[30]

The impact of the hippies on the economy was devastating to the local Hispanic population. Some hippies were able to buy up large parcels of land from the locals, thus inflating real estate values. Others, who were in need of money, drove locals from even the lowest-paying jobs. The 4 percent who lived on welfare used food stamps, which they declared was a political act against a corrupt government. To Hispanic Taoseños, this "act" was a mockery of the poverty they endured involuntarily. Perhaps even more infuriating was the way in which hippies seemed to scorn the deepest-held social and religious beliefs of the Hispanic population, with their practice of uninhibited sex and liberal use of drugs. The hippies also violated health laws with such practices as bathing nude in streams used for drinking water. Repeated articles in the *Taos News* blamed them for increased drug use in the schools and the spread of hepatitis and venereal disease. They were condemned by the Taos Chamber of Commerce, the Taos Ministerial Alliance, and the Taos Municipal Education Association.[31]

The hippies added insult to injury by continuing the practice of "selective ethnophilia," admiring the Taos Indians while denigrating the Hispanics. The majority of Taos Indians received the hippie invasion with bemusement and tolerance because the hippies did not interfere with their land and practices, were enamored of the way they lived, and sought them out as mentors. But the local Anglo and Hispanic populations became increasingly hostile toward the hippies as violent acts began to escalate in the summer of 1970. Government officials in Taos tried to figure out ways to eliminate food stamps, or tighten requirements for them, in order to discourage hippies from staying, which had a punitive affect on many Hispanics.

Convinced that hippies were hurting the tourist trade, local businesses put up signs such as "We will refuse service to anyone we consider a health menace," or "Keep America Beautiful, Take a Hippie to a Carwash," which were combatted by such signs at the hippie General Store as "Health Menaces Served Here." Rapes of hippie and Hispanic women were reported, and it became increasingly difficult for the local population to separate hippies who lived peacefully from drifters and gangs, like the Black Banditos who hung out at the Hot Springs and robbed tourists and hippies alike.[32]

By the late spring and early summer of 1970, hippies themselves began to put out warnings to future recruits: "Northern New Mexico is an arid dry terrain. The wood is sparse. The people are poor and are being invaded. This is a plea for help. Don't come." The *Fountain of Light* all but reversed its utopian vision of the summer before: "The Taos myth is over. We live, not in the land of three cultures, but in a bigoted and provincial society. We have our own brand of Ku Klux Klan occupying our nights, shooting up our houses, burning and dynamiting cars, and beating, threatening and pistol-whipping people. . . . We are caught in a feudal society in which everyone knows everyone and everyone fears everyone. The fears are huge and irrational. They get projected out onto hippies, communists, liberals, artists." The author listed as the most recent violent acts against hippies a VW bus dynamited near Peñasco, a bridge near a commune in Pilar burned down, hitchhikers run down, bomb threats of buildings, cars and houses in Ranchos and San Cristobal that had their windows shot in. The police meted out harsher penalties to hippies than to locals, a fact that Dennis Hopper would learn only too well soon after his move to Taos.[33]

Not all hippies were benighted or indifferent to the reasons they aroused such hostility. Some noted the need for the hippie population to understand that they were regarded by Hispanics "as a new group of Anglo landholders . . . [whose] ignorance of the problems of colonized peoples," and disregard for marriage and family verged "on racist arrogance." The more politicized Anglos who settled in Taos in the late 1960s were well aware of the need to form "a coalition with the oppressed peoples there," and they worked hard to establish such coalitions with Chicano and Indian activists. The two most important organs for these activist voices were the *New Mexico Review,* edited by John Nichols, and *El Grito del Norte* (*The Cry of the North*), published by the militant La Raza movement.[34]

Anglos and Indians made effective common cause in the effort to restore Blue Lake to Taos Pueblo, a cause in which Hopper would involve himself soon after his arrival. On June 12, 1969, John Evans, took out a two-page ad in the *Taos News* intended to rouse the local Anglo populace to action: "THINK BACK! THINK NOW! THINK AHEAD! THIS IS AMERICA! Taos Pueblo is launching a nation-wide public appeal for support of its centuries' old rights to the Blue Lake Area, for religious and ceremonial purposes; rights confirmed when the U.S. Indian Claims Commission, in its decision last September, found that the U.S. Government had illegally taken this land from the Taos Pueblo People in 1906." Once again, as in Luhan's day, national publicity networks were created to further the cause. One of the most successful was WNET-TV's release of the final documentary in their eight-part series, *The Vanishing Wilderness.*

The film, *The Water Is So Clear that a Blind Man Could See,* focuses on Taos Pueblo and the struggle for Blue Lake. It was aired during the debate over the House of Representatives' version of the Blue Lake Bill, and it generated "a flood of letters to the Senate." Perhaps one of the first media uses of Indian culture as a signifier for a growing environmentalist ethic, the film shows a grandfather teaching his grandson about how to love and respect nature. Everyone, the grandfather says, "is a sacred part of the living church." The Blue Lake Bill was signed into law by President Richard Nixon in December 1970, returning the lake and forty-eight thousand surrounding acres to the tribe.[35]

Sylvia Rodriguez has described the emergence of "Hispano ethnic land symbolism" at the same time as the reemergence of the Blue Lake case: "The idea of a stolen homeland was invoked and dramatized in 1967 by Reies López Tijerina, the leader of La Alianza Federal de Los Pueblos Libres, which attracted international attention to the long-buried land grant issue in New Mexico." Tijerina's impact on Taos was both symbolic and political. He gave a name to "what had happened to them as a people" and established the legal and moral entitlement of the Hispanic villagers to the lands they had been granted under the original Spanish land grants.[36]

Tijerina was an evangelical preacher whose charismatic leadership and organization of New Mexico's rural poor culminated in his attempt to reclaim the hundreds of thousands of acres of the Tierra Amarilla and San Joaquin de Rio Chama land grants that had been taken from Hispanic villagers. In 1966 and 1967, the villagers brought petitions to the governor of New Mexico, asking for an investigation of the land claims. When nothing came of it, they "congregated at the Tierra Amarilla Courthouse and voted to re-establish the Pueblo Republica de San Joaquin that had been dissolved by decree in 1882. They proclaimed the 'Free City-State of Tierra Amarilla.'" Several people were arrested at this demonstration. On June 5, 1967, the day they were to be arraigned for "unlawful assembly," members of the Alianza organized a "Citizen's Arrest" of the district attorney at the Rio Arriba courthouse, which was made by a "posse" of twenty armed Hispanic farmers, ranchers, and loggers. The raid resulted in a shoot-out that was heard around the nation and was followed by the arrival of the National Guard in armored tanks.[37]

Tijerina was a messianic figure who presented himself as a disciple of Christ. He often recounted the vision that inspired his activities, when he was asked by three "Angels of Law" to help them. He ascribed his role as a prophet of the mountain villages to "an act of divine revelation," and said that the "Lord had chosen him on a mountain." Tijerina predicted that time was running out for the United States, as blacks, browns, and reds were going to unite. Like Manson, he predicted a racial war, except the results would be the opposite of Manson's racist apocalypse: "After that we will live like brothers. Like one family of races, I believe."[38]

The "Tierra Amarilla courthouse raid and its aftermath became a milestone in the national process of Chicano ethnopolitical mobilization . . . [that] roughly coincided with the emergence of Hispano-Chicano protest activity in Taos in the early 1970s." William deBuys believes that Tijerina and the Alianza's guerilla tactics were particularly effective in spurring important changes in Forest Service policies. To deal with the unrest, the Department of Agriculture agreed to increase spending that would ease local poverty and to make range improvements that would allow for more grazing. For the first time in its history, the Forest Service acknowledged that the local Spanish and Indian cultures were as much "resources" as the wilderness and had to be preserved.[39]

Tijerina's agenda included a desire to organize Pueblos, Hispanics, and hippies as potential allies, a vision that Dennis Hopper would try to connect with after his arrival. The writers for *El Grito* also tried to do their best to help make peace and cooperation possible between groups it saw as natural allies. They publicized the work of the new clinics and agricultural cooperatives that were burgeoning across the Hispanic landscape of northern New Mexico, editorialized on the importance of Indian self-determination, and tried to enlighten hippies as to why they were seen as "gringos," by reminding them of "the 120-year fight by both Hispanics and Indians to get back millions of acres of land taken by Anglo ranchers and lawyers."[40]

But the radical politics of the Alianza further added to the turmoil in Taos. Although they did have allies, primarily among Chicano militants, Taos County's native-born Hispanic population was, for the most part, put off by the group's militancy. There was no Hispanic "community" as such in a region where each small town identified with its birthplace in Spain and regarded other towns with suspicion and hostility. Those who prided themselves on their descent from the Spanish conquistadores of the fifteenth century did not want to be confused with the more recently arrived Mexicans or Mexican Americans, and they were deeply offended by the ethnic label used by Chicanos to proudly affirm their mestizo blood.[41]

One of the most acute Anglo observers of the volatility of the interethnic scene in Taos is the writer John Nichols, a self-described "semi-Marxist-Leninist propaganda arm for a group of quixotic Spanish-speaking septuagenarians locked in mortal combat with the United States government over the preservation of their water rights, their land, their culture, their very historical roots." Nichols was perhaps the first Anglo activist to move to Taos who made the Hispanic population the focus of his energies and interest, an interest that is best known through his novel *The Milagro Bean Field War* (1974) and the film based on it. He moved to Taos in May 1969, burned out from three years of antiwar work in New York, where he had been reading *El Grito* and learning about the dire economic conditions of northern New Mexico's indigenous populations. It didn't take Nichols long to figure out that "the myth of Taos as a community where three cultures lived together in perfect harmony was just that—a Chamber of Commerce–inspired snow job."[42]

From Nichols's perspective, the hippie invasion was

> *probably the most concentrated onslaught on Spanish-speaking culture that has happened in many years. They had no intention, most of them, of accommodating themselves at all to the culture that was here. They had no intention of learning Spanish, they had very little intention of becoming participants at all levels of the social structure. . . . There were serious people, who were interested in some kind of countercultural lifestyle, who remained and have become kind of citizens of the valley. . . . But for the large part it was sort of an influx of . . . freaks, weirdos, who made no commitment to the area, to the culture, to the land, to the history. . . . And they were gone in a few years. In the meantime, however, they . . . caused an awful lot of damage.*[43]

In March 1970, Nichols started the *New Mexico Review,* hoping to make it a muckraking journal that would serve as "the leftist propaganda arm of New Mexico's transplanted-from-New York-radic-lib community." It was also intended to serve as a bridge between cultures, to explain to the various factions within the Taos community what could bring them together rather than drive them apart and thus make allies out of enemies. In the August–September 1970 issue, Nichols wrote an article on human relations in Taos in which he explained why hippies had become "a scapegoat for century-deep fears carried by both the exploited and exploiters of Taos County, and by the many people in between who are simply confused and frightened, as is most of America, by the implications of the endless war in Vietnam."[44]

Nichols's report, in the same issue, of an attempt to open a dialogue about violence in Taos made clear how extremely polarized these factions had become. Harvey Mudd, the Taos County chairman of New Mexico Citizens for Clean Air and Water, descried the police and the courts' inequitable penalties for hippies, while members of the Spanish American community decried the "filth" of "those people who call themselves Flowers of God." In retrospect, Nichols summed up the year 1970, as "hectic, paranoid, and often violent in Taos county." The people of Taos were "divided, conquered, broken up into factions; their outrage over years of exploitation had been expertly diffused during a time of political and intellectual ferment that could have resulted in powerful and lasting social changes guaranteeing to long-time local residents their land and water rights."[45]

The fortieth anniversary celebration of the death of D. H. Lawrence was intended to be part of the intellectual ferment to which Nichols referred. But fifty years after he first sounded his rebel voice in New Mexico, Lawrence's memory survived mainly as a tourist attraction that brought dollars to the needy Taos economy. In September 1970, the town fathers and local literati held a five-day international festival in his honor that included an exhibition of memorabilia, letters, photos, guided tours, and readings and papers by poets and scholars. Poet Robert Bly dubbed Lawrence "the first hippie," a designation that would have horrified the fastidious writer. Bly also acknowledged that the festival did not exactly capture Lawrence's "mood." He condemned the hideous concrete bunkers built by the University of New Mexico to house its conference center as an example "of not keeping good faith with the Lawrence tradition."[46]

Three months earlier, Dennis Hopper had ridden into town, hoping to claim Lawrence's mantle and Mabel's throne. He had already paid tribute to Lawrence in *Easy Rider* when he had Nicholson take his first drink of the morning and toast the day: "Here's to ol' D. H. Lawrence, nik, nik, nik, nik—Indians!" (Hopper and Nicholson had dropped acid at the Lawrence tomb the night before filming Nicholson's utopian speech about the Venutians.) But Hopper soon found that his new home more closely resembled the defensive barricade of the University of New Mexico's militarized bunkers than a launching pad for a guerilla war against mainstream America.[47]

CHAPTER SIX

Hopper Comes to Taos

D. H. Lawrence lived in Taos for nine months.
I was in Taos for nine years.
Dennis Hopper

The stories surrounding Hopper's "discovery" of Taos and the Luhan house have taken on some of the same mythic qualities as those surrounding the burial of D. H. Lawrence's ashes. According to Hopper, his initial arrival in Taos was some kind of karmic mistake. During the filming of *Easy Rider,* he and his production manager were heading east from Los Alamos, and when they reached the divided highway, they had an argument about which way to get to Santa Fe. They went north, instead of south. "I heard that Taos was an artist community and I didn't want to go to any artist community. I was looking for a commune to use." But once he arrived in Taos, Hopper had a problem getting out. "I just suddenly fell in love with it, I mean it was like very mystical to me and I kept trying to get out of town and an Indian would come and say the mountain is smiling on you, you must come and see this, you must come and see that, and so on." After shooting for two weeks in and around Taos, he left saying, "Well, if I ever come back, if I ever make any money, I'm gonna go back and I'm going to live in Taos."[1]

Hopper went to Taos with his friend Leo Garen around Christmas 1969, accompanied by Felicia Fergusson, an eighteen-year-old native Taoseña with whom Dennis was living. Garen had been a theatre producer and director in New York City, where he had first met Dennis during his time at the Actor's Studio. He had come to Los Angeles to work with Antonioni on *Zabriskie Point* and found Dennis a place to stay in the pool house of a large estate where he was living. Felicia was the granddaughter of Terecita Fergusson, the notorious lover of Arthur Manby. She had been accused of cutting off his head in what was perhaps the most famous criminal trial in modern Taos history. Manby was an English remittance man who had rented Mabel her first house in Taos and whose violent death she hoped to convince Robinson Jeffers to make use of in his poetry.[2]

Garen remembers that the three of them stayed at the La Fonda hotel and went to a party up the canyon attended by "acid cowboys and hippie pioneers." Leo passed around thirty or forty tablets of LSD, and Dennis acted as the party's emcee, a role that he loved: "Life was a grand opera in which he is singing the lead and everybody is either a supporting player or an extra." When they drove out to the Luhan house, Hopper was immediately attracted to it: "Ghost-filled places have always fascinated me. . . . When it was time to leave, I couldn't get the door open to get out." Like Mabel he connected the house with the Sacred Mountain visible behind it: "Well, they say the mountain is sacred, I really bought that. You know when I went into the house, like light fell right on certain places, and I came outside and snow was just snowing right where I was standing, you know, and lightning knocked bushes down, you know, I mean it was very bizarre." Hopper returned to buy it in March 1970.

Dennis paid Bonnie Evans somewhere between $140,000 and $180,000. After his brother, David, and his work crew completed repairs to the buildings, Dennis moved in, in June, and started his studio-cum-commune. Its core was to be made up of his then-fiancée, Michelle Phillips, the editors he had worked with on *The Last Movie,* and an assortment of Hollywood friends. Ron Rosenbaum has wittily summarized his ambitious intentions: "Hopper had inherited one of the shrines of the Gnostic, utopian strains of American culture. And he was doing his best to live up to its legacy" when he surrounded himself with "an earnest little commune" who spent fourteen months helping him edit his film. They were devoted to *The Last Movie,* with "an almost messianic faith" that if they could "carve out the right combination of frames from those forty-six hours of film, . . . they would have truly created something more than just a movie. It would be a movie to end all movies, a movie that would pierce the veils of deceit that shrouded the consciousness of ordinary moviegoers and show them the emptiness of the illusions that ordinary movies had them in thrall to. 'The Last Movie' would be . . . The Truth, Nothing less than the Gnostic Gospel of American film."[3]

The Last Movie

The Last Movie almost lived up to its title, although not in the way that Hopper intended, when it came very close to being the last film he ever made. In the United States, the movie was an unmitigated disaster, panned by critics and pulled from movie theaters after a two-week distribution. In Europe, however, Hopper was hailed as a "rebel genius." *Le Monde* described his new movie as "one of the boldest and most advanced works of American cinema," and it won the award for Best Feature Film at the Venice Film Festival in 1971. Both views have merit. To the historian of the 1960s counterculture, it is a fascinating and troubling visual statement about deeply rooted American myths. It reveals Hopper's confused politics as well as the conflicted aesthetics of the postmodern condition he sought to reflect.[4]

The Last Movie is a movie-within-a-movie-within-a-movie, a movie about the making of movies and an attempt to unmask the illusion of reality on which the emotional power of film is based. Its nonlinear, self-reflexive, and disruptive cinematography was reason enough for its failure with mainstream American audiences, who had little patience for the techniques of avant-garde films. What plot there is revolves around the eponymous hero, Kansas (played by Hopper), a stunt man who has accompanied a grade-B film crew and company to Peru to make a low-budget generic western.

Hopper creates an amusing pastiche of every stock element of the classic American western by repeating each element innumerable times: gunshots, falling bodies, the whore with golden heart waiting for the hero to return, who is told by the Henry Hathaway–like director to act more excited when she sees her lover. It soon becomes clear that the good-versus-evil formula is meaningless, the violence random, and the heroes and villains indistinguishable. By the last take, everyone is dead except one lone gunman. Hopper told an interviewer that these scenes were almost all improvisatory, intended as "a ballistic burlesque of a John Wayne western that somehow managed to involve Billy the Kid, D. H. Lawrence, James Dean, Captain Bligh and the Seven Samurai." Hopper allowed himself to give full range to a postmodern sensibility that incorporated "history, fantasy, myth, science, madness and every level of culture from highest mandarin to crassest pop."[5]

Kansas is an American innocent, directly related to the various American Adams in our literature and popular culture. After the film crew packs up and leaves, he decides to stay, in the naive hope that he can make his fortune in Peru, now that Hollywood has "discovered" it. He takes up with a local woman, the virgin-whore Maria, whom he "rescues" from her pimp. We watch them romp through the pristine mountain landscape and make love in a naked embrace beneath a waterfall, evoking the early descriptions of the Americas in which explorers often compared the land's fecundity and its "simple" naked peoples to paradise before the fall.

Kansas tells his lover that all a man needs in life is here: he could be happy just living with her in a "little adobe" perched on top of the mountain. However, it doesn't take long for his imagination to leap from living like Adam in the garden to fantasizing about how he might exploit paradise in order to make his fortune, beginning with his dream of building a ski resort on the mountain behind the village. In the meantime, he rents a California-style bungalow for himself and Maria, who is ripe for corruption—the ravished become ravisher. Once she sees the material ease that the other expatriate Americans in the vicinity enjoy, she demands more goods, turning into a parody of the consumer housewife. Their brief idyll ends in vi-

Outtake from *The Last Movie.*
Photo courtesy of the Museum of Modern Art,
Photo Stills Archive, New York.
(Kansas with Maria, his lover, in their Hollywood bungalow.)

olence, when Hopper prostitutes himself to a wealthy American woman in order to bring home a mink stole that Maria demands, for which he then beats her in order to reaffirm his masculinity.

In the end Hopper brings the movie—and American history—full circle. The Chinchero Indians take over the western town created by the Hollywood film company, create their own movie equipment, and make their own movie. In order to reclaim their native land and religion, they return to pre-Christian forms of celebration, which include ritual sacrifice. Not understanding that moviemaking is "pretend," they assume that when the Hollywood cowboys shot each other, they died; that is, that there were actual consequences to violent actions. Hopper has the Peruvian "director" and his crew claim they are making a real movie with their fake equipment, while Kansas tries to explain to them that the real equipment the Hollywood company used was filming faked violence and death. The Peruvian

Outtake from *The Last Movie.*
Photo courtesy of the Museum of Modern Art,
Photo Stills Archive, New York.
(Dennis joining the Indian fiesta.)

director names the village's movie *La Ultima Pelicula* (*The Last Movie*) and dubs Kansas "the dead man." In what promises to be the climactic scene of the Indians' movie, Kansas will presumably die to pay for the white man's five hundred years of genocide.

Preceding this there is a fiesta scene in which the movie equipment is turned into firecracker propellers, and the actors dance and play in the streets wearing animal masks, much to the chagrin of the local priest who feels his church has been mocked and that the movies have brought devilish ruin to his people. The Indians are finally taking back their own by appropriating the tools of their erstwhile capitalist conquerors, the rich gringos of whom both Maria and the Peruvian director speak with undisguised contempt.

In a *Life* magazine interview he did while on location in Peru, Hopper claimed this was one of the intended readings for his film:

Outtake from *The Last Movie.*
Photo courtesy of the Museum of Modern Art,
Photo Stills Archive, New York.
(Dennis being taken to his "crucifixion.")

It's a story about America and how it's destroying itself. The hero . . . [is] Mr. Middle America. He dreams of big cars, swimming pools, gorgeous girls. He's so innocent. He doesn't realize he's living out a myth, nailing himself to a cross of gold. But the Indians realize it. They stand for the world as it really is, and they see the lousy western for what it really was, a tragic legend of greed and violence in which everybody died at the end. So they build a camera out of junk and re-enact the movie as a religious rite. To play the victim in the ceremony, they pick the stunt man. The end is far-out.

Hopper suggested that the Indians have taken what had become a decadent and life-denying art form and translated it into powerful religiocultural enactment. His appreciation of their premodern sense of the power of art is uncannily similar to the view of tribal ceremonials shared by Luhan and her modernist colleagues.[6]

But Hopper's need to underscore the illusory nature of movies betrayed much of the potentially powerful politics of the film. When Kansas is wounded by a bullet during the fiesta, Hopper comes out of character, replays the scene several times, and asks at one point where his "bloody scar" is. The priest also comes out of character and begins to laugh, while Stella Garcia, the actress who plays Maria, performs cheesecake publicity poses for the film that isn't finished yet. A "scene missing" cue is flashed on the screen, and the movie ends in indeterminacy. Meanwhile, the Peruvian director is acting like a dictator who is no better morally than the Hollywood director he replaces.

The Last Movie can be interpreted as representing the shift that took place from late modernist to postmodernist perspectives in the war-torn decade it climaxed. Hopper's art, and art collection, had always been closely related to those elements of the modernist aesthetic that derived from Surrealism and Dada and thus were closest to the postmodern sensibility—chance, disjunction, fragmentation, collage, a questioning of the boundaries between art and life, truth and fiction, and a fierce determination to violate these boundaries. In *The Last Movie* he gives these ideas full play, ending up with a film that reflects the divided meanings of the postmodern condition and its aesthetics. Hopper's film shows its "revolutionary potential by virtue of its opposition to all forms of meta-narratives . . . and its close attention to 'other worlds' and to 'other voices' that have for too long been silenced." At the same time, however, he is so obsessed with "deconstructing and delegitimating every form of argument" that he ends up negating every claim to validity "to the point where nothing remains of any basis for reasoned action."[7]

Although he seems to empower them, Hopper is equivocal about the minority "voices" that "take over" in his movie. Like D. H. Lawrence before him, Hopper advocated the return of the land stolen by the white fathers to the Indians in order to redeem the West from the blood guilt of the past. (Like Lawrence, he also displaced the story of this guilt from the United States onto Latin American soil.) But while Hopper was less racist than Lawrence, his Indians are little more than stereotypes. They are portrayed as having neither the will nor the intelligence to transcend their "primitive" way of living, except, as in the instances of Maria and the director, by taking on the corrupt attributes of their oppressors. Like *Easy Rider,* but with much more at stake, *The Last Movie* fails because Hopper could not imagine anything beyond the myths and clichés he set out to deconstruct.

It is little wonder that critics and public alike found the aesthetics of Hopper's film impenetrable and its politics unfathomable. He wanted to create an avant-garde film that would transform popular consciousness. But his profound contempt for Hollywood—and, more importantly, its audiences—overrode and buried his radical populist impulses. The film did, indeed, become his "passion," although not in the way that he had intended. Hopper's confused intentions for the film can be seen even more clearly when one examines the making of *The Last Movie,* which replicated some of the very American practices he excoriated in his movie and in the nation at large.

Hopper came to Peru itching to attack the Peruvian government and the Roman Catholic church. No sooner had he landed, than he announced in a press interview that he endorsed pot smoking and homosexuality, and that he lived with a lesbian and enjoyed it. According to *Life* magazine, the clergy and junta were kept outraged by continual rumors about the Hopper entourage's coke snorting, pot smoking, and "whipping parties." Hopper apparently learned a few words of Quechua, as a courtesy to the natives, and promised to leave the whole set, along with building and medical supplies, when the movie was done so that the townspeople could use them for their own purposes. *Esquire's* reporter explained, "He has been told by community leaders that this will help free the people from the power of the priest; they will be able to build a school. . . . 'They're gonna get their town together, man, they're gonna break with that priest and stand on their own.'" Another actor was more explicit: "This movie, man, has shown them the way to revolution!"[8]

A visiting American anthropologist, who was teaching at the University of Cuzco at the time *The Last Movie* was made, saw it as an unambiguous travesty: "The most common complaint concerns the lack of respect shown for local customs and the insensibility of the company toward the problems of the people. Protests have been made that natural settings have been used without payment. The villagers say that the crew has interfered with the performance of rituals. They feel that once again Peruvians are being exploited—this time by a wild group of perverts, Manson-look-alikes with beards and long hair." When he moved to Taos, Hopper also hoped to play the role of liberator to the locals, only to find himself identified as a leader of "the wild-eyed group of perverts" who were despoiling the community.[9]

Communal Dreams

Today, Hopper feels that most of the nine years he owned the Luhan house were wasted time in terms of the downward trajectory of his career

Dennis Hopper in front of Luhan House, n.d.
Photo courtesy of Walter Chappell.

and his personal life: "I think it was really desperate, desperate times. I wasn't really creating. I wasn't really doing anything creative most of the time I was there . . . with the big exception of *The Last Movie,* but after that . . . it was just a lot of bravado and there wasn't anything behind it, because I didn't have any work, so I find that rather pathetic." At the same

Dennis and David Hopper editing *The Last Movie*, n.d.
Photo courtesy of Douglas Magnus.

time, he believes he should share some of the status of the legendary Luhan-Lawrence team that preceded him. "During that period of time, I certainly wasn't Mabel Dodge Luhan but, not to blow smoke around, I must say that probably during the nine years that I was in the house, as many influential people of our time came as Mabel had in that house. And I get a little funny when I go back to Taos and I hear about Lawrence and I hear about Mabel . . . and realize the people that I had in the house and that came there, from McGovern announcing his presidency to God knows what."[10]

Although Hopper's many stories about his time in Taos include some rather tall tales, including the statement that George McGovern announced his candidacy for president there, it is nonetheless true that many notables did pass through the adobe gates of the Mud Palace, including McGovern. It is also true that during Hopper's first year at the Luhan house, the realities of what happened there were at least as fantastic as the legends that he and others would later create about them.

Percy Sandy, *Rainbow Man,* portal, Luhan House.
Photo courtesy of Previews, Inc.

Hopper started off in the right direction, at least in terms of how he took care of the Luhan house, which had fallen into a state of disrepair and which he wished to restore as closely as possible to the way it was when Mabel was in her heyday. (At one point he considered putting a large neon sign on top of the house that said Hopper's Mud Palace, with lights flashing on and off, but he thought better of it.) Dennis spent about eighty thousand dollars to repair collapsed roofs and fallen walls, to install two new septic systems, and to remodel the house to fit its new needs—adding three bedrooms, two bathrooms, a kitchenette apartment in the gatehouse, and converting the log cabin into an editing room. The Awa Tsireh mural that had faded was restored by a Zuni Indian, Percy Sandy, who also designed an original mural of the Rainbow Man on the opposite portal wall. All of the hired labor came from Taos Pueblo and included many families connected with Mabel and Tony—Eliseo Concha, who had built the fireplace in the dining room, Frank Concha, Abe and Annie Trujillo, and Frank

Laura Gilpin, *Portraits—Dennis Hopper,* c. 1970s.
© 1981, Laura Gilpin Collection.
Photo courtesy of Amon Carter Museum, Fort Worth, Texas.
(Hopper is holding a lithograph by Bruce Connor.)

Gomez, who did many of the decorative wall paintings that were scattered throughout the house.

Like Luhan, Dennis Hopper saw his world as a stage on which creativity was in a constant process of happening. As David put it, "Every time Dennis has ever had any money, he has put it into creative space and acquiring the spaces and trying to develop them for use." Where Mabel hung the work of some of the best early American modernists, Hopper hung the works of some of the best late modernists and early postmodernists. Although most of his paintings went to Brooke in their divorce settlement before he moved to Taos, he was still able to pack the Big House to capacity with the works of Andy Warhol (a *Dracula,* a *Madonna,* and a poster from a 1968 Stockholm exhibit in which Warhol is quoted as saying "I never read. I just look at pictures"), Bruce Connor, Ed Ruscha, Walter Berman, Jasper Johns, Roy

Lichtenstein *(Rocket Ships),* Claes Oldenberg, Larry Rivers *(Mona Lisa),* Robert Rauschenberg, Ed Kienholz, and Ad Rinehart *(Black Cross).*

In one corner of Mabel's dining room stood Tony Price's *Mad Scientist Machine* with its ball of pulsating purple lightning that sent off forty thousand watts with each bolt. At the other end of the room was Dennis's *Bomb Drop,* with its seven-foot-long phallic lever. During his years in Taos, Dennis accrued an eclectic collection of folk art that was strewn about the Big House in much the same way that Mabel had mixed her Florentine treasures and brocaded couches with kiva stools and Buddhas: Peruvian Masks, Mexican Trees of Life, Navajo rugs, and a large array of santos, retablos, and Penitente death carts, one of which apparently followed Dennis around the house when he was stoned.

Hopper's visitors were almost as eclectic as his art collection, although they tended much more to the pop culture scene than the elite artists and writers of the Luhan circle. Few of them, however, seemed to have stayed very long or taken creative inspiration from the house or the northern New Mexico landscape, with the notable exceptions of five artist friends who had been part of the L.A. scene in the 1960s—Ken Price, Tony Price, Ron Cooper, Bill Gersh, and Larry Bell. There were some links to Luhan's Taos in the visits of Georgia O'Keeffe and Dorothy Brett, who regaled the Hoppers with stories of the olden days. David recounted one funny story Brett told him about D. H. Lawrence. After taking too much peyote, Lawrence purportedly turned into a coyote. He took off all his clothes and had to be chained to the storehouse in Mabel's courtyard, where he howled until the drug wore off. (David was also told that Lawrence's ashes had been dumped into the acequia.)

Visitors to the Mud Palace included musicians, such as the Everly Brothers, Bo Diddley, Bob Dylan, Kris Kristofferson, and Leonard Cohen, who wrote the lyrics for many of the songs used in the soundtrack for *The Last Movie;* avant-garde artists Bruce Connor and Alan Watts, the beat poet-philosopher; actors, such as John Wayne, Peter Fonda, Jack Nicholson (who came dressed all in black sporting a cape), Susan St. James, Carrie Snodgrass, Warren Oates, Dean Stockwell, Nicholas Ray (director of *Rebel Without a Cause*); filmmakers and art curators Alejandro Jaderowosky (the Russian-Chilean producer of the macabre *El Topo*), Henry Geldzahler of the Metropolitan Museum of Art, and Walter Hopps; politicians David Cargo, governor of New Mexico, and George McGovern; and radical activists Kathleen Cleaver, Paul Krassner, and Reies Tijerina.

One of the more bizarre of the longer-term visitors was the psychic Peter Hurkos, the Dutch immigrant who had been brought in to help solve the Boston Strangler murders. He lived at the house for three months while Hopper contemplated making a film biography of him. According to David Hopper and Tony Price, Hurkos claimed he discovered a secret chamber in the Sacred Mountain, after being taken on a flight over the Sangre de Cristos. Inside that chamber were ancient bodies suspended in ozone, and underneath the chamber ran enough water to irrigate the entire state of New Mexico. David says Hurkos gave him a painting he did of the cave entrance that led to the secret chamber.

These weren't the only secrets that Hurkos ferreted out, as he gained a reputation for being an adept reader of the intimate lives of the family and visitors who kept the Mud Palace humming with wife and lover swapping, and sometimes orgies of sex, drugs, and drink. Hopper raised Luhan's propensity for creating live action drama beyond anything she could have imagined. She had worked to generate creativity from the clash of spirits surrounding her, sometimes by selfishly manipulating those lives to serve her needs and purposes, and sometimes by generously allowing those lives to take what shape they willed. She had enjoyed playing a game called Truth, in which she prodded her guests to self-revelation and revelations of their feelings about others that could be cruel and painful. And she often brought together guests of opposing beliefs and temperaments in order to see what sparks might fly from their confrontations.

Hopper played similar games. Sometimes these games were casual fun, part of the continuing "scene" of reality-unreality that was related to his art and to his desire to subvert mainstream notions of proper behavior. At other times, however, these games were dangerous, and where his female intimates were concerned, they at times turned violent. David described Hopper's methods of playacting as being related both to his advocacy of Method Acting and to sensitivity encounter, which grew out of the 1960s hip psychologies that emphasized the breaking down of individuals' inhibitions in order to help them better relate in groups. Dennis used the same techniques on camera and off, making no distinctions between art and life: "He gets performances out of people by pulling their strings and he knows his own pretty well; he's a pretty good behavioral scientist."

In making movies, Dennis rarely worked from a prepared script; instead, he would let the scene be created among the actors and director. Because he wanted everything in front of the camera to be "real," he used en-

Dennis Hopper and Michelle Phillips in Mabel Dodge Luhan's bedroom, n.d. Photo courtesy of Walter Chappell.

counter techniques to move an actor "off his shit." "Dennis will screw him up, trip him in delivery or whatever until if anything they just break down in not being able to do the structure that they know." Hopper behaved the same way at home. He loved to mix people with conflicting political and social points of view, for example, inviting to dinner Paul Krassner, editor of the radical magazine *The Realist,* and David Cargo, the conservative Republican governor of New Mexico. Cargo must have had to swallow a great deal of distaste in courting Hopper as part of a plan to bring in the film industry to help his state's lagging economy. The one thing all the guests had in common was that they liked to drink.

Hopper's more playful side can be seen in a piece that Tricia Hurst wrote about his early arrival in Taos, the community's reaction to it, and his daily household activities. How he dressed depended entirely on the day and his mood. When Hurst first visited the house, she found everyone dressed in jeans, fur hats, and ponchos, except for Dennis, who was in a Confederate Soldier's uniform, and Michelle Phillips, who was dressed as a southern belle. The electricity was on the fritz, and the diapers of the household's babies were drying on the *Mad Scientist Machine,* while the staff made preparations for George McGovern, who was coming to dinner.[11]

Hurst described the wild wedding that Dennis and Michelle Phillips staged on Halloween night in 1970, when they brought two hundred guests into the house to witness their marriage, lit 150 candles that almost burned down the house, and had their ceremony read from *The Gospel According to Thomas.* Hopper quickly made himself noteworthy by his generosity, allowing the "good ladies" of Taos to give a "tea party" at his "pad," lending his house to raise money for the Taos Artists Association, and giving away large sums of money to friends who were down on their luck. Hurst ended her article by posing the questions that everyone was asking about the meaning of Hopper's entrance into Taos society: "With a chameleon-like quality he choreographs the dance and the players know their parts. But the question still remains. Is he a hopped-up would-be Hippie, a true creative talent, a young genius, a Lord of the Manor, a desirable good neighbor, a Man destined for doom? Or, very simply, maybe just the loneliest man in town!"[12]

Hurst was right on the mark about Hopper's essential loneliness, which no amount of surrounding himself with lovers, family, friends, and visitors could repair. His marriage to Michelle Phillips lasted exactly one week, when she went on the road and called home to say she wasn't coming back. Michelle told Dennis that she didn't want to spend her youth in Taos, and that she didn't like the scene he was creating around himself. When Hopper asked her what he should do, she purportedly asked him if he ever thought of committing suicide. Hopper's self-destructive behavior, marked by increasing alcohol and drug abuse during his years in Taos, may well have been related to his feelings of loss when Phillips left. It is likely that Hopper experienced Phillips's rejection as part of a lifelong betrayal by women that began with his mother's emotional abandonment of him, although it was his violent behavior that seems to have been the primary cause of most of these leave-takings.[13]

When his first wife, Brooke Hayward, was asked what she thought of his role in *Blue Velvet* (1986), where he plays a psychopathic sexual abuser, she said that Dennis could have been seen behaving like Frank at various times throughout the 1960s. Several informants in Taos spoke to me of Hopper's propensity, especially when drunk, to go after any woman within reach, including preadolescent girls, and of his abusive behavior toward women. When I asked one former lover about her relationship with Hopper, she refused to discuss it with me, saying that for her to speak of it would be like asking a Jewish concentration camp survivor to talk about Auschwitz.[14]

Owen Orr, Nancy Gagliano, and unidentified friend in courtyard of Luhan House. Photo courtesy of Walter Chappell.

Hopper did have relationships with women who weren't his lovers in which the very opposite was true—courtesy, gentleness, and mutual respect marked his friendships with photographer Lisa Law and gallery owner Tally Richards. There is little doubt, however, that Hopper treated most women as sex objects or servants rather than as equals. His former sister-in-law, Charlotte Hopper, who headed the female crew that kept the Mud Palace running its first year, talked about how the women were on call day and night to provide food and drink for the all-male film crew, and for any other men on the premises. When she asked Dennis to acknowledge the crucial role that "the ladies of the house" had played as support staff during the fourteen months of editing *The Last Movie,* he refused to put their names in the credits.[15]

As for Tricia Hurst's questions about whether Dennis was a "true creative talent" and "desirable good neighbor," he had high hopes of proving so by putting Taos on the film map with his *Last Movie.* Some of the town fathers went out of their way to get local support for Hopper: "The local radio station tried to sort things out one morning when it asked compadres to try to distinguish between those newcomers who wore strange clothes and had long hair and were a menace to the social health of the community and those newcomers who wore strange clothes and long hair and were our beautiful friends from Hollywood." David Cargo made equipment, such as helicopters, available to Hopper.[16]

Even before Hopper moved to Taos, the film revolution he touted was being prophesied in the local hippie paper as the means to significant social change. Writing in the August 1969 *Fountain of Light,* Roger Sindell spoke of "Taos as a nexus of the planet . . . [where] minute amounts of matter release vast energy stores." These stores were waiting to be harnessed by the filmmakers who were leaving L.A. and New York and "the games of career, success, and personality." John Nichols recalled Dennis's hoped for role in this revolution:

He was supposed to be the great white hope. He was going to make these connections between middle-class Anglos, Hollywood, local people. He was going to be politically involved and set up a film studio where local people, independent filmmakers, could make movies, you know, about their struggle, the struggle about the culture, and all that kind of stuff . . . that was the riff or the dream or something. . . . But you know, for a person of some kind of stature to come into a place like this and have some kind of value they need to be extraordinarily sensitive and in control and tuned in to the area. Dennis didn't have any of that.[17]

It didn't quite "end for Dennis," as Nichols claims, within a few weeks of his arrival. But it is true that when, on the evening of June 16, Hopper got into an argument with some local youths and pulled a gun, his actions had serious and negative consequences, both for himself and the wider Taos community. The incident that triggered these events took place one evening when Hopper, his brother, and two friends, Owen Orr and Ted Markland, were on El Salto Road in Arroyo Seco, apparently heading for the cave that D. H. Lawrence had borrowed to sacrifice Mabel Luhan to the Indian gods in his story "The Woman Who Rode Away." When they stopped to ask some teenagers directions, they were accosted by them. Dennis told them that his brother was married to a Mexican, which only further enraged them. Dennis then pulled out his gun and attempted to make what he called "a citizen's arrest." What happened after that seems to depend on who is doing the telling, and to have escalated over the years in each of Hopper's retellings.[18]

According to Dennis's most recent account, "That day when I knocked the kid out and kicked through the steering wheel and pulled out a gun to hold these six kids, . . . there were like over one hundred farmers with pitchforks and shovels surrounding us." When the police arrived, Dennis told them his life was in danger, and the police allegedly responded, "Shut up, gringo." "When we were in the jail . . . the lynch mob came to get us and the police said we can't hold you any more . . . we're letting you out the back. . . . And then I went the next day and called all my friends, stunt men, ex-marines, to come to Taos and we went into town and bought every rifle and semiautomatic gun we could find." As a result of the citizen's arrest, Dennis was arraigned on charges of assault with a deadly weapon and released on two thousand dollars bond.[19]

Even before this incident, Hopper's brother and sister-in-law and their children had been threatened with rape and beatings by local Hispanic youth. Charlotte was called names and harassed when she and her family walked around town; as a result, she carried a gun in her purse. But she also recalls that the Hoppers met with the parents of the youths whom Hopper tried to arrest and told them that they wanted to work in Taos, that they loved the place and wanted to get along. She recognized that they were making "a big splash in a little pond," one that made a lot of waves because of the poverty in Taos, which contrasted with their material display.

Dennis was not exaggerating when he said that he turned the Luhan house into an armed encampment. Several visitors remember gun patrols on the roof and security guards communicating with one another through walkie-talkies. Hopper also claims to have gone into the high school to warn the kids that more "freaks" were coming, "only these were from Viet Nam, not members of the 'love generation.' . . . I explained to them, 'Macho is macho, and if this keeps up, somebody is going to get hurt around here. Just because these hippies are dropping acid, that doesn't give you the right to rape their women and cut their balls off.' " To show he meant business, he claims that he and David brought automatic rifles with them, which they pulled out from under their ponchos.[20]

In an attempt to further protect himself—and to make amends to the community—Hopper became involved in a number of local political efforts. He bought the El Cortez movie theater in Ranchos de Taos, which he used for the double purpose of showing avant-garde films—the proceeds going to the Blue Lake Fund—and for providing the community children with free Disney cartoons on the weekends. Dennis also helped raise funds for Blue Lake through some of his Hollywood-Washington contacts, including Jacob and Marian Javitz whom he says he brought to the house "to get behind it." He supported La Raza and took to wearing the small gold coyote-head pin that was its emblem. Hopper befriended Reies Tijerina and sought his protection, as another means of diffusing the volatile situation. "Reies put out the word that anybody who touched me was going to have to deal with him."[21]

Dennis housed the Teatro Campesino, the irreverent guerilla theatre that grew out of the United Farm Workers' grape boycott in California, and he paid one hundred dollars for the rental of the Old Martinez Hall in Ranchos de Taos where they performed. Luis Valdez, the founder of the troupe, had grown up in the fields of Delano, the child of migrant workers. Valdez created a kind of "commedia del arte of the farm workers," using the untrained workers to put on bilingual morality plays at roadside picket lines and makeshift union halls that reflected the lives and struggles of the poorest Chicanos. Hopper must have been attracted to Valdez's belief in the prophetic and religious role of art, which he traced back to the Aztec "belief in the power of the arts to remake man." The Teatro's performance in Taos was "a strong affirmation of Chicano culture and Chicano pride."[22]

John Nichols is convinced that Hopper became a pawn in the game that the Anglo and Hispanic power structures were using to help foment hatred between hippies and Hispanics, just at the moment when it looked like a productive alliance might be formed between them: "It is likely that in part the Hippie-Chicano feud was born in hopes that it would divert attention away from the implications of the Tierra Amarilla courthouse raid and various Forest Service sign burnings in Rio Arriba County, incidents which were bringing home to the state's power structure and to America the plight of the Chicano poor, their bitterness about it, and their refusal to accept oppression any longer."[23]

Los Trabajadores was negotiating with Goddard College about the possibility of setting up an accredited college to educate poor Chicanos and Indians; the Teatro Campesino had aroused local Chicano pride; a film crew had come in to make a documentary, and La Raza got an agreement for a percentage of the profits to go to a nonprofit Chicano and Indian educational fund set up by Los Trabajadores. Hopper had committed himself to help teach the local Hispanics something about filmmaking, and the Blue Lake controversy was about to be resolved.

Nichols believes that a state police undercover agent was brought in during the late summer and early fall of 1970 to engage in provocateur activities. The agent told Hopper of "the holocaust that was to hit Taos—the militiamen had bought twenty four-wheel-drive vehicles which they were going to drive into Taos, armed to the teeth. Once inside the city limits they planned to dynamite all exits leading out of town and take over." Hopper was further informed that he "was high on the list to be assassinated, and that one of [his] friends—who was probably the most effective spokesman for Trabajadores and to whom Hopper had given money for the rental of the Martinez Hall—was a member of the militia that had drawn up the death list." In 1972, Nichols wrote in the *New Mexico Review* that as a result of the lies spread by this agent "the ability of Chicanos, Indians, and Anglos to work together and trust each other was seriously impaired. In particular, the relationship between Dennis Hopper, a man who could add much to the educational experience in Taos, and the local people, who could benefit greatly from Hopper's aid and experience, was partially destroyed by mutual confusion and mistrust."[24]

Given what we now know about the FBI's infiltration of many liberal-left organizations in the 1960s, in particular, their COINTELPRO (Counterintelligence Programs) operation against the Black Panther Party and the American Indian Movement (which involved the fabrication of evidence, the spread of disinformation, and the use of infiltrators and agent provocateurs to disrupt these organizations and create suspicion and distrust among potential allies), there is reason to believe that similar activities occurred in Taos at this time. Charlotte Hopper remembers a state undercover agent living at the house during the summer of 1970, and Dennis admits to calling in the FBI himself, for protection, because if the militants were going to "hit him," he believed they would have to come from the Indian land behind the house. He also claims that he realized he was under surveillance by the FBI, but that he used his knowledge of their activities to warn his Chicano friends of what was happening. "I made the community aware of what was going on. I blew their cover right out."[25]

Two years after these events, Hopper still found himself and his family subject to attack by Hispanics in Taos County. When he and his seven-month's pregnant wife, Daria Halprin, went out to Tierra Amarilla with Reies Tijerina in the same car, some locals came up, threw her on the ground, and started to beat him up. Hopper continued to look for ways in which he could integrate himself into the Taos community, but although he stayed in Taos for nine years and was active at various times in the community, he never really found a niche for himself. In retrospect, he understands why he became a lightning rod for so much of the tension and violence that were both latent and real in the community. "I symbolized the fact that I could be bringing other people with me. They didn't want that to happen. They didn't care what it took to keep me saying 'This is a dangerous place.' And it is a dangerous place."[26]

Ghosts

It wasn't only the local community that was giving Hopper troubles. He and his brother and sister-in-law moved out of the Big House after about a year, driven out by what David and Charlotte insist were ghosts—of Tony, Mabel, and local Indians. Charlotte remembers her baby daughter, who was just beginning to talk, pointing at the window in Tony's room and saying "Indian." She and David separately recounted stories of not being able to heat Mabel's room, of hearing people walking and talking in Mabel's room when no one was there, of doors opening and shutting, and of chairs moving and doorknobs jiggling at odd times of the day or night. One evening David awoke to see a woman in white standing by the fireplace.

Mabel seems to have kept her promise to Alice Sprague that she would punish "whatever uncouth or vulgar people have gotten there by mistake." She made her presence felt when Dennis's guests overindulged in drugs and drink and started to bad-mouth her—by knocking paintings off the walls onto the heads of her abusers. She is also rumored to have driven Dennis out of the house, although he claims, "It was more like Tony saying, 'Why don't you come over where I live, out of this insanity?'" David says that he was told by Frank Waters that he should burn "copal" in order to get rid of the ghosts, but apparently this ghost-busting technique didn't work.[27]

Dennis insisted that he had to leave because he didn't seem able to close the house to the hordes of visitors who continually occupied it. The Mud Palace suffered from the same syndrome as the open communes in Taos County—by not turning people away, the space ultimately became uninhabitable: "It was too crazy there. I was too paranoid for it. I'd come downstairs to get something out of the icebox and there'd be thirty people there I'd never seen before. I'd look at the thing and say where's the orange juice and they'd say, 'Who are you?' . . . It was just like open house for anyone who was hungry." The Big House remained occupied until 1977 by visitors, friends, film crews, and various individual artists, artist collectives, rock bands, and random visitors. After selling the Big House in January 1978, Dennis rented the Tony House until 1984, and he continued to make forays into the community with a variety of projects. He also spent a good deal of time abroad working in films, mostly for foreign directors, who still saw him as an important American actor.[28]

American Dreamer

During his first year in Taos, Hopper starred in the underground film *American Dreamer* (1971), which focused on his iconographic role as a leading symbol of the counterculture. Produced by Larry Schiller, it was supposed to be shown only on a tour of college campuses. *American Dreamer* is repellent, tedious, and, intermittently, fascinating. Aesthetically on a par with a badly made home movie, it is nevertheless a revealing statement about the multiple ambiguities and contradictions of Hopper's persona. Hopper behaves in ways that transgress repressive social and gender norms, at the same time that he indulges in the most regressive kinds of sexual fantasies. Ultimately, he refuses to settle on any one among a variety of self-presentations: outlaw, hippie, artist, anarchist, playboy, and drug-tripper.[29]

Not long into the film, one can begin to believe that Mabel Luhan's ghost would have done its best to unseat Hopper from her home, particularly after a very wigged-out Hopper holds up to the camera a photograph of Frieda and D. H. Lawrence and proclaims, "Those were the original freaks here." Then there are the variety of sexual escapades that went well beyond the outer edge of Mabel's somewhat liberal sensibilities. We see Hopper and two women practicing oral sex in a bathtub. We see Hopper taking drugs and experiencing a group grope and sensitivity encounter with about twenty playgirls that Schiller brought in from Topanga Canyon in L.A., as he proclaims: "I'm God and I got this scene together because this is really the scene that I—God deserve."

Hopper's more politicized antics would have been equally unappealing to Luhan, although she might have appreciated his daily gun practice with a repeater rifle in which he used a photograph of J. Edgar Hoover's head as his target. (Thanks to Arthur Manby, Mabel had been subject to a Bureau investigation for purported subversive activities when she first moved to Taos.) Given her dismay at the atomic bomb project at Los Alamos, Mabel might also have understood the gesture of Dennis's walking naked down a suburban street in that town, his voice-over explaining that "taking your clothes off in scientific suburbia with the man who is doing all the big bombs and . . . his wife who he hopes is taking care of the children and him, . . . that was really far out symbolically."[30]

Dennis Hopper, n.d.
Photo courtesy of Walter Chappell.

The most disturbing element of *American Dreamer* is Hopper's simultaneous critique of various forms of oppression in American society—militarism, conformism, intolerance of sexual and artistic difference—and his celebration of forms of violence that are as perverse as the norms they seek to violate. What else can we call it but the politics of nihilism when Dennis speaks of his visiting Charles Manson in prison and blurs the differences between them, both by what he says and how he himself appears in many sequences during the movie. Eschewing any responsibility for his actions, Manson informed Hopper that he had felt he was acting his whole life, but without movie cameras. "If I'm your problem, if I'm your garbage, you made me your garbage."

There are a few haunting moments in the film, when some of the deep reservoirs of Hopper's lifelong pain are revealed. These come out mainly in the sound track. In the opening of the film, Hopper shows us a sepia-tinted family photograph and tells us: "I was very, very unhappy and lonely as a child, and I thought the only way I could stop being unhappy was to become something like an artist, something creative and so beautiful that everybody would say, Wow!" That Hopper is still working out his childhood hurt is evident in a song written by John Buck Wilkins. Wilkins answers the question "Can you ever let them know that you're a star?" with the anguished refrain, "Look at me mama,/Look at me papa,/Look at me,/ It's your boy." The song that best captures Hopper's contradictions is "American Dreamer," which describes him as

Sometimes a faker, sometimes a schemer,
Sometimes a lonely child, sometimes a wise man,
Sometimes a lonely soul, sometimes a great extremist,
But nonetheless the American Dreamer.[31]

Art and Activism

After the critical panning and withdrawal of *The Last Movie* in the fall of 1971, and the concomitant release and removal of *American Dreamer,* Hopper's career began a second downward spiral that eventually led him to various forms of suicidal behavior. This did not happen all at once, and at no time, except toward the very end when he became delusional and had to be institutionalized, did he completely stop performing—either in life or on screen. The tenacity with which he clung to Taos for almost nine years following the fiasco of *The Last Movie* is hard to comprehend. Even after the reestablishment of his career in 1985, he had his brother, David, refurbish the El Cortez theatre into a beautiful apartment and performance space, which he still visits sporadically, as he does the ranch he owns in Lindreth. (He used both as sets for his 1991 video release *Backtrack.*)

Hopper's years in Taos after 1971 did yield some creative and produc-

DENNIS HOPPER
Black and White Photographs
From the 1960's
July 10 through August 8, 1971
Opening Reception Friday, July 9, 9:00 to 11:00 P.M.
For Members, their Guests and Students
CORCORAN
GALLERY OF ART
17th Street and New York Avenue NW Washington DC 20006

Dennis Hopper poster for an exhibit of "Black and White Photographs from the 1960s," 1971, held at the Corcoran Gallery of Art, Washington, D. C.

tive ventures and friendships. He kept up his interest in the arts and, to a lesser degree, in progressive politics. One of the few serious segments of *American Dreamer* shows Dennis with Walter Hopps, looking over some seven thousand photographs that Hopper had taken during the 1960s for a national traveling exhibition that was being mounted of his work. Tally Richards, who first met Dennis in the fall of 1970, not long after opening her gallery of contemporary art, found his knowledge of the avant-garde

Tony Price, *Radioactive Christ,* Santa Fe, 1987.

very helpful to what she saw as a very risky endeavor: "Although I had lived in New York for years and 'felt' art, I was very insecure about having a gallery and being conversant in art. . . . Dennis was exciting to me because he was involved in a world I was simply acquainted with and wanted to know more about. . . . I don't know if what we had was a friendship, but he was supportive, generous, courteous, and understanding whenever I saw him."[32]

Dennis continued to patronize his artist friends from the L.A. school

Tony Price's *Revelations 9 and the Atomic Gongs* on the summer porch in the Luhan courtyard, 1970. Photo courtesy of Walter Chappell.

that he had associated with in the 1950s, some of whom were now living in Taos or Santa Fe. The most innovative of these was Tony Price, an American artist who took literally the biblical proscription of turning "swords into ploughshares." Starting in 1965, when he first came out to New Mexico, he began to buy up nuclear weapons parts that were discarded as salvage by the Los Alamos weapons lab and turn them into sometimes serious and sometimes satirical peace sculptures. He named many after the gods and myths of various world religions, as well as after contemporary political conflicts, for example, *Early Chinese Ancestral Nuclear Bird Bath, Nuclear Nitwit Totem, Angel of Nuclear Forgiveness, The Last Salt Talks*—and perhaps the most powerful one in his contemporary collection—*Radioactive Christ.*

Dennis purchased three or four of Price's creations, including an elaborate and multifaceted set of Tibetan Peace Gongs that were fashioned from used hydrogen bomb casings. Tony set the gongs up on Mabel's canopied summer porch, which stretched across the acequia in her courtyard across from the Big House, where they played a thirty-minute round of richly resonant music whenever they were struck. Price titled the piece *Revelations*

Kenneth Price, detail of *Death Shrine #3, Happy's Curios,* 1972–78.
Mixed media, 256.5 × 274.3 × 182.9 cm.
© 1994, the Art Institute of Chicago.
Restricted gift of Betsy and Andrew Rosenfield, 1981.2.

Nine, referring to a moment on the Day of Judgment when creatures with long hair appear like locusts out of the earth. Charles Manson also referred to this passage to predict his role in the Apocalypse.

One could picture Price and Manson as standing at the two extremes that mark the hippie-countercultural response to the looming apocalypse of total war: with Manson as the Prince of Darkness who lets forth the forces of evil to devour the earth, and Price as the Prince of Peace. In fact, Price believed that he was shamanistically diffusing the destructive energy of nuclear weapons by turning it into creative energy: "I was upset by the nuclear thing, and I thought of a way where I could affect it on an energies level. Conceptually, the idea was to neutralize the nuclear weapons by putting these polar energies together in one object." Like Tally Richards's relationship with Dennis, Tony's was also very positive: "I thought Dennis was a highly intelligent, really gifted and creative guy. He had a great sense of humor."[33]

Jackson Price with vase destroyed by collapsed roof in Luhan Carriage House studio, *Happy's Curios,* 1972.
Photo courtesy of Kenneth Price.

Another artist friend of Hopper's who combined a sense of humor with remarkable originality was the potter Kenneth Price, who first visited Dennis during the Luhan house's armed encampment phase. Ken remembers staying at the Tony House, with his wife, Happy, and that "everyone that Dennis had around him was armed. At the Big House during dinner that night Dennis fired his revolver through the roof." Price says that many of Dennis's friends thought that at the time that he was "courting a violent and glamorous death."[34]

The next year Ken and his wife bought a house in Talpa, where he began his series of quirky, irreverent plates, pots, and shrines that turned into a gallery-size display that he collectively titled *Happy's Curios.* Price used his craft and comic flair to pay homage to the low status of pottery in the art world and to the indigenous traditions of Mexican and American Indian folk pottery. Especially delightful are his cabinets surrounded by fences, which take off from the decorative tradition of the Hispanic death shrines, filled with cactus-shape cups and leeringly funny death's head mugs.[35]

In 1973, Dennis offered Price the use of the gatehouse and a kiln that

Bill Gersh's studio at the Magic Tortoise Commune, 1989.

had been built by the Southern Methodist University art students who had occupied the house in the summer. Price made some of his outsize vases there, but the kiln was poorly designed so he ended up moving back to his studio, north of El Prado. At various times during their three years in Taos, the Price family stayed in most of the Luhan houses, their favorite being the River House in Embudo.

Ron Cooper, *Dennis Hopper Looking at Ron Cooper Looking at Jasper Johns Looking at Marcel Duchamp*, 1989. Watercolor, gouache, wax, charcoal on rag paper, 21½ x 29 inches.

Of all his artist friends, Hopper had the greatest impact on Bill Gersh, whose expressionist sculptures and paintings have much the same satirical edge as his conversation. Bill credited Dennis with helping him get back to work after years of having given up painting: "When I came here there was very little going on with the creative juices that I really needed. . . . I always felt there was like a certain thing that if you would get around Dennis he would take you on these journeys . . . [that] would open you up further than you were already, you'd be involved in this world of acting, of expansion, of opening up your eyes a little more."

Bill described Hopper's "scene" as he remembers it: "You would walk into the place and you would see . . . one of Tony Price's atomic sculptures that was having a continuous erection, like it would go up, and it's eyes would light up. . . . And there's all this energy with people cooking, there's people who are left over from communes and have now assimilated into this scene." Gersh started painting again in 1977 and said that a lot of the impetus "was from Dennis's energy. . . . There was a lot of encouragement from him as another artist and there was a lot of feedback from him. . . .

Ron Cooper, *Portrait Vase—Hopper Head,* 1986.
Bronze on steel base.

The art I was making did not have a very responsive audience and when he would see it he would get charged up."[36]

Hopper's two other L.A. artist friends who moved to Taos are conceptual artists who have their origins in the California "light and space school"—Ron Cooper and Larry Bell. Cooper is one of Hopper's most articulate defenders: "The one most interesting thing about Dennis Hopper for me is his reverence for art and other artists, total reverence and respect for art itself and for its makers." Cooper's respect for Hopper can be seen in a contemporary portrait, in which he traces the evolution of twentieth-century art in the silhouetted profiles of Kandinsky, Duchamp, and

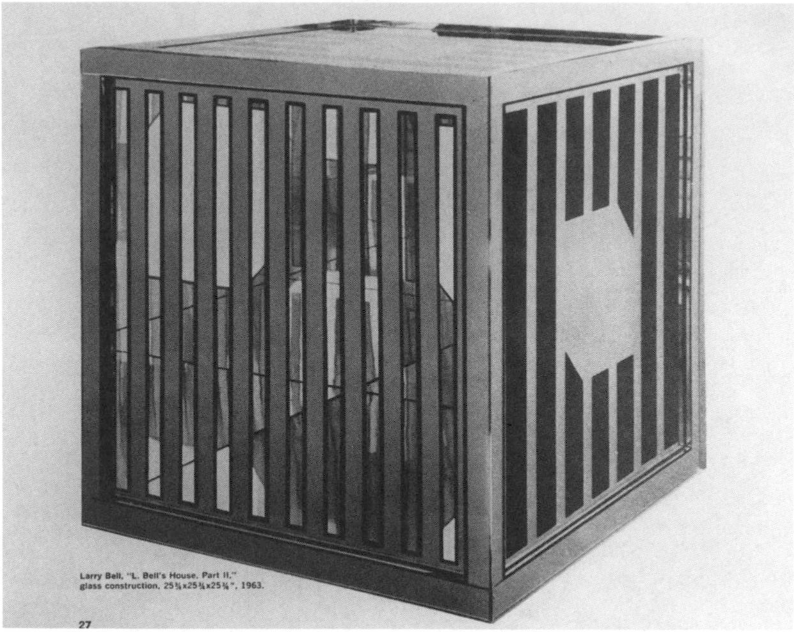

Larry Bell, *L. Bell's House, Part II,* 1962–63.
Mirrored glass, wood, 15 x 25 x 25 inches. Collection of the artist.
Photo by Frank Thomas.

Hopper. Although Hopper bought a lot of his work in the late 1980s, Cooper says that it his "spiritual support" for which he is most grateful.[37]

Cooper's description of his aesthetic shows his descent from the transcendental modernists of Luhan's generation who were drawn to Taos for exactly the same reasons. Light is "a mystery, an energy that is there but a nondefinable energy, the energy being very similar to the human spirit, the spirit of creativity and self-expression . . . not on a personal level but like creation." He has created lamps and vases that at first look like classic Greek designs, and then emerge as the profiles of famous people, when one focuses on what he calls their "negative space. . . . Where the profiles reflecting upon themselves create the lamps, the illumination provides a metaphor for thought, knowledge and understanding."[38]

Larry Bell, who is one of the best-known and most commercially successful artists living in Taos in the early nineties, also has much in common with Hopper and Cooper. All three exemplify the paradoxes of L.A. art, which has taken on its own peculiar resonance from the physical and cultural landscapes of New Mexico. Their work aims at the mystical spirituality of light, yet it is often created out of expensive and insistently ma-

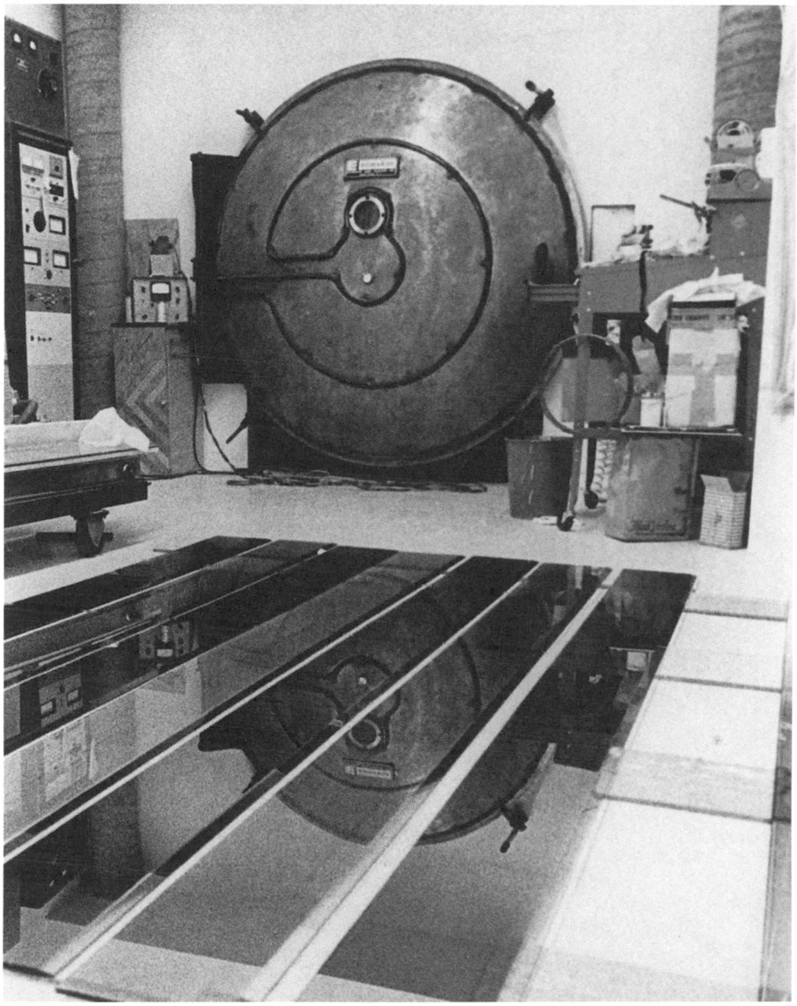

Larry Bell Studio, Taos, 1970s.
Photo courtesy of Larry Bell.

terial materials; they strive for a variety of perceptual illusions in order to unmask the illusory nature of both art and reality; and they seek the classical while being firmly embedded in contemporary techniques and technology. Bell first gained repute in the early 1960s with his glass boxes that were vacuum coated in order to "introduce extremely subtle variations of transparent color onto the surface of the glass." In a 1987 review of his work, he explained: "I like mystery. . . . The pieces I create include the environment. They reflect it, multiply it, transform it—but always engage with it."[39]

[From left to right] James Sternfeld, Katherine Loeffler, David Menongye [Hopi elder], Dennis Hopper, Susie Abbey on the Kaipoworitz Plateau, c. 1976. Photo by Karl Kernberger, courtesy of Jack Loeffler.

Bell first came out to Taos in 1973 to help a friend fix up a house and ended up staying. (Today his studio is one of the largest private buildings on the edge of town, with huge, factorylike spaces, massive ovens, and high-tech equipment). Bell told me that Dennis was one of the first people to buy his work when they both lived in L.A. He described Hopper as "an extremely gifted person," but says he was not too crazy about the "macho types" who were his cronies in the 1970s and thus pretty much kept away from the house.[40]

In 1972, Hopper opened a gallery in town called Dennis Hopper Works of Art, in which he tried, unsuccessfully, to introduce some of the artists he'd collected, like Andy Warhol and Ken Price, to the greater Taos community. In September of 1972, he held the first contemporary western exhibition of the sepia photogravure prints of Edward Curtis, which had been purchased in Boston by Jack Loeffler. Loeffler was desperately trying to keep his environmental action group, the Black Mesa Defense Fund (BMD), financially above water. Dennis heard he had the prints and offered to show them. The sale paid all the bills, although BMD did not last much longer.[41]

Dennis had been a fellow traveler of the BMD, contributing money and engaging in some of their militant protests against the Peabody Coal Company, which was strip mining Hopi Land. According to Loeffler, the group "brought a lot of the people who had been communal hippies into some sort of sense of activism again." They instigated several lawsuits (all of which they lost), and they also engaged in direct action tactics, such as forming brigades that chased down trucks and ran them off the road. In 1976, Dennis accompanied Loeffler to the Kaiparowitz Plateau, north of Lake Powell in Utah (which Edward Abbey called Lake Foul), where they successfully protested the potential development of the site for a power plant.

Hopper accompanied them to a meeting in Page of environmental activists, which included Abbey, Alvin Josephy, editor-in-chief of *American Heritage,* Grace Lichtenstein from the *New York Times,* and a one-hundred-year-old Hopi elder. When Dennis went out to dinner with a few of them that evening, he was arrested by federal agents because he was wearing an eagle feather in his cowboy hat—possession of eagle feathers being a crime for non-Indians. Hopper believes this was done to embarrass the organization. He was released and later was able to prove that he had been given the feather by a member of Taos Pueblo at a ceremony in which he and his brother were made honorary members of the Buffalo clan.[42]

In 1973 or 1974, when the IRS took much of Dennis's art for back taxes, he pretty much stopped collecting (until he made his comeback in the late 1980s). It was his brother, David, who created the most successful artistic venture of the Hoppers' time in Taos—the Return Gallery, which opened in 1977 and stayed in business until 1985. Return was one of those rare galleries graced with an architectural integrity that was as interesting as the best pieces of jewelry displayed within it. It was organized as a cooperative that included Hispanic, Native American, and Anglo craftspeople, including hippies who had stayed on to become serious artists.

A substantial portion of the jewelry at Return was made on the premises of the Luhan house, which was rented out in 1976 to a collaborative called the Sterling Smiths, headed by Pepe Rochon. There are those who remember the Sterling Smiths as having created a great deal of commercialized "junk

Jennifer Sihvonen displaying Larry Herrera/John Hernandez's Winged Scarab, at Luhan house, 1974.
Photo courtesy of David Hopper.

quality" silver jewelry, and at least one Taos artist who is convinced that their chief interest was in buying drugs, not in making art. But the quality of their best work was outstanding. Particularly notable was the metal and semiprecious-stone work of Samuel Quintana, Larry Herrera, and John Hernandez.[43]

Return was designed by David and Charlotte Hopper, and Chuck Banner, the wealthy son of Hollywood producer Bob Banner, who was responsible for much of the financial backing. It was intended to be a replication of the cosmos, with a ground floor divided into two rooms, nature and civilization. The nature room had a waterfall and fireplace, "with references to heaven and earth, as well as mountain and lake, all elements of the *I Ching.*" The civilization room was designed to conjure up images of Chaco Canyon, with the objects on display "like treasures buried in their original surroundings." The second level was a pyramid that contained an octagonal floor depression, like "the sipapu of a kiva."[44]

The gallery was also unusual because it meshed art and politics in ways that were rare in New Mexico in the 1970s, particularly in terms of the cross-fertilization of the triethnic cultures. Some of the Hispanic artists expressed a combination of traditional and hippie mysticism in work that they self-consciously saw as part of the politics of La Raza. Samuel Quintana described his work as Spiritual Surrealism, which was "rooted [both] in the struggle of the people . . . [and] the attempts of humankind to return again to life among the creative forces . . . to a higher spiritual consciousness." The gallery also gave women their due in a way that was rare during Taos's hippie days, with shows such as *Women's Work,* which displayed the craft skills of artists like Rachel Brown and Jennifer Sihvonen, who was the daughter of Joan Loveless, and was married to Pepe Rochon.[45]

Rochon and his fellow workers were noted for the inlaid belt buckles they created, using southwestern landscape and Native American motifs. Their most famous, or infamous, creation was the Bicentennial Concha Belt made by Pepe, Ed Morgan, and Jeff Morris at the Luhan house in 1976. It almost became the official "national" belt until it was discovered that its makers were Anglos, not Indians. The *Taos News* described it as "possibly the most valuable work of art ever produced in Taos." Made of silver and gold with inlaid turquoise, jet, lapis, coral, and ivory, depicting six flags that had flown over the country, and the Great Seal, it was valued at seventy-five thousand dollars. The belt was put on the market to "bring enough money to help sustain the artistic promise of the Mabel Dodge Luhan house."

Pepe Rochon working on the Bicentennial Belt, n.d.
Photo courtesy of David Hopper.

The artists were hoping it would be bought and donated to the Smithsonian by a generous person as "a permanent gift to the American people." Instead, the belt was stolen by a man who said he would sell it, and may have ended up in underworld hands. It has never been seen again.[46]

Hopper at the Movies

Although Dennis had pretty much given up his own use of the Mabel Luhan house by 1972, he did not give up on Taos as a center for filmmaking projects until the late 1970s. In the fall of 1972, he married Daria Halprin. Dennis intended to make movies with Daria, with whom he lived in the Tony House, while reserving the Big House for guests and employees and setting up an editing room in the El Cortez theatre. "For a while he believed that if he just held out long enough in Taos, the opportunities would come." But reports back to Hollywood described him as "an increasingly insane and drugged-out hippie [who] was more rebellious than ever." His increasing combination of drugs, alcohol, and mysticism gave him frightening hallucinations, including "visions of Lawrence's ghost wandering across the patio." Daria Halprin left him after two years and became a practicing clinical psychologist, perhaps motivated by his abusive behavior to her.[47]

Hopper continued to act in movies throughout the 1970s, mostly under foreign directors or those outside the Hollywood system. Despite the fact that almost all the roles he played had a clichéd antisocial edge, some of them contained elements of compelling political and social commentary on the state of the nation. In 1973, he starred in *Kid Blue,* "a social-comedy-tragedy" about a reformed outlaw who tries to go straight, and finds that he can't because of the "rampant capitalism" of American society. After that, the roles he played typically cast him as a mad man. His art more and more uncannily imitated his life, as well as the downward spiral of his country's moral and political life, especially as it was affected by the war in Vietnam.[48]

In Henry Jaglom's film *Tracks* (1976), Hopper played a mad sergeant who was assigned to escort the coffin of a fallen comrade home from Vietnam. The entire movie takes place on the train, which is used metaphorically as "a microcosm of America." Dennis's character, Jack Falen, "has no language with which to describe his experience in Vietnam." By the time he arrives at the train station, and no one is there to claim the body, he has been reduced to inarticulate rage. Not long after this, Hopper left for the Philippines to play the naive and spaced-out journalist who appears at the end of Francis Ford Coppola's antiwar film *Apocalypse Now* (1979) and tries to justify Kurtz's genocide of the Vietnamese.[49]

In between films, Hopper returned to Taos, even though his agent urged him to move back to Hollywood. He had come to be seen as increasingly bizarre and dangerous by most of the community, except perhaps by his artist friends and drinking buddies. In 1975, the *Taos News* noted that Hopper was arrested in Taos Plaza for carrying a .357 magnum and that he resisted arrest and was abusive to the arresting police officer. Three years later, from his drinking chair at the Sagebrush Inn, Hopper recounted his early years in Taos for Mark Goodman, who wrote up the interview in *New Times* under the rubric "Rebel Without a Pause." Although he had just sold the Luhan house, he continued to insist that "I never really felt like I had a home before, but now I do."

Goodman's description of the Tony House reads like a down-at-the-heels caricature of all the past lives Dennis had lived:

> *The tiny dirt courtyard is decorated with Mobil and Penzoil signs, filched signal lights, blue-and-white slot benches, an antique wooden stove. . . . The two-story interior I can only describe as* Aging Radical Gothic: *Pop art of Mao and Monroe, maps of the U.S. with Dennis and Fonda astride the land on their famous bikes, a PCI flag with hammer and sickle. There are Indian drums, serapes, madonnas, African devil masks, quotes from the Torah and Jesus on the cross in terrifying surrealism. . . . Just as Fellini thrives on juxtaposing pre-Christian and post-Christian Rome, so we have here the phantasmagoria of pre-civilization* America *. . . being inhabited by this savage totem of post-civilization* America.[50]

Hopper directed one movie during his final years in Taos that made his claim to create films that "torment the world" as it tormented him more than a self-inflated boast, *Out of the Blue* (1980). Canadian director Paul Lewis brought Hopper to Canada to help out when the film was in trouble. Hopper rewrote the script and roles, directed, and starred in it. It was the first important film over which he had control since *The Last Movie,* and he managed to create a powerful and coherent, if horrific, story out of the materials he reshaped.[51]

Hopper plays a trucker who is incestuously involved with his preteen daughter. The movie opens with him fondling her as he drives his rig into a school bus, killing most of the children. While he is in jail, his wife subsists by shooting heroin and taking a lover, and his daughter by becoming increasingly obsessed with Elvis Presley and punk rockers Sid Vicious and Johnny Rotten. When Hopper returns from prison, he tries to get a buddy of his to initiate his daughter, CeBe, into sex because he is disturbed by her dressing up in men's clothes. Instead, CeBe (nicknamed after the radio in a broken down bus that is parked in their back yard) entices her father to his death by dressing in lace panties and getting him to sniff her vagina, while she stabs him in the back with scissors. She then dynamites the bus with herself and her mother in it.

When the movie was released in the United States in 1982, Hopper responded to those who didn't like it, with atypical understatement, that it was a movie "about the society of North America; the family unit is falling apart. People who say all this doesn't exist in this country—where have they been?" The film was indeed prophetic of the increasing family violence of the 1980s that accompanied the economic and social decline of the Reagan-Bush era: "As the hippie ethos revolted against the basic values of middle-class society (work, the nuclear family, heterosexual monogamy, mindless conformity), punk is the despairing negation of both hippie self-delusion and bourgeois values."[52]

Although Hopper had small parts in a few other films in the early 1980s, his life in and out of Taos more and more came to imitate the no exit of *Out of the Blue.* In 1982–83, he was consuming half a gallon of rum, a few beers, and several grams of cocaine on a daily basis. He slept with a gun under his pillow, used it to challenge people who came to the house, and put bullet holes in several walls while shooting at "phantom intruders." When Rice University decided to put on a retrospective of his paintings and photographs in 1983, appropriately titled *Art on the Edge,* Hopper "celebrated" the event by performing what he called his Russian Suicide Death Chair Act. He placed himself in a chair surrounded by dynamite and had it set off. The "theory" was that he would either survive the blast—if all the dynamite exploded it would create a vacuum around him—or, he would be blown to bits.[53]

Hopper's drug and alcohol addictions were affecting his behavior in other ways. When he went to Mexico to film *Jungle Fever,* he hallucinated, stripped himself naked, and wandered around lost in the jungle, believing that he was Charles Manson. Some friends got him on a plane back to L.A. and checked him into an alcohol rehabilitation center. Terrified by the affects of the antipsychotic drug he was on, he called his lover, Ellen Archuleta, and had her drive him back to Taos. He stayed at the Tony House until early 1984, when he returned to Cedars-Sinai Hospital in L.A. and was put on heavy doses of Thorazine. His friend Bert Schneider "rescued" him, made him see a psychiatrist, and convinced him to join Alcoholics Anonymous.[54]

In 1985, Hopper was finally able to face his past. He reconciled with his mother and his daughters, and he went back to work. Toward the end of his rehabilitation period, when he was counseling other drug addicts and alcoholics, he told a reporter, "I work with people who've bottomed out and want a new life. I don't think people can stop until they've bottomed out, spiritually and morally, or they die. That's how they get off drugs." If Hopper ever came close to living up to the messianic image that he had pursued throughout much of his adult life, it was during this yearlong period when he literally recovered his life.[55]

With the release of *Blue Velvet,* in 1986, Hopper was welcomed, really for the first time in his career, into the arms of Hollywood. The mass media wasted no time in making the most of the drama of his story: "It's the hottest comeback. Dennis Hopper has risen from the ashes of a diabolical past. Four years ago he was in a strait-jacket; now he's headed again for stardom. . . . Hopper talks about his ride to hell and back." Interestingly enough, most of the films that Hopper has made since his comeback do not differ much from those he made during the 1970s and early 1980s. He has continued to probe the cancerous abscesses in American society that most of us would rather ignore, particularly when we go to the movies.[56]

In *Blue Velvet,* Hopper played a sadistic rapist who kidnaps the husband and child of a nightclub singer and uses his power over her to force her into obscenely humiliating sex games. David Lynch's interest here, as with his very popular television series *Twin Peaks,* has been to juxtapose the seemingly serene surface of upper-middle-class American family life with what he sees as its dark underpinnings of violence, sexual terrorism, and exploitation. A more successful and disturbing film that played on this theme was *River's Edge* (1987), although Hopper overacted his role as a drug-peddling, doped-up, ex-biker, who lives with a lifesize inflatable female doll. The movie's power lay partly in the fact that it was based on a real story that took place in a central California town, in which a boy killed his girlfriend and then showed her body to his friends, who helped him cover up the murder. As in *Out of the Blue,* the movie focuses on the psychological and social devastation of a society in which parents have no resources—either monetary or moral—to provide minimal supervision, let alone values for their children.[57]

In the early 1990s, Hopper made two comic-thrillers that refer back to his Taos years, and that offer some insights into the ambiguous roles he has played as an emblem of American popular culture. *Flashback* (1990) is a lightweight but often charming film, particularly for those of us who are both nostalgic about as well as critical of the 1960s. In the peculiar way that Hopper's life has often touched directly on his times, he was hired to play an Abbie Hoffman type who has gone underground and is trying to make a comeback by selling his memoirs. During the filming of the movie, Hoffman died, purportedly from an overdose of pills.

Hopper's character, Huey, has been all but forgotten. In an effort to create interest in his memoirs, he turns himself over to the FBI. The agent who comes for him, played by Kiefer Sutherland, is the child of hippies who had lived in a commune (Rainbow Zen) in Oregon. Originally named Free, he is now totally straight-arrow and uptight. As one might expect, Huey and Free become allies, but not until Dennis drugs him, and switches roles and clothes with him. Free ends up foiling a plot by the district attorney to kill both Huey and him in order to protect his job. When Hopper and Free flee to Rainbow Zen, its one remaining hippie artist (played by the zany Carol Kane) helps them escape in a bus once used to bring draft dodgers across the Canadian border during the Vietnam War. At the end of the film, Free takes off on a motorcycle down the California coast to "find himself," while Huey is seen walking out of City Lights bookstore in San Francisco, whose window is filled with copies of his now best-selling autobiography.

Backtrack (1992) is a more ambitious, but less satisfying film. It started life as a feature and was pulled by Hopper and released as a video when the studio insisted he delete its most interesting—and most bizarre scene. The film stars Jodie Foster, who plays Anne Benten, a Jenny Holzer–like conceptual artist (the art in the film is by Jenny Holzer). Anne inadvertently witnesses a Mafia assassination when she blows a tire on a highway outside L.A. She runs away and is stalked by Dennis Hopper, who plays Milo, a Mafia assassin hired to kill her (and who very unconvincingly falls in love with her).

The most engaging aspect of the film is Hopper's often witty exploration of the connections between postmodern art, organized crime, and contemporary American society. Anne's computer-generated LEDs (light-emitting diodes) turn out to be quite pointed signs of the times. As she tells an interviewer, some of her statements "have great resonance," and "others play off clichés." In the tradition of the Pop artists who preceded her, Anne's art contributes to and critiques a mass-mediated world of cognitive and sensory overload in which it is difficult to tell the meaningful from the meaningless. Anne is both a genuine and a con artist.

Hopper also creates an alliance between the Mafia and the police that underscores the ties between law and lawlessness that have often been intertwined in his films, and in American history. High tech not only allows Anne to maximize her profits by minimizing the amount of time that goes

Dennis Hopper and Jodie Foster during the filming of *Backtrack*, Albuquerque, 1988.
Photo courtesy of Lisa Law.

into her work, but it has also given the police and the mafia access to data, via computer networks and linkups, which make it easier for corruption to occur between them.

After Milo finds Anne, she flees to New Mexico and hides out in Hopper's renovated El Cortez theatre apartment, which is described by an in-joke in the film as belonging to "a loony art collector from El Paso." When Milo discovers his attraction to Anne, we see that the postmodern artist and the hit man are really brother and sister under the skin. Both are loners, disaffiliated from society and family, without real commitment to ideas or to people. Hopper underscores their symbolic plight in the scene that caused the conflict with his production company. A ceremonial, which takes place in back of the Ranchos de Taos Church and across from the El Cortez, combines a Penitente dragging an outsize cross, Indian deer and buffalo dancers, and a burning Zozobra, all enmeshed in a fireworks display. This is Hopper's satiric commentary on the 1980s, in which once affective religious rituals have no power in America except as pastiche and spectacle.[58]

At the end of the movie, Hopper makes dramatic use of the stark contrasts suggested by the ancient inhabitants of New Mexico and the latest tools for dealing death developed by western technology. Anne and Milo

Mabel Luhan's Florentine dining room table in Hopper's postmodern living room, Venice, California, 1988. Photo courtesy of Tim Street-Porter.

flee to Hopper's ranch in Lindreth, where they are safe only momentarily from pursuit. Milo outsmarts the car-posse that comes to get him by fleeing in a helicopter and engaging in what looks like a combat sequence from a Vietnam war film, except that it takes place over Chaco Canyon (which Milo explains to Anne was once "like fuckin' L.A."). Anne and Milo blow up some of "the family" here, and most of the rest in L.A. They then take off to New Zealand on a cargo boat, where they will presumably start a new life, Hopper's final ironic commentary on what it means to live in the postmodern global village.

As he approached sixty, Hopper seemed to have learned how to manage, if not resolve, the doubleness of his lifelong quest: to be perceived as a hard-working, more or less trustworthy and bankable artist, while thumbing his nose at the variety of establishments that have condemned him. He continues to live and work on an ambiguous edge. In 1986 he moved to Venice, California, where he built a home on the dividing line between L.A.'s affluent bohemia and a section known as the Ghetto. Upscale and newsworthy, it has been given spreads in *Vanity Fair,* as well as in the *New York Times* Home section.[59]

Hopper's house was built by Frank Gehry, and the interior designed by Brian Murphy, a "guerrilla designer," according to a friend of Dennis's who recommended him. As Mike Davis has pointed out, Gehry is the perfect "crossover . . . between older, vaguely radical and contemporary, basically cynical styles." So too is Hopper and his house, which looks like a concrete fortress on the outside, while its interiors reveal high, open spaces, with ceilings and walls of exposed wood. Just as Hopper earns his highest income in films that expose the worst of contemporary violence and "urban realism," Frank Gehry has made his reputation and fortune by learning "how to insert high property values and sumptuary spaces into decaying neighborhoods."[60]

Hopper has carried with him into his new home more than a little of his past, as some of his current films do. Along with a collection of the latest Ron Cooper conceptual pieces are Hopper's folk sculptures from Mexico, which he purchased while living in Taos, as well as Mabel Dodge Luhan's dining room table, at which Dennis sat during our second telephone interview. There is something else of Mabel's he's carried with him—a tenacity of spirit that is one of the more likeable qualities these two artists of life share. In her last years, when she was often ill, Mabel had a large-lettered sign placed on the wall across from her bed that read: "ENDURE! ENDURE! ENDURE!" Dennis had printed on the back of the director's chair he used in *Backtrack:* "Age and Treachery Will Win Out Every Time Over Youth and Skill."[61]

PART 3

Las Palomas de Taos (1978–1995)

From the beginning of her experiments with gathering people for open discussions, Mabel Dodge Luhan . . . was concerned with healing of body, mind, and soul, and on a larger scale of communities, societies, nations. Her thinking and the practice of open and free discussion . . . was the model for the institution of Las Palomas that was to be founded by George and Kitty Otero in 1978 on the grounds of her former home. . . . Las Palomas de Taos . . . maintains and creates programs which are a continuation of the global, multicultural concerns that animated Mrs. Luhan.
Las Palomas brochure, 1989–90

The Luhan house, its ambience and staff, have provided a backdrop for some of the most exciting educational development I have ever been associated with.
Robert Sparks, Principal, Green Mountain High School

CHAPTER SEVEN

Legacies of the Sixties

Few contemporary popular analysts are willing to concede that the 1960s produced much of permanent value. In its twenty-year anniversary issue on the counterculture, *Life* magazine was fairer than most when its editors acknowledged: "They wanted to change the world. And in unexpected ways, they did. They helped end the Vietnam War and began the women's movement. Their love of health food, [and] rock and roll, . . . turned those trends into mega-businesses; their fierce outspokenness about nuclear power and the environment and the arms race made those major political issues. They altered American consciousness forever."[1]

One of the most significant legacies of the 1960s is the impact that a generation's raised consciousness has had on schooling in American society. From kindergarten through graduate education, what students read and write about, teachers teach, and scholars publish has undergone a sea change unlike anything that has been experienced before in the history of American education. Whatever their philosophy, it has been all but impossible for universities and school systems over the past two decades not to be affected by the controversies swirling around the various new curricula and pedagogical practices that are under debate throughout the country. It is a measure of the force of these changes that they have been the subject of so much praise and vilification. The mass media, political institutions, religious organizations, professional associations, and a whole subgenre of the book industry have staked their claims on one side or other of what has been dubbed the "political correctness" debate.[2]

In the 1980s, the Mabel Dodge Luhan house achieved a position for itself as an important center of global education and school improvement, especially as they related to the broader ideals of building new kinds of communities that encouraged both personal growth and social responsibility. Under the aegis of Las Palomas, and in the tradition of Deweyan progressivism, these programs envisioned schools as a microcosm of American society that had the potential for modeling a genuinely democratic and pluralist nation. Las Palomas's mission has clear links with the past of the Luhan house, including the utopian dreams and the problematic tensions that have been part of it since its inception. Because their mission has also grown out of the communitarian, multiethnic, and New Age legacies of the 1960s, it is important to understand Las Palomas's place in the wider social and cultural contexts in which these evolved, particularly in Taos.

Taos in the 1980s

The economy, demography, and culture of Taos have not changed a great deal over the past thirty years, except to become increasingly Anglo dominated. (The 1990 census listed the population of the town of Taos as four thousand, and the county as twenty-three thousand.) Between 1975 and 1985, Anglos grew from 7 percent to 27 percent of the population and came to own half the land in Taos County. They dominated not just the tourist industry but real estate as well, with the result that land and homes increased dramatically in cost and value. There were 80 realtors in Taos in 1983; 135, two years later. An acre of irrigated land that sold for $600 in 1960 could sell for as much as $22,000 in 1984. Some Hispanics moved into real estate and banking, but most jobs are still service sector, low paying, and seasonal, with no benefits or security. There have been a few indicators of economic growth, but New Mexico still is one of the five states with the highest unemployment, and race and class are still strongly correlated—and segregated: "The long-manifest, privately acknowledged, yet almost never explicitly articulated ethnographic truth about Taos is its de facto segregation, which obtains virtually everywhere outside the everyday world of business."[3]

During the 1980s and 1990s, there has been intensified development, as tourist-inspired fast-food restaurants and shops on the outlying parts of town continue to encroach ever further north and south on the main highway. Some of this growth is related to the fact that an increasing number of native Taoseños have been forced by skyrocketing land and building costs to move into trailers and low-cost housing. But more of this development can be attributed to wealthy newcomers, known as "amenity migrants." They have caused a housing boom that involves the construction of second and third homes, which are splayed over what were once uninterrupted views of the mountains and mesas.

One of the legacies of the 1960s that has fed northern New Mexico's population and tourist growth are the various spiritual practices associated with New Age religion and medicine. Taos has far more than its demographic fair share of alternative therapies, both physical and mental, some of which have taken their impetus and remedies from Indian and Hispanic cultures. As Stephen Fox explains, "Many practitioners of New Age therapy subscribe to a current myth that transcendent, mystical forces in the Rio Grande valley facilitate healing" which is why "healers and therapists are being drawn here 'by the droves,'" including practitioners of inversion therapy, nutrionics, applied divine light, and orthobionomics. In 1981–82, the number of alternative healers was estimated at about one hundred, approximately equal to the number of painters. In 1992, among the scores of rest and recreation pamphlets available at the newly built chamber of commerce, was the "Taos Guide for Massage and the Healing Arts."[4]

In the spirit of making the most of its magic to increase the tourist trade, Taos has turned to exploiting the names of its famous denizens from the past. Dorothy Brett's house has become the Brett House, an upscale restaurant promising "fine dining and casual elegance." In the early 1990s, a bed-and-breakfast housed on property Mabel owned north of town located itself on Mabel Dodge Lane, while the Mabel Dodge Luhan house uses her name for its toll free number: 1-800-84-MABEL. The Luhan house has also played a role in the continuing saga of the D. H. Lawrence cult, which was perhaps never more fulsomely celebrated than in the 1980 festival attended by some three hundred scholars.

Molly Ivins's account in the *New York Times* sounds like the kind of parody Lawrence himself might have written had he been alive at the time. Before the conference began, the official poster was banned—a portrait of Lady Chatterly "in the altogether" painted by artist R. C. Gorman. The topics of the festival included "sex, blood, death, and the sickness of our civilization," which were illuminated by "intellectuals, wearing neckties and huaraches, . . . crying loud for life red in tooth and claw." Seven male British scholars "solemnly agreed that no one had ever written so accurately about the female orgasm as Lawrence." On Saturday night the conferees "repaired to a costume ball at the home of Mabel Dodge Luhan," where they danced, mostly in their own native dress, to the music of cowboy-disco.[5]

It would have been interesting for the conferees to have heard the stories of Lawrence and Mabel that had been passed down to Hispanic children by their elders. Orlando Romero, whose family has been in the San Gabriel Valley since 1598, has written a fictionalized account based on the overheard conversations of his primos, cousins by blood and friendship, who worked at the Mabel Dodge Luhan house. "Parking on D. H.'s Ashes" recounts the bemusement and disgust of Miguel (from Taos Pueblo) and his friend Juan (from the valley) at the antics of privileged white folk for whom life was more play than work.

Juan: They didn't want to live like the Indian or the Spanish. They wanted things like all Anglos, an Indian to show off, an adobe house, not an adobe home where you have kids, where you live until you die. No these people didn't want to live like us. They wanted things from us, that's all!

Miguel: That English man's wife was always fighting with the wealthy Americana, you know he was that skinny, pale, sickly looking Gringo who lived up the Canyon in San Cristobal. All those crazy Gringos, they seemed so bored! They were always arguing or partying; they couldn't stand each other, but they were always together.

Juan: Where are they now? Even the English writer that looked like a ghost while he was here didn't even die here. He hardly lived here and people come to park on his ashes.[6]

From Communes to Communities

In spite of enduring socioeconomic problems, interethnic hostilities, and the increased tackiness encouraged by the tourist industry, contemporary Taos has also been marked by positive changes. Some of the best of these have grown out of alliances that were created between the natives and those newcomers in the 1960s who sank their roots into the surrounding land and cultures. Their failures, as well as their successes, have much to teach us about the continuing course of the counterculture in American history.

In his book *America's Utopian Experiments* Brian Berry makes a convincing case that the utopian impulses that have arisen and receded throughout American history can be linked to "long-wave crises that periodically have affected American economic development." Thus the severe recession of the 1980s, and what economists have referred to as the massive redistribution of wealth upward that occurred as a result of Reagan-Bush taxation and social welfare policies, helps to account for the growth of "intentional communities" in the 1980s.

Among the 335 such communities founded in the 1980s, Berry discovered a variety of philosophies and goals whose origins he traces back to the 1960s: "preservation of nature, direct action politics, energy self-sufficiency, . . . spiritual healing, ecofeminism, . . . economic democracy, macrobiotics, . . . and spiritual ecology." Unlike the 1960s communes, these intentional communities tend to be structured, carefully financed, and restrictive in membership. According to Berry, who quotes from the 1991 *Dictionary of Intentional Communities,* they reflect the "'theme of the individual intentionally choosing a life-style of social and environmental responsibil-

Lama Foundation, 1989.

ity' which is then transmitted to others, with the hope of creating like-minded groups and networks which will eventually 'influence the larger society.'"[7]

Two examples of transformations from communes into communities in Taos are Lama Foundation and New Buffalo. Lama early on decided to be a closed commune; new members had to be voted on and had to fit into its philosophy of spiritual eclecticism. Its long-term stability has also been helped by the fact that it serves as a temporary retreat. People come to serve their own individual spiritual and personal needs and stay for an average of two years, although they are still obligated to perform certain community tasks (the responsibilities for cooking, gardening, laundry, clean-up, construction, and maintenance are rotated among all members).

Mary Kenney, who was Lama's coordinator in the late 1980s, compared it to "getting an advanced degree in self-awareness," which then encourages graduates to "rejoin" the community at large, "taking Lama-life skills with them." As it did in the 1960s, Lama still pays serious tribute to welcoming many world religious traditions. "We're eclectic in outlook. In the morning a member might praise Allah, then Sufi dance in the afternoon, and light Shabbat candles at sunset." Kenney sees Lama as a model for "how unity in diversity could work in our world, especially in religious matters, where it's so needed today."[8]

Lama Foundation, 1989.

In 1986, New Buffalo commune was transformed into an experimental station of the sustainable agriculture movement, which took hold in New Mexico in 1983 with the creation of the Talavaya Center in Espanola. In 1985, Talavaya's efforts to preserve the genetic diversity of indigenous strains of corn earned them an award from the United Nations Environmental Program. Writing on the growth of the movement in 1989, a *Nation* reporter described the work going on there as "part of the most significant trend in agriculture today."[9]

Talavaya focused on adapting traditional Native American and Hispanic practices to develop crops suited for arid and semiarid conditions, including some of the hundreds of varieties of maize and beans that were part of native diets before the first European contacts in the Americas. John Kimmey, who founded Talavaya with Carol Underhill, explained the need to increase the world's supply of nonhybridized seeds in terms of the fact that they are cheaper to grow, not dependent on chemicals, and are more drought- and frost-resistant. The crisis in Third World agriculture was particularly acute because of the extinction of the majority of open pollinated food crops, and the increasing desertification that has been partially created through ground water contamination by pesticides.

Kimmey's opening of SNAC (Sustainable Native Agriculture) at New

New Buffalo, 1988.

Buffalo was part of a plan to expand the project of helping the often-struggling farmers in northern New Mexico, as well as farmers facing similar terrains in impoverished Third World countries. In 1988, SNAC had five acres of 120 different bean and corn seed varieties under cultivation, and seven people on staff. That summer, a group of students attending a National Youth

John Kimmey (right) and friend, New Buffalo (SNAC), 1988.

Leadership Conference at Las Palomas awarded Kimmey the Pebble in the Pond Award for Making Good Waves. Kimmey's experiment at New Buffalo lasted only three years primarily owing to continuing financial difficulties. In 1992, the Talavaya Center lost its main financial support and was reduced to a one-woman operation run by Carol Underhill.

In spite of these reverses, sustainable agriculture has continued its presence in northern New Mexico, while many of its principles have entered mainstream agriculture. There is a branch of Native Seeds Search, one of the nation's largest nonprofit seed banks, in Albuquerque; an experimental agricultural station in Alcalde run by the State University; and a one-man operation in Embudo, led by Hispanic writer and activist Estevan Arellano, who began with seeds supplied to him by Underhill.[10]

Interethnic Coalitions and Collaborations

The past two decades have witnessed the beginning of a new kind of "ethnically mixed constituency" that has used an increasingly direct "style of activism" to deal with such issues as water disputes and the expansion of Taos Ski Valley. In the early 1980s, they stopped the building of the Indian Camp Dam above Talpa and Ranchos. While supporters claimed it would mean improved irrigation for farmers, it would also have meant increased taxes for local residents in order to support a recreational lake for tourists. Amigos Bravos (Friends of the Wild Rivers) is a coalition of Anglos, Hispanics, and Native Americans that defines as its mission: "to protect, conserve and enhance the biological diversity and important aquatic, wildlife and cultural resources of the upper Rio Grande watershed." Another such organization is Acequias del Norte, a Hispano-Anglo alliance of "ditch associations from several northern counties," that focuses its efforts on real estate development.[11]

Relations between Anglos and the Taos Indians have also sometimes taken on a new cast. Beginning in 1986, R. C. Gordon-McCutchan worked with Taos Pueblo to raise money for the preservation of the old buildings in the center of the pueblo, which were in serious danger of collapsing. (HUD had put up flimsy prefab houses that resulted in most families moving outside the central pueblo, further discouraging its maintenance.) McCutchan developed proposals "that brought 2.5 million dollars to Taos Pueblo for the preservation effort," with funds coming from HUD, private donors, and from the Getty Conservation Institute. At the same time, he initiated the process that won Taos Pueblo World Heritage status in 1992, working with Santana Romero, governor of Taos Pueblo, Alfonso Ortiz, and Laura Feller, from the National Park Service to accomplish this. The preservation project, "under the able direction of tribal member Joe Martinez, spanned five years and resulted in the restoration of the buildings of Taos Pueblo to an immaculate condition."[12]

Yet Taos Pueblo is still faced with enduring problems. Although it has become increasingly savvy about its self-presentation to tourists, it has a hard time implementing long-term economic improvements, in good part because it is caught between old traditions and newer needs. The tribal government changes on a yearly basis, which makes it all but impossible for the decisions made by one regime to be carried into the next, while the moneys that are brought in by tourism support the governor and the tribal council, but not the tribe as a whole. Women are still allowed no formal role in tribal politics, including serving on the tribal council, all of whose fifty members are male. In the past decade, alcoholism, domestic violence, and theft have increased.[13]

A number of young folk understand the need to maintain a strong sense of tradition and at the same time find ways for the tribe to improve its economic and cultural future. In the summer of 1993, a young Taos Pueblo guide talked about the governor's promise of summer jobs to all the youth who went to college, because they are "the future of the pueblo." Yet there are few jobs for the college-educated to come back to (a problem also faced by the Anglo and Hispanic communities). She also spoke frankly about her dissatisfaction with the male-dominated social and political structure, and about how little of the language, and thus of traditional culture, young people were learning.

It was to address this loss of culture that Peter Rabbit and his wife, the poet Anne MacNaughton, began to work with the children of Taos Pueblo in the mid-1980s. They collaborated with three renowned Taos Pueblo artists to form the Taos Children's Theatre, which produced the bilingual *Tiwa Tales:* Bernadette Track, a potter, mask-maker, and Juilliard-trained dancer who has performed all over the world; her sister Soge Track, a writer and art curator; and Robert Mirabal, a playwright, songwriter, and performer. Bernadette's mother told Soge the stories, mostly Coyote tales, in Tiwa, and Bernadette translated them back into English. *Tiwa Tales* was taken over by the Taos Children's Art Center, OO-OONAH, which had a brief life in the early 1970s and was reborn in 1983 under the instigation of Marie Reyna and Joseph Concha. It is a small but important sign of how Taos Indians are beginning to take more control of their cultural heritage, while at the same time reaching out to other communities. In the early 1990s, the Taos Pueblo Children's Art Center brought the play to communities throughout northern New Mexico and participated in a cultural exchange program with other northern Pueblos and with students in Japan.

Soge Track has undertaken an extensive study of the history of Taos Pueblo artists, which includes her discovery of Native Americans who worked in oils in the 1930s and at least one painter, Juan Mirabal, who worked in a modernist idiom during this time. She curated several of the *Annual Art of Taos Pueblo* shows that the Millicent Rogers Museum has held since 1981, including the eleventh-annual exhibit in which she showed the paintings, pottery, beadwork, sculpture, and furniture-making of some forty-three Taos Indians. Among the most notable contemporary Taos Pueblo artists are sculptor John Suazo, whose *Taos Pueblo Family* is in the Millicent Rogers Museum, and filmmaker Diane Reyna, whose fine documentary on Pueblo history and culture, *Surviving Columbus,* was aired on PBS in the fall of 1992, and won a Peabody award.[14]

Multicultural Arts

Peter Rabbit's most successful venture during the 1980s was his creation of SOMOS (Society of the Muse of the Southwest), in 1982. SOMOS grew directly out of Peter's hippie years, when he and his fellow communalists performed happenings and guerilla theatre across the country (at Drop City, they were called Droppings). Peter had always thought of these gigs as a circus, so it seemed natural that when he got together with a group of like-minded Taos poet friends they would come up with the idea of having a Poetry Circus. Intended to democratize the experience of poetry, the Taos Poetry Circus was modeled on the sport of boxing—ten rounds, ten poems. They established a yearly World Championship Poetry Bout, which has grown to have a devoted local, as well as national, audience and that has brought them major grant funding. Their contestants have included Robert Duncan, Allen Ginsberg, Nora Naranjo Morse, Anne Waldman, and Victor Hernandez.

The Poetry Circus grew to include four days of workshops, readings, and other performances. SOMOS and the Taos Poetry Circus became separate entities in 1991, with Peter in charge of the World Poetry Bout Association. In the summer of 1993, Simon Ortiz won the world championship title and the Max Finstein Memorial Poetry Prize (the Max), from Ntozake Shange. SOMOS has continued its weekly writers' reading series in the summer and has published an anthology of excerpts from their works that include such local notables as Natalie Goldberg, John Nichols, Robert Mirabal, and Estevan Arellano.

The Taos Institute for the Arts also has its roots in the 1960s. It opened in the summer of 1989 "with the goal of creating a learning environment in which the creative energies of our tricultural community may be put to use to stimulate and unify our community." One of its chief backers was artist Larry Bell, who worked for two years with more than one hundred artists and local business people, including staff from Las Palomas, to create an integrated curriculum in the arts, humanities, and ecological awareness. The institute hired credentialed as well as traditional artists and opened with students from twenty-two states. They were offered sculpture with Larry Bell, writing with Natalie Goldberg, weaving with Rachel Brown, painting with Ray Vinella, and ceramics with Aliah Sage. Fifty percent of the students are from Taos, and the institute offers a substantial scholarship program for locals only.[15]

Two other community ventures that hark back to Mabel Luhan's generation are the Frank Waters Foundation and the Fechin Institute. The Frank Waters Foundation grew out of the decision by Waters and his wife, Barbara, to establish their property in Arroyo Seco as the basis for a "foundation sheltering the creative spirit." The foundation made its official debut on June 26, 1993, with the announcement that the Waterses had donated eight acres of their land to the Taos Land Trust and were seeking funds to build studios on the remaining fifteen acres, which would provide writers, painters, and musicians with short-term "inspirational living space." Opened in 1981, the Nicolai Fechin Institute is the creation of Eya Fechin, whose goal is to promote international understanding through the arts. Eya restored the Fechin house and studio as a tribute to her father's art, which she displays in annual shows, and as a venue for international exhibitions of Chinese and Russian artists, musical concerts, and art workshops.[16]

Closer to the Luhan house was the transformation of the St. Theresa House into the Lumina Gallery. The first guest house built by Mabel Luhan, it is situated next to the adobe wall that surrounds the Big House. Lumina is owned by Felicia Fergusson, who in her teens was Dennis Hopper's lover, and who is now married to photographer Chuck Henningsen. Although it has undergone interior renovation over the years, much of Mabel's original organic interior, as well as the elegant exterior design remain.[17]

The latest incarnation of the Mabel Dodge Luhan house has grown out of the legacies of the sixties that have promoted the more positive social and cultural endeavors outlined in this chapter. Las Palomas has also suffered from the more debilitating problems of the Taos community, as well as created some of its own. In spite of this, it has contributed a positive legacy to the lives of many among the forty thousand students, teachers, administrators, elderhostelers, and other visitors who have come through its adobe gates seeking respite or renewal.

CHAPTER EIGHT

Las Palomas de Taos

I like what you [Lois] said the other day when you were talking about how Mabel was a well-known figure and Dennis was too and that we are just like everyday-type people. Well, to me, that's exciting, that's hopeful. We all make a difference.
Kitty Otero

The Founding of Las Palomas

The idea of Taos as a microcosm of the global village the world has become is the philosophical underpinning of the third generation to take over the Mabel Dodge Luhan house. As was true for Luhan and Hopper, the sense of place called to its third owners before they actually had any knowledge of its history. The Oteros were seeking to purchase a living-learning center to which they could bring students and teachers interested in global education and school reform.

George Otero was raised in New Mexico, and Kitty moved there at age thirteen, but neither knew anything about the Luhan house before they bought it. They were both born in 1948 and grew up in middle-income neighborhoods in Albuquerque, where stories of life among the high, mighty, and eccentric of Taos were not part of their family and community milieu. George was raised in a half-Hispanic, half-Anglo assimilated family in which no Spanish was spoken.[1]

It is ironic, perhaps, that a young man who lived most of his first twenty-two years within the same few square blocks, and who was able to walk to school from kindergarten through his years at the University of New Mexico, would end up a respected global educator. George describes himself as a "rah-rah" teenager, who was pretty much indifferent to the social and political issues that riddled the 1960s. He was, however, interested in spiritual issues and, from age sixteen to nineteen, performed as a "Southern Baptist preacher boy." Otero's political transformation came in college.

For George, the 1960s came to have ideological meaning while he was student teaching in the Albuquerque public schools with a black homosexual sociology teacher and with a Jewish teacher from the East Coast. He began to focus on the differences that had always been part of his neighborhood, and he felt a growing desire to work through such differences to create community. George left the church when he found his congregation uninterested in the earthly dimensions of his quest, but there is no doubt that the thrust of his religious vocation merged with the sensitivity training he underwent in college to shape his educational philosophy and practice. His evangelical vision has influenced the mission and programming at Las Palomas, and his most consistently praised quality by his peers is his inspirational ability to motivate people toward the kind of self- and community empowerment that leads to personal, institutional, and social change.

The Oteros married when George was a freshman in college. After his

Béla Kalman, *Gates and Birdhouses,* Mabel Dodge Luhan House, 1985.

graduation, his "wonderful little struggling middle-class family" moved to Littleton, Colorado, where he taught in the middle school for four years and Kitty trained to become a nurse. During these years, George took workshops in international relations at the University of Denver, which determined the direction of his career. The doctorate he pursued at the University of Northern Colorado combined international and alternative education, with an emphasis on multicultural education. This led to his being hired by the University of Denver's Center for Teaching International Relations (CTIR) to do teacher-training.

A friend and faculty member at the University of Northern Colorado, Roy Krosky, "reintroduced" Kitty and George to New Mexico. Roy often conducted field trips to the Pueblos because of his interest in having his students understand the connection between learning and spirituality. He was looking for a site in which to live and to do teacher-training in multicultural education in New Mexico. He and his wife, Beverly, had made an initial bid on the Luhan house, which Dennis Hopper rejected, before asking the Oteros to buy in with them. They set out looking for other sites but came back to the Luhan house.

Kitty and George visited the Luhan house with George's mother and grandmother. Kitty remembers the rooms were set up like stalls, each with

Béla Kalman, Interiors of the Luhan house—living room, 1988.

its own wood-burning stove, because Dennis had been forced to rent them out piecemeal. In some rooms, there were nude people walking about, apparently undisturbed by the visitors. Dennis told Kitty about the death cart that followed people around and how he sometimes got locked into the house and couldn't get out. Although George's mother was put off by Hopper, and fearful that if her son and daughter-in-law bought the house and moved in they would turn into hippies, Dennis took an instant liking to the motherly woman, whose presence seemed to ease their negotiations.

After selling their home, borrowing money from George's mother, and getting a loan with the help of a Taos banker, the Oteros raised their half of the $50,000 down payment required on the asking price of $250,000. They and the Kroskys purchased the house in September and the Oteros moved in in December 1977. Not long after the purchase, Kitty says she read Emily Hahn's biography *Mabel* and decided that Mabel was "so horrible" (an opinion she came to revise somewhat) that she didn't want to tell anyone about her. She hadn't known anything about Hopper when they first came, although his return visits to pick up various stashes of drugs he'd left around the house provided some clues as to who he was.

George was immediately taken with the grounds and house, which

Béla Kalman, Interiors of the Luhan house—dining room, 1988.

seemed perfect for his purposes. But it was Kitty who did most of the initial fixing up and dealt with the daily business of keeping the house together. Kitty spent much of their first year working on the kitchen and the log cabin, in which most of the workshops were held. The Kroskys were still living in Greeley and commuting to Taos on the weekends, and George was away most of the time teaching his CTIR courses in Denver and traveling as a consultant in order to earn money. The Oteros' was a fairly traditional marriage and division of labor. This helped to make the place work, but it would have less positive consequences over the years, as Kitty strove to find a place for herself as a professional within the Las Palomas enterprise.

Buying the property was, the Oteros knew, a huge financial risk. The whole project was really quite an extraordinary undertaking for a young couple in their twenties, who had two small children to care for. "But it was so exciting," they both believed they could make it work. The Kroskys provided the first summer's programming on Southwest art and culture and shared the house with the Oteros, but the partnership did not work, and the Oteros bought them out after the first year. For the first three years, Kitty and George put in eighteen-hour days working on the house, which took enormous amounts of energy and money for renovation and mainte-

Béla Kalman, Interiors of the Luhan house—Mabel's bedroom, 1988.
(Mabel's bed, in center, is the only original piece of furniture left).

nance, and talked endlessly—a practice that never stopped over the years—about what kinds of programs would keep it going.

After three years the Oteros had re-adobed the portal, reroofed the house, added a wall in Mabel's bedroom that separated it from what is called Tony's Room, put in a couple of additional bathrooms, restored the gate house, and completed the process of putting the house on the state and national register of historic houses. In 1980, they moved into the apartment they created in the gatehouse, in part because their oldest daughter resented all the time they were putting into the Big House. The tug-of-war between family and personal needs, and between these needs and their devotion to the house and its various projects, would remain an ongoing tension that would ultimately play a role in George and Kitty's separation and divorce.

In 1980, the realization of the Oteros' dreams not only seemed possible, but it was apparently even blessed by Mabel Dodge Luhan herself. Documentary filmmaker Bill Carpenter, who was working on a movie about the haunted houses of northern New Mexico, came to the Luhan house with Ann Jensen, a psychic who was hired to serve as a medium for Mabel's spirit. Jensen lay down in Mabel's bed, the only remaining piece of orig-

Béla Kalman, Interiors of the Luhan house—second-floor bathroom, with the restored painted windows, originally done by D. H. Lawrence and Dorothy Brett, 1988.

inal furniture in the house, and immediately "became Mabel—taking on her personality," according to Carpenter. They got twenty minutes of dialogue on film, during which time Ann "reached out to hold Tony's hand." Both Kitty and George remember "Mabel" telling them that she was pleased with the use they were making of the house. She predicted "it would become more famous than when she was alive." Subsequent to this 1980 visit, Mabel has appeared to many inhabitants of the house, sometimes as a woman in white, sometimes as a presence accompanied by the odor of cinnamon. Unlike the ghost experiences of the Hopper years, those that Kitty collected from Las Palomas family, friends, and visitors, were pleasant.[2]

Kitty did more than collect ghost stories, of course. She arranged the domestic programming, running classes on Southwest foods and cooking, and publishing a cookbook of Las Palomas's best-liked foods. Later, she branched out into more feminist-oriented workshops as she began to deal with her own need for personal growth. During the first decade of programs, George's primary interest was in schooling and how people lived and worked together in school communities. His initial income-generating

Doug Hansen and Nathan Eckhardt drawing at Ranchos de Taos Church, Taos Workshop, Las Palomas, 1986.
Photo courtesy of Bob Campagna.

projects were related to a school improvement network he helped establish with the Albuquerque school system.

From 1980 to 1985, Las Palomas was helped along by a Quaker patron who gave them fifty thousand dollars a year. Until 1982, they benefitted from federal educational grants that were available under the Carter administration. When these grants ran out during the Reagan administration, they hustled to get state and private funds. By 1988, the combination of the profit-making Mabel Dodge enterprise and Las Palomas, the nonprofit foundation that the Oteros established to oversee their educational programming, was bringing in five hundred thousand dollars in grants and income, generated by sixty to eighty weekend and weeklong year-round programs that served two thousand to four thousand people a year. The income came from a wide variety of educational initiatives that included teacher empowerment and student leadership workshops, the development of global and multicultural curricula, and from classes on Southwest art and culture. In 1982, the Oteros began their very successful elderhostel programs, which have run up to fourteen a year. In 1983, they started a bed-and-breakfast in order to bring in more income.

Dancing at Bennie Mondragon's House, summer 1986,
Las Palomas Youth Programs: Taos Adventure and the Taos Workshop.
Photo courtesy of Bob Campagna.

From the beginning, George put into practice the 1960s philosophy that the "personal is the political." Believing that the Luhan house provided an ambience that encouraged personal growth and change, he grounded his programming on its being not just a "retreat," but "a home away from home." This "implies a certain way of being and acting. . . . It becomes a pretty safe, secure place for people to reflect and think about things, [especially] the multi-ethnic communities we all live in." George believes this kind of risk taking is easier in Taos, especially for people from urban areas who no longer have "a sense of place" and whose lack of connectedness to community is one of the reasons for the disempowering alienation they experience in their work and in their daily lives. "We think you have to build learning communities and places where relearning and unlearning are the norms, . . . and where they try to integrate with the environment. We try to model those principles in the place, the staff."

The Oteros saw a clear link between the kind of home they were creating and what Kitty called the idea of "the world [as] our home"—which involved "looking at Taos as a microcosm of the rest of the world." This meant both continuity with and changes from the uses to which the house

Front (L–R) George Otero, Ann Mayes, Bob Campagna.
Back (L–R) Pat Sheets, Kitty Otero, Steve Miller, Paul Mayes, Jan Drum, summer 1987.
Photo courtesy of Bob Campagna.

had been put in the past. Members of the three major ethnic groups have been integrated into the house and professional staffs. Lorencita Lujan, from Taos Pueblo, served on the board of directors for many years, and Bennie Mondragon, Al Lujan, and Ronnie Martinez, among others, have given talks on Pueblo culture. The kitchen staff, which has included Lorencita and Reycita Lujan and Crucita Mondragon, have also given the cooking and pottery classes. Leonila Serna supervised the Title VII Gifted and Talented grant that served Hispanic and Native American middle school students from 1990 to 1992. Sylvia Rodriguez has lectured there, and Larry Torres, a Taos high school teacher, has given numerous talks on Hispanic history and Anglo-Hispanic relations. (His astute and amusing insights into the history of the Luhan house, given as an insider-outsider who has intersected with all three generations, close this book.)

Las Palomas's double sense of home has also included a do-it-yourself philosophy that has at times caused problems with certain clientele who come there. Although the staff pride themselves on the creation of community—on the mixing of races, ages, classes, regions, and different interest groups who rub shoulders in the communal dining room and courtyard—

Reycita Lujan demonstrating pottery-making at Las Palomas, n.d. Photo courtesy of Bob Campagna.

they don't "take care of" or cater to guests. People are expected to scrape their own dishes, share rooms, often with people they don't know, and carry their own bags. As Kitty put it, "It's an alternative place that says you can live in a community and be responsible for yourself." This is particularly important for the youth groups, who have been expected to help with maintenance and repair.

The Oteros' alternative philosophy, and some of their renovations, have been puzzling and off-putting for a number of people. Tourists who expect the kind of service they get from commercial hotels or motels have been disappointed by the lack of modern amenities, as have business people who want private phones and bathrooms where hot and cold water come out of the same tap. The house seems unattractive to some old-timers who remember it from its glory days, when it was beautifully furnished. Architectural and historical purists have been dismayed by its sometimes haphazard and amateur restoration, its unauthentic furnishings, and its loss of certain treasured artifacts, such as the beautiful Awa Tsireh mural, which was covered over when the walls in the portal were re-adobed.

 George Otero explained in a 1983 interview with the *Rocky Mountain*

News: "We want to make Luhan's House into a living museum . . . instead of just another historic landmark you pay two dollars to visit." The changes the house has undergone have entailed certain losses, but the space has continually evolved to meet the needs of those who live in the present. The house has a kind of vitality that is rarely, if ever, evident in historic sites. For me, and for the majority of individuals with whom I have conversed over the years, the Luhan house is a modest palace of delights, conducive to serious and productive conversations, as well as to quiet reflection and the simple pleasures of communing with a landscape that appeals to all one's senses. The closed and protective environment of the living room, dining room, portal, and courtyard gives one a sense of both privacy and community. The backyard that faces the seventy-one thousand acres of Taos Pueblo's rangelands and mountains opens one up in a way that no other landscape has ever done, for me at least.[3]

As one might expect, Las Palomas has also had many of the problems of home, including the larger home of Taos with which it has not always peacefully coexisted. Both Kitty Otero and Susan Chambers-Cook have remarked on the seeming irony that many Taoseños seem to have no idea of what goes on at the Mabel Dodge Luhan house, in spite of the fact that from the early 1980s it has been doing year-round programming that brings in teachers, students, elderhostelers, and visitors from all over the nation. Some locals have thought it was a retirement home, some a home for handicapped children, and others a ranch owned by a wealthy couple. Even among the Taos professionals in the arts, literary, and museum world that I know, I have often been the source of information on what is happening at the Luhan house.

Although less than a mile from the center of town, the house is set apart from the community, in more ways than just being at the end of a dead-end road and surrounded by high adobe walls. Since Mabel's day, it has always had more of a regional and national than a local reach. That tradition continues with Las Palomas, whose most successful programming, with the important exception of their work with New Mexico schools, has been with participants outside the state. The lack of local programming has been in part due to the difficulty of Las Palomas's making money on local events, for which Taos residents expect to be charged less. But it is also due to a lack of a support system in the community, which Kitty once described as "very competitive." As more art and cultural institutions have been built to address Taos's multicultural community, and as bed-and-breakfasts proliferate across the landscape (forty are listed in the 1993 Taos phone book listing), the competition for the tourist dollar has become increasingly fierce. Yet the local economy remains too poor to allow most Taoseños to participate in these programs without financial support.

Taos suffers from the kinds of jealousies and rivalries one often finds in communities whose livelihood is dependent on the arts and tourism. But it is also true that the occupants of the Luhan house have kept themselves somewhat apart, and that the utopian vistas they provide for those who arrive from the outside have not always been realized at home. Because George has spent so much of his work life on the road, he has made few inroads within the local community. There has been continuous turnover among the staff and board of directors. Some of this is related to the stress and burnout that accompany working for an organization that is often under financial duress, and some of it is related to the fact that the owners have had difficulty maintaining workable relationships with their employees. Under the best of circumstances, the kind of programs Las Palomas has offered have barely met the expenses of running the Luhan house. George Otero is a superb educator and mentor, but he has not been a good financial manager. His decision to take out a large loan in 1988, in order to match his expanding vision with larger facilities, brought Las Palomas to the brink of bankruptcy, with the result that the Luhan house was put on the market for sale in 1991—and it has been on and off the market for sale since then.

In spite of the many problems that have faced it over the years, what is most remarkable about the history of Las Palomas is the impressive quality of many of its programs. It is important to remember that its successes, as well as its failures, have taken place within the context of one of the least socially responsible decades in twentieth-century American history. In fact, the situation that the Oteros faced in the 1980s bore some resemblance to the one faced by Mabel and her activist friends in the 1920s. That was a decade of so-called prosperity in which the majority of Americans fared very poorly under three Republican administrations, when the racism of nativist groups like the Ku Klux Klan reached their virulent high point, and when America turned its back on its open policy of immigration to enact severe restrictions for those coming from Eastern and Southern Europe.

Las Palomas was born during the relatively flush times of the Carter administration, but it came of age under the federal axe wielded by Reagan and Bush in the 1980s. Like the 1920s, this was a decade of Republican hegemony during which the very rich cornered the market on most of the increased wealth and income, while the middle and lower classes suffered income and job losses that were accompanied by massive cutbacks in social and human service entitlement programs. During this decade of greed, Las Palomas brought to Taos some twenty thousand youth and adults whose lives were touched by much more community-minded and global understandings of what it means to be an American at the end of the twentieth century. More than a few returned to their home communities to build constructively on the notion of global realities and responsibilities.

The School Improvement Network (SIN)

Some of the most successful programming at Las Palomas is connected to what might loosely be called the school-based reform movement. This movement began to take hold in the late 1970s and early 1980s in response to the all but impossible task public schools faced in meeting a variety of new and sometimes contradictory mandates—for bilingual education, open enrollment, magnet schools, compensatory and special education, sex and drug education programs, and students' rights. These demands were made by conflicting constituencies that included administrators, teachers, parents, taxpayers, and a government that was itself unclear "about the priorities and goals of schooling."[4]

How should public schools deal with the frantic escalation of these demands and with the many teachers and administrators who suffered mounting burnout and frustrations because of them? SIN emphasized the how of change rather than the what, correctly insisting that school improvement only takes place "when schools have the capacity to manage the change process." This capacity is enabled when the entire school system becomes a democratic enterprise in which staff collaboration, cooperative classroom practice, and respect for the intellectual and emotional growth of students and teachers are the bedrock of the school's philosophy and operation.

Building on the pioneering work of John Goodlad and other educational reformers, the New Mexico SIN began its life in the Mabel Dodge Luhan house in 1978, eventually working with more than 150 schools in the state, and with school systems in Colorado, Arizona, and Arkansas. They have helped teachers and administrators learn to analyze the cultural dynamics of their particular schools, and they have provided staff with the means to realize how to use the collective wisdom, talent, and energy they possess for improving the climate of their schools. In the 1980s, Las Palomas was "the hub agency" for SIN's training, developing, and resource sharing. Much of SIN's content focus was related to the twin themes of global (what was then called futures) education and ethnic heritage (diversity) studies, the second supported by a series of grants Las Palomas won under the federal government's Ethnic Heritage Studies Act (1972). This act was another 1960s milestone that encouraged the development of new humanities and social studies curricula that acknowledged the multicultural reality of American history and society.[5]

The Taos schools were some of the first to benefit from the workshops offered by Las Palomas. In 1980, the Taos Federation of Teachers wrote the *Taos News* that they were "treated to the finest in-service program in the entire school year" with George Otero, who offered teachers valuable insights into multicultural education, an issue "vital in Taos." In 1983, the superintendent of Taos Schools told the *Rocky Mountain News* that he wished "there were 10 more George Oteros." George's uncompromising faith in teachers' abilities to improve their work lives and their schools, and his equally passionate belief in the right of every student to learn, come through strongly in this article.[6]

Robert Sparks, principal of Green Mountain High School in Lakewood, Colorado, worked with Las Palomas and SIN for more than a decade, using their consultants to train his staff, and co-consulting with George in his work with other school principals. Sparks feels their efforts were "extremely successful in broadening the perspectives of school teachers and administrators and in developing school cultures which are more capable of responding in creative, cooperative and dynamic ways." Loy Sue Siegenthaler, a school counselor who also worked closely with George and SIN, is proudest of the district team-building that she and George established with the Albuquerque Public Schools. A native New Mexican, Loy Sue first visited the Luhan house in the 1950s when her college roommate, who was from Taos, brought her to have tea with Mabel. She says she found that the ambience—and gossip—"had kind of an elitist specialness to it and a little wickedness, so I could never attach to them as real people. They were figments of their own imagination."[7]

Loy Sue views Las Palomas's work as much more down to earth and real because it tapped "the best anybody who participates . . . has to give of themselves." She also acknowledged George's utopian ambitions for Las Palomas: "It was going to change and transform the world." For Laurie Eastman, a high school English teacher from Colorado, George was "a wizard at bringing material alive and people, people of all ages." Laurie and her teacher-husband, Ben, knew George from his CTIR days at Colorado College, when they all took courses on hunger and the Third World, so they could teach about Asia, Africa, and world religions.

Ben Eastman believes that the mostly white teachers who came from their school to Las Palomas were sensitized to diversity and that these workshops "really did change the nature, the atmosphere of the school. . . . [For] a lot of us who were touched by the sixties, this [was] a real way of making those ideas . . . come alive." Because George practices the kind of democratic strategies that he preaches should be part of school systems, he "pays attention to where the group is and will change on a moment's notice if things are not going well. He doesn't get his ego involved." Some seventy teachers from the Eastmans' school participated in Las Palomas projects, many of them paying out of pocket when the Title IV money dried up. The 25 to 30 percent of their fellow teachers who committed themselves to a multiperspective approach to teaching American history and literature did so, Laurie insisted, "because of this place."[9]

Over the years many innovative curriculum projects have been produced by teachers who have attended SIN workshops. Judy Starr and Karen Casaus, two Albuquerque elementary school teachers, developed a global perspectives unit that helped students discover the commonalities and differences of human behavior across cultures by examining the social structures that most cultures have to organize themselves—art, play, recreation, language, conflict, warfare, education—and asking students to address such questions as, Do you have to be rich to be happy? Do you have to have both parents to be a family? Do you have to go to school to learn? Student games required cooperative learning among students, and affective as well as cognitive responses to the issues that were raised.

Global Realities and Youth Leadership

Las Palomas's national reputation rests on the scores of weeklong workshops that George Otero and his colleagues have run at the Luhan house on the creation of global education curricula and on student empowerment training. During the 1980s, many of the youth programs were cosponsored by the Stanley Foundation of Muscatine, Iowa, under the direction of Jan Drum, who was, until 1992, the foundation's educational support coordinator. Jan began to work with George after meeting him in 1983 at an Ohio global education conference and hearing him voice the same frustration she had with educators who kept doing the same things over and over again, even when they knew they were ineffective. What brought them together was "that sense of truly trying to find a new way to go about things . . . and a sense of caring deeply and truly, respecting any human being as capable of being in charge of their own learning." They shared the philosophy that kids were not just potential leaders but "artists of the future." George and Jan developed some of the most effective workshops that Las Palomas has sponsored—student and youth leadership conferences that dealt with the central planetary issues of economic inequity, ecological imbalance, and the threat of war.

These conferences used the multicultural setting of Taos and the history of the Luhan house to provide a context for the students' understanding of worldwide military and social expenditures. Students interviewed experts in arms and arms control, came up with policy recommendations, and role-played the closing of an auto plant in Detroit and its removal to Brazil. Many of these workshops ended with students and teachers addressing how they could take what they learned home.[9]

One group from Denver established a world affairs conference for their school; a Chicago group created a steering committee for a citywide conference of one thousand youth; and a California group got their community to ban the use of styrofoam. In a 1991 prospectus on their work, Jan quoted one student's joyous response to the impact that these workshops had on her: "Imagine taking a six-inch spike marked AWARENESS and pounding it through your ear with a rose blossom. The Taos conference is about forty-two thousand seconds of life and death and trees and history and beauty and sex and friendship and poetry and fireplaces and shopping and food and music and bad singing and peace—if you care." Between 1986 and 1991, Las Palomas held twenty such programs, involving more than 650 high school students and their teachers.[10]

Jan and George also collaborated on adult workshops in global education, which included religious leaders and community activists. These developed into a series of conferences called the Community of Learners, which focused on personal growth for people who wanted "to integrate the way they live with the way they work and with their belief system." Steve Hughes, a professor of political science at California State University, Stanislaus, wrote of his own growth as part of the Las Palomas Global Education community that the workshops left him "completely committed to changing my attitudes, beliefs, and practices about learning and the classroom." Las Palomas is "fanatical" about the subject of community—"how you build it, how you maximize it for learning, how you develop it in the classroom." Like many others I interviewed, he mentioned the ambience of the Luhan house as being central to the kinds of transformations that occur there: "the feeling of warmth and comfort along with the energy to let go, to experiment."[11]

Steve and George took their programs on the road to Arkansas State University, where they did successful workshops for forty teachers, and to the Tennessee Governor's School for International Studies in Memphis, where George served in an advisory and workshop leader capacity for several years. In 1991, Las Palomas won a four-year, thirty-thousand-dollar-a-year grant from the Mott Foundation for further developing community education around the issues of equity, security, and the environment. Mott designated Las Palomas "a national special issues center with responsibility for developing connections between global issues and community education."[12]

George brought to his role in the global education movement a somewhat unusual stance, according to Jamie Cloud, director of Teacher Education Programs for the American Forum for Global Education, a national clearinghouse for global education information and resources. Jamie met George at a 1984 conference in Washington, D.C., on educating Americans for responsible choice. Whereas most global educators are involved in systematic approaches to structural change, George focuses on "empowering individuals" more than on content: "There's a lot of attention to process, to taking advantage of the expertise in the room. There's very little emphasis on expert and external sources of information."[13]

Cloud also discussed some of the concrete outcomes from Las Palomas-sponsored events, including a three-year institute for professors of education that taught them about international development issues, for which they received incentive grants to redesign the curriculum and the graduation requirements at their schools. Ray Christine, a professor of education at Arizona State, was involved in an Exxon grant that led to "several very successful undergraduate course requirement changes and several excellent teacher education programs at colleges and universities around the country." Other educators whose lives and work have been affected by Las Palomas include Bob Campagna, the "official photographer" of Las Palomas during the four years that he was part of their "creative spirit." Bob was involved in the Taos Workshops and Taos Adventure, two summer programs for adolescents that incorporated art, study, and work in order to "integrate new ways of creating and seeing." Much of what he learned in his work at Las Palomas "translated into my work elsewhere," including workshops he did in Nicaragua and Scotland.[14]

Taos International High School

Taos High School students were involved from the beginning of the student and youth leadership conferences that were held at Las Palomas. Among the most enthusiastic were the children of the flower children of the 1960s commune movement. Nancy Jenkins, a Taos High English teacher who was close to a number of these students encouraged one of them to write a series for the Taos High School student newspaper, the *Tiger's Roar,* about her experiences growing up in Taos in the 1970s and 1980s.

Ananda Read wrote enthusiastically about what she believed her generation had gained from their hippie parents: "They objected to plastic, sterilized and devitalized food, phoney-looking unpractical and uncomfortable clothes, and extravagant and pretentious houses." She reminded her fellow students that the organic food bins in the local supermarket were courtesy of the hippie's shunning of chemicals and preservatives, and she pointed out the unorthodox building materials and the use of solar energy that grew out of their designs for simplified living spaces. Ananda's friends confirmed this when they told her they did not wish they had been brought up as "normal" kids, although some remembered being teased and harassed, and others spoke of their embarrassment at having to eat lunches of wheat bread, tofu, and alfalfa sprouts, rather than baloney, white bread, and Twinkies. Ananda concluded: "Most want to travel and take risks in life, and all are optimistic."[15]

Nancy Jenkins came to Taos with her husband, Ken, in 1969, after leaving Simi Valley High School in California, a school located close to the Manson Family's Spahn Ranch, where a number of their students hung out. She and Ken had gotten a contract from Bobbs-Merrill to write a book about Charles Manson, and they came to Taos because they were told that one of the Manson Family was living there. Soon after their return to California, they quit their teaching jobs and moved to Taos. After one year they became "totally different people." Nancy lost her interest in writing about the "dark side" of the counterculture, although she admitted that there's plenty of dark stuff in Taos: "It makes or breaks marriages and psyches and you can go mad. . . . Shiva is definitely here."[16]

Almost as soon as Nancy arrived, she started to track the first generation

Children of the Counterculture, Taos High School, 1988.
Photo by Lynn Del Margo, courtesy of Nancy Jenkins.

of kids who grew up in the communes. They began to enter the high school around 1984 and were the majority of the Anglos (20 percent) in the school. Although they always felt like a group apart, by the time they arrived at Taos High, they were getting along fairly well with the Indian and Hispanic kids. Nancy spoke of them as "survivors," many of whom had taken care of their parents, and some of whom were on LSD when they were as young as two years old. More politically and socially active than a lot of students, they were especially interested in issues of ecology and community responsibility. A lot of them were in the Honor Society, which voted to use its dues for five years running to sponsor conferences at Las Palomas on issues of peace, world resources and ecology, human rights, civil disobedience, and education reform. George helped them run their conferences. According to Nancy, "He is wonderful at designing situations where students learn themselves."

It was these students, along with the Taos teachers who participated in global education workshops at Las Palomas, that initiated the project of making Taos High the first rural International High School in the nation. The Taos International Studies Program, initially coordinated by Peggy Davis and Bridget Gallegos, won a Quality Education Awards grant from the state in 1989. In 1991, one-third of the faculty offered thirty-one courses with international components, including international math, that served 750 students.

Taos High's 1991 "International Studies Handbook" underscored how dramatically Taos education had changed since the early 1960s when the student body was expected to speak English only and assimilate an Anglo-American curriculum:

The International Studies Program at Taos High is designed to provide students with as many opportunities as possible to explore the world around them. . . . This exploration will begin aqui *[here] in Taos, delving into our tricultural roots and extending to the farthest regions of the globe. . . . The main objective of this program is that students who have been part of it will graduate with a multi-perspective background in viewing the world and with problem-solving skills which will help them deal more effectively with their future, whether a future of fixing cars, fixing people, fixing rock songs or fixing spaceships.*[17]

The New Age Comes to Las Palomas

In the spring of 1988, at age forty, Susan Chambers-Cook walked into the Mabel Dodge Luhan house: "All the hairs on my body stood up, and I knew that I was going to work here. I didn't even know what they did or what it was." Susan described her life as "a struggle to integrate, to find what it was that connected everything," which is why she studied psychology. As a counselor at a performing arts school, she began to perceive the connections between the artistic process and the therapeutic process. Before coming to Taos she had been very ill and come close to death. When she moved to Taos and got the job as codirector of Las Palomas, she felt as though she was beginning "to rise from the ashes."

Susan's role at Las Palomas was to "articulate a newer order of things." This newer order entailed a shift in Las Palomas's philosophy and programming that put greater emphasis on the transformation of the individual: "As you begin to change interior reality, the exterior reality begins to change. . . . The human race has to begin to go within and understand their own dynamic." Whatever we refuse to accept about other nations, cultures, or peoples, is, according to Susan, "really a statement about the rejection of self." Self-acceptance includes accepting one's dark, shadow side. "Being human is not being good, but being whole."[18]

 Susan's interest in mind-body integration and in working toward education and social reform from the inside out resonated strongly with George Otero's evangelical approach to self-empowerment. During my interview with them in July 1988, George spoke of Las Palomas as being "the next step after exposing the disillusionment of the 1960s . . . recovery, integration, wholeness." This next step was clearly related to the exhaustion that George and Kitty, as well as other staff members were experiencing as they faced a question that loomed with increasing urgency that year: How to keep the house going without it taking more from them than it gave?

Susan's vision of spiritual growth and psychological healing brought new energy to Las Palomas, but it also reinforced and expanded George's utopian vistas at a moment in time when the future of his enterprise seemed to be at stake. Susan believed that the decade of the 1990s was going to be "the Las Palomas decade," when it would be at the center of a national paradigm shift: "There have to be new responses to life because the current ways aren't working." She saw this shift not as veering away from, but as fulfilling Las Palomas's true mission: greater self-awareness would reconnect the individual to the larger self of nature and society.

This meant reconceptualizing Las Palomas as "a psycho-spiritual center" in which art and culture programs were renamed "creativity and consciousness." Susan hired Jungian dream analysts Larry and Pat Sargeant to do workshops on self-integration, and she worked with the Omega Institute, a holistic education center headquartered in upstate New York. Gary Cook, her artist-husband, borrowed the "vision quest" concept from Native American cultures and brought it to the painting workshops he did with adolescents. Susan offered workshops on Sacred Landscapes, the Wise Woman Within, and ecopsychology.

In 1989, Susan hired the woman who proved to be the single most successful program draw in Las Palomas's history—the by now renowned Natalie Goldberg, whose writing workshops at Las Palomas drew people from all over the nation and Europe. When Natalie first came to teach at Las Palomas, she knew nothing of the history of the Luhan house. After hearing the lecture I gave to her writing group on the history of the house, she felt that it must have been intended for her to find a teaching home there.

Natalie's deceptively simple formulas—keep your hand moving, pay attention to original detail, write from first mind—have their origins in her alternative school teaching. Building on the Zen paradox that when you "write from first mind" your ego disappears and you get out of the way, she teaches her students that their goal is to have no goal but getting beyond

Natalie Goldberg's writing class, September 1989
(Natalie is standing on left.)

themselves to an authentically genuine direct experience that they don't control: "the mind that doesn't care if you get an A, the mind that connects you with who you are." In Natalie's groups the act of writing is made communal, and no judgments are allowed. When students want to take their writing further and refine it, they are on their own. What she does is a kind of therapy, as well as a disciplined spiritual practice. Many people claim that her workshops and books have "changed their lives" because she has empowered them to use writing as a vehicle of self-knowledge.[19]

Natalie credits the 1960s and her Zen training as the sources of her communal writing practices: "The breakdown of traditional ways of perception that was alive in the hippie generation and in the life of Taos allowed people to experiment with the seemingly ridiculous—building houses out of beer cans or having a writing group where everyone wrote together right there and then read their work aloud." In fact, she lives in a home built of beer cans, constructed by another 1960s émigré to New Mexico, Mike Reynolds. An alternative architect, he achieved the epithet Father Earth for the "earth ships" he created on a mesa north of Taos. These are made almost entirely out of recycled materials—beer cans, rubber tires, glass—and are entirely energy self-sufficient. In a 1993 architecture review, the *New York Times* described Reynolds as using "the detritus of 20th-century civilization" for the "building blocks of a new utopia." [20]

By the summer of 1989, George Otero had settled on an ambitious new building program that he hoped would increase the possibilities for realizing his utopian visions. Susan spoke of Las Palomas's need to "grow or die." She said they needed an income of eight hundred thousand dollars annually, which was impossible to generate with the existing facilities, in order "to show you can make a living running a visionary center." George had clearly found a soul mate who energized his grandest ambitions, and who gave him the support he felt he needed to take the leap beyond running a family business.

Kitty initially embraced Susan's coming as a breath of much-needed fresh air, but she was soon displaced by her. What followed was a sad and bitter contest of persons and wills, in which Kitty returned to Albuquerque, then came back briefly in the summer of 1990 to take over the house, forbidding entrance to Susan. Kitty worked out a personal and business separation with George, which forced Las Palomas to move to downtown offices for a year, its programs directed by Karen Young (who had been Las Palomas's first program director). During that time, Kitty ran Mabel Dodge as a bed-and-breakfast and conference center.

George took out a $1 million loan to refinance the Big House and built two new buildings on the property, including a conference center that doubled the number of people who could be housed on the property (twenty-two in the Big House; up to thirty in the new building). At this point, the majority of his board of directors resigned, arguing that he was risking the whole enterprise of Las Palomas. In the fall of 1990, Kitty moved permanently to Albuquerque, where she began to attend the University New Mexico in order to complete her degree in teaching, and she and George divorced. In the meantime, most of the new programs that Susan instituted did not fill, in spite of her designing for the 1989–90 season the most attractive and expensive brochure ever produced by Las Palomas. George had increasing difficulty paying the mounting bills accrued by the new loan and by the more ambitious advertising campaign Susan had undertaken.

In an attempt to professionalize the running of the business, Susan and George tried to end the mom-and-pop quality of it that had sometimes meant taking care of staff who were not always able to do their jobs. Susan ended

New Office and Conference Center, Las Palomas, 1990.

up firing ten staff people in her first year, with resulting charges of racism and exploitation in the Hispanic and Native American communities. Kitty had a wonderful rapport with many Native American families at the pueblo who worked at Las Palomas. But even before she left, relations with Taos Pueblo turned sour when the then reigning governor made the decision, in the summer of 1988, to put a barbed wire fence behind the Luhan house in order to separate the property from the Indian land, which is about twenty feet behind the house.

The governor of the pueblo, Vincente Lujan, had been told that delivery trucks parked behind the house, and he sent the war chief to demand that the Oteros pay $250 to $300 a month for parking, which George felt were extortion fees. Nineteen eighty-eight was the last year the federal government was giving money to the tribe to fence in its lands, and when George refused to pay the fees, the Indians fenced in the back, telling the Oteros that they would "have to look at it every day." When the fence went up, the staff was in tears, including the Taos Pueblo women who had worked at Las Palomas for most of its existence.[21]

One Taos Pueblo member of the Las Palomas staff, who seemed to un-

Fence put up on boundary between Luhan House and Taos Pueblo, 1988 (photographed in 1989).

derstand the politics involved in this decision, told me that the tribal governor did this because of an old grudge he bore Tony Luhan. In order to understand this, one most know something of the relations that Tony Luhan maintained with the two sides of his family, who have distinctly different memories and perceptions of Mabel and Tony.

The Conchas and the Suazos worked for Mabel and Tony. Mabel's relationship with them was that of the benign patron, and they seem to have willingly accepted her patronage, including her changing Emilia Concha's name to Emily, because there were already two other Emilias working at the house. Emily Concha waited on tables and cooked for the Luhans during the 1930s, and her daughter, Josephine Marcus, was Bonnie Evans's best friend in Taos, where she spent much time in the summers of her adolescence. Josephine and Emily spoke fondly of Mabel's goodness to them, the extra money she gave them, and the clothes she knit when Emily was sick after childbirth. They also recalled the many ice skating and skiing parties and Easter egg hunts that Mabel arranged for the children of Taos pueblo.

The Suazos were the primary beneficiaries of Tony's will, receiving most

Marie Lujan and Lorencita Lujan, Taos Pueblo, 1989.

of his property and some of his finest possessions. Lupe Suazo served as a driver for Tony and Mabel and took care of their horses, sheep, and pigs. He has many beautiful artifacts given him by Tony, including a hunting bow and rifle. Tony was his godfather, and he remembers him as warm and friendly. The Suazos inherited the Tony House, now called the Santiago, or Spanish, House.[22]

For the other side of the family, Mabel and Tony have quite a different character. Alfred and Ernesto Lujan, and their sister, Marie, Tony's nephews and nieces, believe that Tony married Mabel for her money, although Ernesto admitted that he must have really loved her since he put his "soul and faith aside to marry her." They are angry with Tony for having promised their father that he would inherit his property. According to Alfred, Tony's divorce decree from Candelaria stated that all his property would be turned over to Agapito, their father, if she died first. Agapito, along with Trinidad Archuleta, Fred Romero, and Manuel Reyna, had helped to build the Mabel Dodge Luhan house. Julia Anna, Agapito's wife, worked for Mabel. Ernesto feels that Tony played the role of "godfather" in the tribe, that he was "sharp and slick," using his influence with powerful Anglos to get prime land for himself when several thousand acres were

Ernesto Lujan in front of his store, Taos Pueblo, 1989.

George Otero and Susan Chambers-Cook, spring 1994.

returned to the tribe. "He helped the tribe and he helped himself at the same time."[23]

Tony was the richest man in the pueblo, and when he left everything to the Suazos, he left a trail of bitterness. Vincente may well have decided to put up the fence because he was angry that his side of the family had not gotten the property when Tony died. Susan Chambers-Cook felt that what happened was symbolic of the tribe's trying to "fence themselves in" as a means of not dealing with their continuing poverty and loss of culture. While she is not an expert on the pueblo, there is truth in her observations about the ways in which life in Taos Pueblo has often been stymied by the conflict between the old ways and present needs.

As Taos Pueblo has sought to find its way into the future, and Las Palomas struggled to stay alive, their paths converged in other, more positive ways. In 1992, Taos joined with the seven other northern pueblos to begin to stake their claim to environmental leadership in New Mexico, beginning with the appointment of two tribal members to the positions of solid waste manager and manager of natural resources. In the same year, Karen Young, who had been Las Palomas's first program director, and who ran its Elderhostel program for many years, was appointed director of the Northern Pueblos Institute in Española. The institute has developed programs in technical training and assistance for Native Americans in water-quality monitoring, solid waste and hazardous materials management. In the spring of 1993, Karen was the institute's representative at a historic meeting that took place at the Mabel Dodge Luhan house.

Representatives from local government, business, and community groups met with representatives of the Pueblo tribes to "develop a plan of action on environmental and economic issues relevant to the Taos area, including the creation of a county solid-waste transfer facility; water/wastewater reclamation projects that integrate agricultural and community growth issues; and a project related to mining remediation and risk assessment." The meeting was organized by Jim Brown, director of EPOTEC, a nonprofit technology management enterprise. In the summer of 1993, he coordinated the writing of a major federal technology transfer grant that would bring together Las Palomas, the government-funded military labs, the pueblos, the State Environmental Office, and local community agencies to deal with environmental and development issues.[24]

The seeds of such a hope have been scattered across the northern New Mexico landscape for the last two generations, in recent years nurtured by post Cold War expectations of military conversion to peacetime uses. It seemed as though Los Alamos and Sandia would begin to turn away from weapons research and manufacture in order to deal with the wounds our military-industrial complex has inflicted on the earth and its peoples. It is noteworthy that the Santa Fe Institute was founded by physicists who had worked at Los Alamos, and that part of its efforts have been directed toward discussion of how to create a more sustainable world.

But EPOTEC did not get funding for its grant, and the promise of large amounts of federal money for transfer of technology projects has not been realized. While citizens groups are meeting with Los Alamos and Sandia labs about environmental clean up, it is not clear what impact they will have, given the massive government cutbacks in lab personnel and threatened cutbacks in environmental protection.

As this book goes to press, the Mabel Dodge Luhan house is up for sale, and it is impossible to predict its future. But prediction is a treacherous game. As Larry Torres makes clear in the Epilogue, the stories generated by and about the Luhan house for the past seven decades have helped to make Taos, New Mexico, a continually fascinating paradigm of Old World visions and New World dreams. Thus, it is at last reasonable to imagine that the house Mabel built will continue into the next century tantalizing those who wish to construct a world in which we all can be at home.[25]

Andy Mauldin, *Mabel Dodge Luhan House,* 1991. Watercolor.
(Andy is Mabel's great-grandson, a painter who lives and works in Santa Fe.)

Epilogue: Interview with Larry Torres

It is a warm August evening in 1989. Larry Torres and I are sitting in Mabel Luhan's summer house, perched over the acequia that runs through her property. Our four hours of talk and laughter are punctuated by the wind carrying the sound of men singing at Taos Pueblo. Larry is a sixteenth-generation Taoseño, who teaches Spanish, French, Russian, and international studies at Taos High School. His insightful, and sometimes sardonic, memories weave the strands of the Luhan house's history together in a rich tapestry that provides a fitting conclusion for this book.

The Mabel Dodge Luhan Years

It's the mid-1950s. I must be six or seven years old. One of my strongest memories of Mabel was seeing her dressed as a squaw being driven around in a big black car, on a hot day, over and over and over on the plaza, while Noula Karavas, who used to pass as a Greek princess in exile, would look through the lattice work of the La Fonda Hotel. [Noula was the mother of Saki Karavas, owner of La Fonda, which houses the "obscene" paintings of D. H. Lawrence.] The eyes of the two ladies meet; sparks seem to fly for some reason. There was a great rivalry going on there.

Noula will always be called *La Princesa.* Mabel was always *La Luhan.* In Spanish, "la" means "the," so *La Luhan* means "the Luhan Woman." Now if I said the Luhan Woman in English, you'd see that I'm driving toward a specific social standing. We saw her as someone who was always on the periphery of society. She never succeeded in penetrating the culture. So when I talk about the big three goddesses [Noula, Mabel, and Frieda Lawrence], oh yes, they must be controlling the arts somewhere, but they never ever got that big foothold in New Mexico, in Taos, among the native people of this area.

Mabel was very affected—how can I say it—she was playing native. We had known that somehow she had paid money to Tony Luhan's wife, so he could come spend the night over there at her place. Now that was rather unsavory in puritanical Taos. And you have to remember that Victorian Taos lasted almost to the coming of the hippie revolution. This is why it took us so much by surprise. I was raised very Victorian, very proper, very stiff, very moral. Of course, there were always undercurrents, but if someone openly flaunted our way of life, as *La Luhana* did, she would be understood as persona non grata or outcast even among her own kind, although I don't think she gave a royal damn.

The other reason why we kept away from Mabel was because she tried to learn the secrets of the people, but she would not approach them directly. I am speaking of the episode where Mabel and Dorothy Brett were watching a Penitente procession behind the house, and they hid in an arroyo, and they were caught spying on the Penitente rites. This was before my time, but you see the stories here are told all night, night after night, so they remember things like this. Now the Penitente rites are something of a mystery, even to a lot of Spanish people, because they were simply not talked about over the years. And to find out that two Anglo ladies had hidden in the little arroyo just to spy on the ceremonies caused them to be considered very unsavory.

I waited almost nightly [on Dorothy Brett] for seven years, because she used to go to the Casa Cordova, the plushest restaurant in New Mexico [which opened] in the mid-1960s. [Godfried Scheutz, the owner] taught us everything about wine and serving; he tried to make us get rid of our Spanish accents, and to act like French waiters. On slow nights, [Brett] would regale us with life at Windsor Castle, which we never believed, because she was just entertaining us. Among the things she told us was that her own mother was rumored to be the illegitimate daughter of Napoleon Bonaparte. She said that when she wanted to irk Queen Victoria, she would throw marbles at her feet.

Once when I spoke to Georgia O'Keeffe, she said, "You had known Dolly," and I said, "Who the hell is Dolly?" and she said, "Dorothy Brett," and I said, "Yes, I waited on her several times." She said, "Tell me about her." And as I was telling her about her, she got very teary-eyed, and I said, "What's going on?" and she said, "Did you know that she and I had been intimate?" And I said, "No, [but] I know you painted at D. H. Lawrence's ranch together. Why did you break off relations?" She said, "Because she grew progressively more frumpy, more eccentric, and more hard of hearing, and I couldn't abide that. But now that the old broad is gone, I do miss her."

A lot of [Brett's] reminiscences included life at this house, and what would happen behind closed doors over here. Everybody knew that Mabel had built this house to please Tony more than anybody else. They said that she had built it in Pueblo architecture or style. But look at those cobbled corbels over there; you know damn well that this is more Spanish than Pueblo. But because it was multilevel, multitiered, she was complying. She makes her vigas, she paints her vigas, and latillas. But it was not a common practice over here because the people were just busy trying to eke out a living from the earth, without worrying what color the damn latillas were painted, which she wanted to make look like a Navajo blanket, to please Tony again. I don't think Tony would have given much of a damn anyway.

Now the rooster [the ceramic roosters on the roof of the main house] is very symbolic among the Latinos, certainly among us, as a fertility symbol. Certainly the word *gallo,* if you referred to Gaia, or mother earth, the crowing of the rooster in the morning wakes the mother earth. The reason all the doors of all Mabel's houses are painted blue, like all the houses of the Southwest, is because blue dispels evil. Witches cannot fly into your windows.

Tony, who was macho, knew how to control this lady. The lady, I suspect, had finally met her match. She wanted spiritual fulfillment, you said in your book, but sexual fulfillment more than anything else, a man who could tell her what to do, and how to do it, and why to do it. I'm not sure if it was ever what we call a real husband-wife relationship. I think it was always a mentor-student relationship between them. From what I gather among the people Tony was not in a very secure place [in the pueblo]. There are always factions vying for control, and his jig was almost up.

Suddenly this lady can offer him a position where he can move up socially. Now, usually this is not a trait common among the Pueblo people. This is why I feel the man must have been terribly, terribly unusual. This is very much an American trait, this moving up the social ladder. So I don't know if she hit upon a kindred spirit. He did have this quiet dignity as I remember, as he sat smoking. There was a sense of arrogance about him, not pride, there was an arrogance, almost a Spanish arrogance, and that is something I recognize quite well, coming from a long line of those myself.

The Dennis Hopper Years

Nineteen sixty-six. I'm fourteen, I suppose, or something like that. And we were told that the hippies were coming, fifty thousand of them. We had these visions, of fifty thousand longhaired English speakers moving in on us. Now you have to remember that the school system was only consolidated in 1963, here in Taos county. Before that time we all belonged to the little schoolhouses all over the valley. [Now] we are made to speak English formally in the classroom. So we go from a superconservative Hispanic society to an avant-garde society overnight.

Now let's stop and think about it from a historical point of view. This is not a childhood reflection, this is more of a mature reflection, as a linguist, as someone who has traveled abroad for many years. When you consider that the last Moorish stronghold at Granada fell in 1492, and that the Spanish start coming to conquer Mexico, and up the Rio Grande Valley, they are coming straight out of the Middle Ages. They have not undergone the Renaissance, so that the people here are isolated for centuries.

Our religion, our traditions, our customs, our way of looking at people are very medieval, still reflected in the language of today, which is very archaic. Taos Spanish is three hundred years out of fashion, so that we have people, scholars from Spain, who come here to study the language of Cervantes here among us. What happens when you have a society that goes from this to that with no transition or stages? The reason I feel such great empathy for people in the Soviet Union is because they have undergone exactly the same thing. Straight out of the Middle Ages, straight to communism, and modernism, with no transitional period.

[Before the hippies] there had been crackpots, let's call them, because we called them *los locos,* these Anglos, like Mabel. Also we were mistrustful. Something had occurred in Los Alamos and we were not told what it was. They wouldn't let any of us sheepherders up into those mountains anymore. There was great distrust of the Anglo during the times of the Korean war and the pre-Vietnam era. There was a man here in Taos who used to walk around through the Taos fiestas every year. He had long hair, always wore glasses, and always wore a long white dress, a tunic. A lot of the older people distrusted him and would make the sign of the evil eye against him. Other people were seen kissing his hands and feet and treating him like a holy man.

It was not until years later that we found out that this was a government spy who was looking for communists among the literati of Taos. So there is a great mistrust for all Anglo-speaking people in this immediate area. (You're already familiar with the story about Arthur Manby and how he gains control of a lot of the property by manipulating Theresa Fergusson.) So suddenly we are told that fifty thousand hippies are coming out of Haight-Ashbury. We didn't know what Haight-Ashbury was, anyway. But what happened was, they trickled in here . . . without us realizing that they had come.

Now suddenly Mabel's house is revived, and we are high school students, and [we understand that] there are great pot parties going on in this house. The drug scene became very, very, very big. Now again, that was their allure, their enticement for us. Drugs had been virtually unknown to me as a child. The strongest thing I can remember doing is going to the corral and rolling dried horse shit cigarettes. [These are] the same ingredients that give a hallucinogen to the mushroom that is growing in the manure. So for centuries we have been smoking horseshit cigarettes here in Taos, and we were pretty much drugged out, but we didn't know it. And we certainly didn't recognize it as a drug.

Suddenly they come and offer us new and different things, and we are eager for new and different things, because now our English is good enough. Enter Peter Fonda and Dennis Hopper. They came and did *Easy Rider.* They were the first Anglos to give recognition to the Spanish people. They incorporated them into the films; . . . they used locals with no script . . . so that when the film was . . . shown here in Taos, everybody went wild. It was the first time they had seen Anglos and Spanish and Indian people together, saying, "Look! There's so and so. Look!"

A memory of hippie days. I am waiting tables at Casa Cordova, trying to be French. [Dennis and David Hopper and Peter Fonda were] sitting at table four. Gordon Douglas ran in and said, "They killed Sharon, they killed Sharon," and as I was eavesdropping, suddenly the tale of the murder of Sharon Tate comes into focus. [Larry dates this in December but the murders took place in August 1969. He may be conflating memories, since he served Hopper more than once at the restaurant.] I'm pretending that I'm waiting on them, but I am listening with all my soul. I remember Dennis Hopper poking Peter Fonda and saying "We have an eavesdropper," and Peter said, "He's a friend," and he winked at me and wrote me off, which is exactly what I needed to hear the rest of it. Sharon, who had been in *The Valley of the Dolls,* was a friend of all these people, and they were well known, they were the rebels of Hollywood.

It was said that when they were looking for Charles Manson he had fled to the communes of Taos, New Mexico. So I remember there was great fear and trepidation all over the valley for weeks, people locking their doors securely. Already the hippies had made quite an impact. Now suddenly a madman [is coming] who just confirmed everything we ever thought of hippies in the first place, murderers, pot smokers.

Dennis Hopper thought he had made a great many friends in the valley, because he had made Taos famous, although this is not true. He was going up El Salto Road, which is where I live in Arroyo Seco. Suddenly the Seco boys decided they didn't want the goddamn hippie on the road, and they got off the truck and they were going to beat the hell out of Hopper. Now the reason they were going up the road, I suspect, was probably to visit El Salto, the seventh of the seven waterfalls that come down the holy mountain. It was [rumored to have been] used in prehistory for human sacrifice. Now Dennis and his friends were going up there, probably to drink and smoke and just to commune with the spirit of the old generation. Because Dennis Hopper was very much in tune with what had happened here with Mabel and with Lawrence and with Brett, and Willa, and all those others. Suddenly our local boys decided these honkies had no right going up there and getting minted and getting under our falls. So they cornered them against the Indian fence [that borders Taos Pueblo].

Dennis Hopper pulled out a gun. And suddenly they were up in arms, the whole valley. These longhairs pulled a gun on our children! See, the boys never told their fathers that they had plotted to beat the hell out of Hopper. So suddenly I remember there was a meeting at the schoolhouse in Arroyo Seco to see what we were going to do about the hippie problem, and it was decided we'd do something covert. The sheriff, the police department, was called in and they said, "Do what you want, we won't be around when you do it." The ringleaders at the time were great businessmen in town and they didn't like the longhairs. It was a communal effort to drive them out. I remember cornering hippies at the [Manby] spring and although we knew nothing about religion, we'd go up to them and say, "So you guys believe in partying naked, do you?" You know we'd be drinking beers and just trying to goad them into something. And one of them tried to say to us, "Well you guys think you're temples of the holy spirit but you're acting this way." We didn't know what temples of the holy spirit was, so they were beat up anyway.

We had a lot of people who worked at Human Services. Suddenly the bill for food stamps went sky high because these guys were coming in. Do you know what kind of resentment there is from the people who are just trying to eke out a living, who are not given food stamps? Suddenly they see a longhair at the counter buying things that they can't afford with food stamps. So all of these things created such a resentment of this house; when we knew that Hopper was in it [people kept their distance from him]. Dennis himself, when I waited on him, was a lousy tipper for starters, never more than a quarter or fifty cents, which used to irk me. Secondly, he never took off his goddamn hat. It was always dusty and he had two eagle feathers sticking out of it.

Two years after the hippies, 1970, the Chicanos arrive in town. The Brown Berets marched in from California with Che Guevera on their tee shirts and they told us, they told us, who have considered ourselves to be Hispanic all these years, "You're Chicanos." The most anybody had ever told us was that we were Mexicans, and we knew damn well we weren't Mexicans, because Mexicans were wetbacks to us. Any Mexican who made it this far up was a poor man looking for a job. We were centuries-old families over here. Suddenly these guys arrive and tell us we're "Chicanos" and they can't even tell us what a "Chicano" is.

So there's a big identity crisis. Now suddenly not only did we have to deal with the Anglos, we had to deal with our own cultural identity. I go down to New Mexico State in Las Cruces in 1971, and when I arrive in the first Spanish class, they say, "Oh, you're Spanish," in that tone of voice. Already they realized that the people of Taos considered themselves totally different from people elsewhere. So when I look at the cultural roots of where I am, why I became a Russian teacher, number one I think the hippie movement had a greater impact on me than I realized. I became a Russian to become un-American in the early seventies. I didn't like what I saw of American culture. I did not want to become an English American because I hated those longhairs.

I left in 1972 to study in the Soviet Union. I was sent off by the government. They gave me a full stipend, scholarship, and I went off and [got] a degree from the University of Leningrad. It wasn't until I was on the other side of the world that I discovered that all these people that I had known early in life were really interesting, fascinating people. I was amazed once traveling through the Gobi Desert that somebody asked me about the love of Mabel, the love of D. H. Lawrence, and it just floored me.

I had such a terrible, terrible image as an Hispanic, that I became French, instead. It wasn't until years later, that I am living in deep Siberia, or traveling and teaching in France, that I suddenly realize those same things that they are telling me in those little villages over there is what I had. And then I started cultivating my hispanicity again, and my American patriotism again. It wasn't until I started teaching in Memphis, Tennessee, [in 1985] and I made my first trip to Washington, D.C., that I finally felt some patriotism and belonging. But the hurts, the hurts are still there for a lot, a lot of our people.

The Las Palomas Years

When I was offered the teaching position here in Taos after I was ousted out of the Soviet Union in 1983, I would not teach in Taos, I would not. They offered me the job three times before I took it. I finally took it only as a continuing [substitute teacher.] Nobody would associate with [me] for many years because I was the new kid on the block, even though I was native. A big joke to the people of the valley is "Yes, you can say flat tire in ten languages, but you can't change one." And you know, [my father's] still waiting for me to get a real job.

Suddenly I realized that what I was telling to the kids, they were listening to. The kids started nurturing me. I owe these children my life; I really feel that these kids are the source of my strength. Last year when I was voted Teacher of the Year for the State of New Mexico, you know that was the crowning point of my career. And the kids are hungry to hear these same thoughts that I am sharing with you. It always wrenches me apart to talk about Taos. Sometimes, it's something I need to do, kind of like the Ancient Mariner, who has to keep telling the story over and over again.

The reason I do these lectures once a month, at least here at Las Palomas, is because I must or die. It's kind of like a catharsis for me, and in doing so it reminds me to tell the students also, "Look guys, this is the hurt that you have incorporated, maybe this is a prejudice that you have inherited from your own family, but you don't know why you have inherited it." It was like before the coming of Anglo society, the people of Arroyo Seco hated the people of Arroyo Hondo, the people of Arroyo Hondo hated the people of Valdez, the people of Valdez hated the people of— Now how do you account for this? You couldn't, unless you'd been to Spain. Andalucia hates Aragon, Aragon hates Castille, Castille hates Asturias. The people of Arroyo Seco largely come from Asturias, the people from Valdez largely come from Andalucia. . . . You see it is a tribal society, and it is very medieval.

George [Otero] is coyote. Coyote means he is half and half; he is half Spanish, half Anglo. Furthermore he has an Hispanic last name and then he doesn't speak Spanish. You know what kind of shame that is among your own people to have the last name and not to speak [the language]? I think he felt ostracized when he was growing up. [He has told me] how painful it is, number one, to be the son of a minister during a turbulent time, and number two, to be an Hispanic who does not speak Spanish. So he has a great deal of empathy, he reaches out to everybody. In curing everybody else's hurts, you can cure yourself. I found in him a kindred spirit, a man hurting as I had hurt. Someone who was ostracized or not appreciated by his own kind. Somebody who would naturally gravitate to Mabel's, as I have done.

 George moved into town and he wanted to found a cultural or a global center that would reach out beyond even Mabel herself. Suddenly, he is attracting people from Armand Hammer's place up the road, the United World College. Suddenly, he lands grants from the Danforth Foundation. Among the people he attracted was a certain Kate Gooch of Memphis, Tennessee. She is very rich and very influential in Memphis [and became head of the] Governor's School for International Studies. She scanned all over the United States and found that George gave lessons in international relations and community building workshops, and she had herself brought to Taos in 1983. She would listen to my stories of old Taos, and how it fits into the scheme of global realities. [On George's recommendation, she hired Larry to teach Russian.] But George facilitated this for me, or maybe it was the spirit of Mabel.

George had to get credibility outside before gaining credibility here [in Taos and at Taos High School]. There was massive resistance, first of all from the teachers because anybody living in Luhan's house has got to be a crackpot, you see. The thing that gave him the most massive credibility was that grant he landed for the gifted and talented program just last summer. There are still those who refuse to have anything to do with anything here except something that is artsy or weird or dramatic. So, in a way, being here, which I know is a source of his great strength, was also a curse, as far as community relations were concerned. Also, "Who are you Otero who do not speak Spanish to tell us?" Now, he did make good friends, and I count myself among his friends, and I do promote his programs because I think that he is doing very good things over here.

[When George first moved into the Mabel Dodge Luhan house] there was a medium who was brought into the house, and she was asked, "What do you see as the future of this house?" And the medium said to him, "I see a global ed center, far superior to anything Mabel ever did." I am repeating what George told me. See, what he said was that he saw this as a place of harmony, as a place that would become much more famous than even during the time of "the charmed circle." Now, I don't know if George made this up to promote his own whatever; it's very possible.

We all make up stories here in Taos. Because of the fact that when reality cannot be met on your own terms, you make up your own reality. This is why it is so very, very apropos that Don Quixote de la Mancha should be embedded in Mabel's portal. Ever since childhood, I know that there is a patron saint of the mad; it is Don Quixote. And, God help us, we are all men of La Mancha.

Notes

All newspaper and journal articles are given full citations in Notes; primary and secondary texts used as sources are given full citations in Bibliography.

Abbreviations

AAA: Archives of American Art
ASC: Alfred Stieglitz Collection, Beinecke Library, Yale University
ECPC: Elsie Clews Parsons Collection, American Philosophical Society
JCC: John Collier Collection, Sterling Library, Yale University
JTC: Jean Toomer Collection, Beinecke Library, Yale University
MAC: Mary Austin Collection, Huntington Library, San Marino, California
MDLC: Mabel Dodge Luhan Collection, Beinecke Library, Yale University
RJA: Raymond Jonson Archives, University of New Mexico

Preface

1. See Paul Buhle, *Marxism in the USA,* especially chap. 2, "American Socialism, American Culture," where he discusses the indigenous roots of American radicalism in evangelical religion, feminism, and other nonmainstream political movements.
2. See William McLoughlin, *Revivals, Awakenings, and Reform.* McLoughlin discusses the conservative, reformist, and radical elements of what he calls "awakenings," the first of which he locates in the seventeenth century. I am using the concept in a less specifically religious way in referring to the reformist and radical expressions of these cultural moments.
3. On the new western history, see, among others, William Cronon, *Nature's Metropolis;* Patricia Nelson Limerick, *The Legacy of Conquest;* Richard Slotkin, *The Fatal Environment.*
4. See G. William Domhoff, *The Higher Circles* and *The Bohemian Grove.*
5. Some of the most interesting manifestations of this thinking can be found in the work being done at the Santa Fe Institute, the "nerve center" of complexity theory. Their interdisciplinary approach to the sciences and social sciences provides a suggestive analog to the syncretic visions of the artists, writers, and reformers who have populated the Luhan house. See M. Mitchell Waldrop, *Complexity.*

Introduction

1. This story was told to me by Susan Chambers-Cook in September 1989.
2. Page Putnam Miller, who is director of the National Coordinating Committee for the Promotion of History, is responsible for the work involved in nominating the Luhan house for landmark status. She has been a prime mover in the Women's History Landmark Project, which was begun in 1989 as a cooperative agreement between the Organization of American Historians, the Coordinating Committee for the Promotion of History, and the National Park Service. The project's mission is "to increase public awareness and appreciation of women's history by identifying significant sites in women's history and preparing nomination forms for consideration for NHL [National Historic Landmark] status." Miller sent me the project's statement of purpose, from which this quote is taken.

3. Susan Sontag, "The Anthropologist as Hero," *Against Interpretation,* pp. 69–70. I am grateful to Meredith Machen for introducing me to this quote by Sontag, which appears in Machen's dissertation, "Home as Motivation and Metaphor in the Works of Willa Cather."
4. Interview with John Nichols, September 5, 1989.
5. See Stephen Fox, "Healing, Imagination, and New Mexico," *New Mexico Historical Review,* 58, no. 3 (July 1983): 213–37; William deBuys, *Enchantment and Exploitation.*
6. See Lois Rudnick, *Mabel Dodge Luhan,* chaps. 1–4, for the years leading up to Luhan's coming to New Mexico. For a discussion of the idea of the world as home, see Rudnick, "A Feminist American Success Myth: Jane Addams's *Twenty Years at Hull-House,*" in *Tradition and the Talents of Women,* ed. Florence Howe, pp. 145–67; also, Dolores Hayden, *The Grand Domestic Revolution.*
7. See Rudnick, *Mabel Dodge Luhan,* chap. 5. Mabel changed the original spelling of Lu*j*an to Lu*h*an because so many of her friends mispronounced the Spanish "jota."
8. Not all these visitors came at the invitation of Mabel Dodge Luhan or stayed on her property. Carl Jung was brought to Taos by a friend of the Luhans who had "discovered Taos" through them. Aldous Huxley, who stayed at the Lawrence ranch and visited Mabel, came as a result of his friendship with D. H. Lawrence.
9. Ansel Adams quoted in Beaumont Newhall, *Ansel Adams,* p. 48.
10. See Judith Tick, "Ruth Crawford's 'Spiritual Concept': The Sound-Ideals of an Early American Modernist, 1924–1930," *Journal of the American Musicological Society* 44 (Summer 1991): 221–35 (221–61). See Bernard Bell, "Jean Toomer's 'Blue Meridian': The Poet as Prophet of a New Order of Man," in *Jean Toomer: A Critical Evaluation,* ed. Therman O'Daniel, pp. 343–52.
11. Ronald L. Grimes, *Symbol and Conquest,* p. 34.
12. See Marta Weigle, "From Desert to Disney World: The Santa Fe Railway and the Fred Harvey Company Display the Indian Southwest," *Journal of Anthropological Research* 45, no. 1 (Spring 1989): 115–37; also Jackson Rushing, "Feminism, Mysticism, and the Fourth World: Mabel Dodge Luhan on Pueblo Art," paper presented at the New Mexico Art History Conference, Taos, New Mexico, October 1988; and the Introduction in *Ethnic and Tourist Arts,* ed. Nelson Graburn.
13. Barbara Rose, *American Art since 1900,* p. 223; Sandra Starr, *Lost and Found in California,* pp. 12–15; Sandra Stith, *Made in the U.S.A.,* pp. 162–205. On Hopper's inner circle, see Los Angeles Wight Art Gallery, *Forty Years of California Assemblage,* pp. 65–70.
14. The book that eventuated from this research is *The Desert Is No Lady,* eds. Vera Norwood and Jan Monk. For a fuller account of my experiences as Luhan's biographer, see "The Male-Identified Woman and Other Anxieties: The Life of Mabel Dodge Luhan," in *The Challenge of Feminist Biography,* ed. Sara Alpern et al., pp. 116–38.
15. See John Bodine, "Attitudes and Institutions of Taos, New Mexico"; Charles L. Briggs, *Woodcarvers of Córdova;* and Sylvia Rodriguez, "Art, Tourism,

and Race Relations in Taos: Toward a Sociology of the Art Colony," *Journal of Anthropological Research* 45, no. 1 (Spring 1989): 79–97.

16. Mabel Dodge Luhan, *Taos and Its Artists,* p. 11.
17. Interview with Susan Chambers-Cook, August 8, 1988.
18. I want to emphasize the subjectivity of my analysis in the last section of this book, both because of my involvement with the owners and directors and my dependence on oral histories and interviews for much of my information.

Chapter 1

1. See Marc Simmons, *New Mexico;* Arrell Gibson, in *Santa Fe and Taos Colonies,* estimates some 250 artists came to New Mexico during the interwar years; see Weigle and Fiore, *Santa Fe and Taos,* on the some fifty writers who visited or moved there during this period.
2. Whitman quoted in James Kraft and Helen Sloan, *John Sloan in Santa Fe,* pp. 19–20. For an excellent analysis of the relationship between Walt Whitman's poetry and Native American aesthetics see James Nolan, *Poet-Chief.* For more typical late nineteenth-century Anglo views of the Southwest's indigenous peoples, see Susan Kenneson, "Through the Looking-Glass," pp. 262–78. She discusses the first generation of "local colorists" to travel to New Mexico, who were patronizing and racist in their attitudes toward Indians and Hispanics.
3. See Thomas Hartshorne, *The Distorted Image,* for a detailed analysis of the turn-of-the-century debate over national character.
4. Randolph Bourne, "Transnational America," *The Radical Will,* pp. 248–68.
5. See Daniel Joseph Singal, "Towards a Definition of American Modernism," *Modernism in American Culture,* pp. 1–27.
6. See William Homer, *Alfred Stieglitz and the American Avant-Garde;* Edward Abrahams, "Alfred Stieglitz's Faith and Vision," in *1915, The Cultural Moment,* eds. Heller and Rudnick; and James Mellow, "Alfred Stieglitz, Modernist in the Family Parlor," *Art News* (January 1983): 89–92.
7. In the 1920s, Stieglitz's Gallery was called "An American Place." See Bram Djikstra, *The Hieroglyphics of a New Speech,* pp. 80, 90.
8. See Fred Matthews, "The Revolt against Americanism: Cultural Pluralism and Cultural Relativism as an Ideology of Liberation," *Canadian Review of American Studies I,* no. 1 (Spring 1976): 6 (4–31); William Preston, *Aliens and Dissenters.*
9. Both Austin and Luhan indulged in racial typecasting. Mabel was repelled by jazz and disturbed by the African American cultural dynamics that produced it. Austin was more blatant in her stereotyping, attributing "earthiness" to Hispanics, "drive" to Anglos, and asserting that African Americans were culturally inferior. See Austin, *Land of Journey's Ending,* pp. 442–47. Mick Gidley has noted in his work on the photography of Edward Curtis the emergence of the Native American as a "model minority" at the turn of the twentieth century, whose ethnic "purity" was emphasized as an implicit and explicit contrast to the "mongrelized" immigrants from southern and eastern Europe. "Edward Curtis among the Pueblos," paper presented at Continents in Conversation, November 1992, the University of Rouen, France. Gidley confirmed that a 1906 photograph of "Red Willow" by Edward Curtis was a

portrait of Tony Luhan, one of several Curtis portraits of Native Americans that were clearly constructed to look like photographs of the peoples of the Holy Land.

10. Karal Ann Marling, *Woodstock,* n.p.
11. See Laurence Veysey, *The Communal Experience,* chap. 1.
12. See Rudnick, *Mabel Dodge Luhan,* chap. 4; also Richard Maurice Burke, *Cosmic Consciousness.* Mabel's California New Thought guru was Will Lovington Comfort.
13. Veysey, pp. 46–47, 50.
14. See T. Jackson Lears, *No Place of Grace.* On pp. xv-xix, Lears compares himself with Christopher Lasch, Phillip Rieff, and Daniel Bell, who are all grappling "with the self-absorbed nihilism" of American life in the 1980s. Christopher Lasch, *The Culture of Narcissism;* Phillip Rieff, *The Triumph of the Therapeutic,* p. 261, concludes "that a sense of well-being has become the end, rather than the by-product of striving after some superior communal end, announced a fundamental change of focus in the cast of our culture." Veysey, p. 54.
15. See Rudnick, *Mabel Dodge Luhan,* chap. 5, for a full discussion of Mabel's plan.
16. T. S. Eliot, "The Metaphysical Poets," *Selected Essays,* pp. 281–91.
17. Marsden Hartley, "The Red Man," *Adventures in the Arts,* p. 14; Maynard Dixon, *Sketchbook,* p. 52.
18. Mary Austin, "The Indivisible Utility," *Survey Graphic* (December 15, 1925): 327 (306–27); John Collier, "The Red Atlantis," *Survey* (October 1, 1922): 7–20.
19. Richard Eldridge and Cynthia Earl Kerman, *The Lives of Jean Toomer,* pp. 225; Jean Toomer, "Notes on Taos," MS, JTC, n.p.; Frank Waters, *The Masked Gods,* p. 184.
20. Robert Jones, "Notes on the Theatre," *Theatre Arts Monthly* 8 (May 1924): 325 (323–25); Mabel Dodge Luhan, "A Bridge between Cultures," *Theatre Arts Monthly* 9 (May 1925): 297–301.
21. Dane Rudhyar, jacket cover, *String Quartets,* CRI, SD418 (New York: 1979). The phrase is taken from the title of a book by Rudhyar, *The Planetarization of Consciousness* (1969); Leopold Stokowski, *Music for All of Us,* p. 289.
22. John Collier, *Indians of the Americas,* p. 16.
23. Luhan, *Lorenzo in Taos,* p. 3; Robert Rosenblum, "The Primal Scene," in *The Natural Paradise,* ed. Kynaston McShine, p. 37; J. B. Jackson, *The Essential Landscape,* p. 3.
24. Sharyn Udall, "Spirituality in the Art of 20th Century New Mexico," unpublished paper (1990), p. 1. Udall emphasizes the importance of Kandinsky's *Spiritual in Art* on the artists of the Stieglitz circle. See Maurice Tuchman, *The Spiritual in Art,* for a discussion of "the genesis and development of abstract art" as "inextricably tied . . . to a desire to express spiritual, utopian, or metaphysical ideals that cannot be expressed in traditional pictorial terms" (pp. 17–19).
25. Luhan, *Taos and Its Artists,* p. 111; see John Bodine, "Attitudes and Institutions of Taos, New Mexico," pp. 22–27, for discussion of the various theories about how Taos got its name.

26. See Sharyn Udall, "Spirituality in the Art," pp. 14–16, for an analysis of the uses of the mountain in New Mexican art; Joe McGinnis, "Taos," *Southwest* 13 (1927): 41 (36–47); Jean Toomer, "Taos," MS, JTC, n.p. Hodson's theory is cited in Mildred Crews, "A Dash of Taos," *South Dakota Review* 17, no. 8 (1979): 92 (88–109).
27. Alice Henderson, untitled, *Red Earth,* p. 3.
28. See Kenneson, who points out that where the first generation of Anglo pioneers, like Charles Lummis, "lavished praise on rugged individuals and those who met the harsh challenges of the land," the renewed interest in the early twentieth century in community attracted a lot more women to New Mexico (pp. 266, 303–4). See also Barbara Babcock and Nancy Parezo, *Daughters of the Desert,* for a biographical history of the forty-five women anthropologists who were "important in pioneering southwestern research and establishing the field of anthropology" (p. 7).
29. See Sandra Gilbert and Susan Gubar, *No Man's Land,* vols. 1 and 2. Gilbert and Gubar argue that the misogyny found in modernist fiction by male writers is in good part a response to the emergence of feminism at the turn of the century. "The Wilful [*sic*] Woman," the fragment of the novel D. H. Lawrence started on Mabel's life, is in *St. Mawr and Other Stories,* pp. 199–203.
30. See Kay Aiken Reeve, "Pueblos, Poets, and Painters: The Role of the Pueblo Indian in the Development of the Santa Fe–Taos Region as an American Cultural Center," *American Indian Culture and Research Journal,* 5 (no. 4) (1981): 12 (1–19).
31. The quotation about the listener-participant is from Mary Austin, Introduction to *Path on the Rainbow,* pp. xv–xxi; Dickran Tashjian, "Marsden Hartley and the Southwest: A Ceremony for Our Vision, a Fiction for the Eye," *Arts Magazine,* 54, no. 8 (April 1989): 130 (127–31). Reeve makes a similar point when she notes that the Anglo artists' "association with Pueblo art stimulated them not to imitate the Indians' artistic forms, but rather to open their own creative spirit to the indigenous influences of the region" (p. 15).
32. William H. Truettner, "The Art of Pueblo Life," Charles Eldridge et al., *Art in New Mexico,* pp. 67–68; deBuys, *Enchantment and Exploitation,* p. 9.
33. deBuys, p. 9. See Sylvia Rodriguez, "Land, Water, and Ethnic Identity in Taos," in *Land, Water, and Culture,* eds. Charles L. Briggs and J. Van Ness, where she notes that "attachment to a land base" has remained "intrinsic to the ethnic self-identities of both [Native American and Hispanic] groups" (p. 317).
34. Thomas Steele, *Santos and Saints,* pp. 36–37.
35. On the Penitentes, see Marta Weigle, *The Penitentes of the Southwest.*
36. See John Bodine, "A Tri-Ethnic Trap: The Spanish Americans of Taos," in *Spanish-Speaking People of the United States,* ed. J. Helm, pp. 145–54.
37. Rodriguez, "Land, Water, and Ethnic Identity," p. 339; deBuys, pp. 198–211. Taos was incorporated as a town in 1934, at which time it began to promote tourism in earnest. Rodriguez notes that it was then that the battle began between progressives in all three communities who wanted to modernize and traditionalists, artists, and newcomers who "wanted to preserve and enhance Taos's quaint, rustic character." Mabel was in the forefront of this battle, especially after World War II, when returning Pueblo veterans wanted electri-

fication and she sided publicly with the conservatives at the Pueblo who wanted no changes.

38. Peter Nabokov, in *Adobe,* points out that it is "the world's oldest architectural heritage" (p. 18); Gaston Bachelard, *The Poetics of Space,* p. 62.
39. See Bainbridge Bunting, *Taos Adobes,* where he states that the Mabel Dodge Luhan house was one of the first two to be built in Taos in the Pueblo revival style (p. 14); Chris Wilson, "New Mexico Architecture in the Tradition of Romantic Reaction," *Artspace* 13, no. 1 (Winter 1988–89): 22–25 (22–28). Bunting dates the Luhan house 1923, but the first phase of the Big House was completed in December 1918.
40. Jerome Iowa, *Ageless Adobe,* pp. 77–82.
41. Vincent Scully, *Pueblo, Village, Dance,* pp. 9–10, 39; Nabokov, *Adobe,* p. 2. In *Indian Architecture,* Nabokov points out the ways in which Pueblo cosmology reflected in their village design "a distinctive spatial organization which emphasized motifs of ascent, descent, and the four directions" (p. 368).
42. Agnesa Lufkin, "A Rare Place: Mabel Dodge Luhan's Taos Estate," *El Palacio* 86 (Spring 1980): 30 (29–35).
43. Luhan, *Edge of Taos Desert,* pp. 292–93.
44. Beverley Spears, who served as a consultant on the architectural aspects of the Luhan house, says this is the least New Mexican of the rooms because the Pueblo revival features are added-on elements. Spears, "Notes on the Mabel Dodge Luhan House," August 2, 1988, p. 3.
45. Ibid., p. 4. The dining room fireplace is believed to have been built by Tony for his peyote practices.
46. See Bunting, "Architectural Guide to Northern New Mexico," *New Mexico Architecture* 12 (September–October 1970): 30–31, for details on the building of the rooms in the Big House.
47. Bunting, "Residence of Mable [*sic*] Dodge Luhan," *New Mexico Architecture* (September–October 1961): n.p.
48. Bunting, *Early Architecture,* p. 6; interview with John Collier, Jr., July 1, 1986.
49. My understanding of Tony comes from cited published sources, unpublished letters in the MDLC, as well as from interviews with Miriam Hapgood DeWitt, Ben Elkus, Frank Waters, and several relatives of Tony's at Taos Pueblo.
50. Luhan, *Background,* p. 16.
51. Luhan, *Background,* p. 21; Luhan, *European Experiences,* p. 162.
52. See Luhan, *Movers and Shakers,* p. 5.
53. Luhan, *Edge of Taos Desert,* pp. 59, 321.
54. See Jane Nelson, "Journey to the Edge of History: Narrative Form in Mabel Dodge Luhan's *Intimate Memories,*" *Biography* 3, no. 3 (Summer 1980): 240–52; William Spengemann and L. R. Lundquist, "Autobiography and the American Myth," *American Quarterly* 17, no. 3 (Fall 1965): 501–19; and James Nolan, *Poet-Chief,* who points out that for both North and South American "savagists, the American Indian defines the New World paradise, either lost or regained, and points the way to a pre- or post-Christian Eden as the ultimate meaning of America" (p. 49). On Indian captivity narratives, see Annette Kolodny, *The Land before Her,* and Richard Slotkin, *Regeneration through Violence.*

55. Luhan, *Winter in Taos,* pp. 31, 125.

56. Luhan, *Edge of Taos Desert,* p. 331. See my essay, "Renaming the Land," in *The Desert Is No Lady,* for a fuller discussion of the feminist revision of landscape in the works of Luhan, Austin, and Henderson.
57. I am grateful to Annette Kolodny for offering this insight during the panel "Women and the Interpretation Landscape" presented at the 1984 Biennial American Studies Association meeting, Philadelphia, Pennsylvania.

Chapter 2

1. Maurice Sterne, *Shadow and Light,* p. 82. For a discussion of Sterne and Mabel's relationship, see Rudnick, *Mabel Dodge Luhan,* chap. 4. For a discussion of Sterne's art, see H. M. Kallen, *Three American Modernist Painters,* pp. 7–11.
2. Letter quoted in Luhan, *Movers and Shakers,* pp. 534–35.
3. See Rudnick, *Mabel Dodge Luhan,* pp. 143–54. Sterne was not the only artist to be unnerved by the landscape. Both D. H. Lawrence and Jean Toomer responded hostilely at times to the landscape's power to undermine their significance. I have not found any women artists who came to the Luhan house who had this reaction.
4. Van Deren Coke, *Andrew Dasburg,* p. 54.
5. Andrew Dasburg to Mabel Dodge Sterne, [1920], MDLC.
6. Ida Rauh was one of the many multitalented New Women of Greenwich Village. A radical feminist, she was a graduate of New York University's law school, active in the birth control movement and the American Civil Liberties Union, and acknowledged to be the best actress among the early Provincetown Players. The portrait busts she did of Mary Austin and D. H. Lawrence demonstrate that she was also a respectable sculptor. They are in the collection of the University of New Mexico's Harwood Foundation in Taos.
7. Sheldon Reich, *Andrew Dasburg,* pp. 54–55; see also Sharyn Udall, *Modernist Painting,* p. 63. Udall notes that Dasburg's houses are "virtually indistinguishable from the landscape." Dasburg also profited materially from business ventures that involved the marketing of indigenous artifacts. In 1924 he joined with John Evans (Mabel's son), Walter Mruk, and B. J. O. Nordfeldt to form the Spanish and Indian Trading Company, which sold mostly to tourists. Although it is unclear how much they earned from this venture, there is little doubt that they bought cheap and sold dear. They undoubtedly profited more than the village and tribal people from whom they purchased their goods. See Reich, p. 64.
8. Lee Simonson quoted in Mary Henderson, *Theatre in America,* p. 208. In 1920, Jones was also the first scene designer to have his own one-man show. Henderson credits him with liberating American audiences from Belascoism—a totally realist approach to set design established by David Belasco. Few after him, she notes, escaped "the touch of Jones's work" (p. 208).
9. Jones quoted in Henderson, p. 204; Jones, "Notes on the Theatre," p. 323. Jones was very much influenced by George Cram Cook, the cofounder of the Provincetown Players for whom ancient Greek drama was a model for an art that served social and religious purposes. See Robert Sarlos, "Jig Cook and Susan Glaspell: Rule-Makers and Rule-Breakers," in *1915, The Cultural Moment,* pp. 259–59.

10. Maxwell Anderson, *Night Over Taos.* Anderson had never set foot in New Mexico. He was inspired to write the play by a series of articles written by Erna Fergusson. The play was produced by the Group Theatre, which put on several important productions of depression-era playwrights. Although it closed after a two-week run, Jones's sets and costumes were, according to Harold Clurman, the "most highly praised elements of the production." See Harold Clurman, *The Fervent Years,* pp. 76–77, 80.
11. On Hartley's New Mexico work, see Gail Scott, *Marsden Hartley,* pp. 66–72.
12. James Moore, "Marsden Hartley: The New Mexico Period," pp. 8, 19. Hartley's letter to Stieglitz is dated August 1, 1918.
13. Marsden Hartley, *Adventures in the Arts,* p. 14.
14. Scott, p. 69; Moore, p. 20.
15. Scott, p. 66; Udall, *Modernist Painting,* p. 38. Hartley used some of the santos from Mabel's collection for his still lifes, including *El Santo* and *The Virgin Blessing the Melon.*
16. Scott, p. 72. *Recollections* was also, I believe, "colored" by the nightmare of Nazism that Hartley faced on his return.
17. Agnes Pelton, "Biographical Sketch," Archives of American Art, reel 3427; Pelton quoted in Margaret Stainer, *Agnes Pelton,* p. 8.
18. *El Palacio* 6, no. 11 (October 1919): 175.
19. Agnes Pelton to Mabel Luhan, November 21, 1938, MDLC.
20. The Luhan portrait is owned by the Harwood Foundation. See John Young-Hunter's autobiography, *Reviewing the Years.*
21. See Michael Castro, *Interpreting the Indian,* chap. 1, where he points out that early "interpreters" of Indian song, like Austin, used considerable license and often lost or distorted the unique cultural assumptions and meanings of tribal imagery. For biographical details, see Augusta Fink, *I—Mary,* and Esther Lanigan Stineman, *Mary Austin: Song of a Maverick.*
22. Mabel Dodge Sterne to Mary Austin, [ca. June 1919], MAC.
23. See Stineman, pp. 155–71, for an excellent discussion of their friendship. Stineman discovered that Mabel provided Mary not only with living space and transportation, but also monthly stipends. Mary Austin, *Earth Horizon,* p. 32; Mabel Sterne to Mary Austin, May 28, [?], MAC.
24. See *El Palacio,* 6, no. 2 (June 14, 1919): 205–6, for Tony Luhan's rendition of "Br'er Rabbit and the Tar Baby"; *El Palacio,* 7, nos. 7 and 8 (November 30, 1919): 146–53, where Austin discusses the importance of using local folklore to teach New Mexican school children. Austin, *American Rhythm,* p. 6. James Ruppert relates Austin's theory of the landscape line to the modernist literary rebellion, which sought "historical examples of the creative welding of the arts, culture, and the environment." Ruppert, "Mary Austin's Landscape Line in Native American Literature," *Southwest* 68 (Autumn 1983): 376 (376–90).
25. Austin, *Land of Journey's Ending,* pp. 441–42; Austin, "The Indivisible Utility," p. 327. The article was illustrated with a fantastical rendition of Taos Pueblo drawn by Andrew Dasburg.
26. Austin, *Land of Journey's Ending,* p. 89; Austin, *Taos Pueblo,* n.p.
27. Austin, *Starry Adventure,* p. 276. I am grateful to Esther Stineman for bringing this novel to my attention. Like D. H. Lawrence's portraits of Mabel,

Austin's is ambivalent, conveying her fascination and admiration, as well as her loathing.

28. For biographical details, see Lawrence Kelly, *The Assault on Assimilation,* chaps. 1–4; Vine Deloria, *Custer Died for Your Sins,* 157.
29. Collier, "The Red Atlantis," p. 18 (7–20); Larry Kelly, "John Collier and the Discovery of the American Indian," paper presented at the Biennial American Studies meeting, November 1981, Memphis, Tennessee.
30. See Kelly, *The Assault on Assimilation,* chap. 2.
31. Collier, *From Every Zenith,* p. 25.
32. For a much more detailed discussion of the personalities and politics involved in the various Native American rights crusades of the 1920s and 1930s in New Mexico and under Collier's reign as head of the Bureau of Indian Affairs (BIA), including the complications of the land tenure issue and the bias of reformers against Hispanic settlers, see Kelly, *The Assault on Assimilation,* chaps. 5–10; Kenneth Philp, *John Collier's Crusade for Indian Reform;* Rudnick, *Mabel Dodge Luhan,* pp. 172–82, 261–65. For a history of the struggle for Blue Lake, see R. C. Gordon-McCutchan, *The Taos Indians and the Battle for Blue Lake.*
33. Mabel Sterne to John Collier, November 21, [1922?], JCC; Mabel Sterne to Stella Atwood, November 21, 1922, JCC.
34. For details of Collier's Indian New Deal programs, failures as well as successes, see Philp, chap. 8.
35. See Collier, *On the Gleaming Way,* p. 29. Most of this book was written in 1946 after his return from the first session of the General Assembly of the United Nations in London.
36. Uta Gacs, ed. *Women Anthropologists,* p. 287; Peter Hare, *A Woman's Quest for Science,* p. 141.
37. Babcock and Parezo, *Daughters of the Desert,* pp. 1, 15. On p. 7, they note the importance of the Southwest to women as an "alternative to masculine, industrial civilization."
38. See Hare, p. 147; Gacs, p. 287; and Rosemary Lévy Zumwalt, *Wealth and Rebellion,* chap. 11.
39. Mabel's letters to Parsons contain information on such practices as the installation of new officers and funeral rites at the pueblo; on Parsons's use of informants, see Gacs, p. 187. Tony Luhan to Elsie Clews Parsons, April 8, [1932], ECPC; Elsie Clews Parsons to Mabel Luhan, April 11, 1932, MDLC. Tony did not write his own letters, but dictated them, presumably to Mabel.
40. Elsie Clews Parsons to Mabel Luhan, September 15, 1937, MDLC; Parsons to Luhan January 4, 1939, MDLC; copy of January 7 letter to governor and council of Taos Pueblo, MDLC. For a discussion of the furor, see Claire Morrill, *Taos Mosaic,* p. 158; Hare, p. 162; and Zumwalt, pp. 250–56.
41. See Gui de Angulo, *Jaime in Taos,* for biographical notes on his father; quote is on p. 8.
42. Tony Luhan quoted in de Angulo, pp. 37, 46–47.
43. Ibid., pp. 38, 91–93.
44. Ibid., p. 87.
45. Jaime de Angulo to Mabel Luhan, January 16, 1925, MDLC; Barbara Hannah, *Jung, His Life and Work,* p. 161.

46. C. G. Jung, *Man and His Symbols,* p. 76 ; Hannah, pp. 161–62.
47. Jung, "The Spiritual Problem of Modern Man," p. 89; Jung, "The Complications of American Psychology," p. 513, both in *Civilization in Transition.* Some of Jung's ideas about the racial unconscious had fascistic elements, and he himself was sympathetic to the Nazi cause.
48. Luhan, *Lorenzo in Taos,* p. 70.
49. Erich Neumann, *The Great Mother,* 16–17.
50. See James Cowan, *D. H. Lawrence's American Journey;* Lawrence, "America, Listen to Your Own," *Phoenix,* p. 90.
51. Gilbert and Gubar observe that women in the fiction of male modernists are often suggested as the cause of "metaphysical angst," as "modernist formulations of societal breakdown consistently employed imagery of male impotence and female potency." *No Man's Land,* vol. 1, p. 36.
52. For a discussion of Lawrence's use of Mabel's character in his fiction, see Rudnick, *Mabel Dodge Luhan,* pp. 199–201, 219–24. Lawrence was equally ambivalent, for similar reasons, about Native Americans, whom he saw in both redemptive and racist terms.
53. Lawrence, "New Mexico," *Phoenix,* p. 142; "The Hopi Snake Dance," *Mornings in New Mexico,* p. 65. Lawrence's portrait of Hopi may well have influenced Aldous Huxley's portrayal of his "savage" habitat in *Brave New World.* See chap. 3 of this book.
54. Lawrence, "Indians and Englishmen," *Phoenix,* p. 92.
55. Lawrence, *Altitude, Laughing Horse,* no. 20 (Summer 1938): n.p., republished in Sharyn Rohlfsen Udall, ed. *Spud Johnson & Laughing Horse.*
56. Paul Horgan, "So Little Freedom," *The Peace Stone,* p. 171. The story was first published in 1942.
57. See Rudnick, *Mabel Dodge Luhan,* pp. 242–49, for a discussion of Bynner's and Luhan's relationship; Witter Bynner, "A City of Change," *Prose Pieces,* pp. 45–46.
58. Entry on history of Taoism, *Encyclopædia Britannica* vol. 17, 15th ed., 1974, pp. 1044–49.
59. See Spud Johnson, "Poppies," *Horizontal Yellow,* pp. 77–78.
60. Bynner, *Cake,* p. 91.
61. Meredith Machen, "Home as Motivation and Metaphor," p. 9. See also Judith Fryer, "Desert, Rock, Shelter, Legend: Willa Cather's Novels of the Southwest," in *The Desert is No Lady,* pp. 27–46.
62. Cather had already used some of these materials in Tom Outland's story, the interpolated story she embedded in *The Professor's House* (1924), which all but takes over the novel. Tom's trip to Mesa Verde changes the course of his life, as he gives up engineering in order to try to gain recognition for the Indian artifacts he discovers there.
63. Edith Lewis, *Willa Cather Living,* pp. 139–43.
64. Willa Cather, *Death Comes for the Archbishop,* pp. 233–34.
65. Ibid., p. 95; Judith Fryer, "Desert, Rock, Shelter, Legend: Willa Cather's Novels of the Southwest," *The Desert is No Lady,* p. 46.
66. Cather, p. 275.
67. For biographical information on Toomer, see Richard Eldridge and Cynthia

Earl Kerman, *The Lives of Jean Toomer.* On Gurdjieff's teachings, see G. I. Gurdjieff, *Gurdjieff,* and John G. Bennett, *Gurdjieff.*

68. Jean Toomer, "The Gurdjieff Experience," *The Wayward and the Seeking,* p. 130. For a discussion of Toomer and Luhan's relationship, see Rudnick, *Mabel Dodge Luhan,* pp. 225–30.
69. Toomer "Taos," MS., n.d., JTC; Toomer, MS, no title, n.d., JTC.
70. Toomer, *A Drama of the Southwest,* TS, JTC, pp. 35–45.
71. Toomer, "New Mexico," TS, p. 8, JTC; Toomer, "Lost Dance," *Collected Poems,* eds. Robert Jones and Margery Toomer Latimer, p. 39.
72. On Toomer's philosophy of "unitism," see Harry Jones, "Jean Toomer's Vision: Blue Meridian," in *Jean Toomer,* ed. Therman B. O'Daniel, pp. 337–38. Eldridge and Kerman talk about Toomer's messianism and marriage on p. 202.
73. Toomer, "Blue Meridian," *Collected Poems.*
74. John Collier, Jr., told me that he did not think Reyna had any prior experience in wood carving before working for Mabel. The "American Indian Arts" manifesto is quoted in Dorothy Dunn, *American Indian Painting,* p. 29.
75. J. J. Brody, *Indian Painters,* 117. Brody is one of the most critical of the Anglo patrons. See also, Charles Briggs, *The Woodcarvers of Córdova.*
76. Joan Sloan quoted in Dunn, p. 325. Among the most important painters of the first generation are Crescencio Martinez, Alfredo Montoya, Ma-Pe-Wi, and Fred Kabotie. See also Clara Tanner, *Southwest Indian Painting.* Native American painters had worked on canvas and other media with paint before the Dunn school; many of them were self-taught.
77. See Margaret Cesa, "Pop Challee," *New Mexico Magazine* (August 1990). 36–37.
78. Interview with Merina Lujan, August 3, 1990.
79. For biographical information, see Sean Hignett, *Brett: From Bloomsbury to New Mexico;* and Dorothy Brett, "Autobiography: My Long and Beautiful Journey," *South Dakota Review* 5, no. 2 (Summer 1967): 11–71. Mabel quoted in Hignett, pp. 198, 239–41.
80. On Brett's style of painting, see Hignett, p. 199; Dorothy Brett, "Painting Indians," *New Mexico Quarterly,* 21, no. 2 (Summer 1951): 168 (167–73).
81. Brett, "Painting Indians," p. 168. "Stokowski Symphony" was the generic name she gave the series of paintings she did after following Stokowski back to Philadelphia and observing him conduct from backstage.
82. Hignett, p. 213; Brett quoted in Laurie Lisle, "Under the Spell of Taos," *Rocky Mountain Magazine,* (January–February 1981): 61 (59–63).
83. The recovery of Rönnebeck's work is due primarily to the efforts of his daughter, Ursula Works, and Diane Groff who curated the 1990 retrospective, "Arnold Rönnebeck: The Avant-Garde Spirit of the West," in July 1990, for the Denver Art Museum. Groff noted in a letter to me of April 23, 1990, that many of the people Rönnebeck met at Mabel's "were instrumental in the development of his career." Very little of Emerson's work from this period survives, and from what I've seen, it is sentimental and mediocre. The post office mural art that she did under the WPA is more original and interesting. Arnold Rönnebeck to Mabel Luhan, March 20, 1925, MDLC; interview with Arnold Emerson Rönnebeck, August 4, 1990.

84. Diane Groff, notes for exhibition catalogue, "Arnold Rönnebeck: The Avant-Garde Spirit of the West"; Arnold Rönnebeck to Alfred Stieglitz, October 1925, ASC. Rönnebeck did several public commissions, including a beautiful wood sculpture of Indian ceremonials for the La Fonda Hotel in Santa Fe.
85. Arnold Rönnebeck to Alfred Stieglitz, October 9, 1925, ASC. In "Arnold Rönnebeck," a talk presented at the Albuquerque Museum, August 1990, Groff notes that Rönnebeck shares with other modernist artists "the graphic portrayal of musical feelings." I am grateful to Ursula Works for providing me with biographical information about her parents.
86. Eya Fechin, "Teenage Memories," *American West,* 21, no. 6 (November–December 1984): 29–36.
87. Eya Fechin, "Fechin's Home in Taos," *Southwestern Art* 7, no. 1 (1978): 5–12. Eya became a student of Martha Graham, a teacher of modern dance, and a pioneer of dance therapy. Her father painted the Taos landscape and Taos Indians until 1933. He became a naturalized citizen while living in Taos.
88. Mary Balcomb, *Nicolai Fechin,* pp. 60–74. Balcomb quotes Mabel as saying that Willa Cather chose Fechin to paint her because of the "remarkable versatility and mastery" of his portraits (p. 60).
89. Strand quoted in Calvin Tompkins's "Profile," in Paul Strand, *Paul Strand,* p. 23.
90. Strand quoted in Harold Jones, "The Work of Photographers Paul Strand and Edward Weston," p. 92; Yates, *The Transition Years,* p. 44; Paul Strand to Alfred Stieglitz, August 22, 1931, quoted in Yates, p. 29.
91. Strand quoted in Tompkins's "Profile," in Strand, pp. 23–25. The story about Ranchos de Taos church is told in Harold Jones, p. 94.
92. Newhall discussed in Yates, *The Transition Years,* p. 7; Strand, pp. 151–54.
93. Strand's most notable Mexican film was *The Wave,* about a strike by poor fishermen. See Strand, pp. 21–30. Harold Jones states that "the form of portraiture and interpretation of landscapes that Strand first used in New Mexico" influenced the majority of his work in the following forty years (p. vi).
94. Thanks are owed to Suzan Campbell for providing me with biographical information on Rebecca James in her draft essay "Rebecca Salisbury James: An American Original" (1990). See also, Campbell, *Rebecca Salisbury James: A Modern Artist and Her Legacy.*
95. Campbell, "Rebecca Salisbury James," p. 7.
96. Luhan, *Taos and Its Artists,* p. 30. Rebecca divorced Strand in 1933. She married Bill James, a Taos rancher and banker, in 1937.
97. Miriam DeWitt, *A Taos Memory,* p. 2; Rudnick, *Mabel Dodge Luhan,* p. 239.
98. Dewitt, p. 20. Miriam told me in an interview in March 1983 that Tony was "always trying to make love to me," which she found very embarrassing, as he apparently did so "in Mabel's house."
99. Ella Young, *Flowering Dusk,* p. 259; Van Deren Coke, *Marin in New Mexico,* p. 5; John Marin to Alfred Stieglitz, n.d. [1928?], ASC.
100. MacKinley Helm, *John Marin,* pp. 54–65; John Marin, *Letters of John Marin,* ed. Herbert Seligmann, p. 134.

101. Lockwood quoted in Sheldon Reich, "John Marin and the Piercing Light of Taos," *Art News* 73, no. 1 (January 1974): 16 (16–17). See Coke, *Marin in New Mexico,* p. 5, where he discusses Marin's use of the Luhan house motif and his improvisatory transpositions from designs on Indian jewelry and Navajo rugs to his landscapes.
102. John Marin to Paul Strand, September 30, 1930, in Marin, *Selected Writings,* pp. 132–36.
103. For biographical information about O'Keeffe, see Laurie Lisle, *Portrait of an Artist.* Mabel had kept up her correspondence with Stieglitz from the time she came to New Mexico, trying to convince him to visit. Stieglitz, however, believed that he had all he needed in the way of natural inspiration at his family's summer home on Lake George.
104. Bonita Eisler, in *O'Keeffe and Stieglitz,* claims that Mabel and Georgia had an affair in the summer of 1929, but I find her evidence unconvincing (see chap. 19).
105. See Rudnick, *Mabel Dodge Luhan,* pp. 328–41; Georgia O'Keeffe to Russell Vernon Hunter, January 1932, Georgia O'Keeffe, *Georgia O'Keeffe,* pp. 204–5.
106. Elizabeth Duvert, "With Stone, Star, and Earth: The Presence of the Archaic in the Landscape Visions of Georgia O'Keeffe, Nany Holt, and Michelle Stuart," in *The Desert Is No Lady,* pp. 200–1. O'Keeffe's *Wooden Virgin,* seems to interest her for its totemic qualities.
107. O'Keeffe, *Georgia O'Keeffe: Art and Letters,* p. 214.
108. O'Keeffe, *Georgia O'Keeffe,* p. 58.
109. Georgia O'Keeffe to Henry McBride, Summer 1929, in O'Keeffe, *Georgia O'Keeffe: Art and Letters,* p. 189.
110. Georgia O'Keeffe to Mabel Luhan, August 1929, in ibid., p. 192.
111. O'Keeffe, *Georgia O'Keeffe,* p. 64.
112. Ansel Adams quoted in Beaumont Newhall, *Ansel Adams,* p. 48.
113. Weston Neaf, Afterword, in Mary Austin, *Taos Pueblo,* n.p.
114. Ansel Adams, *Letters and Images,* pp. 91–92. Adams was not too fond of Mabel either, though he wrote me that her propensity to "insult, confuse and reject people" was "secondary to her creative contributions." Ansel Adams to Lois Rudnick, February 8, 1984.
115. Ansel Adams to Mabel Luhan, December 6, 1937, MDLC; Adams, *Ansel Adams,* p. 87.

Chapter 3

1. Edmund Wilson, *The American Jitters,* p. 206.
2. Wilson, "Indian Corn Dance," *The New Republic* (October 7, 1931): 202 (202–3). In 1930, New Mexico writer Harvey Fergusson published a novel that dealt in part with "the indiscriminate pillage of wigwam and pueblo" by the "Indian lovers and helpers" of northern New Mexico. It included satiric portraits of Mabel, Tony, and Mary Austin. In the same year, Oliver La Farge published a much more compelling story, "Hard Winter," about an Indian who is corrupted and almost destroyed by a white woman, in which Mabel and Tony also make very unflattering appearances. Fergusson, *Footloose McGarnigal,* pp. 117–30; LaFarge, "Hard Winter," *All the Young Men,* pp. 3–28.

3. Milton Meltzer, *Dorothea Lange,* p. 64. Wesley Burnside, in *Maynard Dixon,* points out that Dixon had a commission from the California auto club to do drawings for the cover of the magazine, and it was on the proceeds of this he stayed in Taos for six months (p. 102).
4. Lange quoted in Meltzer, p. 66. Lange took photographs of Taos, but unfortunately the film she bought could not withstand the high summer temperatures and melted. It's not clear whether Dixon rented the studio from Mabel or she gave it to him gratis.
5. Dixon, *Images of the Native American,* p. 36.
6. Dixon quoted in Meltzer, p. 64; Dixon, *Images of the American Indian,* p. 52.
7. John Roberts, "Huxley and Lawrence," *Virginia Quarterly Review,* 13 (Winter 1937): 546, 548 (546–57).
8. Aldous Huxley, *Brave New World,* p. 29.
9. Ibid., p. 112.
10. Huxley, *Ends and Means,* pp. 20–21.
11. Huxley, *Brave New World,* p. ix.
12. Robinson Jeffers, "New Mexico Mountain," *Selected Poetry,* p. 363.
13. For a discussion of the Jefferses relationship with Luhan, see Rudnick, *Mabel Dodge Luhan,* chap. 7. For information on his life and poetry, see Robert Brophy, *Robinson Jeffers.*
14. Brophy, pp. 277–78.
15. When, by the summer of 1938, it was clear that Jeffers would never fulfill the role she had chosen him for, Luhan perversely helped to direct a scenario in which his life imitated his art. This scenario almost cost Una her life when she shot herself over a love affair that Jeffers was carrying on, at the instigation of Mabel who believed that his creative juices needed reinvigorating.
16. For background on Stokowski's career, see Daniel Oliver, *Leopold Stokowski.*
17. Leopold Stokowski to Mabel Luhan, November 23, 1931; Stokowski to Luhan, [1932], MDLC.
18. Tony Luhan to Leopold Stokowski, n.d.; Stokowski to Mabel Luhan, January 6, 1938, MDLC.
19. Stokowski quoted in Oliver, p. 180; Oliver, p. 282.
20. Stokowski, *Music for All of Us,* pp. 288–89.
21. For biographical information, see Robert Parker, *Carlos Chavez.* On the relationship between Chavez and Stokowski, see Robert Parker, "Leopold Stokowski and Carlos Chavez: The Taos Connection," *Ayer y Hoy en Taos* (Spring 1989):3–7. Chavez first met Stokowski in January 1931 in Mexico, at the same time they both first met Mabel. They both visited her in June 1931.
22. See Oliver, p. 284; Parker, *Carlos Chavez,* p. 109, for a description of the music and the reviews, which were mixed, though more positive about the music than the set design. Eduardo Mata, conductor of the Dallas symphony, has recorded the full score. I am grateful to Lanham Deal, who sent me a copy of the recording and who also informed me that the ballet was commissioned by Catherine Littlefield, founder and head of the Philadelphia Ballet, the first American company to tour Europe performing dances inspired by American music.

23. Carlos Chavez to Mabel Luhan, May 3, 1932; Chavez to Luhan, January 18, 1937. Nothing seems to have come of his attempt to bring the Taos dancers to Mexico.
24. For biographical information see Alfred Morang, *Dane Rudhyar;* "Seed Man: Dane Rudhyar," *Human Dimensions* 4, no. 3 (1975):3–6; Rudhyar, jacket cover, *String Quartets;* Leyla Rudhyar, "The Music of Dane Rudhyar," RJA.
25. Rudhyar's tone suggests they may have met, probably in New York. His letter is dated July 2, no year. I am guessing the date is 1925, since this is the only article Luhan wrote for *Theatre Arts;* yet Graham did not come to New Mexico until the 1930s, nor did Rudhyar, until 1933. Dane Rudhyar to Mabel Luhan, n.d., MDLC.
26. Rudhyar, *Human Dimensions,* p. 8 ; in 1982, he was one of six American composers who had a program devoted to them at the John F. Kennedy Center for Performing Arts in Washington, D.C.
27. Rudhyar,"The Indian Dances for Power," *Dance Observer* 1, no. 6 (August–September 1934): 64. The article is accompanied by a lovely drawing by Brett of a Koshare.
28. Nancy Ruyter, *Reformers and Visionaries,* pp. 67–72.
29. Don McDonoagh, *Martha Graham,* p. 78.
30. Janet Soares, *Louis Horst,* pp. 88, 91–92. See also McDonoagh, pp. 76–77. Graham visited New Mexico four times in the early 1930s. Her first trip was in 1930, at which time Soares says that she visited a Penitente brotherhood, which provided her with "a new inspiration." Graham returned in 1931 and 1932. In July 1933 she stayed at the Luhan house.
31. See Fink, *I—Mary,* on Austin's influence on Graham, p. 245; George Beiswanger, "Martha Graham: A Perspective," in Barbara Morgan, *Martha Graham,* n.p.; Graham quoted in Stephen Polcari, "Martha Graham and Abstract Expressionism," *Smithsonian Studies in American Art,* (Winter 1990): 13 (3–24).
32. Soares suggests that Graham's methods for creating movement were related to O'Keeffe's paintings. Soares and others have noted that the piece was a "unanimously acclaimed masterwork" (pp. 93–95).
33. See Martha Graham's autobiography, *Blood Memory,* pp. 176–77, for her discussion of her trips to the Southwest.
34. Barbara Morgan, "Discussion with Barbara Morgan," *Arts in Society,* 13, no. 2 (Summer/Fall, 1976): 272; Morgan, "Barbara Morgan: Inner Dialogues with the External World," *Quadrille* 5, no. 4 (1971): 15 (11–18).
35. McDonoagh, p., 80.
36. Ibid., p.150.
37. Graham, p. 276.
38. Ward Lockwood, "An Artist's Roots," *Magazine of Art* 33, no. 5 (May 1940): 273 (268–73).
39. Charles Eldridge, *Ward Lockwood,* p. 37. The artist community was neither unaware nor unresponsive to the poverty around them. Miriam DeWitt discusses her own and other artists' involvement in a Benevolent Society that Mabel created in the 1930s to help needy Taoseños. It was in 1936 that Mabel donated a residence she had built for her son as the first county hospital, which served the primarily Hispanic population.

40. Lockwood quoted in Eldridge, pp. 24–25; Eldridge, p. 38.
41. Luhan, *Winter in Taos,* p. 85. In spite of the sympathetic parallels in their work, Lockwood was never an intimate member of the Luhan circle. In fact, he penned one of the most insulting caricatures of Mabel. On a program for an exhibition of American Mural Artists, he doodled a sketch and accompanying limerick: "There was an old harlot: one Mabel/Who was neither brilliant nor able/But when all else would pall/She could always tell all/And it mattered not that t'was all fable" (Lockwood papers, role 535, AAA).
42. Sally Eauclaire, "Edward Weston," *New Mexico Magazine* (June 1989): 61 (58–65).
43. Nancy Newhall, ed., *The Daybooks of Edward Weston,* vol. 2, p. 149.
44. Ibid., pp. 275, 282 ; Lewis Baltz, "Edward Weston in New Mexico," *Artspace* (July–August 1989): 27 (25–27).
45. Harold Jones, "The Work of Photographers Paul Strand and Edward Weston," pp. 128–30.
46. On Knee's New Mexico work, see Tony O'Brien, "A Special Eye," Albuquerque *Journal Magazine* (July 9, 1985): 5.
47. O'Keeffe quoted in E. Boyd, *Cady Wells: Watercolors,* p. 2; Luhan, *Taos and Its Artists,* p. 27.
48. Wells's name appears on several of Luhan's manuscripts at Yale; Kate Duncan, "Cady Wells: The Personal Vision," p. 11.
49. For a discussion of Brinig's and Luhan's relationship, see Rudnick, *Mabel Dodge Luhan,* pp. 302–10.
50. Myron Brinig, *All of Their Lives,* p. 384.
51. Ibid., p. 257.
52. Ibid., p. 471.
53. Ibid., p. 461.
54. There is some debate over who wrote the text of *Taos and Its Artists.* It sounds like Mabel to me, but according to Suzan Campbell, Becky James claims to have done a lot of the writing.
55. Interview with John Candelario, August 13, 1990. In the 1940s, Candelario was given two one-man shows by the Museum of Modern Art in New York, which purchased his first show for their permanent collection.
56. Martha Sandweiss, *Laura Gilpin,* p. 77.
57. Sandweiss, "Laura Gilpin and the Tradition of American Landscape Photography," in *The Desert is No Lady,* pp. 63, 73.
58. Interview with Frank Waters, June 14, 1986.
59. See Fritjof Capra, *The Tao of Physics,* pp. 96–99; Frank Waters, *Mountain Dialogues,* p. 113.
60. See Waters, *Masked Gods,* pp. 144–45.
61. Reporter quoted in Waters, *Masked Gods,* p. 63.
62. Waters, *Masked Gods,* pp. 64–65. Male and female pronouns were often reversed when Pueblos spoke English.
63. Waters, *The Man Who Killed the Deer,* pp. 99–100.
64. Waters, "*The Man Who Killed the Deer:* Thirty Years Later," *New Mexico Magazine* (Winter 1972): 18 (17–23, 49–50).
65. Waters quoted in James Peterson, "Lessons from the Indian Soul," *Psychology Today* (May 1973): 63 (63–72, 99).

66. Waters, *Masked Gods,* pp. 425–26. Waters's work bears a striking resemblance to that of Fritjof Capra in *The Tao of Physics,* which discusses the parallels between western science and Eastern mysticism.
67. Waters, *Mountain Dialogues,* pp. 109–10.

Chapter 4

1. Mabel Luhan to Alice Sprague, August 8, 1946, MDLC.
2. Among other endeavors, Evans contributed to funding the publication of *Oo-Oonah Art* (1968), a beautifully designed book of poetry and drawings by seventh- and eighth-grade pupils of the Taos Pueblo Indian School that was one of the many projects to raise money for the Blue Lake Fund. Frank Waters wrote the introduction.
3. Telephone interview with Bonnie Evans, August 11, 1988.
4. Tricia Hurst, "The Honorable Dorothy Brett," *New Mexican* (July 20, 1975): 14–15.
5. Allen Ginsberg, "Howl," *Howl and Other Poems,* p. 1.
6. Interview with David Hopper, Taos, New Mexico, July 11, 1987. At one point in my research on Hopper, I began to suspect that even his birth date and place may have been invented. I called City Hall, in Dodge City, Kansas, to check on his birth certificate and discovered he was born on May 17, 1936. The woman who gave me the information further verified this by telling me that she was a playmate of his as a young child.
7. Anonymous friend quoted in Brad Darrach, "The Easy Rider Makes a Wild New Movie," *Life* (June 19, 1970): 57 (48–59).
8. Hopper quoted in James Stevenson, "Afternoons with Hopper," *New Yorker* (November 13, 1971): 122 (116–25).
9. Biographical information on Hopper from Elena Rodriguez, *Dennis Hopper.* For biographical information on Dean's life, see David Dalton, *James Dean.*
10. Ron Rosenbaum, "Riding High: Dennis Hopper Bikes Back," *Vanity Fair* (April 1987): 130 (76–83, 130–38).
11. Hopper quoted in Rosenbaum, p. 82. *From Hell to Texas* was released in 1958. It was filmed after *Rebel,* which was not released until 1959, after Dean's death.
12. Henry Hopkins, "Dennis Hopper's America," *Art in America* (May–June 1971): 88 (87–90); Hopper quoted in Darrach, p. 55.
13. Hopper quoted in James Stevenson, pp. 121, 116; Rodriguez, pp. 40–41.
14. Rosenbaum, p. 131; Hopper quoted in Rodriguez, p. 50.
15. Rodriguez, p. 51; Darrach, p. 55. Hopper was reputed to have put together his collection of the artists' early works for about $3,000, which he claimed was worth $1 million in 1970. Most of the paintings went to Brooke in their divorce settlement.
16. Walter Hopps, in Hopper, *Out of the Sixties,* n.p.
17. Hopper quoted in Chris Hodenfield, "Citizen Hopper," *Film Comment* (December 1986): 70 (63–78); Irving Sandler, *The New York School,* p. 164. All of Hopper's Abstract Expressionist works were destroyed in the fire that destroyed his Bel Air home in 1961.
18. Jackson Rushing, "Ritual and Myth: Native American Culture and Abstract Expressionism," in Tuchman, *The Spiritual in Art,* pp. 273, 284.

19. John Ferren, "Epitaph for an Avant-Garde," *Arts* 33 (November 1958): 26 (24–26); Sidra Stith, *Made in the U.S.A,* pp. 7–8. Stith notes the wide-ranging interest in things American in terms of the institutional burgeoning of American Studies in the 1950s and 1960s, the increase in art books, exhibitions, and in American collections in museums. There was even an Americanized analog to the famous Armory Show, which had displayed predominantly European work. In 1958 Madison Square Garden hosted "Art: USA," which showed 1,540 paintings and 300 sculptures by American artists.
20. Sandler, pp. 164–70, 185.
21. Hopper quoted in Hodenfield, p. 70; Terry Southern quoted in Rodriguez, p. 42.
22. Stith, p. 164; Merrild quoted in Los Angeles Wight Art Gallery, *Forty Years,* p. 53; See Knud Merrild, *A Poet and Two Painters,* particularly for his hilarious description of his and Lawrence's arguments over modern aesthetics, pp. 219–24.
23. See Ann Ayres, "Directions in California Assemblage," in *Forty Years,* p. 54. The ordinance was soon rescinded.
24. Peter Boswell, "Beat and Beyond: The Rise of Assemblage Sculpture in California," ibid., 67–68; Barbara Rose, *American Art,* pp. 219, 266.
25. Hopper bought a garage full of Connor's collages and drawings after he made *Easy Rider,* many of which were hung in the Luhan house. Hopper claims that many of the techniques he used in *Easy Rider* were borrowed from Connor's films, especially from *A Movie* (1958), which used stock footage from Hollywood films and arranged them in "a discordant but penetrating mix of pictures of destruction and seduction" (Stith, pp. 166–68); Phillip Brookman, "California Assemblage: The Mixed Message," in *Forty Years,* p. 123.
26. Boswell, p. 68; Ayres, p. 56.
27. Rose, p. 202. See Marshall Berman, *All That Is Solid Melts into Air,* pp. 321, 334.
28. Ayres, pp. 55–56; Robert Dean, "Dennis Hopper," in *Forty Years,* p. 162, where he points out that Hopper's three other extant assemblages also show his interest in exploring "the relationship between real objects and their representation by photographic means," a theme that is central to *The Last Movie.*
29. Hopper quoted in Hopkins, p. 87. Some of his best work can be found in his book *Out of the Sixties.* See *Art Forum* covers, December 1964 and September 1965.
30. Rose, p. 207.
31. Kynaston McShine, *Andy Warhol,* p. 27.
32. Ibid., pp. 36, 57. For an excellent analysis of the double-message of Warhol's art, and in particular his use of commercial products such as Coca-Cola, see Stith, p. 93.
33. Peter Fonda, in *Easy Rider,* eds. Hardin and Schlossberg, p. 28; hereafter cited as *ER.*
34. Dennis Hopper, in *The American Dreamer,* 1971, directed by Lawrence Schiller and L. M. Kit Carson. Hopper attributes this sentiment to Lenin. I am grateful to Mr. Schiller for sending me a copy of this film.

35. Jay Stevens, *Storming Heaven,* p. xiv. Along with writers and popular media heroes such as Allen Ginsberg and the Beatles, who touted the drug, scientists like Timothy Leary and Richard Alpert studied and advocated it, and the military and the CIA experimented with it.
36. There is an interesting parallel between the mystics and anarchists of the early twentieth century, which Veysey discusses in *The Communal Experience,* and the relationship between the early hippie movement and the New Left. On pp. 141–45, Stevens discusses Aldous Huxley's role in advocating LSD as a means of advancing human creativity and the mind's potential. On society's reaction to LSD, see pp. 278–79.
37. See J. Hoberman, *Dennis Hopper,* p. 14.
38. Hopper, *ER,* pp. 8–10.
39. See Seth Cagin and Phillip Dray, *Hollywood Films of the Seventies,* p. 65, on the use of rock music. See Gerald Most, *A Short History of the Movies,* pp. 422–35, on the influence of European new wave on *Easy Rider.*
40. For a fuller discussion of these events, see Todd Gitlin, *The Sixties.*
41. Elizabeth Campbell, *ER,* p. 28; Frederic Tuten, *ER,* p. 37; Jeff Greenfield, "*Easy Rider:* A Turning Point in film? A profound social message? An endless bummer?" *Esquire Film Quarterly* 96, no. 1 (July 1981): 90 (90–91). The film won awards at Cannes and Edinburgh and from the New York film critics. Similar films that came out that year, including several new westerns that cast doubt on the myth of the old frontier, include *The Graduate, Bonnie and Clyde, Midnight Cowboy,* and *McCabe and Mrs. Miller.*
42. I'm grateful to my former student Joyce Linehan for pointing out the direction in which the heroes are moving in her paper "Easy Rider's Relationship to the Western" (1988).
43. It is interesting to note that the local men hired to act in this scene were told by Hopper that he and Fonda were child molesters, presumably to arouse their antagonism. See Sally Hibben, "Easy Rider," *Movies of the Sixties,* ed. Ann Lloyd, p. 202; *ER,* p. 60.
44. *ER,* p. 126.
45. *ER,* pp. 142, 180. See Chris Hugo, "Easy Rider and Hollywood in the 70s," *Movie* 31/32 (Winter 1971): 68 (67–71).
46. Al Auster and Leonard Quart, *American Film and American Society Since 1945,* p. 12; 12; *ER,* pp. 65; Fonda, *ER,* p. 28.
47. On the male bonding tradition, see Tuten, *ER,* p. 36. Joan Mellen, in *Big Bad Wolves,* points out that the 1960s closed with "paeans to male bonding" because "the male hero is so besieged by hostile forces that he rejects all open sexuality" and can only love and trust other men (p. 250).
48. Hopper, *ER,* p. 17.
49. *The Gospel According to Thomas* is quoted in Anthony Macklin, "Easy Rider: The Initiation of Dennis Hopper," *Film Heritage* 5, no. 1 (Fall 1969): 9 (1–12). Macklin says that Hopper once suggested that Billy and Wyatt represented the two thieves who surrounded Christ (George) on the cross. Thanks go to my colleague David Grosser for pointing out the parallel of the final scene with television footage of the Vietnam war.
50. Hopper, *ER,* p. 18. Throughout most of the movie, the music is counterpointed to the action. Here they reinforce one another. "Wasn't Born to

Follow," "Born to be Wild," and "If You Want to be a Bird" accompany Billy's and Wyatt's travels through New Mexico.

Chapter 5

1. *Fountain of Light* (mid-August 1969): 2. The hippies' coming to New Mexico was often spoken of as an "invasion" in the media of the times.
2. *Fountain of Light* (May 1969): 1; (mid-August 1969): 2.
3. Census figures cited in Robert Houriet, *Getting Back Together,* p. 178; rumor of a one-hundred-thousand-acre Earth People's Park reported by John Dean in "The Summer of New Mexico," *Rolling Stone* (July 9, 1970): 28 (25–28); George Michaelson, "Hippies Head for the Hills," *Parade Magazine* (December 14, 1969): 16 (14–16).
4. Houriet, p. xiii; hippie quoted in Keith Melville, *Communes in the Counterculture,* p. 13.
5. Snyder, Corso, and Creeley lived in Placitas, outside Albuquerque. Natalie Goldberg quoted Creeley's statement to me during our September 4, 1989, interview. A decade later, Robert Houriet christened New Mexico "the Aquarian Holy Land" (p. 131).
6. Interview with Peter Rabbit, September 5, 1989. See Joan Loveless, *Three Weavers,* p. 35. Loveless tells the story of their lives and ventures, including the work of their friend and colleague, Kristina Wilson, up through the 1980s.
7. Interview with Jack Loeffler, August 3, 1988.
8. Loeffler read Kropotkin's definition to me during our interview. The quote can be found in Kropotkin, *Modern Science and Anarchism* (1913).
9. Veysey, *The Communal Experience,* p. 200, makes a comparison between Mabel's generation and that of the hippies. Bill Quinn, board member of Lorien Enterprise, quoted in the *Taos News* (February 20, 1970): 1–2.
10. Richard Fairfield, *Communes USA,* pp. 203–9.
11. Interview with Dean Fleming, September 2, 1988. In 1968, Fleming and a few of the leaders of Drop City abandoned the commune and founded the 360-acre Libre community nearby. In 1988, they celebrated their twentieth anniversary, with most of the original twenty-five inhabitants still there.
12. Ram Dass, *Be Here Now,* 1971, n.p. The royalties from his popular guide to life still provide much of the financial support for the activities of the Lama Foundation.
13. Robert Greenfield, *The Spiritual Supermarket,* pp. 253–56. Lama's combination of spiritualism and therapy made it a prototype of the inward-turning New Age movements that burgeoned in the mid-1970s.
14. Interviews with Natalie Goldberg, September 4, 1989, September 15, 1991. See Goldberg, *Long Quiet Highway,* pp. 64–78. Natalie studied Zen formally from 1978 to 1984.
15. Interview with Rick and Terry Klein, July 19, 1993. In the mid-1970s, Rick rented space at the Luhan house from Hopper for his rock band, the Oriental Bluestreaks.
16. Quoted in Houriet, p. 140.
17. Ibid., p. 141.
18. Ibid., pp. 134–52; on New Buffalo's tenth anniversary, see Merilee Danne-

mann, "New Buffalo, 10 Years Old, Still Follows Vision, *Taos News* (July 7, 1977): 3–4.

19. Duncan quoted in Michaelson, pp. 14–15; Houriet, p. 181.
20. Houriet, pp. xx, 181–82.
21. Ibid., p. 182; interview with Bill Gersh, August 7, 1988.
22. Houriet points out that the only other self-consciously political commune, set up by several "ex-Motherfuckers," also failed in its attempted alliance with the Alianza (pp. 181–83).
23. One of the original members of Magic Tortoise moved in the mid-1980s. Another publishes an international newsletter on fractiles, one of the hottest mathematical concepts related to chaos theory. Gersh numbered at perhaps 100 to 150 those who stayed and took root in their communities, spread about in Ranchos, Pilar, Questa, as well as in Taos. In the summer of 1993, Gersh established the Magic Tortoise Foundation, which gave two summers of workshops on art, poetry, and healing. Gersh died suddenly in May 1994.
24. John Rothchild and Susan Wolfe, *The Children of the Counter Culture,* p. 104.
25. Interview with Douglas Magnus, August 8, 1988. See John Dean, p. 27, whose source is a hippie named Brother Daniel. Brother Daniel claimed that Manson lived in a shack called the Goat Shed in 1968 or 1969, that Linda Kasabian and her husband lived there in the winter of 1969, and that she came back there to meet her husband in the fall after the Tate murders.
26. See Vincent Bugliosi, *Helter Skelter,* pp. 322–33.
27. See ibid., pp. 389–91. Bugliosi notes, on p. 296, that for a while after the murders, Manson became a hero to various segments of the counterculture, including the Weathermen and the Yippies. The Yippie paper, *Tuesday's Child,* name Manson Man of the Year and another issue's cover showed him on a cross. There were Manson posters and Free Manson buttons in psychedelic shops. On Kasabian in Taos, see Bugliosi, pp. 389–90.
28. Fox, "Healing, Imagination, and New Mexico," pp. 214, 227–28.
29. See Nichols, If Mountains Die, p. 37.
30. deBuys, *Enchantment and Exploitation,* p. 210; Rodriguez, "Land, Water, and Ethnic Identity," pp. 349–50. In the 1960s, permits for grazing and timber-cutting were cut by 50 percent. John Nichols's novel, *The Milagro Beanfield War,* revolves around the fight that an Hispanic farmer wages with the Forest Service over grazing rights.
31. Rodriguez, "Land, Water, and Ethnic Identity," p. 350; John Nichols, in "Whatever Happened to El Dorado?" *Motive* (April–May 1971): 8–15, notes that in May 1969 one real estate office bragged about selling more than five hundred thousand dollars worth of land to the hippies. In the same year, Nichols reported, tourists outnumbered local New Mexicans fifteen to one. See *Taos News* (March 20, 1969; April 3, 1969; May 16, 1969).
32. Houriet, pp. 177–79; Nichols, "Whatever Happened to El Dorado?," p. 9; Nichols, *If Mountains Die,* pp. 110–15.
33. *Fountain of Light,* no. 12 (April 1, 1970):1; no. 13 (May 1970):2–3.
34. William Rose, "One-Third World; One-Third World; One-Third World," *Caliche,* no. 16 (October 1969): n.p.
35. The first page of Evans's ad had first been published in the *Taos News* in

May 1966. See R. C. Gordon-McCutchan, *The Taos Indians,* p. 203, for an analysis of the impact of the film on the case. For an analysis of how the Taos Indians made use of Anglo ethnophilia see Bodine, *Attitudes and Institutions of Taos,* pp. 255–62. Bodine is somewhat critical of the ways the Taos tribe enhanced the symbolic potency of Blue Lake in order to win their land claim. But he also provided key evidence in support of the tribe's claim. See Gordon-McCutchan, p. 209.

36. Rodriguez, "Land, Water, and Ethnic Identity," pp. 319–23.
37. See Stan Steiner, *La Raza,* pp. 66–81. During the raid, a state policeman and jailer were wounded, and a deputy sheriff and newspaper reporter were kidnapped.
38. Ibid., pp. 88–89.
39. Rodriguez, "Land, Water, and Ethnic Identity," pp. 322–23. La Raza's "Tierra O Muerte" (Land or Death) posters and graffiti could be seen in many villages; Steiner, pp. 208–9, describes the Chicano student movement, which was characterized by student walkouts from schools and demands that Mexican, Spanish, and Indian history and culture be included in the school curriculum. On the Forest Service's changing policies, see deBuys, pp. 258–66.
40. See *El Grito del Norte* 22, no. 11 (November 11, 1969). I am grateful to John Nichols for providing me with a copies of this and other papers from the period.
41. Larry Torres informed me that most of the adults in the Hispanic community saw the Chicano militants as "hippified" Hispanics and rejected them. Some of their children were drawn both to the hippie culture and to the Chicanos. See Torres interview in Epilogue.
42. Nichols, *If Mountains Die,* pp. 13, 37.
43. Interview with John Nichols, September 5, 1989.
44. Nichols, "Human Relations in Taos," *New Mexico Review* (August–September 1970): 16–19.
45. Nichols, *If Mountains Die,* p. 110.
46. Not to be outdone by Bly, Scott Momaday insisted that Jane Austen was really the first hippie. See *Taos News* (September 1, 1970): 1, A2. See also Nichols's article in *Motive,* where he complains about how the town allocated funds for the Lawrence festival that should have gone to the roads, sewer, and school system.
47. *Easy Rider,* p. 126; Lawrence anecdote from telephone interview with Dennis Hopper, August 2, 1988.

Chapter 6

1. Telephone interview with Dennis Hopper, August 2, 1988.
2. Interview with Leo Garen, September 4, 1989. Manby was also notorious among the Hispanic community for his land deals, through which he enriched himself at their community's expense. See Marta Weigle and Peter White, *The Lore of New Mexico,* pp. 299–301. Manby's murder still remains unsolved. For details on Mabel's view of the trial, see her letters to Una Jeffers, reported in Rudnick, *Mabel Dodge Luhan,* pp. 293–94.

3. David Hopper claims the higher price, Dennis the lower. Dennis also

claims the price doubled when word got out he was interested; Ron Rosenbaum, "Riding High: Dennis Hopper Bikes Back," p. 134.

4. See Hoberman, *Dennis Hopper,* p. 21, where reviews are quoted. *The Last Movie* is listed in Harry Medved's *The Fifty Worst Films of All Time.* Quotes from the *New York Times* advertisement, September 26, 1971. In the late 1970s and early 1980s, the film received some serious—and admiring—critical analyses. See Dan Burns, "Dennis Hopper's *The Last Movie*: Beginning of the End," *Film/Literature Quarterly,* 7, no. 2 (1979): 137–47; David James, "Dennis Hopper's *The Last Movie,*" *Journal of the University Film and Video Association,* 25, no. 2 (Spring 1983): 34–46, which he incorporated into his book *Allegories of Cinema* (1989).
5. Hopper quoted in Hoberman, p. 56.
6. Hopper quoted in Darrach, "The Easy Rider Makes a Wild New Movie," p. 51.
7. See David Harvey, *The Condition of Postmodernism,* pp. 43, 116 (chaps. 3 and 6) for an illuminating discussion of the various debates over postmodernism, including whether it represents a continuation of modernism or a new paradigm.
8. Hoberman, p. 52. Hopper was originally supposed to film in Mexico, but apparently the Mexican government threatened to censor his work.
9. Joseph Spielberg, quoted in Alix Jeffrey, "A Gigantic Ego Trip for Dennis Hopper," *New York Times* (May 10, 1970): 14 (11, 14).
10. Telephone interview with Dennis Hopper, July 16, 1990.
11. Tricia Hurst, TS, "The Other Side of the Coin," undated but probably November 1970. I am grateful to Hurst for giving me this article. McGovern remembers having come to dinner after his 1972 presidential campaign was over, but that is unlikely, as he also remembers having been shown *The Last Movie,* which was released in 1971. It is probable that he visited during Thanksgiving of 1970, and although he may not have "announced" his candidacy there, he may well have discussed it. George McGovern to Lois Rudnick, June 6, 1988.
12. Hurst, p. 9.
13. Phillips, conversation reported in Elena Rodriguez, *Dennis Hopper,* p. 84.
14. Brooke Hayward interviewed by Ron Ronsebaum, p. 133. One of Dennis's girlfriends in Taos nicknamed him Dennis "Hop-Head."
15. Interviews with Lisa Law, August 2, 1988; Tally Richards, September 2, 1988 (letter), and Charlotte Hopper, June 24, 1986.
16. Sean Hignett, who was living in Taos at the time, remembered this in *Brett,* pp. 264–65. Charlotte Hopper recalled similar editorials in the local media.
17. Roger Sindell, "The Film Revolution," *Fountain of Light* (August 1969): 6; interview with John Nichols.
18. Hopper's intentions to find the cave are mentioned by Sean Hignett, p. 265.
19. Interview with Dennis Hopper, July 16, 1990; see *Taos News* (July 16, 1970): 1. Charlotte Hopper remembers the judge holding a copy of the *Life* magazine article that described in detail the drugs Hopper used in Peru. Soon after, Dennis went on the Dick Cavett Show, where he denied the charges in the *Life* article that he shot heroin, although he admitted to smoking pot and to taking LSD.

20. Hopper quoted in Mark Goodman, "Rebel without a Pause," *New Times* (October 2, 1978): 53–54 (53–60). The rifle story is quoted in Rosenbaum, p. 136. The Taos high school principal who was there at the time informed me that this incident never happened.
21. Interview with Hopper, July 16, 1990. Once the symbol of Chicano militancy, the coyote has been tamed and made into the leading kitsch trademark of the southwestern tourist trade.
22. The troupe appeared on college campuses and on television. They were awarded an Obie by the Off-Broadway critics, performed before the U. S. Senate's Subcommittee on Migratory Labor, and in the courtyard of the Old Senate Office Building at the invitation of Robert Kennedy, whose brother Ted joined them in singing strike songs. See Stan Steiner, *La Raza,* pp. 325–30; John Nichols, "Whatever Happened to El Dorado?" *Motive,* p. 12.
23. Nichols, "Whatever Happened to El Dorado?," p. 12.
24. In the first version of this story, which he published in the 1971 article in *Motive,* Nichols claimed that the agent was from the FBI. In the second and subsequent versions, published in the *New Mexico Review* (March 1972) and in *If Mountains Die,* pp. 117,120, Nichols says the agent was a state police intelligence officer. The agent is mentioned in the 1972 article in the *New Mexico Review* as having been involved in a shoot-out with two Black Berets in Albuquerque, where he was assigned to a unit on the University of New Mexico campus, whose job was to discredit the militant Chicano movement.
25. On the FBI's infiltration of liberal and radical organizations, such as SNCC and La Raza, see Sanford Ungar, *The FBI;* on COINTELPRO, see Ward Churchill and Jim Vander Wall, *Agents of Repression.* Interview with Dennis Hopper, July 16, 1990.
26. Interview with Dennis Hopper, July 16, 1990.
27. Even before Hopper moved in, Bonnie recalls two young women who rented the log cabin one summer and kept a can of mace to spray the ghosts that visited them. Waters had no memory of giving David advice about getting rid of ghosts by burning copal. One would like to take these ghost stories with a grain of salt, except that they continue into the next generation, where they are told by a variety of respectable and responsible, non-drugged-out, non-alcoholic informants, both children and adults, including yours truly, the entirely sober and skeptical author of this book.
28. Interview with Dennis Hopper, July 16, 1990.
29. See Hoberman, p. 19, where he says that Hopper plays "the prophetic outlaw artist to the max" and that the film "is haunted by the spectre of Charles Manson," to whom Hopper bears more than a slight resemblance during many scenes in the movie.
30. J. Edgar Hoover's photo isn't shown in the movie—David Hopper told me about it. Mabel was under surveillance by Arthur Manby when she first came to Taos; he reported to the Bureau of Investigation that her foreign-accented husband and their guest, Andrew Dasburg, were enemy aliens in league with the Germans, who were presumably planning on invading the United States through Mexico. Luhan also wrote about Los Alamos in a 1946 essay, "Holiday from Science?" *Southwest Review* 31 (1946): 221–24,

that lamented the passing of New Mexico's utopian possibilities with the advent of the atomic bomb.

31. The soundtrack was put out by Mediarts Records. Hopper claims that Schiller tried to release the film commercially and that he had to spend several thousand dollars to block it. The film may have only been shown in a few colleges.
32. Tally Richards to Lois Rudnick, September 2, 1988. Tally's was the first New Mexico gallery to show the works of Fritz Scholder and Larry Bell, who were well known nationally but not that well known in the region until she promoted their work. She also showed Bill Gersh's work for many years.
33. Interview with Tony Price, July 17, 1987. Tony moved to Pecos in 1992, the same year in which he had 120 of his pieces moved to Biosphere II.
34. Ken Price to Lois Rudnick, June 29, 1990. Price lives in L.A. but spends his summers in Taos.
35. See Maurice Tuchman, *Ken Price.*
36. Interview with Bill Gersh.
37. Interview with Ron Cooper, July 9, 1989. Cooper first moved out to New Mexico in 1970 or 1971, settled in Truchas for a while, where he was visited by Larry Bell, went back to L.A., and settled in Taos in 1982.
38. Athena Spear, "Reflections on Close, Cooper, and Jenny, *Arts* 33 (May 1970): 44 (44–47); Miguel Baltierra, "Portrait Vases/Portrait Lamps, *L.A. Architect* (June 1987): 12.
39. Alastair MacIntosh, *Contemporary Artists,* eds. Colin Naylor and Genesis P. Orridge, 1989, p. 81; Bell quoted in Jack Pritchett, "Tripping the Light Fantastic," *Southwest Art* (July 1987): 82. In the late 1980s, Bell began to use this technique with dramatic effect on canvas.
40. Interview with Larry Bell, July 10, 1987.
41. Interview with Jack Loeffler.
42. Interview with Dennis Hopper, July 16, 1990. During our interview, Loeffler pointed out that BMD was in many respects the parent organization of the most militant branch of the environmental movement, Earth First, begun by Dave Forman. Forman began as a Wilderness Society lobbyist in New Mexico, became a national lobbyist, and then decided he wanted to become involved in direct action.
43. See William Wroth, *Hispanic Crafts of the Southwest,* pp. 5–7, for a discussion of the Hispanic crafts revival in the 1970s.
44. See Lisa Sherman, Gallery Review, *Four Winds* (Summer 1982): 80–85.
45. Quintana quoted David Hopper's files on Return Gallery.
46. *Taos News* (February 22, 1976): 1; interviews with Pepe Rochon, June 28, 1986; Ed Morgan, August 11, 1990. Morgan had worked for Hallmark cards before coming to Taos in 1968. He rented the upstairs of the Luhan house for a year and a half and did his engravings in the solarium. Morgan thinks there were drug debts involved with the sale of the belt. Today, Morgan has his own gallery in Taos, where he sells finely crafted engravings on paper.
47. Rodriguez, pp. 107–11.
48. "Kid Blue," *Taos News* (May 23, 1973): B1.
49. Hoberman, p. 25. Hopper's most interesting role during the 1970s was as the "haunted, violent, perhaps insane, at once fascinating and repulsive" ugly American hero of Wim Wenders's *American Friend* (Hoberman, pp. 26–27).

50. Goodman, p. 55. I can vouch for Goodman's description, having visited the Tony house in the summer of 1977, on my first visit to the Luhan estate.
51. Rodriguez, pp. 131–35. *Out of the Blue* was favorably received at the Cannes Film Festival and was a hit in England and France, but not in the United States.
52. Just before her death, CeBe sends out "kill all hippies" messages over the radio. Hopper quoted in Rodriguez, p. 136; Hoberman, *Dennis Hopper,* pp. 29–31.
53. Rodriguez, p. 141.
54. See Rodriguez, pp. 141–54.
55. Hopper quoted in Rodriguez, p. 154.
56. Blurb for Rosenbaum's article, p. 76.
57. Hopper's most controversial film to date is *Colors* (1988), which focused on the dynamics of gang life in L.A. He used real street gang members in the film, from the two most powerful gangs, the Crips and the Bloods. Many communities, fearing that gang violence would break out, banned the film. Hopper defended the film by saying that it did not romanticize gangs, which is true, but the film scarcely provides any analysis of the violence and its causes.
58. There are works by Ron Cooper in the El Cortez apartment, as well as by other artist friends in Taos, along with a ceramic chicken that is missing from the roof of the Luhan house, and the ever-present tortured Christ that seems to follow Hopper from home to home.
59. See *New York Times* (June 18, 1987): pp. C1, C6. Mike Davis, *City of Quartz,* pp. 236–38. Davis notes that Gehry transmutes "*noir* into Pop through a recycling of the elements of a decayed and polarized urban landscape (for example rude concrete, chain link, empty back walls, and so on) into light and airy expressions of a happy lifestyle" (p. 81). For one of Hopper's most recent roles in a high-grossing violent film, see *Speed* (1994) where he plays a mad bomb thrower.
60. Pat Smith, who helped take care of Mabel in her final months, told me about the sign. Interview with Pat Smith, June 18, 1986. The notice on Hopper's chair was mentioned in an *Albuquerque Journal* article on the making of *Backtrack,* July 22, 1988, p. C1.

Chapter 7

1. Quoted in Corinne McLoughlin and Gordon Davidson, *Builders of the Dawn,* p. 93.
2. For one of the most judicious assessments of the debates surrounding the new curriculum, see Gerald Graff, *Beyond the Culture Wars.* His notes cite the most relevant literature on various sides of the debate.
3. Johanna King estimated tourists would spend $2.2 billion in New Mexico by the end of 1989 (*Albuquerque Journal,* [August 27, 1989]: 1, A3). In that same year, the Taos *Visitors Guide* was fifty-five pages, mostly ads. In 1992, a new tourist bureau opened on the south side of town to cater to the increasing numbers that come through town. The population of Taos increased 20 percent between 1980 and 1990, from 3,369 to 4,065, while the county population expanded from 19,456 to 23,118. In 1994, the official

unemployment rate was 14.5 percent and the county rate of food stamp recipiency was 20.9 percent. The 1990 U.S. census showed Taos Pueblo and the town of Taos with poverty rates of 42 and 27 percent respectively. Statistics supplied by Sylvia Rodriguez, "Land, Water, and Ethnic Identity," pp. 357–60, and the Taos Chamber of Commerce.

4. Stephen Fox, "Healing, Imagination, and New Mexico," pp. 231–33.
5. Molly Ivins, "For D. H. Lawrence, Pagan Rites in Desert," *New York Times* (July 22, 1980): C9.
6. I am grateful to Orlando Romero for sharing this story fragment with me. Orlando is a creative writer and historian.
7. See Brian Berry, *America's Utopian Experiments,* chap. 20, "The Wave of the 1990s." See also McLoughlin and Davidson, who make similar points about intentional communities. Berry noted that on the other end of the spectrum are approximately 120 religious-based communities, some of which are fundamentalist cult groups who believe that family breakdown and increasing violence and drugs are bringing us to the verge of "the final holocaust." Among these are the Branch Davidians, most of whom died in a fiery shoot-out in Waco, Texas, when federal agents raided their headquarters in March 1993. See Barlett and Steele, *America: What Went Wrong?,* for statistics on the socioeconomic shifts of the 1980s.
8. Mary Kenney, interviewed in *Taos Magazine* (August 1988): 10–12.
9. Ellen Levy, *Nation* (October 16, 1989): 418. Levy discusses some of the other centers throughout the United States involved in sustainable agriculture and notes that there are several chairs in universities assigned to this kind of research, which is also being supported by the USDA.
10. According to Brett Bakker, who ran the Native Seeds Search operation in Albuquerque in 1993, Native Seeds, whose home office is in Arizona, started around 1978, as an extension of a Freedom from Hunger project. Their sales continued to increase during the 1980s and early 1990s, with the majority of their customers on the East and West coasts. They publish a newsletter, *Seedhead News,* and are working with Native American groups on using diet to control such diseases as diabetes. In 1992, Rick and Terry Klein, the original owners of New Buffalo commune, refurbished it and opened it as a bed-and-breakfast and retreat center. They are working to have it placed on the National Register of Historic Places.
11. Rodriguez, "Land, Water, and Ethnic Identity," pp. 353–54. Information on Amigos Bravos from their 1993 annual report.
12. R. C. Gordon-McCutchan to Lois Rudnick, August 26, 1993. As of 1993 there were 130 World Heritage Sites, including the Taj Mahal and the Grand Canyon. Taos is the first inhabited site to achieve this status, according to Gordon-McCutchan, who explained this designation as an attempt to "protect the earth's most precious natural and cultural sites."
13. See Nancy Wood, *Taos Pueblo.* As of 1989, some one hundred thousand tourists a year were visiting Taos Pueblo.
14. *Tiwa Tales* has been videotaped by Joseph Concha (in Tiwa, with subtitles). I am grateful to Soge Track for telling me about her research and discussing the exhibit she curated at the Millicent Rogers Museum, during my 1993 summer visit. The artists exhibited were Albert Lujan, Albert Looking Elk,

and Juan Mirabal. These impressionist oils look nothing like what most viewers expect "real" Indian art to look like.

15. Taos Institute's Statement of Philosophy provided by Bell. Bell spoke of his hope, in an interview with *Taos Magazine* (November–December 1989): 32–33, that the school would provide some local youth with vocations; interview with Ursula Beck, executive director, TIA, July 13, 1993.
16. See *Frank Waters Foundation Newsletter,* August and December 1993, and *Fechin Institute Newsletter,* 1988–89, 1991, 1994. Several thousand visitors from more than forty-five states and twenty-eight countries have come through the Fechin Institute.
17. Lumina claims to be "the most beautiful art gallery in Taos." The St. Theresa House has had other interesting incarnations. It once belonged to painter Victor Higgins, and is, in fact, still referred to as the Higgins House. In the 1950s, Elizabeth Taylor's brother owned and operated it as an art gallery.

Chapter 8

1. Biographical information on George and Kitty Otero comes primarily from three interviews: June 17, 1986; July 2, 1986; and August 7, 1988.
2. The Carpenter story is told by Tricia Hurst, *Taos Magazine* (Winter 1981): pp. 37–38. The ghost of an Indian girl, presumably Tony's niece who died in the Rainbow Room, has also been sighted, as well as the ghost of a headless conquistador and that of a vaquero who presumably once worked the ranch when it was part of the Spanish land grant.
3. Otero quoted in Patricia Gilmore, "An Old Adobe Mansion Relives the Legend," *Rocky Mountain News* (February 27, 1983): 15 (12–15).
4. These quotes are from a working document produced by New Mexico SIN in 1982: "New Mexico School Improvement Network," by George Otero, Mark Mannes, Jack Jost, and Robert Sparks. It was provided to me by George Otero, as were numerous other documents on curriculum theory and program development produced at Las Palomas or at their home institutions by staff and teachers involved in its programs.
5. See John Goodlad, *The Dynamics of Educational Change* and *A Place Called School.*
6. Letter to the editor, *Taos News* (1980), Las Palomas files; superintendent quoted in Patricia Gilmore, "An Old Adobe Mansion," p. 12.
7. Robert Sparks to Lois Rudnick, November 22 1988; interview with Loy Sue Siegenthaler, August 9, 1988.
8. Interview with Laurie and Ben Eastman, August 9, 1988.
9. Interview with Jan Drum, August 6, 1988. I am grateful to Jan for supplying me with many detailed reports of the conferences in which she was involved, many of them written by her.
10. In 1986, Jan and George began to publish and disseminate a compendium of imaginative "teachable moments," one- or two-page descriptions of easy-to-implement pedagogical and thematic strategies for classrooms from K through 12.
11. Steve Hughes to Lois Rudnick, December 22, 1988.
12. Mott grant proposal titled "Global Issues and Community Education: Nec-

essary Partners for Education in the 21st Century." News release on designation of Las Palomas as National Special Issues Center, March 18, 1991.

13. Telephone interview with Jamie Cloud, January 18, 1990. At that time, there were seven states with global education requirements: California, Florida, Washington, Massachusetts, New York, Arkansas, and Minnesota.
14. Ray Christine to Lois Rudnick, n.d. [1988]; Bob Campagna to Lois Rudnick, December 13, 1989.
15. *Tiger's Roar* articles, given to me by Nancy Jenkins, are dated February 14, 1985; May l, 1986; and May 22, 1986.
16. Interview with Nancy Jenkins, August 13, 1988.
17. Materials and information on the international high school were supplied by Peggy Davis in 1991. She is no longer teaching at Taos High School.
18. Interview with Susan Chambers-Cook, August 7, 1988.
19. Interview with Natalie Goldberg, September 15, 1991.
20. Goldberg, *Long Quiet Highway,* p. 79. On Reynolds, see "Father Earth," *New York Times* (January 10, 1993): Cl, C9.
21. In July 1993, I went to the tribal office seeking an official explanation of the fence and was told by a member of the war chief's staff, John Sandoval, that it went up because there had been "trespassing" on Indian land.
22. Josephine has a fine watercolor of Mabel's hanging in her house. Interviews with Marcus, June 24, 1986; Juan Concha, June 28, 1986; Lupe Suazo, June 28, 1986.
23. Interviews with Ernesto and Al Lujan, June 18, 1986; Marie Lujan, September 6, 1989. Marie said Tony was "kind and generous," but dismissed Mabel as "nosey."
24. The Eight Northern Pueblos Institute is housed in Northern New Mexico Community College, in Espanola. In 1993–94 the institute received an EPA grant to train teachers to use environmental issues in teaching. Information on EPOTEC provided by Jim Brown and George Otero.
25. See Mitchell Waldrop, *Complexity,* pp. 349–53, for a discussion of Murray Gell-Mann's work on global sustainability (which was not supported by the majority of the institute's leadership). See also the institute's working paper "Visions of a Sustainable World," introductory talk at the meeting on the Sustainable World Project, held in Santa Fe, May 1990.

BIBLIOGRAPHY

Adams, Ansel. *Ansel Adams: An Autobiography.* Boston: Little, Brown, 1985.

——. *Images, 1923–1971.* Edited by L. DeCock. Boston: New York Graphic Society, 1974.

——. *Letters and Images, 1916–1984.* Boston: Little, Brown, 1988.

Alpern, Sara, et al., eds. *The Challenge of Feminist Biography: Writing the Lives of Modern American Women.* Urbana: University of Illinois Press, 1992.

Anderson, Maxwell. *Night Over Taos: A Play in Three Acts.* New York: S. French, 1935.

Angulo, Gui de. *Jaime in Taos.* San Francisco: City Lights, 1985.

Auster, Al, and Quart, Leonard. *American Film and American Society Since 1945.* London: MacMillan, 1984.

Austin, Mary. *The American Rhythm.* New York: Harcourt, Brace, 1923.

——. *Earth Horizon.* Boston: Houghton Mifflin, 1932.

——. *Land of Journey's Ending.* Tucson: University of Arizona Press, 1983 (1924).

——. *Starry Adventure.* Boston: Houghton Mifflin, 1931.

——. *Taos Pueblo.* Boston: New York Graphic Society, 1977 (1930).

Babcock, Barbara, and Parezo, Nancy. *Daughters of the Desert: Women Anthropologists and the Native American Southwest, 1880–1980.* Albuquerque: University of New Mexico Press, 1988.

Bachelard, Gaston. *The Poetics of Space.* Translated by Maria Jolas. Boston: Beacon Press, 1969.

Balcomb, Mary. *Nicolai Fechin.* Flagstaff: Northland Press, 1975.

Barlett, David L., and Steele, James B. *America: What Went Wrong?* Kansas City: Andrews and McMeel, 1992.

Bedford, Sybille. *Aldous Huxley: A Biography, Vol. 1, 1894–1939.* London: Chatto and Windus, 1973.

Bennett, John G. *Gurdjieff: Making a New World.* London: Turnstone Books, 1973.

Berman, Marshall. *All That Is Solid Melts into Air: The Experience of Modernism.* New York: Simon and Schuster, 1982.

Berry, Brian. *America's Utopian Experiments: Communal Havens from Long-Wave Crises.* Hanover: University Press of New England, 1992.

Bodine, John. "Attitudes and Institutions of Taos, New Mexico: Variables for Value System Expression." Ph.D diss., Tulane University, 1967.

Bourne, Randolph. *The Radical Will: Selected Writings, 1911–1918.* Edited by Olaf Hansen. New York: Urizen Books, 1977.

Boyd, E. *Cady Wells: Watercolors.* Exh. Cat. Santa Fe: private printing, 1948.

Brett, Dorothy. *Lawrence and Brett: A Friendship.* Philadelphia: J. B. Lippincott, 1933.

Briggs, Charles L. *Woodcarvers of Córdova, New Mexico: Social Dimensions of an Artistic "Revival."* Knoxville: University of Tennessee Press, 1980.

Briggs, Charles L., and Van Ness, J., eds. *Land, Water, and Culture.* Albuquerque: University of New Mexico Press, 1987.

Brinig, Myron. *All of Their Lives.* New York: Farrar and Rhinehart, 1941.

Brody, J. J. *Indian Painters and White Patrons.* Albuquerque: University of New Mexico Press, 1971.

Brophy, Robert J. *Robinson Jeffers: Myth, Ritual, and Symbol in His Narrative Poems.* Cleveland: Case Western Reserve University Press, 1973.

Bugliosi, Vincent. *Helter Skelter.* New York: Bantam Books, 1975.

Buhle, Paul. *Marxism in the USA: From 1870 to the Present Day.* London: Verso, 1987.

Bunting, Bainbridge. *Early Architecture in New Mexico.* Albuquerque: University of New Mexico Press, 1976.

———. *Taos Adobes.* Santa Fe: Museum of New Mexico, 1964.

Burke, Richard Maurice. *Cosmic Consciousness.* New York: E. P. Dutton, 1901.

Burnside, Wesley. *Maynard Dixon: Artist of the West.* Provo: Brigham Young University Press, 1973.

Bynner, Witter. *Cake, An indulgence.* New York: Alfred A. Knopf, 1926.

———. *Prose Pieces.* Edited by James Kraft. New York: Farrar, Straus, Giroux, 1979.

Cagin, Seth, and Dray, Phillip. *Hollywood Films of the Seventies: Sex, Drugs, Violence, Rock'n'Roll, and Politics.* New York: Harper and Row, 1984.

Campbell, Suzan. *Rebecca Salisbury James: A Modern Artist and Her Legacy.* Exh. Cat. Albuquerque: University of New Mexico Museum, 1992.

Capra, Fritjof. *The Tao of Physics.* New York: Bantam Books, 1984.

Castro, Michael. *Interpreting the Indian: Twentieth-Century Poets and the Native American.* Albuquerque: University of New Mexico Press, 1983.

Cather, Willa. *Death Comes for the Archbishop.* New York: Vintage Books, 1971 (1927).

———. *The Professor's House.* New York: Vintage Books, 1973 (1925).

Churchill, Ward, and Vander Wall, John. *Agents of Repression: The FBI's Secret War against the Black Panther Party and the American Indian Movement.* Boston: South End Press, 1992.

Clurman, Harold. *The Fervent Years: The Story of the Group Theatre and the Thirties.* New York: Alfred A. Knopf, 1945.

Coke, Van Deren. *Andrew Dasburg.* Albuquerque: University of New Mexico Press, 1979.

———. *Marin in New Mexico.* Exh. Cat. Albuquerque: University of New Mexico Art Museum, 1968.

Collier, John. *From Every Zenith.* Denver: Sage Books, 1963.

———. *Indians of the Americas.* New York: W. W. Norton, 1947.

——. *On the Gleaming Way: Navahos, Eastern Pueblos, Zunis, Hopis, Apaches, and Their Land.* Chicago: Sage Books, 1962 (1949).

Cowan, James C. *D. H. Lawrence's American Journey: A Study in Literature and Myth.* Cleveland: Case Western Reserve University Press, 1970.

Cronin, George, ed. *The Path on the Rainbow: An Anthology of Songs and Chants from the Indians of North America.* New York: Liveright, 1934 (1918).

Cronon, William. *Nature's Metropolis: Chicago and the Great West.* New York: W. W. Norton, 1991.

Dalton, David. *James Dean: The Mutant King.* New York: St. Martin's Press, 1974.

Dass, Baba Ram. *Be Here Now.* San Cristobal: Lama Foundation, 1971.

Davis, Mike. *City of Quartz.* New York: Vintage Books, 1992.

deBuys, William. *Enchantment and Exploitation: The Life and Hard Times of a New Mexico Mountain Range.* Albuquerque: University of New Mexico Press, 1985.

Deloria, Vine, Jr. *Custer Died for Your Sins: An Indian Manifesto.* New York: Avon Books, 1970.

DeWitt, Miriam. *A Taos Memory.* Albuquerque: University of New Mexico Press, 1992.

Dickstein, Morris. *Gates of Eden: American Culture in the Sixties.* New York: Basic Books, 1977.

Djikstra, Bram. *The Hieroglyphics of a New Speech: Cubism, Stieglitz, and the Early Poetry of William Carlos Williams.* Princeton: Princeton University Press, 1969.

Dixon, Maynard. *Sketchbook.* Flagstaff, Ariz.: Northland Press, 1967.

——. *Images of the Native American.* San Francisco: Academy of Sciences, 1981.

Domhoff, G. William. *The Bohemian Grove and Other Retreats: A Study in Ruling Class Cohesiveness.* New York: Harper and Row, 1974.

——. *The Higher Circles: The Governing Class in America.* New York: Random House, 1970.

Duncan, Kate. *Cady Wells: A Retrospective Exhibition.* Exh. Cat. Albuquerque: University of New Mexico Art Museum, 1967.

——. "Cady Wells: The Personal Vision." Master's thesis, University of New Mexico, 1967.

Dunn, Dorothy. *American Indian Painting of the Southwest and Plains Areas.* Albuquerque: University of New Mexico Press, 1962.

Eisler, Bonita. *O'Keeffe and Stieglitz: An American Romance.* New York: Doubleday, 1991.

Eldridge, Charles. *Ward Lockwood: 1894–1963.* Lawrence: University of Kansas Museum of Art, 1974.

Eldridge, Charles, Schimmel, Julie, and Truettner, William. *Art in New Mexico, 1900–1945: Paths to Santa Fe and Taos.* Washington, D.C.: National Museum of American Art, 1986.

Eldridge, Richard, and Kerman, Cynthia Earl. *The Lives of Jean Toomer: A Hunger for Wholeness.* Baton Rouge: Louisiana State University Press, 1987.

Eliot, T. S. *Selected Essays.* London: Faber and Faber, 1972.

Fairfield, Richard. *Communes USA: A Personal Tour.* Baltimore: Penguin Books, 1972.

Fergusson, Harvey. *Footloose McGarnigal.* New York: Alfred A. Knopf, 1930.

Fink, Augusta. *I—Mary: A Biography of Mary Austin.* Tucson: University of Arizona Press, 1983.

Gacs, Uta. *Women Anthropologists: A Biographical Dictionary.* New York: Greenwood Press, 1988.

Gettings, Frank. *Different Drummers.* Washington, D.C.: Smithsonian, 1988.

Gibson, Arrell M. *Santa Fe and Taos Colonies: Age of the Muses: 1900–1942.* Norman: University of Oklahoma Press, 1983.

Gilbert, Sandra, and Gubar, Susan. *No Man's Land: The Place of the Woman Writer in the Twentieth Century.* New Haven: Yale University Press, 1988–1994.

——. Vol. 1, *The War of the Words,* 1988.

——. Vol. 2, *Sexchanges,* 1989.

Ginsberg, Alan. *Howl and Other Poems.* San Francisco: City Lights, 1956.

Gitlin, Todd. *The Sixties: Years of Hope, Days of Rage.* New York: Bantam Books, 1987.

Goldberg, Natalie. *Long Quiet Highway: Waking Up in America.* New York: Bantam Books, 1993.

——. *Wild Mind: Living the Writer's Life.* New York: Bantam Books, 1990.

——. *Writing Down the Bones: Freeing the Writer Within.* Boston: Shambhala, 1986.

Goodlad, John. *The Dynamics of Educational Change.* New York: McGraw-Hill, 1975.

——. *A Place Called School.* New York: McGraw-Hill, 1983.

Gordon-McCutchan, R. C. *The Taos Indians and the Search for Blue Lake.* Santa Fe: Red Crane Books, 1991.

Graburn, Nelson, ed., *Ethnic and Tourist Arts: Cultural Expressions from the Fourth World.* Berkeley: University of California, 1976.

Graff, Gerald. *Beyond the Culture Wars: How Teaching the Conflicts Can Revitalize American Education.* New York: W. W. Norton, 1992.

Graham, Martha. *Blood Memory.* New York: Doubleday, 1991.

Gray, Cleve. *John Marin.* New York: Holt, Rhinehart, and Winston, 1970.

Greenfield, Robert. *The Spiritual Supermarket.* New York: E. P. Dutton, 1975.

Grimes, Ronald L. *Symbol and Conquest: Public Ritual and Drama in Santa Fe, New Mexico.* Ithaca: Cornell University Press, 1976.

Groff, Diane. *Arnold Rönnebeck: The Avant-Garde Spirit of the West.* Exh. Cat. Denver: Denver Museum of Art, 1990.

Gurdjieff, G. I. *Gurdjieff: Views from the Real World: Early Talks of Gurdjieff.* London: Routledge and Kegan Paul, 1973.

Hannah, Barbara. *Jung, His Life and Work: A Biographical Memoir.* New York: Putnam's, 1976.

Hardin, Nancy, and Schlossberg, Marilyn, eds. *Easy Rider.* New York: Signet, 1969.

Hare, Peter. *A Woman's Quest for Science: Portrait of Anthropologist Elsie Clews Parsons.* Buffalo: Prometheus Books, 1985.

Hartley, Marsden. *Adventures in the Arts.* New York: Boni and Liveright, 1921.

Hartshorne, Thomas, L. *The Distorted Image: Changing Conceptions of the American Character since Turner.* Cleveland: Case Western Reserve, 1968.

Hayden, Dolores. *The Grand Domestic Revolution: A History of Feminist Designs for American Homes, Neighborhoods, and Cities.* Cambridge: MIT Press, 1983.

Harvey, David. *The Condition of Postmodernism: An Inquiry into the Origins of Cultural Change.* Oxford, England: Blackwell, 1989.

Heller, Adele, and Rudnick, Lois, eds. *1915, The Cultural Moment: The New Politics, the New Woman, the New Psychology, the New Art, and the New Theatre in America.* New Brunswick: Rutgers University Press, 1991.

Helm, J., ed. *Spanish-Speaking People of the United States.* Proceedings of the Annual Spring Meeting of the American Ethnological Society. Seattle, 1968.

Helm, MacKinley. *John Marin.* Boston: Pellegrini and Cudahy, 1948.

Henderson, Alice Corbin. *Red Earth: Poems of New Mexico.* Chicago: Ralph Seymour, 1920.

Henderson, Mary. *Theatre in America.* New York: Harry Abrams, 1986.

Highwater, Jamake. *Songs from the Earth: American Indian Painting.* Boston: Little, Brown, 1976.

Hignett, Sean. *Brett: From Bloomsbury to New Mexico.* New York: Franklin Watts, 1983.

Hoberman, J. *Dennis Hopper: From Method to Madness.* Exh. Cat. Minneapolis: Walker Art Center, 1988.

Homer, William I. *Alfred Stieglitz and the American Avant-Garde.* Boston: New York Graphic Society, 1977.

Hopper, Dennis. *Out of the Sixties.* Pasadena: Twelve Tree Press, 1986.

Horgan, Paul. *The Peace Stone: Stories from Four Decades.* New York: Farrar, Straus, Giroux, 1967.

Houriet, Robert. *Getting Back Together.* New York: Coward, McCann and Geoghegan, 1971.

Howard, Gerald. *The Sixties.* New York: Washington Square Press, 1982.

Howe, Florence, ed. *Tradition and the Talents of Women.* Champaign: University of Illinois Press, 1990.

Huxley, Aldous. *Brave New World.* New York: Bantam, 1968 (1932).

———. *Ends and Means: An Enquiry into the Nature of Ideals and into the Methods Employed for Their Realization.* London: Chatto and Windus, 1937.

Iowa, Jerome. *Ageless Adobe: History and Preservation in Southwestern Architecture.* Santa Fe: Sunstone Press, 1985.

Jackson, J. B. *The Essential Landscape: The New Mexico Photographic Survey.* Albuquerque: University of New Mexico Press, 1985.

Jeffers, Robinson. *Selected Poetry of Robinson Jeffers.* New York: Random House, 1938.

Johnson, Spud. *Horizontal Yellow.* Santa Fe: Rydel Press, 1935.

Jones, Harold Henry, III. "The Work of Photographers Paul Strand and Edward Weston with an Emphasis on their Work in New Mexico," Ph.D diss., University of New Mexico, 1970.

Jones, Robert, and Latimer, Margery Toomer, eds. *The Collected Poems of Jean Toomer.* Chapel Hill: University of North Carolina Press, 1988.

Jung, Carl. *Civilization in Transition,* 2d ed. Princeton: Princeton University Press, 1970.

———. *Man and His Symbols.* New York: Dell, 1968.

———. *Memories, Dreams, Reflections.* Edited by Aniela Jaffe. New York: Pantheon Books, 1965.

Kallen, H. M. *Three American Modernist Painters.* New York: Arno Press, 1969.

Kelly, Lawrence C. *The Assault on Assimilation: John Collier and the Origins of Indian Policy Reform.* Albuquerque: University of New Mexico Press, 1983.

Kenneson, Susan, "Through the Looking-Glass: A History of Anglo-American Attitudes towards the Spanish-Americans and Indians of New Mexico," Ph.D diss., Yale University, 1978.

Kolodny, Annette. *The Land before Her: Fantasy and Experience of the American Frontiers, 1630–1860.* Chapel Hill: University of North Carolina Press, 1984.

Kraft, James, and Sloan, Helen. *John Sloan in Santa Fe.* Washington, D.C.: Smithsonian Press, 1981.

Kuh, Katharine. *Break-Up: The Core of Modern Art.* Greenwich, Conn.: New York Graphic Society, 1965.

LaFarge, Oliver. *All the Young Men.* Boston: Houghton Mifflin, 1930.

Lasch, Christopher. *The Culture of Narcissism: American Life in an Age of Diminishing Expectations.* New York: Warner Books, 1979.

Law, Lisa. *Flashing on the Sixties.* San Francisco: Chronicle Books, 1987.

Lawrence, D. H. *Complete Poems of D. H. Lawrence.* Edited by Vivian de Sola Pinto and Warren Roberts. New York: Viking Press, 1964.

——. *The Complete Short Stories,* vols. 2 and 3. New York: Viking Press, 1961.

——. *Mornings in Mexico and Etruscan Places.* London: Heinemann, 1956.

——. *Phoenix: The Posthumous Papers of D. H. Lawrence.* New York: Viking Press, 1972 (1936).

——. *The Plumed Serpent.* New York: Vintage Books, 1959 (1927).

——. *St. Mawr and Other Stories.* Edited by Brian Finney. New York: Cambridge University Press, 1983.

Lears, Jackson. *No Place of Grace: Anti-Modernism and the Transformation of American Culture, 1880–1920.* New York: Pantheon, 1981.

Lewis, Edith. *Willa Cather Living: A Personal Record.* New York: Alfred A. Knopf, 1953.

Limerick, Patricia Nelson. *The Legacy of Conquest: The Unbroken Past of the American West.* New York: W. W. Norton and Company, 1987.

Lisle, Laurie. *Portrait of an Artist: A Biography of Georgia O'Keeffe.* Albuquerque: University of New Mexico Press, 1986.

Lloyd, Ann, ed. *Movies of the Sixties.* London: Orbis Publishing, 1983.

Los Angeles County Museum of Art. *Happy's Curios.* Exh. Cat. Los Angeles: Los Angeles County Museum of Art, 1978.

Los Angeles Wight Art Gallery. *Forty Years of California Assemblage.* Los Angeles: University of California Press, 1989.

Loveless, Joan Potter. *Three Weavers.* Albuquerque: University of New Mexico Press, 1992.

Luhan, Mabel. *Intimate Memories: Background.* New York: Harcourt, Brace, 1933.

——. *European Experiences: Volume Two of Intimate Memories.* New York, Harcourt, Brace, 1935.

——. *Movers and Shakers: Volume Three of Intimate Memories.* New York: Harcourt, Brace, 1936.

——. *Edge of Taos Desert: An Escape to Reality: Volume Four of Intimate Memories.* New York: Harcourt, Brace, 1937.

——. *Lorenzo in Taos.* New York: Alfred A. Knopf, 1932.

——. *Taos and Its Artists.* New York: Duell, Sloan, and Pierce, 1947.

——. *Winter in Taos.* New York: Harcourt, Brace, 1935.

Machen, Meredith R. "Home as Motivation and Metaphor in the Works of Willa Cather," Ph.D diss., University of New Mexico, 1979.

Marin, John. *Letters of John Marin.* Edited by Herbert Seligmann. Boston: Private printing for An American Place, 1931.

——. *Selected Writings of John Marin.* Edited by Dorothy Norman. Boston: Pelegrini and Cudahy, 1949.

Marling, Karal Ann. *Woodstock: An American Art Colony, 1902–1977.* Poughkeepsie: Vassar College Art Gallery, 1977.

McDonoagh, Don. *Martha Graham: A Biography.* New York: Praeger, 1973.

McLoughlin, Corinne, and Davidson, Gordon. *Builders of the Dawn: Community Lifestyles in a Changing World.* Shutesbury, Mass.: Sirius Publishing, 1986.

McLoughlin, William G. *Revivals, Awakenings, and Reform: An Essay on Religion and Social Change in America, 1607–1977.* Chicago: University of Chicago Press, 1978.

McShine, Kynaston, ed. *Andy Warhol: A Retrospective.* Exh. Cat. New York: Museum of Modern Art, 1989.

——. ed. *The Natural Paradise: Painting in America 1800–1950.* New York: Museum of Modern Art, 1976.

Mellen, Joan, *Big Bad Wolves: Masculinity in the American Film.* New York: Pantheon Books, 1977.

Meltzer, Milton. *Dorothea Lange: A Photographer's Life.* New York: Farrar, Straus, Giroux, 1978.

Melville, Keith. *Communes in the Counterculture: Origins, Theories, Styles of Life.* New York: William Morrow, 1972.

Merrild, Knud. *A Poet and Two Painters.* London: Routledge, 1938.

Moore, James. "Marsden Hartley: The New Mexico Period, 1918–1919," Senior thesis, University of New Mexico, 1966.

Morang, Alfred. *Dane Rudhyar: Pioneer in Creative Synthesis.* New York: Lucis Publishing Company, 1939.

Morgan, Barbara. *Martha Graham: Sixteen Dances.* Dobbs Ferry, N.Y.: Morgan and Morgan, 1941.

Morrill, Claire. *A Taos Mosaic: Portrait of a New Mexico Village.* Albuquerque: University of New Mexico Press, 1973.

Most, Gerald. *A Short History of the Movies.* New York: Macmillan, 1987.

Nabokov, Peter. *Adobe: Pueblo and Hispanic Folk Traditions of the Southwest.* Washington, D.C.: Smithsonian Press, 1981.

——. *Indian Architecture.* Santa Fe: Museum of New Mexico, 1988.

Naylor, Colin, ed. *Contemporary Artists,* 3rd edition. London: St. James Press, 1989.

Nelson, Jane. *Mabel Dodge Luhan.* Western Writer's Series, No. 55. Boise: Boise State University Press, 1982.

Neumann, Erich. *The Great Mother: An Analysis of the Archetype.* 2d ed. Princeton: Princeton University Press, 1972.

Newhall, Beaumont. *Ansel Adams: The Eloquent Light.* Millerton, N.Y.: Aperture, 1963.

Newhall, Nancy, ed. *The Daybooks of Edward Weston,* vol. 2. New York: Horizon Press, 1961.

Nichols, John. *If Mountains Die: A New Mexico Memoir.* New York: Alfred A. Knopf, 1977.

———. *Milagro Beanfield War.* New York: Ballantine Books, 1974.

Nolan, James. *Poet-Chief: The Native American Poetics of Walt Whitman and Pablo Neruda.* Albuquerque: University of New Mexico Press, 1994.

Norwood, Vera, and Monk, Janice, eds. *The Desert Is No Lady: Southwestern Landscapes in Women's Writing and Art.* New Haven: Yale University Press, 1987.

O'Daniel, Therman B., ed. *Jean Toomer: A Critical Evaluation.* Washington, D.C.: Howard University Press, 1988.

O'Keeffe, Georgia. *Georgia O'Keeffe.* New York: Viking Press, 1976.

———. *Georgia O'Keeffe: Art and Letters.* Washington, D.C.: National Gallery of Art, 1987.

Oliver, Daniel. *Leopold Stokowski: A Counterpoint of View.* New York: Dodd, Mead, 1982.

Parker, Robert L. *Carlos Chavez: Mexico's Modern-Day Orpheus.* Boston: G. K. Hall, 1983.

Parsons, Elsie Clews. *Taos Pueblo.* Menasha, Wisc.: George Banta, 1936.

Philp, Kenneth. *John Collier's Crusade for Indian Reform, 1920–1945.* Tucson: University of Arizona Press, 1977.

Preston, Robert. *Aliens and Dissenters: Federal Suppression of Radicals, 1903–1933.* Cambridge: Harvard University Press, 1964.

Reich, Sheldon. *Andrew Dasburg: His Life and Art.* Lewisburg, Pa.: Bucknell University Press, 1989.

Reeve, Kai Aiken. *Santa Fe and Taos, 1898–1942: An American Cultural Center.* El Paso, Tx.: Texas Western Press, 1982.

Rieff, Phillip. *The Triumph of the Therapeutic: Uses of Faith After Freud.* New York: Harper and Row, 1966.

Rodriguez, Elena. *Dennis Hopper: A Madness to His Method.* New York: St. Martin's Press, 1988.

Rose, Barbara. *American Art since 1900.* New York: Praeger, 1975.

Rothchild, John, and Wolfe, Susan. *The Children of the Counter Culture.* New York: Doubleday, 1976.

Rubin, William, ed. *Primitivism in the 20th Century: Affinity of the Tribal and the Modern.* New York: Museum of Modern Art, 1984.

Rudnick, Lois. *Mabel Dodge Luhan: New Woman, New Worlds.* Albuquerque: University of New Mexico Press, 1984.

Ruyter, Nancy. *Reformers and Visionaries: The Americanization of Dance.* New York: Dance Horizons, 1979.

Sandler, Irving. *The New York School.* New York: Harper and Row, 1978.

Sandweiss, Martha. *Laura Gilpin: An Enduring Grace.* Fort Worth: Amon Carter Museum, 1986.

San Francisco Museum of Modern Art. *Painting and Sculpture in California: The Modern Era.* San Francisco: Museum of Modern Art, 1977.

Scott, Gail. *Marsden Hartley.* New York: Abbeville Press, 1988.

Scully, Vincent. *Pueblo, Village, Dance.* New York: Viking Press, 1972.

Seth, Sandra, and Laurel Seth, *Adobe! Homes and Interiors of Taos, Santa Fe, and the Southwest.* Stamford, Ct.: Architectural Book Publishing, 1988.

Simmons, Marc. *New Mexico: A History.* New York: W. W. Norton, 1977.

Singal, Daniel Joseph. *Modernism in American Culture.* Belmont, Calif.: Wadsworth Publishing, 1991.

Slotkin, Richard. *The Fatal Environment: The Mythology of the Frontier in the Age of Industrialization, 1800–1900.* Middleton, Conn.: Wesleyan University Press, 1985.

——. *Regeneration through Violence: The Mythology of the American Frontier, 1600–1860.* Middletown, Conn.: Wesleyan University Press, 1975.

Soares, Janet. *Louis Horst: Musician in a Dancer's World.* Nashville: Duke University Press, 1992.

Sontag, Susan. *Against Interpretation, and other essays.* New York: Farrar, Straus and Giroux, 1966.

Spears, Beverly. *American Adobes: Rural Houses of New Mexico.* Albuquerque: University of New Mexico Press, 1986.

Stainer, Margaret. *Agnes Pelton.* Exh. Cat. Ohlone College Art Gallery, Fremont, Calif., 1989.

Starr, Sandra. *Lost and Found in California: Four Decades of Assemblage Art.* Santa Monica: James Corcoran Gallery, 1988.

Steele, Thomas J. *Santos and Saints: The Religious Folk Art of Hispanic New Mexico.* Santa Fe: Ancient City Press, 1974.

Steiner, Stan. *La Raza: The Mexican Americans.* New York: Harper and Row, 1971.

Sterne, Maurice. *Shadow and Light: The Life, Friends, and Opinions of Maurice Sterne.* Edited by Charles Mayerson. New York: Harcourt, Brace, 1965.

Stevens, Jay. *Storming Heaven: LSD and the American Dream.* New York: Harper and Row, 1988.

Stineman, Esther Lanigan. *Mary Austin: Song of a Maverick.* New Haven: Yale University Press, 1989.

Stith, Sidra. *Made in the U.S.A.: An Americanization in Modern Art, the '50s and 60s.* Berkeley: University of California Press, 1987.

Stodelle, Ernestine. *Dance Song: The Dance Story of Martha Graham.* New York: Schirmer Books, 1984.

Stokowski, Leopold. *Music for All of Us.* New York: Simon and Schuster, 1943.

Strand, Paul. *Paul Strand: Sixty Years of Photographs.* Millerton, N.Y.: Aperture, 1976.

Tanner, Clara Lee. *Southwest Indian Painting,* 2d ed. Tucson: University of Arizona Press, 1973.

Toomer, Jean. *The Wayward and the Seeking: A Collection of Writings by Jean Toomer.* Edited by Darwin Turner. Washington, D.C.: Howard University Press, 1980.

Tuchman, Maurice. *Ken Price: Happy's Curios.* Exh. Cat. Los Angeles: Los Angeles County Museum of Art, 1978.

———. *The Spiritual in Art: Abstract Painting, 1890–1985.* Exh. Cat. Los Angeles: Los Angeles County Museum of Art and Abbeville Press, 1986.

Turner, Darwin. *In a Minor Chord: Three Afro-American Writers and Their Search for Identity.* Carbondale: Southern Illinois University Press, 1971.

Udall, Sharyn Rohlfsen. *Modernist Painting in New Mexico, 1913–1935.* Albuquerque: University of New Mexico Press, 1984.

Udall, Sharyn Rohlfsen, ed. *Spud Johnson & Laughing Horse.* Albuquerque: University of New Mexico Press, 1994.

Ungar, Sanford. *The FBI.* Boston: Little, Brown, 1976.

Veysey, Laurence. *The Communal Experience: Anarchist and Mystical Counter-Cultures.* New York: Harper and Row, 1973.

Waldrop, M. Mitchell. *Complexity: The Emerging Science at the Edge of Order and Chaos.* New York: Simon and Schuster, 1992.

Waters, Frank. *The Man Who Killed the Deer.* Chicago: Swallow Press, 1970 (1940).

———. *Masked Gods: Navajo and Pueblo Ceremonialism.* New York: Ballantine Books, 1960 (1950).

———. *Mountain Dialogues.* Athens, Ohio: Swallow Press, 1981.

Weigle, Marta. *The Penitentes of the Southwest.* Santa Fe: Ancient City Press, 1970.

Weigle, Marta, and Fiore, Kyle. *Santa Fe and Taos: The Writer's Era, 1916–1941.* Santa Fe: Ancient City Press, 1982.

Weigle, Marta, and White, Peter. *The Lore of New Mexico.* Albuquerque: University of New Mexico Press, 1988.

Wilson, Edmund. *The American Jitters: The Year of the Slump.* New York: Scribner's, 1932.

Wood, Nancy. *Taos Pueblo.* New York: Alfred A. Knopf, 1989.

Wroth, William. *Hispanic Crafts of the Southwest.* Exh. Cat. Colorado Springs: Taylor Museum of the Colorado Springs Fine Arts Center, 1977.

Yates, Stephen. *Edward Weston in New Mexico.* Exh. Cat. Santa Fe: Museum of New Mexico, 1989.

———. *The Transition Years: Paul Strand in New Mexico.* Exh. Cat. Santa Fe: Museum of New Mexico, 1989.

Young, Ella. *Flowering Dusk: Things Remembered Accurately and Inaccurately.* New York: Longmans, Green, 1945.

Young-Hunter, John. *Reviewing the Years.* New York: Crown, 1962.

Zakian, Michael. *Agnes Pelton: Poet of Nature.* Exh. Cat. Palm Springs: Palm Springs Desert Museum, 1995.

Zumwalt, Rosemary Levy. *Wealth and Rebellion: Elsie Clews Parsons, Anthropologist and Folklorist.* Urbana: University of Illinois Press, 1992.

INDEX

B

D

I

J

M

O

P

T

U

V

W